Plays by
A. W. Pinero

THE SCHOOLMISTRESS
THE SECOND MRS TANQUERAY
TRELAWNY OF THE 'WELLS'
THE THUNDERBOLT

Edited with an introduction and notes by
George Rowell

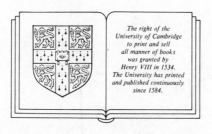

*The right of the
University of Cambridge
to print and sell
all manner of books
was granted by
Henry VIII in 1534.
The University has printed
and published continuously
since 1584.*

CAMBRIDGE UNIVERSITY PRESS

Cambridge

London   New York   New Rochelle

Melbourne   Sydney

Published by the Press Syndicate of the University of Cambridge
The Pitt Building, Trumpington Street, Cambridge CB2 1RP
32 East 57th Street, New York, NY 10022, USA
10 Stamford Road, Oakleigh, Melbourne 3166, Australia

© Cambridge University Press 1986

First published 1986

Printed in Great Britain at
the University Press, Cambridge

British Library cataloguing in publication data

Pinero, Arthur Wing
Plays. – (British and American playwrights 1750–1920)
I. Title   II. Rowell, George   III. Series
822′.8   PR5181

Library of Congress cataloguing in publication data

Pinero, Arthur Wing, Sir, 1855–1934.
Plays.
(British and American playwrights, 1750–1920)
'The plays of A. W. Pinero'
Bibliography: p.
Contents: The schoolmistress – The second Mrs Tanqueray –
Trelawny of the 'Wells' – [etc.]
I. Rowell, George.   II. Title.   III. Series.
PR5181.R6   1985   822′.8   85–17504

ISBN 0 521 24103 0 hard covers
ISBN 0 521 28440 6 paperback

CE

GENERAL EDITORS' PREFACE

It is the primary aim of this series to make available to the British and American theatre plays which were effective in their own time, and which are good enough to be effective still.

Each volume assembles a number of plays, normally by a single author, scrupulously edited but sparingly annotated. Textual variations are recorded where individual editors have found them either essential or interesting. Introductions give an account of the theatrical context, and locate playwrights and plays within it. Biographical and chronological tables, brief bibliographies, and the complete listing of known plays provide information useful in itself, and which also offers guidance and incentive to further exploration.

Many of the plays published in this series have appeared in modern anthologies. Such representation is scarcely distinguishable from anonymity. We have relished the tendency of individual editors to make claims for the dramatists of whom they write. These are not plays best forgotten. They are plays best remembered. If the series is a contribution to theatre history, that is well and good. If it is a contribution to the continuing life of the theatre, that is well and better.

We have been lucky. The Cambridge University Press has supported the venture beyond our legitimate expectations. Acknowledgement is not, in this case, perfunctory. Sarah Stanton's contribution to the series has been substantial, and it has enhanced our work.

Martin Banham
Peter Thomson

CONTENTS

ILLUSTRATIONS

INTRODUCTION

In most theatrical records the two suitors who woke the Sleeping Beauty of Victorian drama from a century's slumber were Wilde and Shaw, and the popularity of their plays in the modern repertory supports this view. But a dramatic critic assessing the state of the English stage in 1899 would have formed a very different opinion. Wilde's career as a playwright in effect lasted four years, during which he produced three diverting but flawed 'dramas of modern life' and one comedy for all time, but his trial and imprisonment then banished his plays from the stage. By 1899 Shaw had written ten plays, of which only one had received a public performance in London. Had his cycling accident near Edgware in 1897 proved fatal, he would now appear in English theatre history as a successful critic and failed playwright. Both the press and the public at the end of Victoria's reign named as the leading English dramatist Arthur Wing Pinero, whose range and output placed him well ahead of his nearest rival, Henry Arthur Jones. Devotees of Hilaire Belloc's *Cautionary Tales* will recall the fate of that untruthful miss, Matilda, and may remember that the treat her aunt denied her was 'to see that interesting play, *The Second Mrs Tanqueray*/ . . . A deprivation just and wise,/ To punish her for telling lies'.

Pinero's reputation as the masterbuilder of the new English drama was built on stout and substantial foundations. Born in 1855 into a London family of Portuguese origin (the name had been anglicised from Pinheiro), he followed his father into a solicitor's office but at eighteen threw up the law for the stage. Valuable experience in leading 'stock' companies, notably the Theatre Royal, Edinburgh, and the Alexandra, Liverpool, led to his engagement at the Lyceum with Irving in 1876. It may be deduced that, like Shakespeare or his cherished Tom Robertson, Pinero was never greatly gifted as an actor. His most responsible assignment at the Lyceum seems to have been Roderigo, and though his Desdemona, Ellen Terry, observed loyally: 'He was always good in the "silly ass" type of part, and no one could say of him he was playing himself',[1] it is not a leading role. Later at the Haymarket, Squire and Marie Bancroft entrusted him with Sir Anthony Absolute in their production of *The Rivals*, but his performance was generally judged to be ineffective, and this reaction may have contributed to his decision to give up acting (at the age of twenty-nine) in favour of full-time writing. The following year he wrote *The Magistrate* and achieved widespread recognition, both at home and abroad.

What his acting experience, first in the provinces and then in London's two leading playhouses, did provide was a command of the needs and scope of

1

stage performance which was to distinguish all his best work for the next forty years. Though the standing of that work has varied, with once 'major' achievements like *The Notorious Mrs Ebbsmith* or *The Gay Lord Quex* suffering eclipse, and 'minor' pieces such as the Court farces or *Trelawny of the 'Wells'* growing in stature, that respect for the theatre which Pinero learnt under Irving and the Bancrofts has earned him a solid, even formidable, reputation ever since. Moreover it was the Lyceum under Irving and the Haymarket under the Bancrofts that helped to train him as a playwright as well as an actor. *Two Can Play at That Game, Daisy's Escape* and *Bygones* were three of his earliest pieces with which Irving filled out the Lyceum bill, and *Lords and Commons*, produced at the Haymarket while he was associated with the Bancrofts, one of his first full-length serious plays. Many actors aspire to write for the stage, some achieve a certain success, and a handful have confirmed that success. Pinero's particular achievement was to attain in his writing a human insight which as an actor he could not command but knew was lacking in the drama of the day.

While playing at the Lyceum and Haymarket he was also busy writing for other theatres and companies, notably two light-hearted pieces, *Hester's Mystery* and *Girls and Boys*, for the veteran farceur J. L. Toole, and another, *In Chancery*, for the popular comedian Edward Terry. But more significant was his work for the increasingly fashionable St James's (with which Pinero was to be associated throughout his career). Some of this work was routine adaptation from the French, but two early contributions caught the public's and critics' attention, not least for the opportunities offered to the redoubtable Madge Kendal. In *The Money-Spinner* she portrayed a wife prepared to cheat at cards to save her husband from bankruptcy, and in *The Squire* another wife concealing her marriage (and risking scandal) for her husband's sake. Both pieces are tentative and often trite, but the resolve to extend the range of character-drawing is apparent and points forwards.

Pinero's decision in 1884 to devote himself to writing produced handsome rewards over the next three years in the shape of his three major farces for the Court Theatre. *The Magistrate, The Schoolmistress* and *Dandy Dick* are distinguishable not only from other farces of the period but also from Pinero's own later work in this vein, like *A Wife Without a Smile* or *Preserving Mr Panmure*, even when designed for the same address and much the same company as were *The Cabinet Minister* and *The Amazons*. The first three Court farces have a lightness of touch and a respect for good intentions which is endearing as well as richly entertaining. Their humanity and warmth are especially apparent when they are compared with other favourite farces of the period. Adaptation from the French was the standby of most Victorian playwrights, from Nicholas Nickleby onwards. *Pink Dominos* (1877), taken by James Albery from *Les Dominos Roses* by Hénnequin and Delacour, typifies the 'sophisticated' article discreetly diluted for English consumption.

ACKNOWLEDGEMENTS

This volume is devoted to the playwright recognised by his own generation as the champion of a new English drama, and it is timely that its preparation should coincide with the centenary of his turning full-time writer and the fiftieth anniversary of his death. I am therefore particularly grateful to the Cambridge University Press, and to Martin Banham, one of the General Editors of the series, for entrusting me with it.

I am happy to acknowledge the permission of the Trustees of the Royal Literary Fund as literary executors of Pinero's estate to draw on unpublished and copyright material, notably the manuscripts of *The Schoolmistress* and *The Second Mrs Tanqueray*, and to the Fales Library, New York University, and the Houghton Library, Harvard University, where these manuscripts are respectively held.

Amongst a number of scholars and authorities to whom I have turned, I should mention particularly Dr Peter Wearing of the University of Arizona, who generously made available to me his collation of the manuscript and author's prompt copy of *The Second Mrs Tanqueray*; Martin Banham, who drew my attention to the original ending of *The Schoolmistress*, contained in the manuscript; the Garrick Club, of which Pinero was a member for 47 years; Mr Brian Oulton; Mr John Bedding of Samuel French; and two colleagues, Brenda Jackson and Christopher Robinson, for their valued help in the preparation of the text.

The residuary beneficiaries of Pinero's will were the Middlesex Hospital, the Royal Literary Fund and the Garrick Club – evidence of the breadth of his sympathies and extent of his generosity. It is to be hoped that his work, now in the public domain, will continue to demonstrate that sympathy, and that the availability of four of his plays in this volume may contribute something to the process.

G.R.

1984

Both *Pink Dominos* and *The Magistrate* propel married couples to clandestine assignments in a dubious restaurant, but Albery's farce aspires no higher than titillation, whereas Aeneas and Agatha Poskett in *The Magistrate* visit the Hôtel des Princes to save their nearest and dearest from distress.

Charley's Aunt (1892), which like *The Schoolmistress*, focuses on an educational establishment, is energetically English, but if Brandon Thomas's work is all his own and clean as a whistle, it is equally shrill, which perhaps accounts for the public's readiness to hear it. *The Schoolmistress*, on the other hand, is the most delicate of Pinero's farces. While *The Magistrate* and *Dandy Dick* trace their situations within the framework of the majestic, essentially male, world of the Law and the Church, it is set inside the petticoat principality of Volumnia College, and much of the humour derives from the struggles of the menfolk to throw off their silken chains. The outbreak of the fire provides the male sex with a momentary advantage, but in the end feminine enterprise triumphs. Even the Admiral's wife mutinies, and whereas Poskett and Dean Judd are content to hush up their adventures and stuff the family skeleton back in the cupboard, Miss Dyott renounces pedagogy and glories in the disclosure that she is Queen of the Opera Bouffe. *The Schoolmistress* is also notable for letting youth call the tune. Although Miss Dyott gives her name to the play, she is absent for most of the crucial second act and the controlling force is really Peggy Hesslerigge, so that an apter title might be *The Pupil Teacher*. Pinero's manuscript reveals that Peggy even claimed the curtain speech (see Appendix A, below, pp. 73–4) but Mrs John Wood, the Court's leading lady, evidently objected and could not be denied.

It is customary to hail Pinero's precision engineering in his farces and contrast its comic impact with the calculation and contrivance of the social dramas. Of course sound construction is essential if a farce is not to collapse from overloaded incident, but at their best Pinero's farces offer more than technical excellence. The range of their characterisation has already been stressed and the affection with which the characters are presented distinguished Pinero not only from Gilbert or Brandon Thomas but also from Labiche and Feydeau. The dialogue too has a quaint formality which contrasts eloquently with the familiar, functional note of earlier Victorian farce. In later, more oracular plays this note was to earn him charges of pompousness and artificiality, but here it counterpoints the development of the action. Even in emergencies the characters are never lost for words. When the guests in *The Schoolmistress* decline to listen to the Fire Brigade's *raconteur* while awaiting rescue by ladder, only Pinero could have provided the superintendent's protest: 'Really gentlemen, I must say I've never heard Mr Goff treated so hasty at any conflagration', with its firm avowal of professional and personal loyalty.

Between his first major success with *The Magistrate* and his recognition as the leading dramatist of the day with *The Second Mrs Tanqueray*, Pinero experimented widely. Since he lacked the gift of satire his essays in this vein (*The Hobby Horse, The Weaker Sex, The Times*) were always laboured and usually spoilt by sentiment. He was in fact much more successful with undiluted sentimentality, as in the modest but greatly loved *Sweet Lavender*, a tale of romance, past and present, and barristers, broken or beginning. Nevertheless an insistent call to attempt serious drama of social significance is detectable in the plays of this period. The time and temper of the theatre fostered such a call. Though Pinero claimed: 'When I wrote *The Profligate* [produced 1889] I had no knowledge of Ibsen, nor have I, I believe, been influenced in the smallest degree by his works',[2] he could not continue unaware of the strength of feeling English performances of Ibsen provoked in the early 1890s, and must have been considerably impressed to tell William Archer: 'I went down on my knees to Irving, begging him to do *Hedda Gabler* at the Lyceum with himself and Ellen Terry as Lövborg and Hedda'[3] (an odd suggestion – Ellen Terry was in her mid-forties by 1891 when Archer's translation was published, and Irving nine years older).

Whether conceived as an English response to Ibsen or not, Pinero's social dramas of the 1890s took up the serious note of *The Squire* or *Lady Bountiful* and modulated it towards unity of tone and tragic resolution. This end he felt to be only attainable in terms of high society. In an interview with William Archer in 1901 he claimed 'not only that wealth and leisure are more productive of dramatic complications than poverty and hard work, but that if you want a certain order of ideas expressed or questions discussed you must go pretty well up the social scale'.[4] His first fully articulate demonstration of this belief was *The Profligate*, and his first *raisonneur* or spokesman for the establishment Lord Dangars in that play. Its impact has been weakened by other plays (including some of Pinero's) on the theme of the philanderer whose past interposes to ruin his happiness just as he grasps it, but the manager, John Hare, took fright at its tragic conclusion, with the young husband drinking poison, and forced a conventional curtain achieved by the wife's forgiveness. Pinero's acquiescence nevertheless stiffened his resolve to pursue the theme to its logical end in *The Second Mrs Tanqueray*, with the 'other woman' moved to the centre of the story and the profligate a late though fatal intruder.

This centrality followed logically from Pinero's earlier essays in a serious vein. *The Squire, The Money-Spinner, The Hobby Horse, Lady Bountiful* all pivot on the dilemma in which the heroine finds herself, and may have been a conscious reaction against the conventions of melodrama, which was essentially a man's world with the heroine kept waiting in the wings to be rescued from starvation or seduction. But the emphasis placed on the *woman* with a past was also a concession to the taste of the fashionable element in the late Victorian audience. The stalls patrons at the St James's and other smart

houses could recognise the authenticity with which the stage mirrored their drawing-rooms, but looked to the playwright to introduce a character they would never willingly admit to their own homes, the mysterious female without a pedigree whose efforts to 'acquire some relations as soon as possible', in Lady Bracknell's words, provided the plot of so much Society drama of this period. Doubtless the notoriety attaching at this time to certain of Ibsen's heroines, particularly Rebecca West and Hedda Gabler, added a savour to the audience's taste, though Shaw contemptuously dismissed the English playwrights' response: 'It seemed to them that most of Ibsen's heroines were naughty ladies. And they tried to produce Ibsen plays by making their heroines naughty. But they took great care to make them pretty and expensively dressed.'[5]

Pinero's portrait of Paula Tanqueray is better assessed by comparing her with the 'naughty ladies' of his British colleagues Wilde and Henry Arthur Jones than with Ibsen's. Mrs Erlynne in *Lady Windermere's Fan* and Mrs Cheveley in *An Ideal Husband* are flamboyant and entertaining figures but their situations do not demand serious consideration, while Mrs Arbuthnot in *A Woman of No Importance*, though wholly serious, is neither flamboyant nor entertaining. Jones's cautious handling in *The Case of Rebellious Susan* and *The Liars* of a wife tempted by her husband's callousness to pay him out in kind stops short of real candour and therefore lasting comedy, while Mrs Dane is ultimately dismissed as a woman more sinning than sinned against. Uniquely in the Society dramas of this period, Paula is presented as a human being compounded of strength and weakness, charm and coarseness. She has been exploited and discarded by her 'protectors', but her own caprice and shallowness contribute to her ruin. It was the subtlety with which the virtually unknown Mrs Patrick Campbell realised this complex character that ensured the play's original impact. Later productions have had to contend with its legendary reputation and appeal to mature actresses (including Mrs Campbell, who went on playing Paula in her fifties), but the National Theatre revival of 1981, by casting the *gamine* but incisive Felicity Kendal, showed convincingly how the woman her husband calls 'dear baby' could nevertheless be driven to suicide.

The play took risks. John Hare turned it down as 'immoral' and George Alexander originally proposed it for matinées only. But there were other grounds on which the St James's audience might have taken offence. Pinero had reduced the profligate's part, yet he was increasingly severe on the profligate's behaviour. Aubrey Tanqueray condemns not only Hugh Ardale and such unseen 'protectors' of Paula as Selwyn Ethurst and Peter Jarman, but also himself for leading what many of Pinero's public accepted as 'a man's life'. In the original text even Cayley Drummle, the acknowledged *raisonneur*, pleaded guilty to this charge, and the play finished with his General Confession:

> And I – I've been hard on this woman! Good God, men are hard on all women![6]

Evidently Pinero found this overemphatic and reverted to the purely visual – Ellean 'beats her breast' and 'faints upon the ottoman' – for the final tableau. A modern playgoer does not need the dual moral code of Victorian Society spelled out, but the play's boldness calls for acknowledgement.

The success of *Mrs Tanqueray* confirmed Pinero's pre-eminence not only as a dramatist but as a director of his own work. Possibly as a reaction to his treatment over *The Profligate*, he took a firm hold of rehearsals and continued master of any stage on which his work was being prepared. Frequent accounts (not always appreciative) by actors whom he rehearsed are confirmed by the meticulously detailed promptbooks he kept and by the texts of his plays published from 1891 onwards. This insistence on controlling the performance and publication of his work constituted Pinero's stand against actor–managerial exploitation, which in preceding decades had treated the writer's word as a draft scenario on which to enlarge, and was a crucial step in establishing the self-sufficiency of English drama. It aligned him with Robertson and Gilbert as a dramatist–director, and prepared the ground for Shaw to rule over his rehearsals. Robertson and Gilbert, however, had worked with semi-permanent ensembles offering a clearly established genre. Pinero brought his work to life at different theatres with companies specially assembled, and evidently felt the need for an even stricter discipline.

Greatly as this discipline raised the standards of performance, it tended to codify what is essentially a spontaneous and shared process, and to confer on some of his more delicate pieces (*The Princess and the Butterfly*, *The 'Mind-the-Paint' Girl*) an impression of love's labours lost. It is understandable that an author directing his own play should want to impose on the cast his own interpretation and should view unsolicited suggestions as unwelcome (Noel Coward is a more recent example of this approach). But a logical development from the dramatist–director was the independent director, and it is not surprising that the younger Dion ('Dot') Boucicault, who created Sir William Gower for Pinero and married his Rose Trelawny, Irene Vanbrugh, should emerge as the first major independent director in the English theatre. Marie Tempest, herself not the most malleable of material, declared of Boucicault: 'I was a blank page on which he was able to write at will, and if he ever created anything, Dion Boucicault created me as an actress.'[7] But such uncompromising methods inevitably provoked a reaction. The call for imagination and insight from the actors themselves, voiced by Granville Barker and the intellectual movement in the theatre, was in some sense a protest against the dramatist–director as formidably personified by Pinero.

After *The Second Mrs Tanqueray* the struggle of an intelligent woman to achieve independence in a society that allowed her only one career – as wife

and mother – increasingly obsessed Pinero. Agnes in *The Notorious Mrs
Ebbsmith* is the child of one unhappy marriage and the survivor of another
who has turned to political agitation and atheism until called on to nurse a
rising politician separated from his wife. The two became lovers, but while
Agnes dreams of sharing his study rather than his bed, Lucas Cleeve drifts
towards the compromise his worldly brother-in-law, the Duke of St Olpherts,
puts forward, in which an apparent reconciliation allows him to return to
political life while establishing Agnes as his mistress. From this point the play
suffers a terminal decline into theatrical gesture (Agnes discards her sexless
black dress in favour of a concubine's finery, then hurls into the fire a bible
offered her by a well-meaning clergyman, only to burn herself in retrieving it)
and anti-climax: Cleeve's wife appeals successfully to her to forgo her claims
and thus reactivate his career. The weakness of the conclusion is underlined
by the strength of the exposition.

Unquestionably the seriousness of Pinero's intentions in examining these
heroines is blunted by the assumption that they cannot support themselves
and by the enervating affluence in which they live. In *Iris* a young widow who
will lose her fortune on remarriage turns down the honourable advances of a
young admirer about to make his way to Canada. When her wealth vanishes
with her financial adviser, she accepts the dishonourable proposals of a
ruthless 'protector'. The return of her suitor, now able to support her, leads
to rejection by both men and humiliation (apparently) on the streets. In *His
House in Order* (which achieved Pinero's longest London run amongst his
social dramas) a governess finds herself married to a humourless widower and
harried by his disdainful in-laws. Chance places in her hands evidence that the
first wife was unfaithful and her child illegitimate, yet the *raisonneur*
persuades her to 'wear a halo' and give up her revenge. An audience is likely
to be less forgiving. Zoe Blundell in *Mid-Channel* suggests a more sensitive
cousin to H. A. Jones's rebellious Lady Susan or flirtatious Lady Jessica. Like
them she has been neglected by a brutish and inconstant husband and turns
for consolation to a series of admirers, the last of whom proves all too
accommodating. When the husband finds out, Pinero engineers her suicide,
whereas a modern observer wishes so intelligent a woman would take a tip
from an exact contemporary, Kate in Barrie's *The Twelve Pound Look*, and
go in search of typing lessons.

Pinero is far happier in the theatrical world of *Trelawny of the 'Wells'*, or
more accurately its two theatrical worlds, those of Sadler's Wells after the
departure of Phelps (his local playhouse as a child in Islington) and of the
Prince of Wales's in the time of Robertson (whose triumphs he witnessed as a
boy). Pinero seems disposed to make light of this piece, describing it as 'a
comedietta' on the title-page and 'this little play' in an author's note. It was
written at the summit of his success as a 'modern' playwright and perhaps
viewed as an exercise in nostalgia. Irene Vanbrugh, who played the heroine,

recalled 'that first night each individual entrance was hailed with a good deal of laughter',[8] presumably on the grounds that last year's fashions are always funnier than last century's. But it is neither simple to stage nor slight in content. The theatrical types are exaggerated but never ridiculous. The aspiring playwright, Tom Wrench, is not only recognisable as Robertson-in-the-making (Pinero's notes for the play[9] reveal that he first used the name Tom Robinson); he is also touching in his devotion to Rose Trelawny, the young actress who outgrows the fustian of *The Pedlar of Marseilles* and is ready for what Robertson's critics called 'cup-and-saucer comedy', but perhaps could be termed 'ball-of-wool-gathering' in *Life*, as Tom Wrench conceives it.

Moreover it is not just contrast in theatrical convention that distinguishes the play. The rigidity of the Cavendish Square household in which Rose's engagement to Arthur Gower enmeshes her is sketched with insight and wit. Above all, Sir William Gower, its tyrant, grows in understanding and humanity as the play develops. Unlike the lordly Dangars, St Olpherts and Quex, he comes to appreciate Rose's predicament and waives his own 'rules' to assist her. Their discovery of a mutual bond in Edmund Kean, 'the splendid gipsy', adds a third theatrical perspective, and the conclusion – with Arthur, Rose and Tom about to challenge fortune – is far more stirring than the contrived endings of so many plays of the period. *Trelawny of the 'Wells'* is not only Pinero's happiest inspiration but a key-document in Victorian drama.

The intrusion of a working girl (again played by Irene Vanbrugh) into the boudoirs of high society is a feature of his next two comedies. In *The Gay Lord Quex* Sophie Fullgarney is the efficient manageress of a manicurists' salon, skilfully presented, but her involvement in the private lives of the Marquis of Quex and the Duchess of Strood is only brought about by the unlikely device of making her a foster-sister to the play's nominal heroine. It was a considerable success, owing to the elaborate (though wholly decorous) bedroom-scene, but Sophie's persistence in arranging her protégée's future grows increasingly obtrusive. *Letty* is an equally careful portrait of three City girls and their followers, with meticulous accounts of a rooftop reception and a restaurant supper-party, though the heroine is anaemic in every sense and neither her difficulty in deciding between the coarse but legitimate proposal of her employer and the illicit luxury offered by a married admirer, nor her ultimate destiny as a suburban wife and mother, fires the imagination.

By 1908 the theatrical climate had undergone notable change. Shaw's position as a challenging if controversial playwright was assured by the *réclame* of the Court Theatre seasons, and his lead was being taken up not only in London but in Manchester, where at the Gaiety Miss Horniman was brewing provincial repertory with her inheritance from the family tea business. It is tempting to see *The Thunderbolt* as Pinero's response to these

developments. Its setting and background (Midland and middle class) seems a deliberate break with the West End/East End contrasts of the plays that preceded it. The stage directions themselves suggest a closer familiarity with the lives of the author's fellow men than his society dramas convey. 'The room and everything in the room are eloquent of narrow means, if not of actual poverty'; 'The architecture, decorations, and furniture are pseudo-artistic and vulgar'; 'The whole suggests the home of a common person of moderate means who has built himself a "fine house"' – these are three such directions, and they contrast strongly with 'A rich and tastefully decorated room'; 'Everything to suggest wealth and refinement'; 'Everything charming and tasteful' (comparable directions from *The Second Mrs Tanqueray*). In moving away from Mayfair Pinero's dialogue acquires a sharper edge, as does the crowded but compact gallery of family portraits. Clayton Hamilton, the American editor of Pinero's *Social Plays*, recorded with some surprise the author's insistence that he 'loved' the Mortimores.[10] No doubt that surprise sprang from a comparison with the engaging company at Volumnia College or Sadler's Wells Theatre. But presumably Pinero's comment implied that he loved what he had achieved in drawing the Mortimores – imperfect beings, but recognisably human despite (or rather because of) their failings and follies.

Technically, too, the play exhibits an economy and discipline not always apparent in the relaxed and almost invertebrate structure of (say) *The Princess and the Butterfly*. One feature often commended by critics is the 'overlap' between the Second and Third Acts: the latter starts at a point preceding that reached by the end of Act Two and 'catches up' with Thaddeus' arrival at the family conclave. More integral to the play's taut design is the almost total absence of sub-plot or side-issue. Except for the (merely touched on) romantic attachment of young Trist to Helen Thornhill, the entire business of the play concerns itself with the disposal of Edward Mortimore's estate. Even the obtrusive (to modern taste) figures of Thaddeus' children are part and parcel of this design, since their future is involved and their mother's action undertaken for their sake. It is this solidity of structure, as opposed to the sometimes overwrought fabric of the Society plays, that gives *The Thunderbolt* its special strength. There is a momentum to the story which is all the more remarkable since the 'mystery' is exploded early by Phyllis's confession to her husband before the play is half over.

If it is tempting to see *The Thunderbolt* as Pinero's recognition of a new horizon opened up in English drama by the repertory movement, it is also tempting to compare the play with one of Granville Barker's contributions to the Court Theatre programme, *The Voysey Inheritance*. The background here is suburban and professional, not provincial and commercial, but the display of family ties shattered and family expectations dashed by a skeleton in the cupboard and unsuspected death duties is common to the two plays. Pinero shows his more traditional training by employing the materials of the well-made play (a missing will, an illegitimate child), whereas Barker's method is shaped by specialist legal processes. There are traces too of the coy humour of Pinero's early work in the comic curate and precocious children. But the overall tone is clear and compelling, and the story maintains its grip to the 'open' end. Since he stood for the theatrical establishment against which the Court enterprise and the repertory movement had issued their challenge, it was predictable that he should offer the play to the St James's, whose audience found the setting drab and the casting of George Alexander as a run-down music-teacher unacceptable. It might have earned a very different response played by Manchester's skilled ensemble with authentic accents. Because of this initial rejection *The Thunderbolt* has made very little impression on the English stage; it deserves another chance to strike home.

Between the muted impact of *The Thunderbolt* and the deep waters of *Mid-Channel* Pinero followed Gilbert as the second dramatist to be knighted for services to the theatre. (Forerunners had been honoured for their services to literature, an achievement open to question in the case of F. C. Burnand.) There was aptness, if also foreboding, about the timing in Edward VII's last Birthday Honours. Pinero continued to write almost until his death in 1934 but found himself increasingly disregarded. His attempt to present a Rose Trelawny of the musical comedy stage in *The 'Mind-the-Paint' Girl* struck few chords; his last piece for the St James's, *The Big Drum*, failed to divert a wartime audience, and *The Enchanted Cottage* tackled a theme more suited to Barrie. His was too oracular a voice for a generation attuned to the staccato tones and scepticism of Maugham, Lonsdale and Coward. While his new work withered in performance, revivals of some of his successes were welcomed as period pieces, notably *Trelawny of the 'Wells'* at the Old Vic in 1925 – in a revised text positively identifying Rose's training-ground as Sadler's Wells, to whose rebuilding the production was dedicated. This objective was achieved in 1931, three years before the playwright's death.

Pinero's plays reflect a leisurely age: his characters travel by carriage or train, communicate by letter, have time to converse in complete sentences, or even whole paragraphs. His tempo therefore seemed over-deliberate and his tone too measured for playgoers who drove fast cars, depended on the telephone and talked in broken phrases spiced with slang. But his best work was inspired by love of the theatre and theatrical method, and marked by respect for his public's judgement. Respect usually begets respect, and Pinero has retained critical regard for his craftsmanship. Love on the other hand does not necessarily engender love in return, so that the theatre fifty years after his death favours Wilde's glittering epigrams and Shaw's thrusting argument before his solid worth. But there will always be admiration for the proud workmanship of his writing and deep affection for the warm humanity of his people.

NOTES

1 Ellen Terry, *Memoirs* (London, 1933), p. 161.
2 Letter to H. H. Küther, dated 10 May 1932, printed in J. P. Wearing (ed.), *The Collected Letters of Sir Arthur Pinero* (Minneapolis, Minn., 1974), p. 288.
3 Letter dated 27 November 1907, printed in Wearing, (ed.), p. 209.
4 *Real Conversations* (London, 1901), p. 21.
5 Preface to *Three Plays for Puritans* (Harmondsworth, 1946), p. xliii.
6 See footnote to p. 131.
7 Quoted in Norman Marshall, *The Producer and the Play* (London, 1957), p. 258.
8 *To Tell My Story* (London, 1948), p. 49.
9 In the Library of the Garrick Club.
10 *The Social Plays of Arthur Wing Pinero*, 4 vols. (New York, 1922), IV, 22.

BIOGRAPHICAL RECORD

24 May 1855	Born at 21 Dalby Terrace, Islington, London. Father: John Daniel Pinero, solicitor; mother: Lucy Daines Pinero.
1860–5	Attended Exmouth Street School, Clerkenwell, London.
1865–70	Worked in father's office
1870–4	Solicitor's clerk, Lincoln's Inn Fields, London. Studied elocution at Birkbeck College, London, appearing in numerous productions.
1871	Father died.
1874	Joined company at Theatre Royal, Edinburgh, under R. H. Wyndham.
1875	Joined company at Royal Alexandra Theatre, Liverpool, under Edward Saker.
15 April–4 July 1876	Played Mr Darch in *Miss Gwilt* (by Wilkie Collins) at Globe, London.
18 September–9 December 1876	Toured with Irving and Lyceum company.
16 December 1876–22 July 1881	With Irving's company. Parts included: 29 January 1877 Lord Stanley (*Richard III*) 26 December 1877 Lambert (*The Lyons Mail*) 28 December 1877 Marquis of Huntley (*Charles I*) 16 January 1878 Dr Zimmer (*The Bells*) 18 May 1878 Montgomery Clutterbuck (*Two Can Play at That Game*) 30 December 1878 Guildenstern (*Hamlet*) 20 September 1879 Augustus Cadell (*Daisy's Escape*) 1 November 1879 Salarino (*The Merchant of Venice*) 18 September 1880 Alfred Maynard (*The Corsican Brothers*) 2 May 1881 Mazzoni (*Bygones*) Roderigo (*Othello*)

26 November 1881–28 July 1882	With Bancrofts' company at Theatre Royal, Haymarket Parts included: 26 November 1881 Marquis de Cevennes (*Plot and Passion*) 19 January 1882 Sir Alexander Shendryn (*Ours*) 26 January 1882 Diggory (*She Stoops to Conquer*) 25 April 1882 Mr Hanway (*Odette*)
19 April 1883	Married Myra Emily Hamilton, née Moore, widow of John Angus Hamilton, stage name Myra Holme. Moved to 10 Marlborough Crescent, Bedford Park, London.
3 May–19 July 1884	Rejoined Bancrofts to play Sir Anthony Absolute (*The Rivals*).
20 July 1885	Played Adolphus Spanker in *London Assurance* for Bancrofts' Farewell, Theatre Royal, Haymarket. Moved to 64 St John's Wood Road, London.
1887	Elected to Garrick Club
1891	Contributed introduction to Tolstoy, *The Fruits of Enlightenment* (Heinemann).
1892	Moved to 70A Hamilton Terrace, London
1896	Contributed prefatory letter to William Archer, *The Theatrical World of 1895* (Scott).
1900	Contributed prefatory note to W. L. Courtney, *The Idea of Tragedy in Ancient and Modern Drama* (Constable).
1902	Moved to 14 Hanover Square, London.
1903	Lectured to Philosophical Institution, Edinburgh, on 'Robert Louis Stevenson as a Dramatist'.
1906	Chairman, Executive Committee, Ellen Terry Jubilee Celebrations.
June 1909	Knighted Moved to 115A Harley Street, London. Gave evidence to Parliamentary Committee on Theatrical Censorship. Elected first President, Dramatists' Club.

1910	Fellow, Royal Society of Literature.
1914	Chairman, 1st Battalion, United Artists' Rifles.
1918	Contributed introduction to Leonard Merrick; *The Position of Peggy Harper* (Hodder and Stoughton).
30 June 1919	Death of wife
1929	Contributed 'The Theatre in the Seventies' to *The Eighteen Seventies: Essays by Fellows of the Royal Society of Literature*, ed. Harley Granville Barker (Cambridge)
1932	Contributed 'Robert Browning as a Dramatist' to *Transactions of the Royal Society of Literature*, 2nd series, 31, pp. 255–68 Contributed 'The Theatre in Transition' to *Fifty Years: Memories and Contrasts. A Composite Picture of the Period 1882–1932* (Butterworth)
23 November 1934	Died at the Marylebone Nursing Home, London.

A NOTE ON THE TEXTS

The texts of *The Schoolmistress* and *The Thunderbolt* are those printed by Heinemann in the series *Plays of Arthur Pinero*, dated respectively 1894 and 1909.

An Appendix provides an alternative ending to *The Schoolmistress* as it appears in Pinero's manuscript now in the Fales Library of New York University.

The published text of *The Second Mrs Tanqueray* (Heinemann, 1895) has been collated with that of the manuscript, now in the Houghton Library of Harvard University and with Pinero's prompt-copy (itself a marked copy of the privately printed edition by J. Miles, dated 1892), now in the British Library (pressmark: Cup. 401 c.2).

The text of *Trelawny of the 'Wells'* is that published by Samuel French in 1936 'as altered for the revival of the play at the Victoria Theatre – the "Old Vic" – in 1925'. This revival was directed by Pinero himself. Variations between this edition and that published by Heinemann in the *Plays of Arthur Pinero* series (1899) are printed as footnotes. The stage directions have been simplified to conform with those employed in the other plays in this volume, and follow the usage adopted in the Heinemann edition.

THE SCHOOLMISTRESS

A farce in three acts

First produced at the Royal Court Theatre, London, on 27 March 1886, with the following cast:

THE HON. VERE QUECKETT	Mr Arthur Cecil
REAR-ADMIRAL ARCHIBALD RANKLING, C. B. (of H.M. Flag-ship *Pandora*)	Mr John Clayton
LIEUT. JOHN MALLORY (of H.M. Flag-ship *Pandora*)	Mr F. Kerr
MR SAUNDERS (Mr Mallory's Nephew, of the Training-ship *Dexterous*)	Mr Edwin Victor
MR REGINALD PAULOVER	Mr H. Eversfield
MR OTTO BERNSTEIN (a Popular Composer)	Mr Chevalier
TYLER (a Servant)	Mr W. Phillips
GOFF	Mr Fred Cape
JAFFRAY	Mr Sugg
MRS RANKLING	Miss Emily Cross
MISS DYOTT (Principal of Volumnia College for the Daughters of Gentlemen)	Mrs John Wood
DINAH RANKLING	Miss Cudmore
GWENDOLINE HAWKINS	Miss Viney
ERMYNTRUDE JOHNSON	Miss La Coste
PEGGY HESSLERIGGE (an Articled Pupil)	Miss Norreys
JANE CHIPMAN	Miss Roche

a 'Oh, you vexing girl!'

b 'For heaven's sake, don't touch the pudding.'

c 'Oh, crikey! This must be for *him*!'

I *The Schoolmistress*, 1886. Photographs of the original cast:
(*a*) Act I – Peggy Hesslerigge (Rose Norreys), the Hon. Vere Queckett (Arthur Cecil); (*b*) Act II – Mr Saunders (Edwin Victor), Lieut. John Mallory (Fred Kerr), Rear-Admiral Archibald Rankling, C.B. (John Clayton); (*c*) Act I – Peggy Hesslerigge (Rose Norreys), Tyler (W. Phillips), Ermyntrude Johnson (Miss La Coste), Dinah Rankling (Miss Cudmore), Gwendoline Hawkins (Miss Viney)

THE FIRST ACT: THE MYSTERY

The Scene is the Reception-room at MISS DYOTT'*s seminary for young ladies, known as* Volumnia College, Volumnia House, *near Portland Place. The windows look on to the street, and a large door at the further end of the room opens to the hall, where there are some portmanteaus standing, while there is another door on the spectator's right.*
JANE CHIPMAN, *a stout middle-aged servant, and* TYLER, *an unhealthy-looking youth, wearing a page's jacket, enter the room, carrying between them a large travelling-trunk.*

TYLER: (*breathlessly*) 'Old 'ard – 'old 'ard! Phew! (*They rest the trunk on the floor,* TYLER *dabs his forehead with a small dirty handkerchief, which he passes on to* JANE.) Excuse me not offering it to you first, Jane.

JANE: (*dabbing the palms of her hands*) Don't name it, Tyler. Do you 'appen to know what time Missus starts?

TYLER: Two-thirty, I 'eard say.

JANE: It's a queer thing her going away like this alone – not to say nothing of a schoolmistress leaving a lot of foolish young gals for a month or six weeks.

TYLER: (*sitting despondently on the trunk*) Cook and the parlourmaid got rid of too – it's not much of a Christmas vacation we shall get, you and me, Jane.

JANE: You're right. (*sitting on the sofa*) Let's see – how many of our young ladies 'aven't gone home for their 'olidays?

TYLER: Well, there's Miss 'Awkins.

JANE: Her people is in India.

TYLER: Miss Johnson.

JANE: Her people is in the Divorce Court.

TYLER: Miss Hesslerigge.

JANE: Oh, she ain't got no 'ome. She's an orphan, studying for to be a governess.

TYLER: Then there's this new girl, Miss Ranklin'.

JANE: Dinah Ranklin'?

TYLER: Yes, Dinah Ranklin'. Now, why is *she* to spend her Exmas at our College? She's the daughter of Admiral Ranklin', and the Ranklin's live jest round the corner at Collin'wood 'Ouse.

JANE: Oh, she's been fallin' in love or something, and has got to be locked up.

TYLER: Well then, last but not least, there's the individual who is kicking his 'eels about the 'ouse, and giving himself the airs of the 'aughty.

JANE: (*mysteriously*) What – Missus's husband?

TYLER: Yes – Missus's husband.

JANE: Ah! Mark my word, if ever there was a Mystery, there's one.

TYLER: *Who* is he? Missus brings him 'ome about a month ago, and doesn't introduce him to us or to nobody. The order is she's still to be called Miss Dyott, and we don't know even his nasty name.

JANE: (*returning to the trunk*) She calls him Ducky.

TYLER: Yes, but *we* can't call him Ducky. (*pointing to the handkerchief which*

Volumnia College: presumably so called because it serves as a Roman matron to its pupils.
Collin'wood 'Ouse: Collingwood House. Admiral Collingwood took command of the British fleet at Trafalgar after Nelson's death.

JANE *has left upon the sofa*). My 'andkerchief, please. I don't let *anybody* use it.

JANE: (*returning the handkerchief*) Excuse me. (*In putting the handkerchief into his breast-pocket, he first removes a handful of cheap-looking squibs.*) Lor'! You will carry them deadly fireworks about with you, Tyler.

TYLER: (*regarding them fondly*) Fireworks is my only disserpation. There ain't much danger unless anybody lunges at me. (*producing some dirty crackers from his trousers pockets, and regarding them with gloomy relish*) Friction is the risk I run.

JANE: (*palpitating*) Oh, don't, Tyler! How can you 'ave such a 'ankering?

TYLER: (*intensely*) It's more than a 'ankering. I love to 'oard 'em and meller 'em. To-day they're damp – to-morrow they're dry. And when the time comes for to let them off –

JANE: Then they don't go off –

TYLER: (*putting the fireworks away*) P'r'aps not – and it's their 'orrible uncertainty wot I crave after. Lift your end, Jane.

> (*They take up the trunk as* GWENDOLINE HAWKINS *and* ERMYNTRUDE JOHNSON, *two pretty girls, the one gushing, the other haughty in manner, appear in the hall.*)

GWENDOLINE: Here are Miss Dyott's boxes – she is really going to-day. I am so happy!

ERMYNTRUDE: What an inexpressible relief! Oh, Tyler, I am dissatisfied with the manner in which my shoes are polished.

GWENDOLINE: Yes – and, Tyler, you never fed my mice last night.

TYLER: It ain't my place. Birds and mice is Jane's place.

GWENDOLINE: You are an inhuman boy! (*shaking* TYLER)

ERMYNTRUDE: You are a creature!

JANE: Don't shake him, Miss, don't shake him!

> (PEGGY HESSLERIGGE *enters through the hall, and comes between* TYLER *and* GWENDOLINE. PEGGY *is a shabbily dressed, untidy girl, with wild hair and inky fingers; her voice is rather shrewish and her actions are jerky; altogether she has the appearance of an overwise and neglected child.*)

PEGGY: Leave the boy alone, Gwendoline Hawkins! What has he done?

GWENDOLINE: He won't feed my darling pets.

ERMYNTRUDE: And he is generally a Lower Order.

PEGGY: Go away, Tyler. (TYLER *and* JANE *deposit the trunk in the hall with the other baggage, and disappear.*) You silly girls! To make an enemy of the boy at the very moment we depend upon his devotion! It's just like you, Ermyntrude Johnson!

ERMYNTRUDE: Don't you threaten me with your inky finger, Miss Hesslerigge, please.

PEGGY: Ugh! Haven't we sworn to help Dinah Rankling with our last breath? Haven't we sworn to free her from the chains of tyranny and oppression, and never to eat much till we have seen her safely and happily by her husband's side!

---

meller: perhaps Cockney version of 'mellow' = 'mature'.

ERMYNTRUDE: Yes – but we can't truckle to a pale and stumpy boy, you know.

PEGGY: We can – we've got to! If Dinah's husband is ever to enter this house we must crouch before the instrument who opens the door – however short, however pasty.

DINAH: (*calling ouside*) Are you there, girls?

PEGGY: (*jumping, and clapping her hands*) Here's Dinah!

ERMYNTRUDE *and* GWENDOLINE: (*calling*) Dinah!

> (*They run up to the door to receive and embrace* DINAH, *who enters through the hall.* DINAH *is an exceedingly pretty and simple-looking girl of about sixteen.*)

GWENDOLINE: We've been waiting for you, Dinah.

PEGGY: And now you're going to keep your promise to us, ain't you?

DINAH: My promise?

PEGGY: To tell us all about it 'from beginning to end.

DINAH: (*bashfully*) Oh, I can't – I don't like to.

PEGGY: You must; we've only heard your story in bits.

DINAH: But where's Miss Dyott?

PEGGY: Out – out – out.

DINAH: And where is *he* – Miss Dyott's husband?

PEGGY: What – the Mystery? (*skipping across to the left-hand door, and, going down on her knees, peering through the keyhole*) It's all right. One o'clock in the day, and he's not down yet – the imp! I'd cold sponge him if I were Miss Dyott. Places, young ladies. (ERMYNTRUDE *sits with* DINAH *on the sofa,* GWENDOLINE *being at* DINAH's *feet.* PEGGY *perches on the edge of the table, with her feet on a chair.*) H'm! Now then, Mrs — What's your name, Dinah?

DINAH: (*drooping her eyelids*) Paulover – Mrs Reginald Paulover.

PEGGY: Attention for Mrs Paulover's narrative. Chapter One.

DINAH: Well, dears, I met him at a party – at Mrs St Dunstan's in the Cromwell Road. He was presented to Mamma and me by Major Padgate.

PEGGY: Vote of thanks to Major Padgate; I wish *we* knew him, young ladies. Well?

DINAH: I bowed, of course, and then Mr Paulover – Mr Paulover asked me whether I didn't think the evening was rather warm.

PEGGY: He soon began to rattle on, then. It was his conversation that attracted you, I suppose?

DINAH: Oh no, love came very gradually. We were introduced at about ten o'clock, and I didn't feel really drawn to him till long after eleven. The next day, being Ma's 'At home' day, Major Padgate brought him to tea.

PEGGY: Young ladies, what is your opinion of Major Padgate?

ERMYNTRUDE: I think he must be awfully considerate.

DINAH: He's not – he called my Reginald a 'young shaver'.

PEGGY: That's contemptible enough. How old is your Reginald?

DINAH: He is much my senior – he was seventeen in November. Well, the following week Reginald proposed to me in the conservatory. He spoke very sensibly about settling down, and how we were not growing younger; and how he'd seen a house in Park Lane which wasn't to let, but which very likely would be to let some day. And then we went into the drawing-room and told Mamma.

PEGGY, ERMYNTRUDE *and* GWENDOLINE: Well, well?

DINAH: (*breaking down and putting her handkerchief to her eyes*) Oh, I shall never forget the scene! I never shall.

PEGGY: Don't cry, Dinah!
(*They all try to console her.*)

DINAH: Mamma, who is very delicate, went into violent hysterics and tore at the hearthrug with her teeth. But a day or two afterwards she grew a little calmer, and promised to write to Papa, who was with his ship at Malta.

PEGGY: And did she?

DINAH: Yes. Papa, you know, is Admiral Rankling. His ship, the 'Pandora', has never run into anything, and so Papa is a very distinguished man.

GWENDOLINE: And what was his answer?

DINAH: He telegraphed home one terrible word – 'Bosh'!

PEGGY, ERMYNTRUDE *and* GWENDOLINE: (*indignantly*) Oh!

PEGGY: He ought to be struck into a Flying Dutchman!

DINAH: The telegraphic rate from Malta necessitates abruptness, but I can never forgive the choice of such a phrase. But it decided our fate. Three weeks ago, when I was supposed to selecting wools at Whiteley's, Reginald and I were secretly united at the Registry Office.

GWENDOLINE: Oh, how lovely!

ERMYNTRUDE: How romantic!

DINAH: We declared we were much older than we really are, but, as Reginald said, trouble had aged us, so it wasn't a story. At the doors of the Registry Office we parted.

ERMYNTRUDE: How horrible!

GWENDOLINE: I couldn't have done that!

DINAH: And when I reached home there was a letter from Papa ordering Mamma to have me locked up at once in a Boarding School; and here I am – torn from my husband, my letters opened by Miss Dyott, quite friendless and alone.

PEGGY: No, that you're not, Dinah. Listen to me! Miss Dyott is going out of town to-day, and I'm left in charge. I'm a poor governess, but playing jailer over bleeding hearts is not in my articles, and if your husband comes to Volumnia House and demands his wife, he doesn't go away without you – does he, young ladies?

GWENDOLINE *and* ERMYNTRUDE: No.

PEGGY: We will do as we would be done by – won't we?

GWENDOLINE *and* ERMYNTRUDE: Yes!
(*The street-door bell is heard, the* GIRLS *cling to each other.*)

PEGGY, ERMYNTRUDE *and* GWENDOLINE: (*in a whisper*) Oh!

DINAH: (*trembling*) Miss Dyott!
(TYLER *is seen crossing the hall.* PEGGY *runs to the window, and looks out.*)

PEGGY: No, it isn't – it's the postman.

DINAH: A letter from Reginald!

Flying Dutchman: the legendary sailor featured in Wagner's opera and many plays.
Whiteley's: a large store in Queensway.

(TYLER *enters with three letters.*)

PEGGY: (*sweetly*) Anything for us, Tyler dear?

TYLER: (*looking at the letters, which he guards with one arm*) One for Miss Dinah Ranklin'!

DINAH: Oh! (*snatching at her letter, which* TYLER *quickly slips into his pocket.*)

TYLER: My orders is to hand Miss Ranklin's letters to the missus. (*handing a letter to* PEGGY) Miss Hesslerigge.

PEGGY: (*surprised*) For me?

TYLER: (*looking at the third letter*) Oh, look 'ere, here's a go!

GIRLS: What's that?

TYLER: (*dancing with delight*) Oh, crikey! this must be for *him*!

PEGGY: Miss Dyott's husband!

GIRLS: The Mystery!

        (*The* GIRLS *gather round* TYLER *and look over his shoulder.*)

PEGGY: (*reading the address*) It's re-addressed from the Junior Amalgamated Club, St James's Street. (*snatching the letter from* TYLER) Gracious! 'The Honourable Vere Queckett'!

GWENDOLINE: The Honourable!

ERMYNTRUDE: The Honourable!

TYLER: What's that mean?

PEGGY: Young ladies, we have been entertaining a swell unawares! (*returning letter to* TYLER) Take it up.

TYLER: Swell or no swell, the person who siles two pairs of boots *per diem* daily is no friend o' mine.

        (TYLER *goes out.*)

PEGGY: (*opening her letter*) Oh! From Dinah's Reginald!

DINAH: No, no!

PEGGY: Addressed to me. (*referring to the signature*) 'Reginald Percy Paulover'!

DINAH: Read it, read it!

        (PEGGY *sits on the sofa, the three girls clustering round her;* DINAH *kneeling at her feet expectantly.*)

PEGGY: (*reading.*) 'Montpelier Square, West Brompton. Dear Miss Hesslerigge, – Heaven will reward you. The letter wrapped round a stone which you threw me last night from an upper window of Volumnia House was handed to me after I had compensated the person upon whose head it unfortunately alighted. The news that Dinah has one friend in Volumnia House enabled me to get a little rest between half-past five and six this morning.'

GWENDOLINE: *One* friend!

ERMYNTRUDE: What about us?

        (DINAH *kisses them.*)

DINAH: Go on!

PEGGY: (*reading*) 'Not having closed my eyes for eleven nights, sleep was of distinct

---

Honourable: Queckett's father is (or was) a peer of the rank of baron or above; the sons of such are allowed the courtesy title of 'Honourable'.

siles = soils.

value. Now, dear Miss Hesslerigge, inform Dinah that our apartments are quite
ready – '

GWENDOLINE *and* ERMYNTRUDE: Oh!

PEGGY: 'And that I shall present myself at Volumnia College, to fetch away the dear
love of my heart, to-night at half-past nine.' To-night!

GWENDOLINE *and* ERMYNTRUDE: To-night!

DINAH: Oh, I've come over so frightened!

PEGGY: To-night!
> (*Waving the letter and dancing round with delight.*)

GWENDOLINE: Finish the letter.

PEGGY: (*resuming her seat, and reading with emotion*) 'Please assure Dinah that I
shall love her till death, and that the piano is now moving in. Dinah is my one
thought. The former is on the three years' system. Kiss my angel for me. Our
carpet is Axminster, and, I regret to say, second-hand. But, oh! our life will be a
blessed, blessed dream – the worn part going well under the centre table. This
evening at half-past nine. Gratefully yours, Reginald Percy Paulover. P.S. – I
shall be closely muffled up, as the corner lamp-post under which I stand is visible
from the window of Admiral Rankling's dining-room. You will know me by my
faithful, trusty respirator.' Oh! I'm so excited! I wish somebody was coming for
me!

ERMYNTRUDE: I know – we shall be frustrated by Jane!

GWENDOLINE: Or Tyler!

PEGGY: Leave them to me – I'll manage 'em!

DINAH: But there's Miss Dyott's husband!

PEGGY: What? Let the mysterious person who has won Miss Dyott pause before he
steps between a young bride and bridegroom! Ladies, Miss Dyott's husband is
ours for the holidays. One frown from him and his dinners shall be wrecked, his
wine watered, his cigars dampened. He shall find us not girls but Gorgons!
> (*A loud knock and ring are heard at the front door. JANE crosses the
> hall.*)

ERMYNTRUDE, GWENDOLINE, *and* DINAH: (*under their breath*) Miss Dyott!
Miss Dyott!
> (*They quickly disappear. PEGGY remains, hastily concealing the
> letter. MISS DYOTT enters. She is a good-looking, dark woman of
> dignified presence and rigid demeanour, her dress and manner being
> those of the typical schoolmistress.*)

MISS DYOTT: Is that Miss Hesslerigge?

PEGGY: (*demurely*) Yes, Miss Dyott.

MISS DYOTT: How have the young ladies been employing themselves?

PEGGY: I have been reading aloud to them, Miss Dyott.

MISS DYOTT: Is Mr Que— is my husband down yet?

PEGGY: I've not had the pleasure of seeing him, Miss Dyott.

MISS DYOTT: You can join the young ladies, thank you.

PEGGY: Thank you, Miss Dyott.

---

respirator: 'apparatus of gauze etc. worn, over mouth to warm or filter inhaled air' (*OED*).

(*In the doorway she waves Reginald's letter defiantly, but quickly disappears as* MISS DYOTT *turns round.*)

MISS DYOTT: Now, if Vere will only remain upstairs a few moments longer! (*She goes hurriedly to the left-hand door, listens, and turns the key, then to the centre door, listens again and appears satisfied, after which she throws open the window and waves her handkerchief, calling in a loud whisper*) Mr Bernstein! Mr. Bernstein! I have left the door on the latch. Come in, please (*closing the window and going to the door. Very shortly afterwards,* OTTO BERNSTEIN, *a little elderly German, with the air of a musician, enters the room.*) Thank you for following me so quickly. (*closing the door and turning the key*)

BERNSTEIN: You seemed so agitated that I came after your cab mit anoder.

MISS DYOTT: Agitated – yes. Tell me – miserable woman that I am – tell me, what did I sound like at rehearsal this morning?

BERNSTEIN: Cabital – cabital. Your voice comes out rich and peautiful. Marks my vord – you will make a hit to-night. Have you seen your new name in de pills?

MISS DYOTT: The pills?

BERNSTEIN: The blay-pills.

MISS DYOTT: I should drop flat on the pavement, if I did.

BERNSTEIN: It looks very vine. (*Quoting*) 'Miss Gonstance Delaporte as Queen Honorine, in Otto Bernstein's new Gomic Opera, "Pierrette", her vurst abbearance in London.'

MISS DYOTT: Oh, how disgraceful!

BERNSTEIN: Disgraceful! To sing such melodies! No – no, please. Disgraceful! Vy did you appeal to me, dree weeks ago, to put you in the vay of getting through the Christmas vacation?

MISS DYOTT: (*tearfully*) You don't know everything. Sit down! I can trust you. You are my oldest friend, and were a pupil of my late eminent father. Mr Bernstein, I am no longer a single woman.

BERNSTEIN: Oh, I am very bleased. I wish you many happy returns of the – eh – no – I congratulate you.

MISS DYOTT: I am married secretly – secretly, because my husband could never face the world of fashion as the consort of the proprietress of a scholastic establishment. You will gather from this that my husband is a gentleman.

BERNSTEIN: H'm – so – is he?

MISS DYOTT: It had been a long-cherished ambition with me, if ever I married, to wed no one but a gentleman. I do not mean a gentleman in a mere parliamentary sense – I mean a man of birth, blood, and breeding. Respect my confidence – I have wedded the Honourable Vere Queckett.

BERNSTEIN: (*unconcernedly*) Ah! Is he a very nice man?

MISS DYOTT: Nice! Mr Bernstein, you are speaking of a brother of Lord Limehouse!

BERNSTEIN: Oh, am I? Lord Limehouse – let me tink – he is very – very – vot you gall it? – very popular just now. Yah – yah – he is in the Bankruptcy Court!

MISS DYOTT: (*with pride*) Certainly. So is Harold Archideckne Queckett, Vere's youngest brother. So is Loftus Martineau Queckett, Vere's cousin. They have always been a very united family. But, dear Mr Bernstein, you have accidentally probed the one – I won't say fault – the one most remarkable attribute of these great Saxon Quecketts.

BERNSTEIN: Oh yes, I see; you have to pay your husband's leedle pills.

MISS DYOTT: Quite so – that is it. I have the honour of being employed in the gradual discharge of liabilities incurred by Mr Vere Queckett since the year 1876. I am also engaged in the noble task of providing Mr Queckett with the elaborate necessities of his present existence.

BERNSTEIN: I know now vy you vanted mine help.

MISS DYOTT: Ah yes, Volumnia College is not equal to the grand duty imposed upon it. It is absolutely ncessary that I should increase my income. In my despair at facing the genial season I wrote to you.

BERNSTEIN: Proposing to turn your cabital voice to account, eh?

MISS DYOTT: Quite so – and suggesting that I should sing in your new Oratorio.

BERNSTEIN: Well, you are going to do zo.

MISS DYOTT: What! When you have induced me to figure in a comic opera!

BERNSTEIN: Yah, yah – but I have told you I have used the music of my new Oratorio for my new Gomic Opera.

MISS DYOTT: Ah, yes – that is my only consolation.

BERNSTEIN: Vill your goot gentleman be in the stalls to-night?

MISS DYOTT: In the stalls – at the theatre! Hush, Mr Bernstein, it is a secret from Vere. Lest his suspicions should be aroused by my leaving home every evening, I have led him to think that I am visiting a clergyman's wife at Hereford. I shall really be lodging in Henrietta Street, Covent Garden.

BERNSTEIN: Oh, vy not tell him all about it?

MISS DYOTT: Nonsense! Vere is a gentleman; he would insist upon attending me to and from the theatre.

BERNSTEIN: Vell, I should hope so.

MISS DYOTT: No – no. He is himself a graceful dancer. A common chord of sympathy would naturally be struck between him and the *coryphées*. Oh, there is so much variety in Vere's character.

BERNSTEIN: Vell, you are a plucky woman; you deserve to be happy zome day.

MISS DYOTT: Happy! Think of the deception I am practising upon dear Vere! Think of the people who believe in the rigid austerity of Caroline Dyott, Principal of Volumnia College. Think of the precious confidence reposed in me by the parents and relations of twenty-seven innocent pupils. Give an average of eight and a half relations to each pupil; multiply eight and a half by twenty-seven and you approximate the number whose trust I betray this night!

BERNSTEIN: Yes, but tink of the audience you will delight tonight in my Oratorio – I mean my Gomic Opera. Oh, that reminds me. (*taking out a written paper from a pocket-book*) Here are two new verses of the Bolitical Song for you to commit to memory before this evening. They are extremely goot.

MISS DYOTT: (*looking at the paper*) Mr Bernstein, surely here is a veiled allusion to – yes, I thought so. Oh, the unwarrantable familiarity! I can't – I can't even vocally allude to a perfect stranger as the Grand Old Man!

Grand Old Man: William Ewart Gladstone, Liberal statesman and four times Prime Minister.

BERNSTEIN: Oh, now, now – he von't mind dat!

MISS DYOTT: But the tendency of the chorus – (*reading*) 'Doesn't he wish he may get it!' is opposed to my stern political convictions! Oh, what am I coming to?

>   (QUECKETT's *voice is heard.*)

QUECKETT: (*calling outside*) Caroline! Caroline!

MISS DYOTT: Here's Vere! (*hurriedly to* BERNSTEIN) Good-bye, dear Mr Bernstein – you understand why I cannot present you.

BERNSTEIN: (*bustling*) Good-bye – till to-night. Marks my vord, you vill make a great hit.

QUECKETT: (*calling*) Caroline!

MISS DYOTT: (*unlocking the centre door*) Go – let yourself out.

BERNSTEIN: Goot luck to you!

MISS DYOTT: (*opening the door*) Yes, yes.

BERNSTEIN: And success to my new Oratorio – I mean my Gomic Opera.

MISS DYOTT: Oh, go!

>   (*She pushes him out and closes the door, leaning against it faintly.*)

QUECKETT: (*rattling the other door*) I say, Caroline!

MISS DYOTT: (*calling to him*) Is that my darling Vere?

QUECKETT: (*outside*) Yes.

>   (*She comes to the other door, unlocks and opens it.* VERE
>   QUECKETT *enters. He is a fresh, breezy, dapper little gentleman of
>   about forty-five, with fair curly hair, a small waxed moustache, and a
>   simple boyish manner. He is dressed in the height of fashion and wears a
>   flower in his coat, and an eye-glass.*)

QUECKETT: Good morning, Caroline, good morning.

MISS DYOTT: How is my little pet to-day? (*kissing his cheek, which he turns to her for the purpose*) Naughty Vere is down later than usual.

QUECKETT: It isn't my fault, dear; the florist was late in sending my flower.

MISS DYOTT: What a shame!

QUECKETT: (*shaking out a folded silk handkerchief*) Oh, by the bye, Carrie, I want some fresh perfume in my bottles.

MISS DYOTT: My Vere shall have it.

QUECKETT: Thank you – thank you. (*sitting before the fire, opening the newspaper, and humming a tune*) Let me see – let me see. Ah, here we are – 'Court of Bankruptcy – before the Official Receiver'. Limehouse came up again for hearing yesterday. How they bother him! They bothered me in '75. Now here's a coincidence, Carrie. In 1875 my assets were *nil* – in 1885 dear old Bob's assets are *nil*. Now that's deuced funny.

MISS DYOTT: Vere, dear, have you forgotten what to-day is?

QUECKETT: (*referring to the head of paper*) December the twenty-second.

MISS DYOTT: Yes, but it's the day on which I am to quit my Verey.

QUECKETT: Oh, you've stuck to going, then! Well, I daresay you're right, you know. You've a very bad cold. Nothing like a change for a bad cold – change of scene, change of pocket-handkerchiefs, and so on.

MISS DYOTT: But you don't say anything about your own lonely Christmas. I have married a man who is too unselfish.

(*The centre door opens slightly, and the heads of the three girls,* PEGGY, GWENDOLINE, *and* ERMYNTRUDE *appear one above the other, spying.*)

QUECKETT: (*putting down his paper*) Lonely? By Jove, those inquisitive pupils of yours won't let a fellow be lonely! Upon my soul, they are vexing girls.

MISS DYOTT: But they are a source of income, dear.

QUECKETT: They are a source of annoyance. I've never had the measles – I've half a mind to catch it and give it to 'em. Now if I could only while away my evenings somewhere, these vexing girls wouldn't so much matter. (*He rises, the heads disappear, and the door closes. Listening*) What was that?

MISS DYOTT: The front door, I think.

QUECKETT: I thought it might be those vexing girls – they're always prying about. I was going to say, Carrie, why not let me withdraw my resignation at the Junior Amalgamated Club and continue my membership?

MISS DYOTT: Ten guineas a year for such an object I cannot afford, and will not pay, Vere.

QUECKETT: Upon my soul, I might just as well be nobody, the way I'm treated.

MISS DYOTT: Oh, my king, don't say that! Have you thought about the Christmas expenses?

QUECKETT: Frankly, my dear, I have not.

MISS DYOTT: Have you forgotten that my rent is due on Friday?

QUECKETT: Completely.

MISS DYOTT: And then think – only think of your boots!

QUECKETT: Oh, dash it all – what man of any position ever thinks of his boots? (*producing a letter*) The fact is, Caroline, I have had a note – sent on to me from the Club – from my friend, Jack Mallory. He is first lieutenant on the 'Pandora', you know, and just home after four years at Malta. He reached London yesterday, and writes me – (*reading*) 'Now, old chap, do let's have one of our old rollicking nights together, and –'

MISS DYOTT: What!

QUECKETT: Eh? (*correcting himself*) He writes me – (*referring to the letter*) 'Now, old chap, do let me give you the details of our new self-loading eighty-ton gun.' Well, Carrie, what the deuce am I to do? It seems a nice gun. (*She shrugs her shoulders.*) Carrie, what is your Vere to do? (*She makes no answer, he approaches her and touches her on the shoulder.*) Carrie. Carrie, look at your Vere. Vere speaks to you. (*He sits on her lap, she looks up affectionately.*) Carrie, darling, you know old Jack is such a devil –

MISS DYOTT: Eh?

QUECKETT: A nice devil, you know – an exceedingly nice devil. Now I can't show up at the Club after sending in my resignation – they'd quiz me awfully. But I must entertain poor old Jack. (*coaxingly*) Eh? Resignation sent in through misunderstanding, eh? (*pinching her cheek*) Ten little ginny-winnies, eh?

MISS DYOTT: Not a ginny-winny! For a Club, not half a ginny-winny!

QUECKETT: Caroline, you forget what is due to me.

MISS DYOTT: I wish I could forget what is due to everybody. Don't be cross, Vere. I'll fetch your hat and coat, and Vere shall go out for his little morning stroll.

And if he promises not to be angry with his Caroline, there are five shillings to spend.

> (*She gives him some silver; he looks up beamingly again.*)

QUECKETT: My darling!

MISS DYOTT: (*taking his face between her hands, and kissing him*) Um – you spoilt boy!

> (*She runs out.*)

QUECKETT: Now what am I to do about Jack? I can't ask him here. Carrie would never allow it, and if she would I couldn't stand the chaff about marrying a Boarding School. No, I can't ask Jack here. *Why* can't I ask Jack here? Everybody in bed at nine o'clock – square the boy Tyler to wait. Bachelor lodgings, near Portland Place. Extremely good address. Jack *shall* give me the details of that eighty-ton gun. Yes – and we'll load it, too. While I'm out I'll send this wire to Jack. (*taking a telegraph form from the stationery-cabinet, and writing*) 'Come up to-night, dear old boy. Nine-thirty sharp. Diggings of humble bachelor. 80, Duke Street, Portland Place. Bring two or three good fellows. – Vere.' How much does that come to? (*counting the words rapidly*) One – two – three – four – five – no. (*getting confused*) One – two – three – four – five – six – no. One – two – three – four – five – six. (*counting to the end*) I think it is one and something halfpenny – but it's all luck under the new regulations. Oh, and I haven't addressed it! Where's Jack's letter?

> (*He takes the letter from his pocket.* PEGGY *enters quietly. Seeing* QUECKETT, *she draws back, watching him.*)

PEGGY: (*to herself*) What is he doing now – the Guy Fawkes?

QUECKETT: (*referring to the letter*) Ah, 'Rovers' Club'! (*addressing the telegram*) 'John Mallory, Rovers' Club'. Let me see – that's in Green Street, Piccadilly. (*writing*) 'Green Street, Piccadilly'. Or am I thinking of the 'Stragglers'? I've a Club list upstairs – I'll go and look at it. (*Humming an air, he shuts up the telegraph form in the blotting-book, and rises, still with his back to* PEGGY.) I feel so happy!

> (*He goes out.*)

PEGGY: (*advances to the blotting-book, carrying some luggage labels.*) Miss Dyott has sent me to address her luggage labels. I am compelled to open that blotting-book. (*She sits on the chair lately vacated by* QUECKETT, *and opens the blotting-book mischievously with her forefinger and thumb. Seeing the telegraph form*) Ah! (*Reading it greedily with exclamations*) Oh! 'Dear old boy!' Oh! 'Diggings of humble bachelor!' Oh! 'Bring two or three good fellows!' Oh–oh! (*Sticking the telegraph form prominently against the stationery-cabinet, facing her, and addressing a luggage label*) 'Miss Dyott, passenger to Hereford.'

QUECKETT: (*re-entering gaily*) It *is* in Green Street, Piccadilly.

> (*He sees* PEGGY, *and stands perplexed, twisting his little moustache.*)

PEGGY: (*writing solemnly*) 'Miss Dyott, passenger to Hereford.'

QUECKETT: (*coughing anxiously*) H'm! I fancy I left an eighty-ton gun – I mean, I think I've mislaid a – er – (*Without looking up,* PEGGY *re-adjusts the telegraph*

Guy Fawkes: i.e. conspirator. Guy Fawkes was a leading figure in the 'Gunpowder Plot' (1605) to blow up the Houses of Parliament.

form against the cabinet.) Oh! H'm! That's it. (*He makes one or two fidgety attempts to take it, when* PEGGY *rises with it in her hand. She reads it silently, forming the words with her lips.*) Oh, you vexing girl! What do you think of doing about it? (*She commences to fold the form very neatly.*) You know I sha'n't send it. I never meant to send it. I say, I shall not send it. (*nervously holding out his hand*) Shall I? (PEGGY *doubles up the form into another fold without speaking.*) You *are* a vexing girl.

MISS DYOTT: (*calling outside*) Miss Hesslerigge!

    (PEGGY *quietly slips the telegraph form into her pocket.*)

QUECKETT: Oh! You won't tell my wife! You will not *dare* to tell my wife! (*mildly*) Will you?

MISS DYOTT: (*calling again*) Miss Hesslerigge!

QUECKETT: (*in agony*) Oh! (*between his teeth*) Do you – do you know any bad language?

PEGGY: I went to the Lord Mayor's Show once; I heard a little.

QUECKETT: Then I regret to say I use it to you, Miss Hesslerigge – I use it to you!

    (MISS DYOTT *enters, carrying* QUECKETT's *hat, gloves, and overcoat.*)

MISS DYOTT: You can address the labels in another room, Miss Hesslerigge, please.

QUECKETT: (*to himself*) Will she tell?

PEGGY: (*to herself*) He is in our power!

    (PEGGY *goes out.*)

MISS DYOTT: (*putting the hat on* QUECKETT's *head*) You look sickly, my Vere.

QUECKETT: I shall be better after my stroll, Caroline.

    (*A knock and ring are heard.*)

MISS DYOTT: (*assisting* QUECKETT *with his overcoat*) As you have some solitary evenings before you, you may lay in a few cigars, Vere darling.

QUECKETT: Thank you Carrie.

MISS DYOTT: (*helping him to put on his gloves like a child*) But, for the sake of our depressed native industries, I beg that you will order those of purely British origin and manufacture. (TYLER *enters carrying a large common black tea-tray upon which is a solitary visiting-card.*) Where's the salver, you bad boy!

TYLER: (*pointing to* QUECKETT, *sullenly*) 'E slopped his choc'late over it.

MISS DYOTT: (*taking the card*) Admiral and Mrs Rankling – Dinah's parents! I must see them.

QUECKETT: (*hastily turning up his collar to conceal his face*) No, no! They know me – they are old friends of my family's!

    (TYLER *shows in* ADMIRAL *and* MRS RANKLING. MRS RANKLING *is a thin, weak-looking, faded lady with a pale face and anxious eyes. She is dressed in too many colours, and nothing seems to fit very well.* ADMIRAL RANKLING *is a stout, fine old gentleman with short crisp grey hair and fierce black eyebrows. He appears to be suffering inwardly from intense anger.*)

MISS DYOTT: My dear Mrs Rankling.

    (*The ladies shake hands.* TYLER *goes out.*)

Lord Mayor's Show: annual procession of floats, etc., through the main streets of London to mark the start of a Lord Mayor's term of office.

MRS RANKLING: (*pointing to* RANKLING) This is Admiral Rankling.
>   (MISS DYOTT *bows ceremoniously.* RANKLING *returns a slight bow and glares at her.*)
MISS DYOTT: (*to* MRS RANKLING) Pray sit by the fire.
>   (*As the ladies move to the fire,* QUECKETT, *who has been watching his opportunity, creeps round at the back and goes out.*)
MRS RANKLING: (*warming her feet at the fire*) The Admiral has called upon you, Miss Dyott, with reference to our child, Dinah.
>   (RANKLING, *with a smothered exclamation of rage, sits on the sofa.*)
MISS DYOTT: Whom we find the charming daughter of charming parents.
>   (RANKLING *gives her a fierce look, which frightens* MISS DYOTT, *who is most anxious to conciliate the* ADMIRAL.)
MRS RANKLING: Dinah's obstinacy is a very serious shock to the Admiral, who is naturally unused to insubordination.
MISS DYOTT: Naturally.
>   (RANKLING *glares at her again; she puts her hand to her heart.*)
MRS RANKLING: The Admiral has been stationed with his ship at Malta for a long period – in fact the Admiral has not brightened our home for over four years.
MISS DYOTT: How more than delightful to have him with you again!
>   (RANKLING *gives* MISS DYOTT *a fearful look; she clutches her chair.*)
MRS RANKLING: The Admiral has one of those fine English tempers – generous but impetuous. You may guess the sad impression Dinah's ingratitude has produced upon him. It is an open secret that the Admiral made three wills yesterday, and read King Lear's curse after supper in place of Thanksgiving.
RANKLING: (*sharply*) Emma!
MRS RANKLING: (*starting*) Yes, Archibald.
RANKLING: Leave the fire – you'll be chilled when we go. Come over here.
MRS RANKLING: Yes, Archibald. (*crossing the room in a flutter and sitting beside* RANKLING, *who makes insufficient room for her*)
MRS RANKLING: Thank you, Archibald. I have been sitting up with the Admiral all night, and it is owing to my entreaties that he has consented to give Dinah one last chance of reconciliation.
RANKLING: (*who has been eyeing her*) Emma!
MRS RANKLING: Yes, Archibald.
RANKLING: Your bonnet's on one side again.
MRS RANKLING: (*adjusting it*) Thank you, Archibald. We leave town for the holidays to-morrow; it rests with Dinah whether she spends Christmas in her papa's society or not.
RANKLING: Don't twitch your fingers, Emma – don't twitch your fingers.
MRS RANKLING: (*nervously*) It's a habit, Archibald.
RANKLING: It's a very bad one.
MRS RANKLING: All we require is that Dinah should personally assure us that she has banished every thought of the foolish young gentleman she met at Mrs St Dunstan's.

King Lear's curse: on his daughters (*King Lear*, i.iv).

MISS DYOTT: (*rising and ringing the bell*) If I am any student of the passing fancies of a young girl's mind –

RANKLING: Speak louder, ma'am – your voice doesn't travel.

MISS DYOTT: (*nervously – with a gulp*) If I am any student of the passing – fancies – ` (RANKLING *puts his hand to his ear:*) Oh, don't make me so nervous.

> (JANE *enters, looking untidy, her sleeves turned up, and wiping her hands on her apron.*)

MISS DYOTT: (*shocked*) Where is the man-servant?

JANE: On a herring, ma'am.

MISS DYOTT: Ask Miss Dinah Rankling to be good enough to step down-stairs.

> (JANE *goes out.* RANKLING *rises, with* MRS RANKLING *clinging to his arm.*)

MRS RANKLING: You will be calm, Archibald – you will be moderate in tone. (*with a little nervous cough*) Oh, dear! poor Dinah!

RANKLING: Stop that fidgety cough, Emma. (*stalking about the room, his wife following him*)

MRS RANKLING: Even love-matches are sometimes very happy. Ours was a love-match, Archibald.

RANKLING: Be quiet – we're exceptions.

> (*Pacing up to the door just as it opens, and* PEGGY *presents herself. Directly* RANKLING *sees* PEGGY, *he catches her by the shoulders, and gives her a good shaking.*)

MISS DYOTT: Admiral!

MRS RANKLING: Archibald!

PEGGY: (*being shaken*) Oh – oh – oh – oh!

RANKLING: (*panting, and releasing* PEGGY) You good-for-nothing girl! Do you know you have upset your mother?

MRS RANKLING: Archibald, that isn't Dinah!

MISS DYOTT: That is another young lady.

RANKLING: (*aghast*) What – not – Who – who has led me into this unpardonable error of judgment?

MRS RANKLING: (*to* PEGGY, *who is rubbing her shoulders and looking vindictively at* RANKLING) Oh, my dear young lady, pray think of this only as an amusing mistake. The Admiral has been away for more than four years – Dinah was but a child when he last saw her. (*weeping*) Oh, dear me!

RANKLING: Be quiet, Emma – you'll make a scene.

MISS DYOTT: (*to* PEGGY) Where is Miss Rankling?

PEGGY: Miss Rankling presents her compliments to Miss Dyott, and her love to her papa and mamma, and, as her mind is quite made up, she would rather not cause distress by granting an interview.

> (RANKLING *sinks into a chair.*)

MRS RANKLING: Archibald!

MISS DYOTT: (*to* PEGGY) The port wine!

> (PEGGY *advances with the cake and wine.*)

---

herring = errand.

MRS RANKLING: (*kneeling to* RANKLING) Archibald, be yourself! Remember, you have to respond for the Navy at a banquet to-night. Think of your reputation as a genial after-dinner speaker!

RANKLING: (*rising with forced calmness*) Thank you, Emma. (*to* MISS DYOTT) Madam, my daughter is in your charge till you receive instructions from my solicitor. (*glaring at* PEGGY) A short written apology shall be sent to this young lady in the course of the afternoon. (*to his wife*) Emma, your hair's rough – come home.

> (*He gives* MRS RANKLING *his arm. They go out.* MISS DYOTT *sinks exhausted on sofa.* PEGGY *offers her a glass of wine.*)

MISS DYOTT: Oh, my goodness! (*declining the wine*) No, no – not that. It has been decanted since Midsummer.

> (QUECKETT, *his coat collar turned up, appears at the door, looking back over his shoulder.*)

QUECKETT: What's the matter with the Ranklings? (*seeing* MISS DYOTT *and* PEGGY) Oh! has that vexing girl told Caroline?

> (*The clock strikes two.*)

MISS DYOTT: (*to herself*) Two o'clock – I must remove to Henrietta Street. (*seeing* QUECKETT) My darling.

QUECKETT: My love. (*to himself*) All right.

MISS DYOTT: I am going to prepare for my journey – the train leaves Paddington at three.

> (*As* MISS DYOTT *goes towards the centre door,* JANE *enters carrying about twenty boxes of cigars, which she deposits on the floor and then goes out.*)

MISS DYOTT: What is this?

QUECKETT: H'm! my cigars, Carrie – brought 'em with me in a cab.

MISS DYOTT: Oh! (*reading the label of one of the boxes*) 'Por Carolina'. Ah, poor Caroline.

> (*She goes out. Directly she is gone,* PEGGY *and* QUECKETT, *by a simultaneous movement, rush to the two doors and close them.*)

QUECKETT: Now, Miss Hesslerigge!

PEGGY: Sir.

QUECKETT: We will come to a distinct understanding.

PEGGY: If you please.

QUECKETT: In the first place, you will return me my telegram.

PEGGY: I can't.

QUECKETT: You mean you won't.

PEGGY: No, I can't.

QUECKETT: Why not?

PEGGY: I have just sent it to the telegraph office by Tyler.

QUECKETT: Despatched it!

PEGGY: Despatched it – it was one and fourpence.

QUECKETT: Oh, you – you – you vexing girl! Mr Mallory will be here to-night.

PEGGY: Yes – and will 'Bring two or three good fellows.' At least we hope so.

QUECKETT: Hope so!

PEGGY: (*standing over him with her arms folded*) Listen, Mr Vere Queckett. (*He*

starts.) We ladies are going to give a little party to-night to celebrate a serious
event in the life of one of us. We have invited only one young gentleman; your
friends will be welcome.

QUECKETT: Oh!

PEGGY: Without us your party must fail, for we command the servants. Let it be a
compact – your soirée shall be our soirée, and our soirée your soirée.

QUECKETT: And if I indignantly decline?

PEGGY: (*solemnly*) Consider, Mr Queckett – your Christmas holidays are to be
passed with us. Think in which direction your comfort and freedom lie – in
friendship or in enmity? Even now, Ermyntrude Johnson is trimming the holly
with one of your razors.

QUECKETT: But what explanation could I give Mr Mallory of your presence here?

PEGGY: Every detail has been considered. You are our bachelor uncle.

QUECKETT: Uncle!

PEGGY: We are your four nieces.

> (QUECKETT *looks up – is tickled by the idea and bursts out laughing.*
> PEGGY *joins.*)

QUECKETT: I don't see why that shouldn't be rather jolly.

PEGGY: (*roguishly*) D'ye consent?

QUECKETT: Can't help myself – can I?

PEGGY: (*delighted*) That you can't.

QUECKETT: Let's be friends, then – shall we? Have you girls got any money?

PEGGY: No. Have you?

QUECKETT: No! that is, all mine's invested.

MISS DYOTT: (*outside*) Tyler, fetch a cab. (QUECKETT *makes a bolt from the
room, and* PEGGY *vigorously re-arranges the furniture as* MISS DYOTT *enters,
dressed as if for a journey, and carrying her umbrella and hand-bag again.*)
Where is my husband?

PEGGY: (*looking about her*) Your hand-bag, Miss Dyott?

> (QUECKETT *re-enters.*)

MISS DYOTT: Still in your overcoat, dear?

QUECKETT: Of course, Carrie. I'll drive with you to Paddington.

MISS DYOTT: No, no – I insist on going alone.

QUECKETT: (*taking off his coat with alacrity*) Oh, Carrie, I am disappointed!
(DINAH, GWENDOLINE *and* ERMYNTRUDE *come through the hall into
the room, and form a group.* JANE *enters the hall.* TYLER *joins her there.*)

MISS DYOTT: Miss Hesslerigge – young ladies. I regret to say I am compelled to – to
quit Volumnia House for a time. The length of my absence depends upon how
long it runs – (*correcting herself in confusion*) – upon how long it runs to it, to
employ a colloquialism of the vulgar. But I depart with a light heart, because I
leave my husband in authority. He will find a trusty lieutenant in Miss
Hesslerigge. Ladies, to abandon for the moment our mother tongue, *Je vous
embrasse de tout mon cœur – soyez sages!*

GIRLS: (*together*) *Au revoir, Mademoiselle Dyott! Bon voyage, Mademoiselle Dyott!*
> (PEGGY *joins the girls and they talk earnestly. A cabman is seen
> carrying out the boxes from the hall, assisted by* TYLER. MISS
> DYOTT *produces some paper packets of money from her hand-bag.*)

MISS DYOTT: (*as she gives the packets to* QUECKETT) Vere, the house-agent will apply for the rent – there it is. Our fire insurance expired yesterday – post the premium to the Eagle Office at once. Jane's wages are due next week – deduct for the broken water-bottle. When you need exercise, dear one, tidy up the back yard – the recreation ground. A charwoman assists Jane on Fridays – three-quarters of a day, and leaves before her tea. Good-bye, Vere.

TYLER: The cab's a-waitin', ma'am.

      (MISS DYOTT *takes* QUECKETT'S *arm.*)

GIRLS: Good-bye, Miss Dyott.

      (MISS DYOTT *and* QUECKETT *go out through the hall.* PEGGY, ERMYNTRUDE, *and* GWENDOLINE *run over to the windows and look out.* DINAH *sits apart, thinking.*)

ERMYNTRUDE: There they are!

GWENDOLINE: Miss Dyott's in the cab!

PEGGY: She's off!

THE THREE: Hurrah! Hurrah!

      (QUECKETT *returns, the girls surround him demonstratively.*)

PEGGY: Dinah – young ladies – (*pointing to* QUECKETT) – Uncle Vere!

ERMYNTRUDE *and* GWENDOLINE: (*together*) Uncle Vere! Uncle Vere!

      (QUECKETT *tries to maintain his dignity, and pushes the girls from him.* TYLER, *with* JANE, *is seen letting off a squib in the hall.*)

      END OF THE FIRST ACT

THE SECOND ACT: THE PARTY

The Scene is a plain-looking School-room at MISS DYOTT'*s. Outside the two windows runs a narrow balcony, and beyond are seen the upper stories and roofs of the opposite houses. There are two doors facing each other. The room is decorated for the occasion with holly and evergreen, and a table is laid with supper.*

PEGGY *is standing on a chair, with a large hammer in her hand, nailing up holly.*

PEGGY: (*surveying her work*) There! I'm sure Miss Dyott wouldn't recognise the dull old class-rooms. (*descending*) I think it's time I dressed. (QUECKETT *enters slowly; he is in a perfectly-fitting evening dress, with a flower in his button-hole, but looks much depressed. He and* PEGGY *regard each other for a moment silently.*) Oh, I'm so glad you're ready early! How good it makes one feel, giving pleasure to others – doesn't it? Aren't you well?

QUECKETT: Yes – no. I deeply regret plunging into the vortex of these festivities.

PEGGY: Oh, I suppose you're nervous in society.

QUECKETT: (*drawing himself up*) Nervous in society, Miss Hesslerigge?

PEGGY: What do you think of the decorations? Artistic, aren't they?

QUECKETT: A treat at a Sunday School!

PEGGY: Then you shouldn't have locked up the rooms downstairs.

QUECKETT: I daren't allow the neighbours to see the house lighted up downstairs. I wish I could have locked up all you vexing girls.

Eagle Office: Eagle Insurance, a prominent company then and now.

PEGGY: That's not the spirit to give a party in! (*contemplating the table*) How many do you think your friend, Mr Mallory, will bring?

QUECKETT: I don't think Mr Mallory will find his way here at all. Have you observed the fog?

PEGGY: Is it foggy?

QUECKETT: You can't see your hand before you outside. I sincerely hope my friend will *not* come.

PEGGY: There's hospitality! Ours will.

QUECKETT: Who *is* your friend?

PEGGY: Mr Paulover.

QUECKETT: And who the devil is –

PEGGY: I don't think that's the language for a party, Mr Queckett!

QUECKETT: I beg your pardon. Who is Paulover? (TYLER *enters with a bill in his hand, with his hair stiffly brushed and greased, and wearing an expression of intense wonderment.*) What's this?

TYLER: A beautiful large lobster salid is come, sir.

QUECKETT: (*looking at* PEGGY) *I* haven't ordered a lobster salad. (*in an undertone*) You know, this is getting extremely vexing. (*He takes from his pocket the packets of money previously given him by* MISS DYOTT.) I've already paid a bill for some oysters and a *pâté de foie gras*. Jane's wages went for that. (*opening a packet*) Now, here's a salad. That breaks into next week's household expenses. (*handing the money to* TYLER, *who goes out*)

PEGGY: We're only girls, you know. And you seem to forget you're our uncle.

QUECKETT: (*irritably*) I am *not* your uncle.

PEGGY: To-night you are. But you needn't be our uncle to-morrow.

QUECKETT: (*gloomily*) Somebody will have to be *my* uncle to-morrow. Then I understand there's a lark pudding ordered for half-past nine. I can't allow the account to be sent in to – to –

PEGGY: To Auntie?

QUECKETT: Well – to – to Auntie. Who pays for the lark pudding?

PEGGY: You couldn't well ask girls to do it; besides, it's your party.

QUECKETT: It is *not* my party, and it is *your* lark pudding.

PEGGY: It may be our lark – but it's your pudding.

> (TYLER *enters, still much astonished, and with another bill.*)

QUECKETT: (*taking the bill*) What's that?

TYLER: Sich a lot of champagne's come, sir!

PEGGY: Champagne! Who ordered that? *I* didn't.

QUECKETT: Hush! I did – I did – I did.

PEGGY: Then it *is* your party?

QUECKETT: Part of the party is my party (*opening another packet*) I've broken into the rent. (*He hands* TYLER *the bill and some money, pocketing the remainder.* TYLER *goes out.*) The Fire Insurance alone remains intact. (*opening the last packet*) Postal Orders for thirty shillings. I'll despatch that, at any rate. (*He sits*

---

uncle = slang term for pawnbroker.

at the writing-table and begins to write. PEGGY *hammers up the last piece of holly as* QUECKETT *tries to write.*) Oh, you vexing girl!

PEGGY: Beg pardon; this is the last blow.

> (*She gives another knock as* JANE *enters, carrying a large ornamental wedding-cake.* JANE *is in a black gown and smart cap and apron; her eyes are wide open with pleasure and astonishment.* JANE *deposits the cake upon the writing-table before* QUECKETT.)

JANE: 'Scuse me, sir; the confectioner's jest brought the things.

QUECKETT: What's that? *That* isn't the lark pudding.

JANE: Oh, lor', no, sir!

> (*She goes out.*)

PEGGY: Oh, that's the wedding-cake.

QUECKETT: Oh, come – it isn't my wedding-cake.

PEGGY: (*laughing*) Oh, don't,'you funny man! No, it's Mr Paulover's.

QUECKETT: Who the dev –

PEGGY: Hush!

QUECKETT: Let's settle one thing at a time. Who is Paulover?

PEGGY: Dear Dinah's husband.

QUECKETT: Dear Dinah?

PEGGY: Your niece – Dinah Rankling.

QUECKETT: Married?

PEGGY: Secretly. To Mr Paulover.

> (QUECKETT *puts his hand to his brow.*)

QUECKETT: Oh, that's old Paulover, is it?

PEGGY: *Young* Paulover. They were married really three weeks ago, but without any breakfast – I don't mean a bacon breakfast, I mean a proper breakfast. But we girls think they ought to have a wedding-cake and everything complete to start them in life together: and that's why you're giving this party, you know.

QUECKETT: Now, understand me, I will not be dragged into such a conspiracy!

PEGGY: But you're in it.

QUECKETT: The Ranklings are acquaintances of mine, almost relatives; Admiral Rankling's cousin married the sister of the man who bought my brother's horses. (*rubbing his hands together*) I wash my hands of all you vexing girls.

PEGGY: Don't fret about it, please. Nothing can ever make Mrs Paulover Miss Rankling again. I'll go and dress while you finish your letter.

QUECKETT: (*impatiently*) Oh!

> (*He resumes writing at the table.*)

PEGGY: (*going to the door*) The girls will be here directly. Be nice, won't you?

> (*She goes out.* JANE *enters with tarts and confectionery on dishes which she places on the table before* QUECKETT.)

JANE: 'Scuse me, sir.

> (QUECKETT *rises with his letter and the inkstand, and goes impatiently over to the other side of the room, where he continues writing on the top of piano.*)

QUECKETT: They won't let me write to the Insurance Office.

> (TYLER *enters with some boxes of bon-bons. The writing-table being crowded,* JANE *waves him over to the piano and goes out.* TYLER

puts the bon-bons on the top of the piano before QUECKETT, *who snatches up his letter and inkstand again and goes to the centre table.*)

QUECKETT: I *will* write to the Insurance Office.

(TYLER *goes out as* JANE *re-enters.*)

JANE: (*presenting a bill*) The pastrycook's bill, sir.

QUECKETT: Great Scot! (*diving his hand into his pocket, bringing out some loose money and giving it to* JANE) There! (JANE *goes out.*) I've written to the Insurance Office. (*sealing the letter*) My mind's easy – done my duty to poor Caroline.

(*He puts the letter in his breast-pocket as* TYLER *enters.*)

TYLER: (*more astonished than ever, announcing*) Miss Gwendoline Hawkins.

(GWENDOLINE *enters, dressed in a simple and pretty party-dress.* TYLER *goes out.*)

GWENDOLINE: (*bashfully, seeing nobody but* QUECKETT) Oh, I'm first; I shall come back again.

(*She is going.*)

QUECKETT: Come in – come in. How d'ye do. (GWENDOLINE *advances.* QUECKETT *shakes hands with her.*) Delighted to see you – so glad you've come – won't you sit down? (*to himself with satisfaction*) Illustrations of Deportment and the Restrictions of Society – Vere Queckett. Carrie would be delighted.

(TYLER *re-enters, still more astonished.*)

TYLER: Miss Hermyntrude Johnson, and – and – and Mrs Reginald Paulover!

QUECKETT: This is a little too vexing! (ERMYNTRUDE *and* DINAH *enter, both prettily dressed –* DINAH *in white.* TYLER *goes out. Angrily*) How d'ye do – so glad you've come – won't you sit down?

DINAH: We're very well, thank you.

ERMYNTRUDE: Awfully well.

(*They sit, the three girls in a row.* DINAH *in the centre,* GWENDOLINE *and* ERMYNTRUDE *taking her hands.*)

QUECKETT: (*to himself*) Instructions in Polite Conversation. (*brusquely to* DINAH) How is Paulover?

DINAH: I think he's very well, thank you

QUECKETT: (*to himself*) Carrie would be pleased. (*to the girls*) H'm! I suppose you young ladies distinctly understand that I occupy a painfully false position this evening?

DINAH: I am sure it is very, very kind of you to give this party.

QUECKETT: (*to himself*) Well, now, that's exceedingly appropriate, the way in which that is put. Carrie really does do her duty to the parents of these girls.

GWENDOLINE: Peggy says you insist on our calling you Uncle.

QUECKETT: Does she! (*to himself*) Peggy is the one I've turned against.

ERMYNTRUDE: We think you'll be an awfully jolly uncle.

QUECKETT: (*pleased*) Thank ye – thank ye. (*to himself*) I begin to like helping Carrie with the pupils. (PEGGY *enters. She is quaintly but untidily dressed in poor, much-worn, and old-fashioned finery. In her hand she carries a pair of soiled, long white gloves.*) Hallo! (*Without speaking a word,* PEGGY *hurries*

across the room and goes out.) What is the matter with that vexing girl now?
(PEGGY *re-enters with* TYLER, *pushing him forward.*)

TYLER: (*announcing*) Miss Margaret Hesslerigge.

> (PEGGY *advances to* QUECKETT, *holding out her hand.*)

PEGGY: How do you do?

QUECKETT: (*savagely*) How d'ye do – delighted to see you – for goodness' sake, sit down!

> (*He turns away to the fire. The three girls rise to greet* PEGGY.)

DINAH: (*anxiously*) I don't think it's nearly half-past nine yet.

PEGGY: (*rather proudly, produces a huge old-fashioned watch*) Twenty to ten.

DINAH: I thought it was.

> (DINAH, GWENDOLINE, *and* ERMYNTRUDE *run to one window, pull aside the blind, and look out.* PEGGY *goes to the other window, pulls up the blind, and opens the window.*)

QUECKETT: What are you doing?

PEGGY: I can just see him, under his lamp post.

DINAH: The fog will hurt him.

PEGGY: Hush! I told him we'd whistle twice.

DINAH: Do it!

> (PEGGY *makes two or three ineffectual attempts to whistle.*)

PEGGY: Girls, it's ominous – my whistle has left me. (*to* QUECKETT, *taking his arm*) Come and whistle!

QUECKETT: No – no.

PEGGY: (*leading* QUECKETT *to the open window*) Whistle, or you'll catch cold.
(QUECKETT *whistles twice, desperately, then returns to the fireplace, annoyed.*)
He's heard it. (*She closes the window and pulls down the blind.*) Now, listen. (*to* GWENDOLINE *and* ERMYNTRUDE) You two girls count five.

GWENDOLINE: One.

ERMYNTRUDE: Two.

DINAH: Oh, how slowly you count!

GWENDOLINE: Three.

ERMYNTRUDE: Four.

DINAH: (*clasping her hands*) Five!

> (*There is a distant ring at the bell; with a little cry* DINAH *runs out.* PEGGY *begins to put her gloves on.* ERMYNTRUDE *and* GWENDOLINE *go to the door, open it and listen.*)

PEGGY: (*to* QUECKETT) Thank you for whistling. I shall never make a 'Whistling woman', shall I?

QUECKETT: A wide knowledge of humanity, in its highest and lowest grades, Miss Hesslerigge, does not enable me even to conjecture the possibilities of your future.

PEGGY: No compliments, please. Thank you. (*She holds out her gloved hand for him to button the glove. After a look of astonishment he complies.*) You know my idea about my future, don't you?

'*Whistling woman*': possibly a popular performer or song of the period.

QUECKETT: No.

PEGGY: That I only need one essential to become a Duchess.

QUECKETT: What is that?

PEGGY: A Duke.

GWENDOLINE: They're coming upstairs!

PEGGY: (*to* QUECKETT) Now you'll see Mr Paulover. Oh, I do hope he'll take to you!

QUECKETT: Well, really, I'm –

> (*He walks angrily away as* DINAH *enters with* REGINALD PAULOVER, *a good-looking lad, rather sheepish when in repose, but fiery and demonstrative when out of temper. He is in evening dress, overcoat and muffler, and wears a respirator, which he removes on entering.*)

DINAH: (*introducing the three girls*) Reggie, these are my three dear friends – Miss Hawkins – Miss Johnson –

REGINALD: (*Bowing*) Awfully pleased to meet you.

DINAH: and Miss Hesslerigge.

> (PEGGY *advances and shakes hands with* REGINALD.)

REGINALD: Thank you very much for being so kind to – my wife.

ERMYNTRUDE: (*to* GWENDOLINE, *disappointed*) No whiskers or moustache! Oh!

PEGGY: (*to* REGINALD) Had you been waiting long?

REGINALD: Ten minutes. I was jolly glad to hear my wife's dear little whistle. I should know it from a thousand.

PEGGY: H'm! Dinah dear, make Mr Paulover and Mr Queckett known to each other.

> (QUECKETT *comes forward with a disagreeable look.* REGINALD *glares at him.*)

DINAH: (*timidly*) Reggie dear, this is Mr Queckett.

> (QUECKETT *bows stiffly.* REGINALD *nods angrily.*)

REGINALD: (*to* DINAH) Dinah, what is a man doing here? You know I can't bear you to talk to a man.

DINAH: Oh, Reggie, why are you always so jealous?

PEGGY: Mr Queckett is giving the party.

REGINALD: What party?

PEGGY: Your wedding-party.

REGINALD: Is he! (*to* QUECKETT, *angrily*) I'm much obliged to Mr Queckett.

PEGGY: (*pacifying* REGINALD) Mr Queckett is so nice – he calls himself Dinah's uncle.

REGINALD: Does he! Then it's a liberty – that's all I can say.

QUECKETT: Do you know you're in my house, sir?

REGINALD: I'm not in your house, sir! Come away, Dinah!

PEGGY: Hush! Mr Queckett is Miss Dyott's –

QUECKETT: Be quiet – mind your own business.

REGINALD: (*to* QUECKETT) At any rate it's my business, sir.

QUECKETT: I'm afraid you're a cub, sir.

REGINALD: What!

DINAH: Oh Reggie, don't!
> (*A loud knock and ring are heard.*)
PEGGY: (*to* QUECKETT) Your friend.
REGINALD: Whose friend?
QUECKETT: *My* friend.
REGINALD: Another man, I suppose – Dinah!
PEGGY: Ladies, do explain everything to Mr Paulover.
> (DINAH *seizes* REGINALD'S *arm.* GWENDOLINE *and*
> ERMYNTRUDE *gather round them,* REGINALD *protesting.*)
REGINALD: (*handing his card as he passes* QUECKETT) My card, sir.
QUECKETT: Pooh, sir! (*throwing the card in the fire. The three girls hurry*
> REGINALD *out of the room.*)
PEGGY: (*to* QUECKETT) I'm so sorry – he *hasn't* taken to you.
QUECKETT: He needn't trouble himself! Upon my soul, this is going to be a nice
> party!
> (TYLER *enters.*)
TYLER: Three gentlemen, sir: I was to say the name of Mallory.
QUECKETT: *Three* gentlemen!
PEGGY: (*delighted, to* QUECKETT) Oh, he's brought some good fellows!
> (*reckoning on her fingers*) That's one for Ermyntrude – and one for me – and
> one for –
QUECKETT: (*to* PEGGY) Be quiet. (*to* TYLER) I'll come down.
MALLORY: (*outside*) Queckett!
QUECKETT: Yes, Jack!
> (JACK MALLORY *enters. He is a good-looking, jovial fellow of about*
> *thirty-six, with a bronzed face. He is in evening dress and overcoat.*
> TYLER *goes out.*)
MALLORY: (*shaking hands heartily with* QUECKETT) Ah, Queckett – dear old
> chap – well, I am glad to see you.
QUECKETT: How are you Jack?
MALLORY: Quaint diggings you have up here. The hanging committee have skied
> you, though, haven't they? (*seeing* PEGGY) I beg your pardon.
QUECKETT: (*confused*) Oh – ah – yes. I didn't mention it. I have my – my nieces
> spending Christmas with me.
MALLORY: (*bowing to* PEGGY) Delighted. (*to* QUECKETT) Did you say niece or
> nieces?
QUECKETT: Nieces. (*softly to* PEGGY, *quickly*) How many? I forget.
PEGGY: (*to* QUECKETT) Three.
QUECKETT: Three.
PEGGY: Three, not counting me.
QUECKETT: Three, not counting me. I mean three, not counting that vexing girl –
> Peggy – Margaret.

My card: proffering one's card was an accepted form of challenge to a duel.
hanging . . . you: the Royal Academy's selectors decide where canvases accepted for their
exhibitions shall be hung.
Skied = high on the wall.

MALLORY: (*bowing*) It would be impossible not to count Miss – Margaret.

PEGGY: (*simpering*) Oh!

> (QUECKETT *assists* MALLORY *to take off his overcoat, first darting an angry look at* PEGGY.)

PEGGY: (*to herself*) I shall give Gwendoline and Ermyntrude the two that are downstairs.

QUECKETT: H'm! You're not alone, are you, Jack?

MALLORY: No – they're coming up.

QUECKETT: (*grimly*) Are they?

MALLORY: The old gentleman takes his time with the stairs.

QUECKETT: (*with forced ease*) Poor old gentleman! Who the deuce – ?

MALLORY: The fact is, there's been a big Navy dinner to-night at the Whitehall Rooms. The enthusiasm became rather forced – 'Britannia rules the waves', and all that sort of thing – so I gladly thought of finishing up with you. I've brought my nephew – hallo, here he is! (MR SAUNDERS *enters. He is a pretty boy, almost a child, in the uniform of a naval cadet.*) My nephew – Horatio Nelson Drake Saunders, of the Training Ship 'Dexterous'.

SAUNDERS: (*with the airs of a little man, but in a treble voice*) How do you do? Awfully pleased to come here.

QUECKETT: Glad to see you, Mr Saunders

MALLORY: (*laughing, to* SAUNDERS) I say, you shouldn't have left the old gentleman.

SAUNDERS: (*laughing*) He sent me up to count how many more stairs there were.

QUECKETT: (*impatiently*) Jack, I don't put the question on theological grounds, but who *is* the old gentleman?

MALLORY: Oh, I beg your pardon – and his. We persuaded an old acquaintance of yours to join us – Admiral Rankling.

QUECKETT: (*aghast*) What!

MALLORY: Do you mind?

QUECKETT: Mind!

RANKLING: (*outside*) Mr Saunders!

SAUNDERS: Here, sir.

> (PEGGY *makes a bolt out of the room.* SAUNDERS *goes to the door, and returns with* RANKLING. RANKLING *is in evening dress, overcoat and muffler, and is much out of breath.*)

RANKLING: Ah, Mr Queckett, how do you do? We haven't met anywhere lately; I've been away, you know.

QUECKETT: I am delighted to renew our acquaintance, Admiral Rankling.

RANKLING: (*puffing*) Mr Mallory suggested that we should smoke our last cigar at your lodgings. I can't stay, for I've a long distance to drive home. At least, I suppose I have, for I really don't know quite where we are. What quarter of London have you brought me to, Mr Mallory? Oh, thank ye!

> (*He turns to* SAUNDERS, *who is offering to remove his overcoat. The door is slightly opened, and the heads of all the girls are seen.*)

---

the old gentleman = a common euphemism for the devil.

QUECKETT: (*hastily to* MALLORY) He doesn't know where he is!

MALLORY: The fog's as thick as a board outside.

QUECKETT: He isn't aware he lives a hundred and fifty yards off!

MALLORY: No – does he?

QUECKETT: Hush, don't tell him! Jack, don't tell him! I'll explain why by and bye.

      (QUECKETT *turns to assist* SAUNDERS *who, mounted on a chair, is struggling ineffectually to relieve* RANKLING *of his overcoat.*)

RANKLING: Thank ye – bits o' boys, bits o' boys.

MALLORY: (*to himself*) There's a wild look about poor Queckett I don't like. It's his lonely bachelor life, I suppose. Curious place too – he used to be such a swell in the Albany. (*looking about him. The door shuts and the heads disappear.*)

RANKLING: (*to* QUECKETT) Thank ye – thank ye (*panting*) Ouf!

      (RANKLING *sits down, and* MALLORY *talks to hims.* SAUNDERS *has seated himself on the sofa and is dozing off, quite tired out.*)

QUECKETT: Oh, what a party!

      (*The door opens, and* PEGGY'S *head appears.*)

PEGGY: (*hurriedly to* QUECKETT) Who'd have thought of this?

QUECKETT: It might be worse – he doesn't recognise the house he is in.

PEGGY: Doesn't he?

QUECKETT: Get rid of his daughter and that horrid Paulover.

PEGGY: Certainly not; I know he won't recognise his daughter.

QUECKETT: Won't recognise his own dau– You'll drive me mad!

      (*They continue to talk in undertones.* SAUNDERS *is now fast asleep.*)

RANKLING: (*to* MALLORY) No – *I* don't like the look of poor Queckett.

MALLORY: He seems altered.

RANKLING: Altered – he glares like the devil. He's not married, is he?

MALLORY : No.

RANKLING: Then, what does he mean by it? Queer rooms too. (*catching sight of the wedding-cake on the table*) Lord, look there!

MALLORY: (*looking at the cake*) Hallo!

RANKLING: Why, it's like the thing we had at my wedding breakfast. Phew! I shall go.

MALLORY: No, no! The fact is poor old Queckett has some nieces staying with him.

RANKLING: Nieces?

MALLORY: Four of 'em. I've seen one, and I fancy by the look of her mischievous little face, that they're too much for him.

PEGGY: (*to* QUECKETT) Leave everything to me. Don't spoil the party, uncle.

QUECKETT: Dash the party!

      (PEGGY *retiring hastily, the door bangs, at which* RANKLING *and* MALLORY *look round.*)

---

bits o' boys: presumably a reference to Saunders' youth.

Albany: a luxurious block of apartments between Burlington Gardens and the Royal Academy built in 1802–3 by Henry Holland and traditionally occupied by wealthy bachelors. Although Miss Prism in the first draft of *The Importance of Being Earnest* judged Ernest as 'bad as any young man who has chambers in the Albany', Pinero viewed the address as highly desirable. See *The Second Mrs. Tanqueray* Act I (below, p. 77).

RANKLING: Oh, Queckett, where are your nieces?

QUECKETT: Nieces – nieces? Oh, they retire at eight o'clock. Early to bed, early
to rise –

> (GWENDOLINE *and* ERMYNTRUDE *enter, visibly pushed on by*
> PEGGY.)

RANKLING: (*rising*) Um, this doesn't look like early to bed.

QUECKETT: (*weakly*) Just got up, I suppose. Gwendoline – Ermyntrude – my dears
– Admiral Rankling – Mr Mallory – (*looking about for* SAUNDERS) Mr – Mr –
Oh, Mr Saunders is asleep!

> (ERMYNTRUDE *and* GWENDOLINE *advance to* RANKLING.)

RANKLING: (*to the girls*) How do you do? And whose daughters are you?

> (GWENDOLINE *and* ERMYNTRUDE *look frightened, and shake
> their heads.*)

QUECKETT: Oh, these are my sister Isabel's girls.

RANKLING: Why, all your sister Isabel's children were boys.

QUECKETT: *Were* boys, yes.

RANKLING: (*irritably*) *Are* boys, sir.

QUECKETT: Are *men* now. H'm! I should have said these are my sister Janet's
children.

RANKLING: Oh! I've never heard of your sister Janet.

QUECKETT: No – quiet, retiring girl, Janet.

RANKLING: Well, then, whom did Janet marry?

QUECKETT: Whom *didn't* Janet marry! I mean, whom *did* Janet marry? Why,
Finch-Griffin of the Berkshire Royals!

RANKLING: Dear me, we're going to meet Major Griffin and his wife on Christmas
Day at the Trotwells'.

QUECKETT: *Are* you? (*to* GWENDOLINE *and* ERMYNTRUDE) Go away.
(PEGGY *enters.*) Oh – ahem! This is Margaret – Peggy.

RANKLING: Oh – another of Mrs Griffin's.

QUECKETT: Yes, yes!

RANKLING: Large family.

QUECKETT: Rapid – two a year.

RANKLING: (*eyeing* PEGGY) Why, we've met before to-day!

QUECKETT: Eh – where?

RANKLING: At a miserable school near my house in Portland Place.

PEGGY: Oh, yes. Our holidays began this afternoon.

RANKLING: Why, Queckett, my daughter Dinah and Miss Griffin are school-
fellows!

QUECKETT: No!

RANKLING: Yes!

QUECKETT: No!

RANKLING: Yes, sir.

QUECKETT: How small the world is!

RANKLING: Do you happen to know anything about the person who keeps that
school? What's the woman's name – Miss – Miss – ?

Berkshire Royals: an army regiment.

QUECKETT: Miss – Miss – Miss –

PEGGY: Miss Dyott. Oh, yes, Uncle knows her to speak to.

RANKLING: What about her, Queckett?

QUECKETT: (*looking vindictively at* PEGGY) Er – um – rather not hazard an opinion.

> (*He hastily joins* MALLORY, GWENDOLINE *and* ERMYNTRUDE.)

RANKLING: (*confidentially to* PEGGY) Er – um – my dear Miss Griffin, did you receive a short but ample apology from me this afternoon – addressed: 'To the young lady who was shaken'?

PEGGY: Yes, and oh! I shall always prize it!

RANKLING: No, no don't! You haven't bothered your Uncle about it, have you, dear?

PEGGY: No – not yet.

RANKLING: I shouldn't, then; I shouldn't. He seems worried enough. Shall I take you and your sisters to see the pantomime?

PEGGY: Yes – please.

RANKLING: Then you'd better give me back that apology.

PEGGY: Oh, no – you'd use it again.

RANKLING: One – two – three. Mr Mallory says you have *four* nieces with you, Mr Queckett.

QUECKETT: Ah, but Jack's been dining, you know. I beg your pardon, Jack.

PEGGY: Oh, yes, there is one more. Mrs – Mrs – Parkinson is here with her husband.

QUECKETT: H'm! my brother Tankerville's eldest girl.

RANKLING: I've never heard of your brother Tankerville!

QUECKETT: No – he's Deputy Inspector of Prisons in British Guiana. Quiet, retiring chap.

PEGGY: I'll go and fetch them.

> (*She runs out.*)

QUECKETT: (*to* RANKLING) To make a clean breast of it, the girls have been preparing a little festival to-night in honour of Mr and Mrs – Mr and Mrs – the name Peggy mentioned. My niece was married, very quietly, some weeks ago to a charming young fellow – a charming young fellow – and these foolish children insist on cutting a wedding-cake and all that sort of nonsense. I didn't want to disturb you with their chatter –

RANKLING: You forget, Queckett, you are speaking to a father.

QUECKETT: No – I don't, indeed.

> (PEGGY *re-enters, followed by* REGINALD *and* DINAH.)

PEGGY: My cousin and Mr Parkinson.

RANKLING: How do you – (*staring*) What an extraordinary likeness to my brother Ned! (*taking her hand slowly, still looking at her*) And how do you do?

DINAH: (*palpitating*) Thank you, I am very well.

RANKLING: Do you know, your voice is exceedingly like my sister Rachel's!

REGINALD: (*thrusting himself between* DINAH *and* RANKLING) I am sorry to differ – I think my wife resembles no one but herself.

RANKLING: (*hotly*) I beg your pardon, sir.

REGINALD: (*hotly*) Pray, don't!

RANKLING (*to himself*) *That's* not a charming young fellow!

PEGGY: (*presenting* MALLORY *to* DINAH) Mr Mallory.

MALLORY: (*gallantly, to* DINAH) I am delighted to have the opportunity of congratulating my old friend's niece upon her recent marriage. (*taking her hand*) I think myself especially fortunate in being present on such –

REGINALD: (*thrusting himself between* DINAH *and* MALLORY, *and giving* DINAH *his arm*) How do you do, sir?

PEGGY: Mr Mallory – Mr Parkinson.

>(*They bow abruptly, glaring at each other.*)

MALLORY: (*to himself*) Is *that* a charming young fellow?

>(DINAH *expostulates in undertones with* REGINALD; *he answering with violent gestures and glaring at* RANKLING, *who mutters comments on* DINAH's *resemblance to various members of his family.* PEGGY *endeavours to pacify* MALLORY *who is evidently annoyed, and altogether there is much hubbub, with signs of general ill-feeling.*)

QUECKETT: (*sinking back in his chair*) Oh, what a party!

>(JANE *enters*)

JANE: (*quietly to* QUECKETT) The pudding is in the arey, sir, waiting to be paid.

QUECKETT: I'll come to it. (JANE *goes out. To* PEGGY) Margaret, show Admiral Rankling and Mr Mallory where the cigarettes are – they may like – (*to himself*) Years are going off my life!

>(*He goes out.*)

PEGGY: (*to* MALLORY) May I take you to the cigarettes?

MALLORY: (*to* PEGGY) You may take me anywhere.

PEGGY: (*bashfully*) Oh! (*to* RANKLING) The cigarettes are in the next room, Admiral Rankling.

RANKLING: (*not hearing* PEGGY, *but still eyeing* DINAH) That girl has a look of Emma's sister Susan.

>(PEGGY *and* MALLORY *go out.* REGINALD *seeing* RANKLING *is still looking at* DINAH, *abruptly takes her over to the door, glaring at* RANKLING *as he passes.*)

REGINALD: (*to* DINAH, *fiercely*) Come away, Dinah!

DINAH: (*to* REGINALD, *tearfully*) Oh, Reggie, dear Reggie, you are so different when people are not present.

>(*They go out.* RANKLING *watches them through the doorway.* GWENDOLINE *has meanwhile seated herself beside* SAUNDERS, *whose head has gradually fallen till it rests upon her shoulder. She is now sitting quite still, looking down upon the boy's face.*)

ERMYNTRUDE: (*watching them enviously*) Well, considering that Mr Saunders was introduced to us asleep, I don't think Gwendoline's behaviour is *comme il faut*! (*She bumps gently against* RANKLING.) Oh!

RANKLING: (*looking at* ERMYNTRUDE, *rather dazed*) My dear, I am quite glad to see somebody who isn't like any of my relations. Come along.

>(*They go out.* SAUNDERS *moves dreamily and murmurs.*)

---

arey = area, i.e. 'sunk court, railed off from pavement, and giving access to basement' (*OED*).

SAUNDERS: (*waking*) All right, ma dear, I'll come down directly. (*He raises his head and kisses* GWENDOLINE, *then opens his eyes and looks at her, startled.*) Oh, I've been dreaming about my ma! I – I don't know you, do I?

GWENDOLINE: It doesn't matter. Mr Saunders. You've had such a good sleep. (*She kisses his forehead gently.*)

SAUNDERS: Oh, that's just like my ma! Where are the others?

GWENDOLINE: (*arranging his curls upon his forehead*) I'll take you to them.

SAUNDERS: Thank you. What's your name?

GWENDOLINE: Gwendoline.

SAUNDERS: Gwen's short for that, isn't it? (*rubbing his eyes with his fists, then offering her his arm*) Permit me, Gwen.
> (*They go out.* QUECKETT, *his hair disarranged, his appearance generally wild, immediately enters, followed by* JANE *and* TYLER.)

QUECKETT: I can't help it! I am in the hands of fate. Arrange the table. I cannot help it!
> (TYLER *and* JANE *proceed to arrange the table and the seats for supper.* PEGGY *enters quietly.*)

PEGGY: It is supper-time. Oh, what's the matter, Uncle Vere?

QUECKETT: Well, in the first place, there are no oysters.

PEGGY: I've seen them!

QUECKETT: I've gone further – I've tasted them.

PEGGY: Bad!

QUECKETT: Well, I should describe them as Inland oysters. A long time since *they* had a fortnight at the seaside.

PEGGY: Oh, dear! Then we must fall back on the lark pudding.

QUECKETT: You'll injure yourself seriously if you do.

PEGGY: Tell me everything. It has not come small?

QUECKETT: It has come ridiculously small.

PEGGY: It was ordered for eight persons.

QUECKETT: Then it is architecturally disproportionate.

PEGGY: (*to herself*) Something must be done. (*She runs to the writing-table and begins to write rapidly on three half-sheets of paper, folding each into a three-cornered note as she finishes it.*) The girls must be warned. (*writing*) 'For goodness' sake, don't taste the pudding.' Poor girls – what an end to a happy day!

QUECKETT: (*to himself*) Oh, if the members of my family could see me at this moment! I, whose suppers in the Albany were at one time a proverb! Oh, Caroline, Caroline, even you little know the sacrifice I have made for you!

PEGGY: (*to* QUECKETT, *handing him the notes*) Quick, please quick – give them these notes.

QUECKETT: (*taking the notes*) What for?

PEGGY: Oh, don't ask; you will see the result.

QUECKETT: But you mustn't write to people you –!

PEGGY: (*angrily*) Go away!
> (*He hurries out.* PEGGY *wipes her eyes.*)

JANE: Oh, don't be upset, Miss!

PEGGY: No, I won't, I won't. But I am only a girl, and the responsibility is very great for such young shoulders.

(*There is a murmur of voices outside.* JANE *and* TYLER *go out as*
RANKLING *enters with* ERMYNTRUDE, *followed by*
REGGIE *and* DINAH. REGINALD *is endeavouring to keep*
her away from MALLORY, *who comes after them.*
SAUNDERS *and* GWENDOLINE *follow next, and*
QUECKETT *brings up the rear. There is much talking as*
QUECKETT *indicates the seats they are to occupy.*)
PEGGY: (*quietly to* QUECKETT) Did you give the girls the notes?
QUECKETT: (*surprised*) No.
PEGGY: Oh! Never mind – I'll whisper to them now.
(*She whispers hurriedly to* DINAH, GWENDOLINE *and*
ERMYNTRUDE.)
QUECKETT: (*to himself*) I didn't understand they were for the *girls*.
(*He goes to the head, of the table as* RANKLING, MALLORY *and*
SAUNDERS *come suddenly together, each carrying a note.*)
RANKLING: (*to* MALLORY) Mallory, we were right – there is some horrible
mystery about Queckett. (*looking to see they are not observed*) I've had an
anonymous warning. 'For heaven's sake, don't touch the pudding!'
MALLORY: I know.
RANKLING: Tell the boy.
MALLORY: (*to* SAUNDERS) I say – don't you say yes to pudding.
SAUNDERS: I know. Tell the old gentleman.
MALLORY: (*to* SAUNDERS) He knows. (*to* RANKLING) He knows.
(*With a simultaneous gesture they pocket the notes and go to find their*
seats at table. They all sit. The lobster salad and the pâté have been
placed by TYLER *at the end of the table.* TYLER *now enters carrying*
nine large plates, which he places before QUECKETT.)
QUECKETT: (*with assumed composure and good spirits*) There is a spontaneity
about our jolly little supper which will perhaps – ah'm! – atone for any absence
of elaboration.
RANKLING: Don't name it, Mr Queckett.
MALLORY: Just as it should be, my dear fellow.
(TYLER *goes out*)
QUECKETT: The language of the heart is simplicity. Our little supper is from the
heart.
MALLORY: Ah, I shall never forget your little suppers in the Albany – where were
they from?
QUECKETT: Gunter's, Jack. (*with a groan*) Oh!
(JANE, *at the door, hands to* TYLER *a very small pudding in a silver*
basin, which he places before QUECKETT.)
RANKLING, MALLORY *and* SAUNDERS: (*to themselves*) The pudding!
(*They exhibit great eagerness to get a view of the pudding.*)
PEGGY: (*behind* MALLORY'S *back*) Oh, how shameful it looks!
QUECKETT: (*falteringly*) Here is a homely little dish which has fascinations for

---

Gunter's: a high-class restaurant which supplied meals and staff in customers' own homes. See
The Second Mrs Tanqueray, Act I (below, p. 88).

many, though I never touch it myself – I never touch it myself. (RANKLING, MALLORY, *and* SAUNDERS *exchange significant looks*.) Ah'm! A pudding made of larks. (*He glances round, all look down, there is deep silence.*) A pudding – made – of larks. (*to* DINAH) My dear – a very little?

DINAH: No, thank you, Uncle.

QUECKETT: Perhaps you're right. Gwendoline, a suggestion?

GWENDOLINE: No, thank you, Uncle.

QUECKETT: (*to* PEGGY) Margaret, I know what your digestion is – I won't tempt you. (*to* ERMYNTRUDE) Ermyntrude – the least in the world?

ERMYNTRUDE: No, thank you, Uncle.

QUECKETT: (*to himself*) Ah! How lucky!

PEGGY: (*to herself*) Brave girls; I was afraid they'd falter.

QUECKETT: (*heartily*) Now then – Admiral Rankling?

RANKLING: No, thank you.

QUECKETT: No pudding?

RANKLING: I haven't long dined, thank you, Queckett.

QUECKETT: (*to* REGINALD – *coldly*) May I?

REGINALD: (*distantly*) I never eat suppers, thank you.

QUECKETT: (*to* SAUNDERS) My dear Mr Saunders?

SAUNDERS: No, Mr Queckett, thank you.

QUECKETT: (*getting desperate – to* MALLORY) Jack – a lark?

MALLORY: No, thanks, old fellow.

QUECKETT: Well, I – (*throwing down his knife and spoon, and leaning back in his chair. To* TYLER) Take it away!

(TYLER *removes the pudding; they all watch its going.*)

TYLER: (*handing it to* JANE) Keep it warm, Jane.

QUECKETT: Jack, a lobster salad and a small *pâté de foie gras* are at your end of the table.

MALLORY: (*looking round.*) May I?

(*There is a general reply of* 'No, thank you', *expressed in symbols by the ladies.*)

PEGGY: (*to herself*) Poor girls, what sacrifices they make for these men!

MALLORY: (*with a plate in his hand*) May I – ?

RANKLING, SAUNDERS *and* REGINALD: (*together*) No, thank you.

QUECKETT: (*to himself*) What a supper party! Tyler, the champagne.

(TYLER *fetches a bottle of champagne, and proceeds to open it.*)

RANKLING: (*behind* ERMYNTRUDE *and* PEGGY, *to* MALLORY) If we see the cork drawn, shall we risk it?

MALLORY: (*to* RANKLING) Risk it.

RANKLING: Risk it.

(REGINALD *has risen from the table and is seen tapping* SAUNDERS *upon the shoulder and speaking to him rapidly and excitedly.*)

SAUNDERS: No, I have not!

(*Talking together,* REGINALD *and* SAUNDERS *go out hurriedly.*)

MALLORY: What's the matter with that charming young fellow now? (*to the table*) Excuse me.

(*He follows them out.*)

DINAH: (*tearfully to* GWENDOLINE) Reginald's jealousy gets worse and worse. I am sure it will cloud our future.
GWENDOLINE: (*to* DINAH) Mr Saunders wasn't looking at you, I am positive. The poor little fellow was stroking my hand.
(MALLORY *returns with* SAUNDERS *and* REGINALD, *who both look excited, and their hair is disarranged.*)
REGINALD: (*to* MALLORY *and* SAUNDERS) I beg your pardon; I may have been mistaken. I imagined that Mr Saunders was regarding my wife in a way which overstepped the borders of ordinary admiration.
(*They hastily shake hands all round and hurry back to their seats.* TYLER *has poured out the champagne, and now departs.* ADMIRAL RANKLING *rises.* QUECKETT *taps the table for silence.*)
QUECKETT: Please – please.
RANKLING: Ah'm!
MALLORY: (*to himself*) I thought the old gentleman wouldn't resist the temptation.
RANKLING: My dear Mr Queckett, it would ill become an old man – himself the father of a daughter, nearly, if not quite, of the age of the young lady opposite me – to lose an opportunity of saying a few words on the pleasant, the – the extremely pleasant – condition of the British Naval Forces – ah'm! no –
MALLORY: (*to himself*) I knew that would happen.
RANKLING: Pardon me, I have been speaking on other subjects to-night. I should say, the extremely pleasant occasion which brings us together.
QUECKETT: Certainly, my dear Rankling, how nice of you!
RANKLING: Not only am I the commander – the father – of a ship – of a daughter whom it is my ambition to see happily wedded to the man of her choice –
PEGGY: Hear, hear!
QUECKETT: (*in an undertone, glaring at her*) You vexing girl.
RANKLING: But I am also the husband of a heavily-plated cruiser – er – um – h'm! of a dear lady to whose affection and society I owe the greatest happiness of my life.
PEGGY: (*to herself*) How different some gentlemen are when their wives are not present.
RANKLING: If I have the regret of knowing that my acquaintance with Mrs – Mrs –
PEGGY: Parkinson.
RANKLING: Thank you, I know – Parkinson – has begun only to-night, I have also the pleasure of inaugurating a friendship with that delightful young lady, which on my side shall be little less than paternal. I – I – I –
MALLORY: Oh, gracious!
RANKLING: I – I cannot sit down –
MALLORY: (*wearily*) Why not?
RANKLING: I will not sit down without adding a word of congratulations to Mr – Mr –
PEGGY: Parkinson.
RANKLING: Thank you, I know – Parkinson – the young gentleman whose ingenious construction and sea-going qualities –
MALLORY: No – no.
RANKLING: Er – um – whose amiability and genial demeanour have so favourably impressed us. As an old married man I welcome this recruit to the service.
PEGGY: Hear, hear!

RANKLING: It is one of hardship and danger – of stiff breezes and dismal night watches. But it is because Englishmen never know when they are beaten –
MALLORY: No, no.
RANKLING: Yes, sir – it is because Englishmen never know when they are beaten that they occasionally find conjugal happiness. I ask you all to drink to the Navy – to – Mr and Mrs – thank you, I know – Jenkinson.
> (*All except* DINAH *and* REGINALD *rise and drink the toast* 'Mr and Mrs Parkinson', *then, as they resume their seats,* REGINALD *rises sulkily.*)
REGINALD: Admiral Rankling.
> (JANE *appears at the door, wildly beckoning to* QUECKETT.)
JANE: (*in a whisper*) Sir – Sir – !
QUECKETT: (*angrily*) Not now – not now – go away.
THE GIRLS: Hush!
> (*The* GIRLS *motion* JANE *away; she retires.*)
QUECKETT: (*to* REGINALD) I beg pardon.
REGINALD: All I have to say is that the highest estimation Admiral Rankling can form of me will not do justice to my devotion to my wife.
PEGGY: (*sotto voce*) Oh, beautiful!
REGINALD: (*fiercely*) And I should like to know the individual, old or young, who would take my wife from me!
MALLORY:(*to himself*) Many a husband would like to know *that* person.
REGINALD: In conclusion – as for Admiral Rankling's offer of a paternal friendship, I trust he will remember that offer if ever we should have occasion to remind him of it. (*looking at his watch*) And now I regret to say –
> (*The girls rise, the men follow.*)
PEGGY: No, no – not before we have danced one quadrille.
GWENDOLINE *and* ERMYNTRUDE: Oh, yes – oh, yes! A quadrille!
PEGGY: Uncle Vere will play for us.
QUECKETT: No, Uncle Vere will not!
MALLORY: Oh, yes you will, Queckett, old fellow – eh?
QUECKETT: Well – I – with pleasure, Jack. (*to himself*) How dare they!
PEGGY: Clear the floor!
> (SAUNDERS *and* MALLORY, *assisted by* ERMYNTRUDE *and* GWENDOLINE, *put back the table and chairs.*)
RANKLING: (*getting very good-humoured*) Upon my soul, I never saw such girls in my life! I wonder whether my Dinah is anything like 'em!
> (DINAH *and* REGINALD *are having a violent altercation.*)
DINAH: A wife shouldn't dance with her husband – it is horrible form!
REGINALD: I can't see you led out by a stranger.
DINAH: It is merely a quadrille.
REGINALD: Merely a quadrille! Woman, do you think I am marble!
DINAH: (*distractedly, turning to* RANKLING) Admiral Rankling, are you going to dance?
RANKLING: (*gallantly*) If you do me the honour, my dear Madam.
> (*She takes his arm.*)
REGINALD: (*madly, to* DINAH) Ah, flirt!

QUECKETT: (*to* PEGGY) Get rid of them soon, or I shall become a gibbering idiot!

MALLORY: (*slapping* QUECKETT *on the back*) Now then Queckett. (QUECKETT *goes to the piano. To* PEGGY) Will you make me happy, dear Miss Peggy?

PEGGY: Thank you, Mr Mallory, I never dance. (*taking his arm*) But I don't mind this once. Uncle!

QUECKETT: (*to himself*) I wash my hands of the entire party!

> (*He plays the first figure of a quadrille, while they dance –* RANKLING *and* DINAH, SAUNDERS *and* GWENDOLINE, MALLORY *and* PEGGY, ERMYNTRUDE *and* REGINALD. *They dance with brightness and animation, but whenever* REGINALD *encounters* DINAH *there is a violent altercation. As the figure ends* JANE *enters again, and runs to* QUECKETT *at the piano.*)

QUECKETT: What is it?

JANE: Oh, sir, do come down-stairs – as far down as you can get.

QUECKETT: What do you mean?

JANE: That boy, Tyler, sir!

QUECKETT: Tyler – well?

JANE: He went off bang in the kitchen, sir, about ten minutes ago. Them fireworks!

QUECKETT: Fireworks! Where is he?

JANE: Gone for the engines, sir.

QUECKETT: (*rising*) The engines!

ERMYNTRUDE: Uncle!

GWENDOLINE: Uncle Vere!

PEGGY: Now then, Uncle!

QUECKETT: Excuse me – let somebody take my place at the piano. I – I'll be back in a moment!

> (JANE *hurries out, he following her.*)

PEGGY: (*running to the piano and commencing a waltz*) A waltz! Change partners!

> (RANKLING *dances with* ERMYNTRUDE, SAUNDERS *with* GWENDOLINE. REGINALD *is left out, but is wildly following* DINAH, *who is dancing with* MALLORY.)

RANKLING: (*puffing*) Not so fast, Miss Griffin – not so fast.

REGINALD: (*in* DINAH'S *ear*) I shall require some explanation, Madam.

DINAH: Oh, Reginald!

> (*There is the sound of a prolonged knocking at the street door, followed by a bell ringing violently.*)

PEGGY: (*playing*) Somebody wants to come in, evidently.

> (*Suddenly the music and the dancing stop and everybody listens; then they all run to the windows and look out.*)

RANKLING: What's that?

MALLORY: What's wrong?

SAUNDERS: Oh, look there!

PEGGY: Oh, there's such a crowd at our house?

> (QUECKETT *re-enters with* JANE, *who sinks into a chair.* QUECKETT *looks very pale and frightened.*)

QUECKETT : Listen to me, please.

ALL: What's the matter?

QUECKETT: Don't be alarmed. Look at me. Imitate my self-possession.

ALL: What *is* the matter?

QUECKETT: The matter? The weather is so unfavourable that the boy Tyler has been compelled to display fireworks on the premises.

THE GIRLS: Oh!

THE MEN: What has happened?

QUECKETT: Pray don't be disturbed. There is not the slightest occasion for alarm. We have now the choice of one alternative.

RANKLING *and* MALLORY: What's that?

QUECKETT: To get out without unnecessary delay.

THE GIRLS: (*clustering together*) Oh!

RANKLING: (*assuming the tone of a commander*) Mr Mallory! Mr Saunders!

MALLORY: Yes, sir.

SAUNDERS: Yes, sir.

> (MALLORY *and* SAUNDERS *place themselves beside* RANKLING.)

RANKLING: Ladies, fetch your cloaks and wraps preparatory to breaking up our pleasant little party. Who volunteers to assist the ladies?

MALLORY: I, sir!

SAUNDERS: I, sir!

REGINALD: I do!

QUECKETT: I do!

RANKLING: Mr Mallory, tell off Mr Queckett and Mr Jenkinson to help the ladies.

> (*The* GIRLS *run out, followed by* REGINALD, QUECKETT *and* JANE.)

RANKLING: Mr Mallory! Mr Saunders!

MALLORY *and* SAUNDERS: Yes, sir.

RANKLING: Our respective coats.

> (*They bustle about to get their coats as the door quietly opens and* JAFFRAY, *a fireman, appears.*)

JAFFRAY: Good evening, gentlemen. Can you tell me where I'll find the ladies?

MALLORY: They're putting on their hats and cloaks.

JAFFRAY: Thank you, gentlemen, I'm much obliged to you. (*He goes to the window, pulls up the blind, and throws the window open; the top of a ladder is seen against the balcony.*) Are you coming up, Mr Goff?

GOFF: (*out of sight*) Yes, Mr Jaffray.

> (GOFF, *a middle-aged, jolly-looking fireman, enters by the balcony and the window.*)

JAFFRAY: Gentlemen, Mr Goff – one of the oldest and most respected members of the Brigade. Mr Goff tells some most interesting stories, gentlemen.

RANKLING: (*impatiently*) Stories, sir! Call the ladies, Mr Mallory.

> (MALLORY *goes out.*)

GOFF: I shouldn't hurry them, sir – ladies like to take their time. Now I remember an instance in October '78 –

RANKLING: Confound it, sir, you're not going to relate anecdotes now!

JAFFRAY: I beg your pardon, sir, Mr Goff is one of the most experienced and entertaining members of the Brigade.

RANKLING: I tell you I don't care about that just now! Where are the ladies?
(SAUNDERS *goes out.*)
JAFFRAY: Excuse me, sir, Mr Goff's reminiscences are well worth hearing while you wait.
RANKLING: But I don't wish to wait!
(MALLORY *and* PEGGY, SAUNDERS *and* GWENDOLINE, REGINALD *and* DINAH, *followed by* JANE, *enter. The girls are hastily attired in all sorts of odd apparel and carrying bonnet-boxes, parcels, and small hand-bags.* ERMYNTRUDE *carries, amongst other things, a cage of white mice,* GWENDOLINE, *a bird in a cage, and* DINAH *a black cat, and* PEGGY *a pair of skates and a brush and comb.*)
THE GIRLS: We're ready. Take us away!
JAFFRAY: I must really ask you, ladies and gentlemen, to take it quietly for a few minutes.
ALL: Take it quietly! What for?
JAFFRAY: The staircase isn't just the thing for ladies and gentlemen at the present moment. I shall have to ask the ladies and gentlemen to use the Escape.
ALL: (*turning to the window*) The Escape! Where is it?
JAFFRAY: It'll be here in two minutes. In the meantime, I think Mr Goff could while away the time very pleasantly with a reminiscence or two. Ladies, Mr Goff –
THE GIRLS: Oh, take us away! Take us away!
(MALLORY, SAUNDERS *and* REGINALD *soothe the ladies,* JAFFRAY *goes to the window and looks out.*)
GOFF: (*pleasantly seating himself and taking off his helmet*) Well, ladies, I don't know that I can tell you much to amuse you – however –
RANKLING: Be quiet, sir – we will not be entertained!
JAFFRAY: (*carrying a hose from the window to the door*) Really, gentlemen, I must say I've never heard Mr Goff treated so hasty at any conflagration.
(*He carries the hose out.*)
RANKLING: A fireman full of anecdote! I decline to appreciate any reminiscence whatever. So do we all!
REGINALD: Certainly!
MALLORY: All of us!
GOFF: It was in July '79, ladies – my wife had just brought my tea to the Chandos Street Station –
(JAFFRAY *re-enters, and goes to the window.*)
MALLORY: Will you be silent, sir?
REGINALD: Get up and do something!
SAUNDERS: Go away!
JAFFRAY: The Escape, ladies and gentlemen – that window – one at a time.
(*There is a general movement and hubbub.* GOFF *rises, he and* JAFFRAY *disappear by the window on the left.* MALLORY *throws open the other window, and* JAFFRAY *appears outside and receives* DINAH, GWENDOLINE, ERMYNTRUDE, PEGGY *and* JANE *as they escape.*)
RANKLING: Mr Mallory – Mr Saunders – good evening!

(REGINALD *disappears by the right-hand window.* SAUNDERS *goes after him,* MALLORY *is about to follow when* QUECKETT *enters hurriedly.* QUECKETT *is in a tall hat, a short covert coat, and carries gloves and an umbrella. He is flourishing a letter.*)

QUECKETT: (*pulling* MALLORY *back*) Jack – Jack!

MALLORY: Hallo!

QUECKETT: I'm going back to save some valuables. Directly you get down, post that letter. Oh, Jack, it's so important.

MALLORY: (*looking at the letter*) To the Eagle Fire Insurance Company.

QUECKETT: Quite so – slipped my memory.

(MALLORY *disappears.* JAFFRAY *follows him.*)

RANKLING: (*hurrying to* QUECKETT) My dear Queckett, it is the commander's duty to be the last to leave the ship – you are master here. Thank you for your hospitality. Good-night.

QUECKETT: My dear Rankling, thank *you* for coming to see me. Good-night.

(JAFFRAY *appears at the window.*)

JAFFRAY: It's all right, gentlemen – there's a kind lady down below who is taking everybody into her house for the night – Mrs Rankling of Portland Place.

RANKLING: Mrs Rankling – that's my wife!

(QUECKETT *disappears.*)

JAFFRAY: Is she, sir? Glad to hear it. Then they are all your visitors till to-morrow.

RANKLING: Confound it, sir, where do I live?

JAFFRAY: Just at the corner here, sir – a hundred yards off.

RANKLING: Then where am I now?

JAFFRAY: Miss Dyott's boarding school, sir – Volumnia College.

RANKLING: What!

(*He and* JAFFRAY *go out by the window on the right as* GOFF *enters by the window on the left.*)

GOFF: Where is he? (*calling at the door*) Sir, here's the lady of the house – rode up on an engine from Piccadilly – make haste – she says she will come up the ladder.

(QUECKETT *enters quickly dragging after him several boxes of cigars.*)

QUECKETT: A lady! What lady? (MISS DYOTT *appears at the window. She is in the gorgeous dress of an opera-bouffe Queen, with a flaxen wig, much disarranged, and a crown on one side. Recoiling*) Caroline!

MISS DYOTT: (*entering and taking him by the collar*) Come down!

(*She drags him towards the window.*)

END OF THE SECOND ACT

THE THIRD ACT: NIGHTMARE

The Scene is a well-furnished, tastefully decorated Morning-room in the house of ADMIRAL RANKLING. *At the further end of the room there are two double doors facing each other, one with glazed panels opening to a conservatory, the other to a dark room. There are also two doors near to the pillars that support an archway spanning the*

---

covert coat: 'a short light overcoat' (*OED*).

room. *All is darkness save for a faint glow from the fire, and a blue light coming through the conservatory windows.*

PEGGY, *dressed as before, enters quietly, looking about her.*

PEGGY: (*in a whisper*) Where have I got to now, I wonder? What a dreadful wilderness of a house to wander about in, in the dark, all alone. Oh, for the daylight! (*looking at her watch*) Half-past six. Why, gracious! here's a spark of fire! Oh, joy!

> (*She goes down on her knees, and replenishes the fire with coal from the scuttle. The door opens, and* GWENDOLINE *peeps in.*)

GWENDOLINE: (*in a whisper*) What room is this? (*entering noiselessly*) Will the day never break? (*frightened, and retreating as* PEGGY *makes a noise blowing up the fire*) Oh!

PEGGY: (*frightened*) Oh! Who is that? (*looking round*) Gwendoline!

GWENDOLINE: Peggy!

PEGGY: Are you wandering about too?

GWENDOLINE: Yes. I can't sleep – can you?

PEGGY: (*shivering*) Sleep? No. As if I could sleep in a strange bed in a strange house, in one of Admiral Rankling's night-gowns. You didn't meet any daylight on the stairs, did you?

> (*Another door opens, and* ERMYNTRUDE *enters noiselessly.*)

GWENDOLINE: (*clinging to* PEGGY) Oh, look there!

ERMYNTRUDE: (*in a whisper*) I wonder where I am now.

PEGGY: Ermyntrude!

ERMYNTRUDE: (*clinging to a chair*) Ah!

PEGGY: Be quiet! It's we – it's us – it's her and me! Oh, my grammar's going now!

ERMYNTRUDE: Can't you girls get to sleep?

GWENDOLINE: I should think not.

PEGGY: There wasn't any daylight in your room when you came down, was there?

ERMYNTRUDE: I thought I saw a glimmer through the window on the first floor landing.

PEGGY: Ah, perhaps that's some of yesterday's. I know! I've made up the fire; let us bivouac here till daybreak. Two by the fire, and take it in turns for the sofa.
(picking up a bear-skin rug and carrying it to the sofa) Who's first for the sofa?

GWENDOLINE: Ermyntrude.

ERMYNTRUDE: Gwendoline.

PEGGY: Come along, Gwendoline. (GWENDOLINE *puts herself upon the sofa, and* PEGGY *covers her with the bear-skin.*) There – as soon as you drop off to sleep it will be Ermyntrude's turn. (*looking through the conservatory doors*) Oh, how the snow is coming down!

> (*Joining* ERMYNTRUDE, *who is warming her hands by the fire. She sits in an arm-chair.*)

ERMYNTRUDE: Peggy – do you know what has become of poor Dinah?

PEGGY: Yes, she's locked up upstairs till the morning. Admiral Rankling locked her up.

GWENDOLINE: (*from the sofa*) It's a shame!

PEGGY: Go to sleep! Oh, what a scene there was! Admiral Rankling foamed at the mouth. It was lucky they got Mr Queckett away from him in time.

GWENDOLINE: (*sleepily*) Where is Mr Queckett?

PEGGY: Go to sleep.

ERMYNTRUDE: (*leaning against* PEGGY's *knees*) Mr Queckett is locked up too, isn't he?

PEGGY: Of course he is – till the morning. Miss Dyott locked *him* up – very properly I think.

ERMYNTRUDE: And where's Miss Dyott?

PEGGY: Upstairs, in the room next to mine, in hysterics. Hush! I do believe Gwendoline has gone off. Are you pretty comfortable?

ERMYNTRUDE: (*her head on* PEGGY's *lap – sleepily*) Yes, thank you.

PEGGY: (*wearily*) Oh!

> (*The door quietly opens, and* SAUNDERS *appears.* PEGGY *and* ERMYNTRUDE *are hidden from him by the arm-chair.*)

SAUNDERS: (*sleepily*) I can't sleep in my room. Where have they put Uncle Jack, I wonder? (*seeing* GWENDOLINE, *who is sleeping, with the light from the conservatory windows upon her*) Oh – what's that? (*going softly up to* GWENDOLINE, *and looking at her*) Why, here's my Gwen. I wonder if she'd mind my sitting near her. (*turning up his coat collar and sitting gently on the footstool, he leans against the head of the sofa, drowsily*) Now if any robbers wanted to hurt Gwen, I could kill them. (*closing his eyes wearily*)

> (*Soon there is a sound of heavy regular breathing from the four sleeping figures. The door opens, and* MALLORY *enters.*)

MALLORY: (*shivering*) Can't get a blessed wink of sleep. Where have I wandered to? Why, this is the room where the awful row was. (*seeing* GWENDOLINE) Hallo, here's one of those school-girls – (*discovering* SAUNDERS) – and – well, this nephew of mine is a devil of a fellow! That isn't a glimmer of fire, surely. (*Walking towards the fireplace, he nearly stumbles over* ERMYNTRUDE.) More girls.

> (*He accidentally knocks over the scuttle. They all wake up with a start.*)

PEGGY *and* ERMYNTRUDE: What's that?

GWENDOLINE *and* SAUNDERS: Who is it?

MALLORY: Hush, don't be frightened! It's only I.

PEGGY: Mr Mallory.

MALLORY: I've been wandering about – can't sleep.

PEGGY: No – we can't sleep either.

MALLORY: Well I don't know about that.

> (ERMYNTRUDE *lights the candle on the mantelpiece.*)

PEGGY: Why haven't you and Mr Saunders gone home? You're not burnt out.

MALLORY: Perhaps not; but Admiral Rankling asked me to remain, and, if he hadn't, I'm not going to leave this house till my friend Queckett is out of danger.

PEGGY: Out of danger?

MALLORY: Yes. Are you aware that you young ladies have brought very grave difficulties upon that unfortunate gentleman?

PEGGY: (*crying*) He encouraged us! He's a man!

MALLORY: Now, pray don't cry, my dear Miss – what is your name this morning?

PEGGY: Hesslerigge, and I wish I'd never been born!

MALLORY: Hesslerigge, and you wish you'd never been born. (*taking her hand*)

Well, Miss Hesslerigge, the serious aspect of the affair is that Admiral Rankling has a most violent, ungovernable temper.

PEGGY: (*tearfully*) I know. I've never seen a gentleman foam at the mouth before. It's quite a new experience.

MALLORY: (*soothingly*) Of course – of course – and therefore I'm apprehensive for poor Mr Queckett's bodily safety. Meanwhile I won't disturb you any longer; come along, Saunders.

PEGGY: Where are you going?

MALLORY: To the front door – to speak a word or two of encouragement to that young fellow, Paulover.

PEGGY: Oh, he is outside still? In the snow!

MALLORY: Why, he has been walking up and down on the other side of the way all night.

PEGGY: (*indignantly*) And you haven't let him in!

MALLORY: How could I! You forget that our host has forbidden him the house.

PEGGY: No, I don't; I saw them roll out into the road together. Girls, shall we open the front door, or shall we remain the mere slaves of etiquette?

GWENDOLINE: I should like to let him in.

ERMYNTRUDE: Certainly – why not?

SAUNDERS: Come along – I know the way.

> (SAUNDERS, GWENDOLINE, *and* ERMYNTRUDE *go out quietly.*)

MALLORY: (*to* PEGGY) Well, you'll perhaps pardon my saying that you are a devil-may-care little school-girl!

PEGGY: You make a great mistake. I am not a school-girl; I am struggling to be a governess.

MALLORY: Ah, I hope you'll make your way in your profession.

> (PEGGY *has discovered the spirit-stand on the sideboard and now places it on the table.*)

MALLORY: What are you going to do now?

PEGGY: Brew poor Mr Paulover something hot. (*bringing the kettle and spirit lamp to the table*) Light this lamp for me, please. (*He lights the lamp.*) If you can recommend me at any time to a lady with young daughters I shall be grateful.

MALLORY: I will – I will.

PEGGY: I think I am almost capable of finishing any young lady now.

MALLORY: I am sure you are. (*looking at the spirit lamp*) Is that alight? (*They put their heads down close together to look at the lighted lamp.*) That's all right.

PEGGY: Seems so.

> (*They rise and look at one another.*)

MALLORY: We'd better watch it, perhaps, in case it goes out. (*They bob down again with their heads together, and both sit on the same chair.*) You'll get into an awful scrape over your share in last night's business, won't you?

PEGGY: Frightful; the thought depresses me.

MALLORY: Do you think Miss Dyott, or Mrs Queckett, or whatever she is, will send you home?

PEGGY: She can't – she's got me for ever. She took me, years ago, for a bad debt.

MALLORY: How can she punish you then?

PEGGY: I think she will withdraw her confidence from me.

MALLORY: You won't despair, will you?

PEGGY: I'll try not to.

MALLORY: What a jolly little sailor's wife you'd make – brewing grog like this.

PEGGY: I hope I should do my duty in any station of life to which I might be called.

MALLORY: *I'm* a sailor, you know.

PEGGY: No – are you?

MALLORY (*taking her hand and putting it to his lips*) You know I am.

PEGGY: (*suddenly*) It's going to boil over! (*They jump up quickly*, MALLORY *retreats.*) Oh, no, it isn't. (GWENDOLINE *and* ERMYNTRUDE *enter, leading* REGINALD, *with* SAUNDERS *following.* REGINALD *is in a deplorable condition, covered with snow and icicles, his face is white, and his nose red.*) Oh, poor Mr Paulover!

SAUNDERS: He's frost-bitten!

PEGGY: Thaw him by degrees.

> (PEGGY *mixes the grog.* GWENDOLINE *and* ERMYNTRUDE *lead* REGINALD *to a chair before the fire, he uttering some violent but incoherent exclamations.*)

ERMYNTRUDE: He's annoyed with Admiral Rankling.

> (*The girls chafe his hands while he still mutters, with his eyes rolling.*)

PEGGY: It's a good job his language is frozen.

> (*Putting the glass of grog to his lips.*)

REGINALD: (*reviving*) Thank you. Take my hat off, please – I bought it from a cabman. (GWENDOLINE *removes his hat, which is very shabby.*) Good morning! Where's my wife Dinah?

PEGGY: She's quite safe.

REGINALD: I must see her – speak to her!

PEGGY: You can't – she's locked up.

REGINALD: Then I must push a long letter under her door. She *must*, she *shall* know that I am going to walk up and down outside this house all my life! (*faintly*) Bring writing materials!

MALLORY: I'll hunt for the pen and ink.

SAUNDERS: So will I.

REGINALD: (*to* PEGGY) No – no – you do it. These men are bachelors – they can't feel for me!

MALLORY: Here's a writing-table.

> (PEGGY *runs to* MALLORY *and opens the lid of the writing-table.*)

PEGGY: Note-paper and envelopes – where's the – (*Opening one of the small drawers – she starts back with a cry.*) Oh!

> (*They all turn and look at her.*)

ALL: What's the matter?

PEGGY: (*taking from the drawer a large bunch of keys, each with a small label, which she examines breathlessly*) Duplicate keys of all the rooms in the house! What gross carelessness – to leave keys in an open drawer! Girls, why should not we impress this fact upon Admiral Rankling by releasing Dinah immediately?

GWENDOLINE *and* ERMYNTRUDE: Oh, yes, yes!

REGINALD: (*seizing* PEGGY's *hand*) Oh, Miss Hesslerigge, my father-in-law is
  entertaining an angel unawares.

MALLORY: Oh, stop, stop, stop – I don't think we're quite justified –

REGINALD: (*scornfully*) Hah, I told you he was merely a bachelor! (*pointing to*
  SAUNDERS) So is his companion. Give *me* the keys!

PEGGY: No – no – I take the responsibility of this. I am a girl! (*going towards the
  door, and looking at* MALLORY *and* SAUNDERS *as they make way for her*) I
  hope you will repent your line of conduct, gentlemen.
      (*She goes out.*)

MALLORY: I think we *all* shall.
      (*There is a sudden noise, as of some one falling down a couple of stairs.
      They start and listen.*)

GIRLS: Oh!

MALLORY: What's that?

ERMYNTRUDE: (*looking out at door*) Here's Admiral Rankling!
      (*There is a suppressed exclamation with a silent scamper to the further
      end of the room.*)

MALLORY: (*indignantly*) What the deuce does a respectable man want out of bed at
  this unearthly hour?

RANKLING: (*in a rage, outside the door*) Confound that!

GIRLS: Oh!

REGINALD: (*opening the door leading to the dark room*) Here's a room here. Shall
  we condescend to hide?

ALL: Yes.
      (*They disappear hastily as* RANKLING *appears in a dressing-gown, his
      face pale and his eyes red and wild.*)

RANKLING: Hallo! Some one has been sitting up – candles – and a fire. Ah! (*sniffing
  and walking about the room, he goes straight to the mantelpiece, upon which
  REGINALD's grog has been left, and takes up the tumbler.*) It's Mallory. (*with
  suppressed passion*) It's against the rules for anybody to sit up in my house!
  (*calmly*) But I don't mind Mallory – I don't – (*looking at sofa*). Hallo – Mallory
  has been turning in here. (*going to the sofa and sitting there shaking with anger*)
  Are we never going to have any more daylight? How long am I to wait till that
  miserable schoolmistress releases the worm Queckett! Queckett! *Uncle Vere!*
  The reptile who has made a fool of me in the eyes of my wife and daughter! Ugh!
  But I must husband my strength for Queckett. I have been a very careful man all
  my life; as far as muscular economy goes, Queckett shall have the savings of a
  lifetime. (*lying down and pulling the rug over him*) Uncle Vere! Ah – I was a
  wild, impetuous, daring lad once – (*going to sleep*) – and I can be unpleasant
  even now. I can! The Admiralty doesn't know it – Emma doesn't know it –
  Queckett shall know it.
      (*He breathes heavily. The others have been peeping from their hiding-
      place, and as they close the door,* PEGGY *enters alone, quickly but
      silently. She looks for the others, then almost falls over* RANKLING *on
      the sofa, at which she retreats with a suppressed screech of horror.*
      MALLORY *opens the further door and gesticulates to her violently to
      be silent.*)

PEGGY: (*Petrified*) Oh, my goodness gracious!
> (MALLORY *comes and bends over* RANKLING, *listening to his breathing, he then goes to* PEGGY.)
MALLORY: He's dropped off. Where is Mrs Paulover?
PEGGY: She's not on that side of the house.
MALLORY: I've a plan for disposing of the old gentleman. Try the other side.
PEGGY: I'm going to. (*turning and clutching* MALLORY) But, oh, Mr Mallory, what *do* you think I've done?
MALLORY: That's impossible to conjecture.
PEGGY: I've made a mistake about the doors and – I have unlocked Mr Queckett!
> (*She goes out quickly,* MALLORY *thinks for a moment, then bursts into a fit of silent laughter.*)
MALLORY: I love that girl!
> (REGINALD *appears at the further door, gesticulating.*)
REGINALD: (*in a hoarse whisper*) Where is my wife? I cannot live longer without her! Where is Dinah!
MALLORY: Hush! She'll be here in a minute. Come out of there and lend me a hand. (SAUNDERS, GWENDOLINE, *and* ERMYNTRUDE *enter on tiptoe. To* REGINALD) Now then – gently.
> (MALLORY *and* REGINALD *each take an end of the sofa and carry* RANKLING *out through the door into the dark room.*)
GWENDOLINE: (*breathlessly*) If they bump him, all's lost!
> (MALLORY *and* REGINALD *re-appear.*)
REGINALD: I feel warmer now.
MALLORY: Turn the key.
> (REGINALD *turns the key as* DINAH *and* PEGGY *enter cautiously.*)
GWENDOLINE *and* ERMYNTRUDE: Dinah!
DINAH: Reggie!
REGINALD: My wife!
> (REGINALD *rushes down to* DINAH *and embraces her frantically. There is a general cry of relief as* MALLORY *embraces* PEGGY, *and* GWENDOLINE *throws her arms round* SAUNDERS. *Suddenly there is the sound of some one stumbling downstairs, accompanied by a smothered exclamation.*)
ALL: (*listening*) What's that?
ERMYNTRUDE: (*peeping out at door*) Here's Uncle Vere got loose. He has fallen downstairs.
REGINALD: Oh, bother! Come along, Dinah.
> (REGINALD *and* DINAH, SAUNDERS, ERMYNTRUDE *and* GWENDOLINE *go out quickly.*)
PEGGY: (*to* MALLORY) Rather bad taste of your nephew and those girls to run after a newly married couple, isn't it?
MALLORY: Yes; *we* won't do it.
PEGGY: No; but we don't want to be bothered with your old friend, Queckett, do we?
MALLORY: No – he's an awful bore. Is the conservatory heated?

PEGGY: (*taking his arm*) I don't mind if it isn't.

> (*They disappear into the conservatory. The door opens, and* QUECKETT, *his face pale and haggard, enters, still wearing his hat and the short covert coat over his evening dress, and carrying his gloves and umbrella.*)

QUECKETT: To whom am I indebted for being let out? Was it by way of treachery, I wonder? Somebody has been sitting up late, or rising early! Who is it? (*sniffing and looking about him, then going straight to the mantelpiece, taking up the tumbler and smelling the contents*) I am anxious not to do any one an injustice, but that's Peggy. Oh, what a night I've passed! I have no hesitation in saying that the extremely bad behaviour of Caroline – of the lady I have married – and the ungovernable rage of Rankling, are indelibly impressed upon me. (*looking round nervously*) Good gracious! I am actually in the room where Rankling announced his intention of ultimately dislocating my vertebræ. I shall certainly not winter in England. (*The clock strikes seven, he looks at his watch.*) Seven. It will be wise to remain here till the first gleam of daylight, and then leave the house – unostentatiously. I will exchange *no* explanations with Caroline. I shall simply lay the whole circumstances of my injudicious, boyish marriage before my brother Bob and the other members of my family. Any allowance which Caroline may make me shall come through them. (*There is a sound of something falling and breaking outside the room.*) The deuce! What's that? (*going on tiptoe over to the door, and peeping out*) Somebody has knocked something over. (*snatching up his hat, gloves and umbrella*) I shan't wait till daybreak if they're breaking other things. (*He hurries to the other door, opens it, looks out and closes it quickly.*) People sitting on the stairs! Is this a plot to surround me? the conservatory? (*He goes quickly to the conservatory doors, opens them, then draws back closing them quickly.*) Two persons under a palm tree. (*There is a knock at the door on the right.*) Oh! (*seeing the door leading to the dark room*) Where does that lead to? (*He tries the door, unlocks it and looks in.*) A dark room! Oh, I'm so thankful!

> (*He disappears, closing the door after him. The knocking outside is repeated, then the door opens and* MISS DYOTT *enters. She is dressed in her burlesque queen costume, her face is pale. She carries the head, broken off at the neck, of a terra-cotta bust of a woman.*)

MISS DYOTT: I have broken a bust now. It is an embarrassing thing to break a bust in the house of comparative strangers. Oh, will it never be daylight? Does the milkman *never* come to Portland Place! I have been listening at the keyhole of Vere's room – not a sound. He can sleep with the ruin of Volumnia College upon his conscience while I – (*sinking into a chair*) Ah, I realise now the correctness of the poet's observation – 'Uneasy lies the head that wears a crown!'

> (QUECKETT *comes quietly from the dark room, much terrified.*)

QUECKETT: Rankling's in there – asleep. In the dark I sat on him. Oh, what a

---

'*Uneasy . . . crown*': *2 Henry IV*, III.i.

narrow escape I've had! (*coming behind* MISS DYOTT *and suddenly seeing her*)
Caroline! Scylla and Charybdis!

(*He bolts back into the dark room.*)

MISS DYOTT: (*rising alarmed*) What's that?

(MRS RANKLING *enters, in a peignoir.*)

MRS RANKLING: I heard something fall. (*seeing* MISS DYOTT) Mrs Queckett!
(*distantly*) Instructions were given that everybody should be called at eight. I
had arranged that a more appropriate costume should be placed at your
disposal. (*seeing the broken bust*) Ah, what has happened?

MISS DYOTT: I knocked over the pedestal.

MRS RANKLING: (*Distressed*) Oh, bust of myself by Belt! I saw him working on it!
Oh, Mrs Queckett, is there no end to the trouble you have brought upon us?

MISS DYOTT: The trouble *you* have brought upon me.

MRS RANKLING: What! Why didn't you tell us you had a husband?

MISS DYOTT: Why didn't you tell me that Dinah had a husband?

MRS RANKLING: We didn't know it.

MISS DYOTT: Well, if you didn't know your own daughter was married, how can you
wonder at your ignorance of other people's domestic complications?

MRS RANKLING: But that's not all. You have informed us that you are now actually
contributing to a nightly entertainment of a volatile description – that you are
positively being laughed at in public.

MISS DYOTT: Isn't it better to be laughed at in public, and paid for it, than to be
sniggered at privately for nothing!

MRS RANKLING: Mrs Queckett, you are revealing your true character.

MISS DYOTT: It is the same as your own – an undervalued wife. Let me open your
eyes as mine are opened. We have engaged to love and to honour two men.

MRS RANKLING: *I* have done nothing of the kind.

MISS DYOTT: I mean one each.

MRS RANKLING: Oh – excuse me.

MISS DYOTT: Now – looking at him microscopically – is there much to love and to
honour in Admiral Rankling?

MRS RANKLING: He is a genial after-dinner speaker.

MISS DYOTT: Hah!

MRS RANKLING: It is true he is rather austere.

MISS DYOTT: An austere sailor! All bows abroad and stern at home. Well then –
knowing what occurred last night – is there anything to love and to honour in Mr
Queckett?

MRS RANKLING: Nothing whatever.

MISS DYOTT: (*annoyed*) And yet he is undoubtedly the superior of Admiral
Rankling. Very well then – do as I mean to do – put your foot down. If heaven
has gifted you with a large one, so much the better.

Scylla and Charybdis: in classical mythology, Scylla was a monster which threatened mariners
from a cave separated by a narrow passage from the whirlpool Charybdis, between the Italian
mainland and Sicily. Classical map-makers attached their names to the two features which still
bear them. Hence the allusion is to two opposite dangers to be avoided.

(*The voices of* QUECKETT *and* RANKLING *are heard suddenly raised in the adjoining room.*

RANKLING: (*outside*) Queckett.

QUECKETT: (*outside*) My dear Rankling!

MISS.DYOTT: Vere!

MRS RANKLING: The Admiral has released your husband.

RANKLING: (*in the distance*) I'll trouble you, sir!

QUECKETT: Certainly, Rankling.

MISS DYOTT: (*to* MRS RANKLING) Come away, and I will advise you. Bring your head with you.

      (MISS DYOTT *and* MRS RANKLING, *carrying the broken bust, hurry out as* QUECKETT *enters quickly, followed by* RANKLING.)

QUECKETT: Admiral Rankling I shall mark my opinion of your behaviour – through the post.

RANKLING: Sit down.

QUECKETT: Thank you – I've been sitting. I sat on you on the sofa.

RANKLING: Sit down. (QUECKETT *sits promptly*.) As an old friend of your family, Mr Queckett, I am going to have a quiet chat with you on family matters.

      (RANKLING *wheels the arm-chair near* QUECKETT.)

QUECKETT: (*to himself*) I don't like his calmness – I don't like his calmness

      (RANKLING *sits bending forward, and glaring at* QUECKETT.)

RANKLING: (*grimly*) How is your sister Janet? Quite well, eh? (*fiercely*) Tell me – without a moment's delay, sir – how is Janet?

QUECKETT: Permit me to say, Admiral Rankling, that whatever your standing with other members of my family, you have *no* acquaintance with the lady you mention.

RANKLING: Oh, haven't I (*drawing his chair nearer* QUECKETT) Very well, then. Is *Griffin* quite well – Finch-Griffin of the Berkshire Royals?

QUECKETT: I do not know how Major Griffin is, and I feel I do not care.

RANKLING: Oh, you don't. Very well, then (*drawing his chair still nearer* QUECKETT) Will you answer me one simple but important question?

QUECKETT: If it be a question a gentleman may answer – certainly.

RANKLING: How often do you hear from your brother Tankerville?

QUECKETT: Oh!

RANKLING: (*clutching* QUECKETT'*s knee*) He's Deputy Inspector of Prisons in British Guiana, you know. Doesn't have time to write often, does he?

QUECKETT: Admiral Rankling, you will permit me to remind you that in families of long standing and complicated interests there are regrettable estrangements which should be lightly dealt with. (*affected*) You have recalled memories (*rising*) Excuse me.

RANKLING:(*rising*) No sir, I will not excuse you!

QUECKETT: Where are my gloves?

RANKLING: Because, Mr Queckett, I have your assurance as a gentleman that your brother Tankerville's daughter is married to a charming young fellow of the name of Parkinson. Now I've discovered that Parkinson is really a charming young fellow of the name of Paulover, so that, as Paulover has married my daughter as well as Tankerville's, Paulover must be prosecuted for bigamy, and as you knew that Paulover was Parkinson, and Parkinson Paulover, you connived at the crime, inasmuch as knowing Paulover was Tankerville's daughter's husband you deliberately aided Parkinson in making my child Dinah his wife. But that's not the worst of it!

QUECKETT: Oh!

RANKLING: (*continuing, rapidly and excitedly*) Because I have since received your gentlemanly assurance that Tankerville's daughter is *my* daughter. Now, either you mean to say that I've behaved like a blackguard to Tankerville – which will be a libel; or that Tankerville has conducted himself with less than common fairness to me – which will be a divorce. And, in either case, without wishing to anticipate the law, I shall personally chastise you, because, although I've been a sailor on the high seas for five and forty years, I have *never* during the whole of that period listened to such a yarn of mendacious fabrications as you spun me last night!

QUECKETT: (*beginning carefully to put on his gloves*) It would be idle to deny that this affair has now assumed its most unpleasant aspect. Admiral Rankling – the time has come for candour on both sides.

RANKLING: Be quick, sir!

QUECKETT: I am being quick, Rankling. I admit, with all the rapidity of utterance of which I am capable, that my assurances of last night were founded upon an airy basis.

RANKLING: In plain words – lies, Mr Queckett.

QUECKETT: A habit of preparing election manifestoes for various members of my family may have impaired a fervent admiration for truth, in which I yield to no man.

RANKLING: (*advancing in a determined manner*) Very well, Sir!

QUECKETT: (*retreating*) One moment, Rankling. One moment – *if not two*! I glean that you are prepared to assault –

RANKLING: To chastise!

QUECKETT: Well, to inconvenience a man at whose table you feasted last night. Do so!

RANKLING: I will do so!

QUECKETT: I say, do so. But the triumph, when you kneel upon my body – for I am bound to tell you that I shall lie down – the triumph will be mine!

RANKLING: You are welcome to it, sir. Put down that umbrella!

QUECKETT: What for?

RANKLING: *I* haven't an umbrella.

QUECKETT: You haven't? Allow me to leave this room, my dear Rankling, and I'll beg your acceptance of this one.

(RANKLING *advances fiercely;* QUECKETT *retreats;* MISS DYOTT *enters.*)

QUECKETT: Caroline!

MISS DYOTT: Stop, Admiral Rankling, if you please. Any reprimand, physical or otherwise, will be administered to Mr Queckett at my hands.

QUECKETT: (*to himself*) I would have preferred Rankling. Rankling I could have winded.

(*He goes out quickly.* MISS DYOTT *following in pursuit.*)

MISS DYOTT: (*as she goes*) Vere!

RANKLING: I am in my own house, madam –

(MRS RANKLING *enters, carrying the broken bust.*)

RANKLING: Emma, go back to bed.

MRS RANKLING: Archibald Rankling, attend to me. Don't roll your eyes – but attend to me.

RANKLING: Emma, your tone is dictatorial

MRS RANKLING: It is meant to be so, because, after seventeen years of married life, I am going to speak my mind, at last. (*holding up the head before him*) Archibald, look at that.

RANKLING: What's that?

MRS RANKLING: Myself – less than ten years ago – the sculptor's earliest effort.

RANKLING: Broken – made of bad stuff – send it back.

MRS RANKLING: It is your memory I wish to send back. Ah, Archibald, do you see how round and plump those cheeks are?

RANKLING: People alter. You were stout then.

MRS RANKLING: I was.

RANKLING: In those days I was thin.

MRS RANKLING: Frightfully.

RANKLING: Very well, then – the average remains the same. Some day we may return to the old arrangement.

MRS RANKLING: If you ever find yourself a spare man again, Archibald, it won't be because I have worried and fretted you with my peevish ill-humour –

RANKLING: Emma!

MRS RANKLING: As you have worried and worn me with yours.

RANKLING: Emma, you have completely lost your head. (*She raises the broken bust.*) I don't mean that confounded bust. That was an ideal.

MRS RANKLING: And if a mere sculptor could make your wife an ideal, why shouldn't you try? So, understand me finally, Archibald, I will not be ground down any longer. Unless some arrangement is arrived at for the happiness of dear Dinah and Mr Paulover, I leave you.

RANKLING: Leave me!

MRS RANKLING: This very day.

RANKLING: Wantonly desert your home and husband, Emma?

MRS RANKLING: Yes.

RANKLING: (*with emotion*) And I don't know where to put my hand upon even a necktie!

(*covering his face with his handkerchief*)

MRS RANKLING: All the world shall learn how highly you thought of Dinah's marriage at Mr Queckett's party last night.

RANKLING: (*to himself*) Oh!

MRS RANKLING: And what a very different man you have always been in your own home. (*beginning to cry*) And take care, Archibald, that the verdict of posterity is not that you were less a husband and father than a tyrant and oppressor.

(QUECKETT *enters, with* MISS DYOTT *in pursuit; she follows him out.*)

MISS DYOTT: (*as she goes*) Vere!

(RANKLING *blows his nose and wipes his eyes, and looks at* MRS RANKLING)

RANKLING: (*in a conciliatory tone*) Emma! Emma!

MRS RANKLING: (*weeping*) Oh, dear, oh, dear!

RANKLING: Emma. (*irritably*) Don't tuck your head under your arm in that way! (*She puts the broken bust on the table.*) Emma – there have been grave faults on both sides. Yours I will endeavour to overlook.

MRS RANKLING: Ah, now you are your dear old self again.

RANKLING: But, Emma, you are occasionally an irritating woman to live with.

MRS RANKLING: You are the first who has ever said that.

RANKLING: So I should hope, Emma.

MRS RANKLING: And poor Dinah – you will forgive her?

RANKLING: On condition that she doesn't see Paulover's face again for five years.

MRS RANKLING: Oh, there will be no difficulty about that.

(REGINALD *and* DINAH *enter; she is dressed for flight.*)

DINAH: Papa!

REGINALD: My father-in-law!

(*They retreat hastily.*)

RANKLING: (*madly*) Who let you out? Who let you in?

(*He goes out after them* – MRS RANKLING *follows.*)

MRS RANKLING: (*As she goes out*) Archibald! continue your dear old self.

(QUECKETT *enters by another door,* MISS DYOTT *following him – both out of breath. They look at each other, recovering themselves.*)

QUECKETT: I understand that you wish to speak to me, Caroline.

MISS DYOTT: Oh, you – you paltry little man! You mean ungrateful little creature! You laced-up little heap of pompous pauperism! You – you – I cannot adequately describe you. Wretch!

QUECKETT: (*putting on his gloves again*) Have you finished with me, Caroline?

MISS DYOTT: Finished with you! I shall never have finished with you! Never till you leave me!

QUECKETT: (*rising*) Till I leave you?

MISS DYOTT: Till you leave me a widow.

QUECKETT: (*resuming his seat, disappointed*) Oh!

MISS DYOTT: You don't think I expect you to leave me anything else. Oh, what could I have seen in you!

QUECKETT: I take it, Caroline, that, in the language of the hunting-field, you 'scented' a gentleman.

MISS DYOTT: Scented a gentleman! In the few weeks of our marriage I have scented you and cigaretted you, wined you and liqueured you, tailored and hatted and booted you. I have darned and mended and washed you – gruelled you with a cold, tinctured you with a toothache, and linimented you with the gout. (*fiercely*) Have I not? Have I not?

QUECKETT: You certainly have had exceptional privileges. Familiarity appears to have fulfilled its usual functions and bred –

MISS DYOTT: The most utter contempt. Have I not paid your debts?

QUECKETT: (*promptly*) Not at my suggestion.

MISS DYOTT: And all for what?

QUECKETT: I assume, for Love's dear sake, Carrie.

MISS DYOTT: For the sake of having the vestal seclusion of Volumnia College telegraphically denominated as Bachelor Diggings!

QUECKETT: Any collection of young ladies may be so described. The description is happy but harmless. As for the subsequent conflagration –

MISS DYOTT: Don't talk about it!

QUECKETT: I say with all sincerity that from the moment the fire broke out till I escaped no one regretted it more than myself. *That* was Tyler!

MISS DYOTT: Tyler! What Tyler! I make no historical reference when I say what Tyler was it who abruptly tore aside the veil of mystery which had hitherto shrouded the existence of champagne and lobster salad from four young girls? It was you!

QUECKETT: No, it wasn't, Carrie, upon my word!

MISS DYOTT: Bah!

QUECKETT: Upon my honour!

MISS DYOTT: (*witheringly*) Hah!

QUECKETT: Those vexing pupils played the very devil with me. After you left, the pupils, as it were, dilated.

MISS DYOTT: Yes, and you ordered them champagne glasses, I suppose! Oh, deceiver!

QUECKETT: You talk of deception! What about the three o'clock train from Paddington?

MISS DYOTT: It was the whole truth – there was one.

QUECKETT: But you didn't travel in it! What about the clergyman's wife at Hereford?

MISS DYOTT: Go there – you will find several!

QUECKETT: But you're not staying with them. Oh, Carrie, how can you meet my fearless glance when you recall that my last words yesterday were: 'Cabman, drive to Paddington – the lady will pay your fare'?

MISS DYOTT: I cannot deny that it is by accident you have discovered that I am Queen Honorine in Otto Bernstein's successful comic opera.

QUECKETT: And what do you think my family would think of that?

MISS DYOTT: It is true that the public now know me as Miss Constance Delaporte.

QUECKETT: (*indignantly*) Oh! Miss Constance Delaporte!

MISS DYOTT: The new and startling contralto – her first appearance.

QUECKETT: And have I, a Queckett, after all, gone and married a Connie?

MISS DYOTT: You have! It is true, too, that last night, while you and my pupils were dilating, I was singing – aye and at one important juncture, dancing!

QUECKETT: (*with horror*) No, no – not dancing!

MISS DYOTT: Madly, desperately, hysterically, dancing!

QUECKETT: And to think – if there was any free list – that my brother Bob may have been there.

---

what Tyler: a pun on Wat Tyler (originally Walter Tyler) who led a rebellion against Richard II in 1381.

free list: Victorian theatrical practice included a 'free list' (usually of tradesmen exhibiting playbills) which provided free admission when space allowed.

MISS DYOTT: But do you guess the one thought that prompted me, buoyed me up, guided my steps, and ultimately produced a lower G of exceptional power?

QUECKETT: (*with a groan*) No.

MISS DYOTT: The thought that every note I sang might bring a bank-note to my lonely Vere at home.

QUECKETT: Carrie!

MISS DYOTT: I went through the performance in a dream! The conductor's *bâton* beat nothing but, 'Vere, Vere, Vere', into my eyes. Some one applauded me! I thought, 'Ah, that's worth a new hat to Vere!' I sang my political verse – a man very properly hissed. 'He has smashed Vere's new hat', I murmured. At last came my important solo. I drew a long breath, saw a vision of you reading an old copy of *The Rock* by the fireside at home – and opened my mouth. I remember nothing more till I found myself wildly dancing to the *refrain* of my song. The audience yelled with approbation – I bowed again and again – and then tottered away to sink into the arms of the prompter with the words, 'Vere, catch your Carrie'!

QUECKETT: But my family – my brother Bob –

MISS DYOTT: What have they ever done for you? While I – it was my ambition to devote every penny of my salary to your little wants.

QUECKETT: And isn't it?

MISS DYOTT: No – Vere Albany Bute Queckett; it isn't! The moment I dragged you down that ladder last night and left behind me the smouldering ruins of Volumnia College, I became an altered woman.

QUECKETT: Then I will lay the whole affair before my family.

MISS DYOTT: Do, and tell them to what your selfishness has brought you – that where there was love there is disdain, where there was claret there will be beer, where there were cigars there will be pipes, and where there was Poole there will be Kino!

QUECKETT: Oh, why didn't I wait and marry a lady?

MISS DYOTT: You *did* marry a lady! But scratch the lady and you find a hardworking comic actress!

QUECKETT: Be silent, madam!

MISS DYOTT: Ha! Ha! This is my revenge, Vere Queckett! To-night I will dance more wildly, more demonstratively than ever!

QUECKETT: I forbid it!

MISS DYOTT: *You* forbid it! *You* dictate to Constance Delaporte – the hit of the opera! I am queen Honorine!

> (*She slaps her hands and sings with great abandonment, and in the pronounced manner of the buffo queen, the song she is supposed to sing in* BERNSTEIN's *opera. Singing*)

'Rine, 'Rine, Honorine!

Mighty, whether wife or queen;

The Rock: an Anglican publication, strongly Evangelical in tone, which appeared between 1868 and 1905.

Poole (for Pool): 'a game played on a billiard table' (*OED*).

Kino (or Keno): 'a game of chance based on the drawing of numbers (c.f. Lotto)' (*OED*).

> Firmer ruler never seen,
> Than 'Rine, 'Rine! *La!*

QUECKETT: (*indignantly*) I will write to my married sisters!

MISS DYOTT: Do – and I will call upon them! (*singing*)

> Man's a boasting, fretting fumer,
> Smoking alcohol consumer,
> Quick of temper, ill of humour!

QUECKETT: Oh, you shall sing this to my family!

MISS DYOTT: I will! (*singing with her hands upon her hips*)

> Woman has no petty vices,
> Cuts her sins in good thick slices,
> With a smile that sweet and nice is!

QUECKETT: (*writhing*) Oh!

MISS DYOTT: (*boisterously*) Refrain! (*singing and dancing*)

> 'Rine, 'Rine, Honorine!
> Mighty, whether wife or queen,
> Firmer ruler never seen,
> Than 'Rine, 'Rine! *La!*
> (*With a burst of hysterical laughter she sinks into a chair.*)

QUECKETT: Oh, I will tell my brother of you!

> (*Daylight appears through the conservatory doors.* MRS RANKLING *and* DINAH *enter.* MALLORY *and* PEGGY *enter from conservatory, 'spooning'.*)

MRS RANKLING: My dear Mrs Queckett, I owe everything to you – my treatment of the dear Admiral has had wonderful results. What do you think! The Admiral and Mr Paulover are quite reconciled and understand each other perfectly (RANKLING *and* PAULOVER *enter, glaring at each other and quarrelling violently in undertones.*) Look – the Admiral already regards him as his own child.

> (SAUNDERS, ERMYNTRUDE *and* GWENDOLINE *enter and join* PEGGY *and* MALLORY.)

DINAH: (*sobbing*) But we are to be separated for five years. Oh, Reggie, you trust me implicitly, don't you?

REGINALD: (*fiercely*) I do. And that is why I warn you never to let me hear of you addressing another man.

DINAH: Oh, Reggie!

> (*They embrace.*)

RANKLING: Don't do that! You don't see me behaving in that way to Mrs Rankling – and we've been married for years

MRS RANKLING: (*to* DINAH) But you and Mr Paulover are to be allowed to meet once every quarter.

REGINALD: Yes – in the presence of Admiral Rankling and a policeman!

> (MRS RANKLING, RANKLING, DINAH *and* REGINALD *join the others.* OTTO BERNSTEIN *enters quickly and excitedly, carrying a quantity of newspapers.*)

BERNSTEIN: I beg your pardon. I must see Miss Constance Delaporte – I mean, Miss Dyott.

MISS DYOTT: Mr Bernstein.

BERNSTEIN: Your house is burnt down. It does not madder. You have made a gread hit in my new oratorio – I mean my Comic Opera. I have been walking up and down Fleet Street waiting for the babers to gome out. (*handing round all the newspapers*) Der 'Dimes' – Der 'Delegraph' – Der 'Daily News' – Der 'Standard' – Der 'Bost' – Der 'Ghronicle'! Dey are all gomplimentary except one, and dat I gave to the gabman.

MISS DYOTT: (*reading*) 'Miss Delaporte – a decided acquisition.'

BERNSTEIN: Go on!

QUECKETT: (*reading*) 'Miss Delaporte – an imposing figure.' (*indignantly*) What do they know about it?

BERNSTEIN: (*excitedly*) Go on! Go on! I always say I do not read the babers, but I *do*! (*to* MISS DYOTT) You will get fifty bounds a week in my next oratorio – I mean, my gomic opera.

QUECKETT: Fifty pounds a week! My Carrie! I shall be able to snap my fingers at my damn family.

MRS RANKLING: How very pleasing! (*reading*) 'A voice of great purity, a correct intonation, and a lower G of decided volume, rendered attractive some music not remarkable for grace or originality.'

(BERNSTEIN *takes the paper from* MRS RANKLING.)

BERNSTEIN: I did not see dat – I will give *dat* to the gabman. Goo-bye – I cannot stay. I am going to have a Turkish bath till the evening babers gome out. I always say I do not read the evening babers – but I *do*!

(*He bustles out.*)

MRS RANKLING: Mrs Queckett, I shall book stalls at once to hear your singing.

RANKLING: No, Emma – dress circle.

MRS RANKLING: Stalls, Archibald.

RANKLING: (*glaring*) Dress circle!

MRS RANKLING: Stalls, Archibald, or I leave you for ever!

RANKLING: (*mildly*) Very well, Emma. I have no desire but to please you.

QUECKETT: I take this as a great compliment, my dear Rankling. Carrie and I thank you. But I can't hear of it. I insist on offering you both a seat in my box.

MISS DYOTT: *Your* box!

QUECKETT: (*softly to her*) Hush! Carrie, my darling! Your Vere's private box!

MISS DYOTT: Mr Queckett's private box, during my absence at night, will be our lodgings, where he will remain under lock and key.

(PEGGY *laughs at* QUECKETT.)

QUECKETT: (*to* PEGGY) Oh, you vexing girl!*

MALLORY: (*annoyed*) Excuse me, my dear Queckett, but while looking at the plants in the conservatory, I became engaged to Miss Hesslerigge.

(*There is a general exclamation of surprise.*)

REGINALD: (*to* MALLORY) Ah, coward, you haven't to wait five years!

(JANE *enters.*)

JANE: Oh, if you please ma'am, Tyler –

---

*For alternative ending from this point, see Appendix A (below, pp. 73–4).

MISS DYOTT, QUECKETT, PEGGY *and* DINAH: Tyler!

JANE: Tyler wants to know who is to pay him the reward for being the first to fetch the fire engines last night?

QUECKETT: I will!

MISS DYOTT: No – I will. Tyler has rendered me a signal service. He has demolished Volumnia College. From the ashes of that establishment rises the Phœnix of my new career. Miss Dyott is extinct – Miss Delaporte is alive, and, during the evening, kicking. I hope none will regret the change – I shall not, for one, while the generous public allow me to remain a Favourite!

THE END

APPENDIX A

Alternative ending for *The Schoolmistress* (from Pinero's manuscript, now in the Fales Library, New York University)
(See above p. 72.)

MISS DYOTT: Mr Queckett's private box, during my absence at night, will be our lodgings, where he will remain under lock and key. (PEGGY *laughs*.)

QUECKETT: Oh, you vexing girl!

MISS DYOTT: As for Miss Hesslerigge – !

PEGGY: (*advancing to* MISS DYOTT, *humbly*) Yes, Miss Dyott?

MISS DYOTT: I have done with her and her mischievous tricks for ever.

PEGGY: (*weeping*) Oh, dear – oh, dear! After the way I slaved at the party!

QUECKETT: (*advancing to* PEGGY) Certainly we have done with you – my roof no longer shelters you.

PEGGY: You haven't got a roof – you've burnt it.

QUECKETT: (*retiring*) Quite so – forgot that.

DINAH: Peggy, you shall come and live here.

RANKLING: No, that she shan't!

MALLORY: (*advancing to* PEGGY) Excuse me, Admiral Rankling, but while looking at the plants in your conservatory I became aware of Miss Hesslerigge's many noble qualities. (*to* PEGGY) Miss Hesslerigge, may I ask you one question?

PEGGY: (*bashfully*) Certainly – if no one is listening.

MALLORY: Have you ever thought of marrying?

PEGGY: Frequently.

MALLORY: Then will you try to think of marrying me?

PEGGY: (*tearfully*) Oh, Mr Mallory, I'm only a poor struggling girl, but I've always been very determined and energetic – and I will try my hardest.

MALLORY: (*embracing her*) Hurrah!
          (*A general exclamation.*)

REGINALD: Ah, coward! You haven't to wait five years!

PEGGY: (*to* MALLORY) I shan't come to you empty-handed – I have a wedding-cake. And, oh, I feel so happy. I've only one misgiving.

MALLORY: What's that?

PEGGY: It's nothing to do with you. (*to the audience*)
          There is a spot, which no one ever mentions,
          Paved, it is said, with excellent intentions.
          If those around me, eager to traduce,
          Declare that Peggy's played the very deuce,
          Yet still I've taught the moral to the letter –
          For my intentions couldn't have been better.

Schoolmates and Playmates! One reward bequeath:
A Flow'r to place on Peggy's bridal wreath –
View facts with charitable eye and say
'Tis all you can expect from mortal clay.
Give me one helping hand ere you depart
And carry Peggy's image in your heart!
       CURTAIN

THE SECOND MRS TANQUERAY

A play in four acts

First produced at the St James's Theatre, London, on 27 May 1893, with the following cast:

AUBREY TANQUERAY	Mr George Alexander
SIR GEORGE ORREYED, BART.	Mr A. Vane Tempest
CAPTAIN HUGH ARDALE	Mr Ben Webster
CAYLEY DRUMMLE	Mr Cyril Maude
FRANK MISQUITH, Q.C., M.P.	Mr Nutcombe Gould
GORDON JAYNE, M.D.	Mr Murray Hathorn
MORSE	Mr Alfred Holles
LADY ORREYED	Miss Edith Chester
MRS CORTELYON	Miss Amy Roselle
PAULA	Mrs Patrick Campbell
ELLEAN	Miss Maude Millett

Servants

The Scene of the First Act is laid at Mr Tanqueray's rooms, No. 2x the Albany, in the month of November; the occurrences of the succeeding Acts take place at his house, 'Highercoombe', near Willowmere, Surrey, during the early part of the following year.

'I'm a good woman! I swear I am!'

II *The Second Mrs Tanqueray*, 1893. Artist's impression by André Sleigh of Act IV: Ellean (Maude Millett), Paula (Mrs Patrick Campbell), Aubrey Tanqueray (George Alexander)

THE FIRST ACT

AUBREY TANQUERAY's *Chambers in the Albany – a richly and tastefully decorated room, elegantly and luxuriously furnished: on the right a large pair of doors opening into another room, on the left at the further end of the room a small door leading to a bedchamber. A circular table is laid for dinner for four persons which has now reached the stage of dessert and coffee. Everything in the apartment suggests wealth and refinement. The fire is burning brightly.*
AUBREY TANQUERAY, MISQUITH *and* JAYNE *are seated at the dinner-table.*
AUBREY *is forty-two, handsome, winning in manner, his speech and bearing retaining some of the qualities of young-manhood.* MISQUITH *is about forty-seven, genial and portly.* JAYNE *is a year or two* MISQUITH's *senior; soft-speaking and precise – in appearance a type of the prosperous town physician.* MORSE, AUBREY's *servant, places the little cabinet of cigars and the spirit-lamp on the table beside* AUBREY, *and goes out.*

MISQUITH: Aubrey, it is a pleasant yet dreadful fact to contemplate, but it's nearly
    fifteen years since I first dined with you. You lodged in Piccadilly in those days,
    over a hat-shop. Jayne, I met you at that dinner, and Cayley Drummle.
JAYNE: Yes, yes. What a pity it is that Cayley isn't here to-night.
AUBREY: Confound the old gossip! His empty chair has been staring us in the face
    all through dinner. I ought to have told Morse to take it away.
MISQUITH: Odd, his sending no excuse.
AUBREY: I'll walk round to his lodgings later on and ask for him.
MISQUITH: I'll go with you.
JAYNE: So will I.
AUBREY: (*opening the cigar-cabinet*) Doctor, it's useless to tempt you, I know.
    Frank –
        (MISQUITH *and* AUBREY *smoke*)
    I particularly wished Cayley Drummle to be one of us to-night. You two fellows
    and Cayley are my closest, my best friends –
MISQUITH: My dear Aubrey!
JAYNE: I rejoice to hear you say so.
AUBREY: And I wanted to see the three of you round this table. You can't guess the
    reason.
MISQUITH: You desired to give us a most excellent dinner.
JAYNE: Obviously.
AUBREY: (*hesitatingly*) Well – I – (*glancing at the clock*) – Cayley won't turn up now.
JAYNE: H'm, hardly.
AUBREY: Then you two shall hear it. Doctor, Frank, this is the last time we are to
    meet in these rooms.
JAYNE: The last time?
MISQUITH: You're going to leave the Albany?
AUBREY: Yes. You've heard me speak of a house I built in the country years ago,
    haven't you?

---

the Albany: see *The Schoolmistress*, Act II (above, p. 43).

MISQUITH: In Surrey.

AUBREY: Well, when my wife died I cleared out of that house and let it. I think of trying the place again.

MISQUITH: But you'll go raving mad if ever you find yourself down there alone.

AUBREY: Ah, but I shan't be alone, and that's what I wanted to tell you. I'm going to be married.

JAYNE: Going to be married?

MISQUITH: Married?

AUBREY: Yes – to-morrow.

JAYNE: To-morrow?

MISQUITH: You take my breath away! My dear fellow, I – I – of course, I congratulate you.

JAYNE: And – and so do I – heartily.

AUBREY: Thanks – thanks.

(*There is a moment or two of embarrassment.*)

MISQUITH: Er – ah – this is an excellent cigar.

JAYNE: Ah – um – your coffee is remarkable.

AUBREY: Look here; I daresay you two old friends think this treatment very strange, very unkind. So I want you to understand me. You know a marriage often cools friendships. What's the usual course of things? A man's engagement is given out, he is congratulated, complimented upon his choice; the church is filled with troops of friends, and he goes away happily to a chorus of good wishes. He comes back, sets up house in town or country, and thinks to resume the old associations, the old companionships. My dear Frank, my dear good doctor, it's very seldom that it can be done. Generally, a worm has begun to eat its way into those hearty, unreserved, prenuptial friendships; a damnable constraint sets in and acts like a wasting disease; and so, believe me, in nine cases out of ten a man's marriage severs for him more close ties than it forms.

MISQUITH: Well, my dear Aubrey, I earnestly hope –

AUBREY: I know what you're going to say, Frank. I hope so, too. In the meantime let's face dangers. I've reminded you of the *usual* course of things, but my marriage isn't even the conventional sort of marriage likely to satisfy society. Now, Cayley's a bachelor, but you two men have wives. By the by, my love to Mrs Misquith and to Mrs Jayne when you get home – don't forget that. Well, your wives may not – like – the lady I'm going to marry.

JAYNE: Aubrey, forgive me for suggesting that the lady you are going to marry may not like our wives – mine at least; I beg your pardon, Frank.

AUBREY: Quite so; then I must go the way my wife goes.

MISQUITH: Come, come, pray don't let us anticipate that either side will be called upon to make such a sacrifice.

AUBREY: Yes, yes, let us anticipate it. And let us make up our minds to have no slow bleeding-to-death of our friendship. We'll end a pleasant chapter here to-night, and after to-night start afresh. When my wife and I settle down at Willowmere it's possible that we shall all come together. But if this isn't to be, for Heaven's sake let us recognise that it is simply because it *can't* be, and not wear hypocritical faces and suffer and be wretched. Doctor, Frank – (*holding out his hands, one to* MISQUITH *the other to* JAYNE) – good luck to all of us!

MISQUITH: But – but – do I understand we are to ask nothing? Not even the lady's name, Aubrey?

AUBREY: The lady, my dear Frank, belongs to the next chapter, and in that her name is Mrs Aubrey Tanqueray.

JAYNE: (*raising his coffee-cup*) Then, in an old-fashioned way, I propose a toast. Aubrey, Frank, I give you 'The Next Chapter!'.

(*They drink the toast saying, 'The Next Chapter!'.*)

AUBREY: Doctor, find a comfortable chair; Frank, you too. As we're going to turn out by and by, let me scribble a couple of notes now while I think of them.

MISQUITH *and* JAYNE: (*together*) Certainly – yes, yes.

AUBREY: It might slip my memory when I get back.

(*AUBREY sits at the writing-table at the other end of the room, and writes.*)

JAYNE: (*to* MISQUITH, *in a whisper*) Frank –

(*MISQUITH quietly leaves his chair and sits nearer to* JAYNE, *above table.*)

What is all this? Simply a morbid crank of Aubrey's with regard to ante-nuptial acquaintances?

MISQUITH: H'm! Did you notice *one* expression he used?

JAYNE: Let me think –

MISQUITH: 'My marriage is not even the conventional sort of marriage likely to satisfy society.'

JAYNE: Bless me, yes! What does that suggest?

MISQUITH: That he has a particular rather than a general reason for anticipating estrangement from his friends, I'm afraid.

JAYNE: A horrible *mésalliance*! A dairymaid who has given him a glass of milk during a day's hunting, or a little anaemic shop-girl! Frank, I'm utterly wretched!

MISQUITH: My dear Jayne, speaking in absolute confidence, I have never been more profoundly depressed in my life.

(*MORSE enters.*)

MORSE: (*announcing*) Mr Drummle.

(*CAYLEY DRUMMLE enters briskly. He is a neat little man of about five-and-forty, in manner bright, airy, debonair, but with an undercurrent of seriousness. MORSE retires.*)

DRUMMLE: I'm in disgrace; nobody realises that more thoroughly than I do. Where's my host?

AUBREY: (*who has risen*) Cayley.

DRUMMLE: (*shaking hands with him*) Don't speak to me till I have tendered my explanation. A harsh word from anybody would unman me.

(*MISQUITH and* JAYNE *shake hands with* DRUMMLE.)

AUBREY: Have you dined?

DRUMMLE: No – unless you call a bit of fish, a cutlet and a pancake dining.

AUBREY: Cayley, this is disgraceful.

JAYNE: Fish, a cutlet, and a pancake will require a great deal of explanation.

MISQUITH: Especially the pancake. My dear friend, your case looks miserably weak.

DRUMMLE: Hear me! hear me!

JAYNE: Now then!

MISQUITH: Come!

AUBREY: Well!

DRUMMLE: It so happens that to-night I was exceptionally *early* in dressing for dinner.

MISQUITH: For which dinner – the fish and cutlet?

DRUMMLE: For *this* dinner, of course – really, Frank! At a quarter to eight, in fact, I found myself trimming my nails, with ten minutes to spare. Just then enter my man with a note – would I hasten, as fast as cab could carry me, to old Lady Orreyed in Bruton Street? – 'sad trouble'. Now, recollect, please, I had ten minutes on my hands, old Lady Orreyed was a very dear friend of my mother's and was in some distress.

AUBREY: Cayley, come to the fish and cutlet!

MISQUITH *and* JAYNE: Yes, yes, and the pancake!

DRUMMLE: Upon my word! Well, the scene in Bruton Street beggars description; the women servants looked scared, the men drunk; and there was poor old Lady Orreyed on the floor of her boudoir like Queen Bess among her pillows.

AUBREY: What's the matter?

DRUMMLE: (*to everybody*) You know George Orreyed?

MISQUITH: Yes.

JAYNE: I've met him.

DRUMMLE: Well, he's a thing of the past.

AUBREY: Not dead!

DRUMMLE: Certainly, in the worst sense. He's married Mabel Hervey.

MISQUITH: What!

DRUMMLE: It's true – this morninng. The poor mother showed me his letter – a dozen curt words, and some of those ill-spelt.

MISQUITH: (*walking up to the fireplace*) I'm very sorry.

JAYNE: Pardon my ignorance – who *was* Mabel Hervey?

DRUMMLE: You don't – ? Oh, of course not. (*He sits.*) Miss Hervey – Lady Orreyed, as she now is – was a lady who would have been, perhaps had been, described in the reports of the Police or the Divorce Court as an actress. Had she belonged to a lower stratum of our advanced civilisation she would, in the event of judicial inquiry, have defined her calling with equal justification as that of a dressmaker. To do her justice, she is a type of a class which is immortal. Physically, by the strange caprice of creation, curiously beautiful; mentally, she lacks even the strength of deliberate viciousness. Paint her portrait, it would symbolise a creature perfectly patrician; lance a vein of her superbly-modelled arm, you would get the poorest *vin ordinaire*! Her affections, emotions, impulses, her very existence – a burlesque! Flaxen, five-and-twenty, and feebly frolicsome; anybody's, in less gentle society I should say everybody's, property! That Doctor, was Miss Hervey who is the new Lady Orreyed. Dost thou like the picture?

MISQUITH: Very good, Cayley! Bravo!

AUBREY: (*laying his hand on* DRUMMLE's *shoulder*) You'd scarcely believe it, Jayne, but none of us really know anything about this lady, our gay young friend here, I suspect, least of all.

DRUMMLE: Aubrey, I applaud your chivalry.

AUBREY: And perhaps you'll let me finish a couple of letters which Frank and Jayne have given me leave to write (*Returning to the writing-table*) Ring for what you want, like a good fellow!

   (AUBREY *resumes his writing.*)

MISQUITH: (*to* DRUMMLE) Still, the fish and cutlet remain unexplained.

DRUMMLE: Oh, the poor old woman was so weak that I insisted upon her taking some food, and felt there was nothing for it but to sit down opposite her. The fool! the blackguard!

MISQUITH: Poor Orreyed! Well, he's gone under for a time.

DRUMMLE: For a time! My dear Frank, I tell you he has absolutely ceased to be.

   (AUBREY, *who has been writing busily, turns his head towards the speakers and listens. His lips are set, and there is a frown upon his face.*)

For all practical purposes you may regard him as the late George Orreyed. To-morrow the very characteristics of his speech, as we remember them, will have become obsolete.

JAYNE: But surely, in the course of years, he and his wife will outlive –

DRUMMLE: No, no, Doctor, don't try to upset one of my settled beliefs. You may dive into many waters, but there is *one* social Dead Sea – !

JAYNE: Perhaps you're right.

DRUMMLE: Right! Good God! I wish you could prove me otherwise! Why, for years I've been sitting, and watching and waiting.*

MISQUITH: You're in form to-night, Cayley. May we ask where you've been in the habit of squandering your useful leisure?

DRUMMLE: Where? On the shore of that same sea.

MISQUITH: And, pray, what have you been waiting for?

DRUMMLE: For some of my best friends to *come up*.

   (AUBREY *utters a half-stifled exclamation of impatience; then he hurriedly gathers up his papers from the writing-table. The three men turn to him.*)

   Eh?

AUBREY: Oh, I – I'll finish my letters in the other room if you'll excuse me for five minutes. Tell Cayley the news.

   (*He goes out.*)

DRUMMLE: (*hurrying to the door and speaking off*) My dear fellow, my jabbering has disturbed you! I'll never talk again as long as I live!

MISQUITH: Close the door, Cayley.

   (DRUMMLE *shuts the door.*)

JAYNE: Cayley –

DRUMMLE: (*advancing to the dinner-table*) A smoke, a smoke, or I perish! (*He selects a cigar from the little cabinet.*)

---

*Pinero's autograph manuscript (MS) and prompt-copy (PP) add:

MISQUITH: Watching – What?

DRUMMLE: (*with an action of the hand*) An awful widening circle – the wheel of the spindle of Lachesis turning upon a bubble.

MISQUITH: You're in form tonight . . .

LACHESIS: with Clotho and Atropos, constituted the three Fates.

JAYNE: Cayley, marriages are in the air.

DRUMMLE: Are they? Discover the bacillus, Doctor, and destroy it.

JAYNE: I mean, among our friends.

DRUMMLE: Oh, Nugent Warrinder's engagement to Lady Alice Tring. I've heard of that. They're not to be married till the spring.

JAYNE: Another marriage that concerns us a little takes place to-morrow.

DRUMMLE: Whose marriage?

JAYNE: Aubrey's.

DRUMMLE: Aub – ! (*looking towards* MISQUITH,) Is it a joke?

MISQUITH: No.

DRUMMLE: (*looking from* MISQUITH *to* JAYNE) To whom?

MISQUITH: He doesn't tell us.

JAYNE: We three were asked here to-night to receive the announcement. Aubrey has some theory that marriage is likely to alienate a man from his friends, and it seems to me he has taken the precaution to wish us good-bye.

MISQUITH: No, no.

JAYNE: Practically, surely?

DRUMMLE: (*thoughtfully*) Marriage in general, does he mean, or *this* marriage

JAYNE: That's the point. Frank says –

MISQUITH: No, no, no; I feared it suggested –

JAYNE: Well, well. (*to* DRUMMLE) What do you think of it?

DRUMMLE: (*after a slight pause*) Is there a light there? (*lighting his cigar*) He – wraps the lady – in mystery – you say?

MISQUITH: Most modestly.

DRUMMLE: Aubrey's – not – a very – young man.

JAYNE: Forty-three.

DRUMMLE: Ah! *L'âge critique*!

MISQUITH: A dangerous age – yes, yes.

DRUMMLE: When you two fellows go home, do you mind leaving me behind here?

MISQUITH: Not at all.

JAYNE: By all means.

DRUMMLE: All right. (*anxiously*) Deuce take it, the man's second marriage mustn't be another mistake! (*With his head bent he walks up to the fireplace.*)

JAYNE: You knew him in his short married life, Cayley. Terribly unsatisfactory, wasn't it?

DRUMMLE: Well – (*looking at the door*) I quite closed that door?

MISQUITH: Yes.

(*He settles himself on the sofa;* JAYNE *is seated in an armchair.*)

DRUMMLE: (*smoking, with his back to the fire*) He married a Miss Herriot; that was in the year eighteen – confound dates – twenty years ago. She was a lovely creature – by Jove, she was; by religion a Roman Catholic. She was one of your cold sort, you know – all marble arms and black velvet. I remember her with painful distinctness as the only woman who ever made me nervous.

MISQUITH: (*softly*) Ha, ha!

DRUMMLE: He loved her – to distraction, as they say. Jupiter, how fervently that poor devil courted her! But I don't believe she allowed him even to squeeze her fingers. She *was* an iceberg! As for kissing, the mere contact would have given him chapped lips. However, he married her and took her away, the latter greatly to my relief.

JAYNE: Abroad, you mean?

DRUMMLE: Eh? Yes. I imagine he gratified her by renting a villa in Lapland, but I don't know. After a while they returned, and then I saw how woefully Aubrey had miscalculated results.

JAYNE: Miscalculated – ?

DRUMMLE: He had reckoned, poor wretch, that in the early days of marriage she would thaw. But she didn't. I used to picture him closing his doors and making up the fire in the hope of seeing her features relax. Bless her, the thaw never set in! I believe she kept a thermometer in her stays and always registered ten degrees below zero. However, in time a child came – a daughter.

JAYNE: Didn't that – ?

DRUMMLE: Not a bit of it; it made matters worse. Frightened at her failure to stir up in him some sympathetic religious belief, she determined upon strong measures with regard to the child. He opposed her for a miserable year or so, but she wore him down, and the insensible little brat was placed in a convent, first in France, then in Ireland. Not long afterwards the mother died strangely enough, of fever, the only warmth, I believe, that ever came to that woman's body.

MISQUITH: Don't, Cayley!

JAYNE: The child is living, we know.

DRUMMLE: Yes, if you choose to call it living. Miss Tanqueray – a young woman of nineteen now – is in the Loretto convent at Armagh. She professes to have found her true vocation in a religious life, and within a month or two will take final vows.

MISQUITH: He ought to have removed his daughter from the convent when the mother died.

DRUMMLE: Yes, yes, but absolutely at the end there was reconciliation between husband and wife, and she won his promise that the child should complete her conventual education. He reaped his reward. When he attempted to gain his girl's confidence and affection he was too late; he found he was dealing with the spirit of the mother. You remember his visit to Ireland last month?

JAYNE: Yes.

DRUMMLE: That was to wish his girl good-bye.

MISQUITH: Poor fellow!

DRUMMLE: He sent for me when he came back. I think he must have had a lingering hope that the girl would relent – would come to life, as it were – at the last moment, for, for an hour or so, in this room, he was terribly shaken. I'm sure he'd clung to that hope from the persistent way in which he kept breaking off in his talk to repeat one dismal word, as if he couldn't realise his position without dinning this damned word into his head.

JAYNE: What word was that?

DRUMMLE: Alone – alone.

(AUBREY *enters*)

AUBREY: (*advancing to the fire*) A thousand apologies!

DRUMMLE: (*gaily*) We are talking about you, my dear Aubrey.

(*During the telling of the story*, MISQUITH *has risen and gone to the*

fire, and DRUMMLE *has thrown himself full length on the sofa.*
AUBREY *now joins* MISQUITH *and* JAYNE.)

AUBREY: Well, Cayley, you are surprised?

DRUMMLE: Surp – I haven't been surprised for twenty years.

AUBREY: And you're not angry with me?

DRUMMLE: Angry! (*rising*) Because you considerately withhold the name of a lady with whom it is now the object of my life to become acquainted? My dear fellow, you pique my curiosity, you give zest to my existence! And as for a wedding, who on earth wants to attend that familiar and probably draughty function? Ugh! My cigar's out.

AUBREY: Let's talk about something else.

MISQUITH: (*looking at his watch* Not to-night, Aubrey.

AUBREY: My dear Frank!

MISQUITH: I go up to Scotland to-morrow, and there are some little matters –

JAYNE: I am off too.

AUBREY: No, no.

JAYNE: I must: I have to give a look to a case in Clifford Street on my way home.

AUBREY: (*going to the door*) Well!

(MISQUITH *and* JAYNE *exchange looks with* DRUMMLE.)

(*Opening the door and calling*) Morse, hats and coats! I shall write to you all next week from Genoa or Florence. Now, Doctor, Frank, remember, my love to Mrs Misquith and to Mrs Jayne!

(MORSE *enters with hats and coats*.)

MISQUITH *and* JAYNE: Yes, yes – yes, yes.

AUBREY: And your young people!

(*As* MISQUITH *and* JAYNE *put on their coats there is the chatter of careless talk*.)

JAYNE: Cayley, I meet you at dinner on Sunday.

DRUMMLE: At the Stratfields'. That's very pleasant.

MISQUITH: (*putting on his coat with* AUBREY'S *aid*) Ah–h!

AUBREY: What's wrong?

MISQUITH: A twinge. Why didn't I go to Aix in August?

JAYNE: (*shaking hands with* DRUMMLE) Good night, Cayley.

DRUMMLE: Good night, my dear Doctor!

MISQUITH: (*shaking hands with* DRUMMLE). Cayley, are you in town for long?

DRUMMLE: Dear friend, I'm nowhere for long. Good night.

MISQUITH: Good night.

(AUBREY, JAYNE *and* MISQUITH *go out, followed by* MORSE; *the hum of talk is continued outside*.)

AUBREY: A cigar, Frank?

MISQUITH: No, thank you.

AUBREY: Going to walk, Doctor?

JAYNE: If Frank will.

MISQUITH: By all means.

AUBREY: It's a cold night.

(*The door is closed*. DRUMMLE *remains standing with his coat on his arm and his hat in his hand*.)

DRUMMLE: (*to himself, thoughtfully*) Now then! What the devil – !
   (AUBREY *returns.*)
AUBREY: (*eyeing* DRUMMLE *a little awkwardly*) Well, Cayley?
DRUMMLE: Well, Aubrey?
   (AUBREY *walks up to the fire and stands looking into it.*)
AUBREY: You're not going, old chap?
   (DRUMMLE *deliberately puts his hat and coat on the sofa and*
   sits.)
DRUMMLE: No.
AUBREY: (*after a slight pause, with a forced laugh*) Hah! Cayley, I never thought I
  should feel – shy – with you.
DRUMMLE: Why do you?
AUBREY: Never mind.
DRUMMLE: Now, I can quite understand a man wishing to be married in the dark, as
  it were.
AUBREY: You can?
DRUMMLE: In your place I should very likely adopt the same course.
AUBREY: You think so?
DRUMMLE: And if I intended marrying a lady not prominently in Society, as I
  presume you do – as I presume you do –
AUBREY: Well?
DRUMMLE: As I presume you do, I'm not sure that *I* should tender her for
  preliminary dissection at afternoon tea-tables.
AUBREY: No?
DRUMMLE: In fact, there is probably only one person – were I in your position
  to-night – with whom I should care to chat the matter over.
AUBREY: Who's that?
DRUMMLE: Yourself, of course. (*Going to* AUBREY *and standing beside him*) Of
  course, yourself, old friend.
AUBREY: (*after a pause*) I must seem a brute to you, Cayley. But there are some acts
  which are hard to explain, hard to defend –
DRUMMLE: To defend – ?
AUBREY: Some acts which one must trust to time to put right.
   (DRUMMLE *watches him for a moment, then takes up his hat and*
   coat.)
DRUMMLE: Well, I'll be moving.
AUBREY: Cayley! Confound you and your old friendship! Do you think I forget it?
  Put your coat down! Why did you stay behind here? Cayley, the lady I am going
  to marry is the lady – who is known as – Mrs Jarman.
   (*There is a pause.*)
DRUMMLE: (*in a low voice*) Mrs Jarman! are you serious?
   (*He walks up to the fireplace, where he leans upon the mantelpiece,*
   uttering something like a groan.)
AUBREY: As you've got this out of me I give you leave to say all you care to say.
  Come, we'll be plain with each other. You know Mrs Jarman?
DRUMMLE: I first met her at – what does it matter?
AUBREY: Yes, yes, everything! Come!

DRUMMLE: I met her at Homburg, two – three seasons ago.

AUBREY: *Not* as Mrs Jarman?

DRUMMLE: No.

AUBREY: She was then – ?

DRUMMLE: Mrs Dartry.

AUBREY: Yes. She has also seen you in London, she says.

DRUMMLE: Certainly.

AUBREY: In Aldford Street. Go on.

DRUMMLE: Please!

AUBREY: I insist.

DRUMMLE: (*with a slight shrug of the shoulders*) Some time last year I was asked by a man to sup at his house, one night after the theatre.

AUBREY: Mr Selwyn Ethurst – a bachelor.

DRUMMLE: Yes.

AUBREY: You were surprised therefore to find Mr Ethurst aided in his cursed hospitality by a lady.

DRUMMLE: I was unprepared.

AUBREY: The lady you had known as Mrs Dartry?

> (DRUMMLE *inclines his head slightly.*)

There is something of a yachting cruise in the Mediterranean too, is there not?

DRUMMLE: I joined Peter Jarman's yacht at Marseilles, in the spring a month before he died.

AUBREY: Mrs Jarman was on board?

DRUMMLE: She was a kind hostess.

AUBREY: And an old acquaintance?

DRUMMLE: Yes.

AUBREY: You have told your story.

DRUMMLE: With your assistance.

AUBREY: I have put you to the pain of telling it to show you that this is not the case of a blind man entrapped by an artful woman. Let me add that Mrs Jarman has no legal right to that name, she is simply Miss Ray – Miss Paula Ray.

DRUMMLE: (*after a pause*) I should like to express my regret, Aubrey, for the way in which I spoke of George Orreyed's marriage.

AUBREY: You mean you compare Lady Orreyed with Miss Ray?

> (DRUMMLE *is silent.*)

(*Coming down towards* DRUMMLE *hotly*) Oh, of course! To you, Cayley, all women who have been roughly treated, and who dare to survive by borrowing a little of our philosophy, are alike. You see in the crowd of the Ill-used only one pattern; you can't detect the shades of goodness, intelligence, even nobility there. Well, well, how should you? The crowd is dimly lighted! And, besides, yours is the way of the world.

DRUMMLE: My dear Aubrey, I *live* in the world.

AUBREY: The name we give our little parish of St James's.

Homburg: German spa popular with members of English society.

St James's: St James's Church, Piccadilly; also the fashionable district surrounding St James's Square which included the St James's Theatre in King Street at which this play was first performed.

DRUMMLE: (*laying a hand on* AUBREY'*s shoulder*) And you are quite prepared, my friend, to forfeit the esteem of your little parish?

AUBREY: I avoid mortification by shifting from one parish to another. I give up Pall Mall for the Surrey hills; leave off varnishing my boots and double the thickness of the soles.

DRUMMLE: And your skin – do you double the thickness of that also?

AUBREY: I know you think me a fool, Cayley – you needn't infer that I'm a coward into the bargain. No! I know what I'm doing, and I do it deliberately, defiantly. I'm alone; I injure no living soul by the step I'm going to take; and so you can't urge the one argument which might restrain me. Of course, I don't expect you to think compassionately, fairly even, of the woman whom I – whom I am drawn to –

DRUMMLE: My dear Aubrey, I assure you I consider Mrs – Miss Jarman – Mrs Ray – Miss Ray – delightful. But I confess there is a form of chivalry which I gravely distrust, especially in a man of – our age.

AUBREY: Thanks. I've heard you say that from forty till fifty a man is at heart either a stoic or a satyr.

DRUMMLE: (*protestingly*) Ah! now –

AUBREY: I am neither. I have a temperate, honourable affection for Mrs Jarman. She has never met a man who has treated her well – I intend to treat her well. That's all. And in a few years, Cayley, if you've not quite forsaken me, I'll prove to you that it's possible to rear a life of happiness, of good repute, on a – miserable foundation.

DRUMMLE: (*offering his hand*) Do prove it!

AUBREY: (*taking his hand*) We have spoken too freely of – of Mrs Jarman. I was excited – angry. Please forget it!

DRUMMLE: My dear Aubrey, when we next meet I shall remember nothing but my respect for the lady who bears your name.

(MORSE *enters, closing the door behind him carefully.*)

AUBREY: What is it?

MORSE: (*hesitatingly*) May I speak to you, sir? (*in an undertone*) Mrs Jarman, sir.

AUBREY: (*softly to* MORSE) Mrs Jarman! Do you mean she is at the lodge in her carriage?

MORSE: No, sir – here. (AUBREY *looks towards* DRUMMLE, *perplexed.*) There's a nice fire in your – in that room, sir. (*glancing in the direction of the door leading to the bedroom*)

AUBREY: (*between his teeth, angrily*) Very well.

(MORSE *retires.*)

DRUMMLE: (*looking at his watch*) A quarter to eleven – horrible! (*Crossing to sofa and taking up his hat and coat*) Must get to bed – up late every night this week. (AUBREY *assists* DRUMMLE *with his coat.*) Thank you. Well, good night, Aubrey. I feel I've been dooced serious, quite out of keeping with myself; pray overlook it.

AUBREY: (*kindly*) Ah, Cayley!

DRUMMLE: (*putting on a neck-handkerchief*) And remember that, after all, I'm merely a spectator in life; nothing more than a man at play, in fact; only, like the old-fashioned playgoer, I love to see certain characters happy and comfortable at the finish. You understand?

AUBREY: I think I do.

DRUMMLE: Then, for as long as you can, old friend, will you – keep a stall for me?

AUBREY: Yes, Cayley.

DRUMMLE: (*gaily*) Ah, ha! Good night! (*bustling to the door*) Don't bother! I'll let myself out! Good night! God bless yer!

> (*He goes out; AUBREY follows him. MORSE enters by the other door, carrying some unopened letters which after a little consideration he places on the mantelpiece against the clock. AUBREY returns.*)

AUBREY: Yes?

MORSE: You hadn't seen your letters that came by the nine o'clock post, sir; I've put 'em where they'll catch your eye by and by.

AUBREY: Thank you.

MORSE: (*hesitatingly*) Gunter's cook and waiter have gone, sir. Would you prefer me to go to bed?

AUBREY: (*frowning*) Certainly not.

MORSE: Very well, sir.

> (*He goes out.*)

AUBREY: (*opening the upper door*) Paula! Paula!

> (*PAULA enters and throws her arms round his neck. She is a young woman of about twenty-seven: beautiful, fresh, innocent-looking. She is in superb evening dress.*)

PAULA: Dearest!

AUBREY: Why have you come here?

PAULA: Angry?

AUBREY: Yes – no. But it's eleven o'clock.

PAULA: (*laughing*) I know.

AUBREY: What on earth will Morse think?

PAULA: Do you trouble yourself about what servants *think*?

AUBREY: Of course.

PAULA: Goose! They're only machines made to wait upon people – and to give evidence in the Divorce Court. (*looking round*) Oh, indeed! A snug little dinner!

AUBREY: Three men.

PAULA: (*suspiciously*) Men?

AUBREY: (*decisively*) Men.

PAULA: (*penitently*) Ah! (*sitting at the table*) I'm so hungry.

AUBREY: Let me get you some game pie, or some –

PAULA: No, no, hungry for this. What beautiful fruit! I love fruit when it's expensive.

> (*He clears a space on the table, places a plate before her, and helps her to fruit.*)

I haven't dined, Aubrey dear.

AUBREY: My poor girl! Why?

Gunter's: see *The Schoolmistress*, Act II (above, p. 48).

PAULA: In the first place, I forgot to order any dinner, and my cook, who has always loathed me, thought he'd pay me out before he departed.

AUBREY: The beast!

PAULA: That's precisely what I –

AUBREY: No, Paula!

PAULA: What I told my maid to call him. What next will you think of me?

AUBREY: Forgive me. You must be starved.

PAULA: (*eating fruit*) *I* didn't care. As there was nothing to eat, I sat in my best frock with my toes on the dining-room fender, and dreamt, oh, such a lovely dinner-party.

AUBREY: Dear lonely little woman!

PAULA: It was perfect. I saw you at the end of a very long table, opposite me, and we exchanged sly glances now and again over the flowers. We were host and hostess, Aubrey, and had been married about five years.

AUBREY: (*kissing her hand*) Five years.

PAULA: And on each side of us was the nicest set imaginable – you know, dearest, the sort of men and women that can't be imitated.

AUBREY: Yes, yes. Eat some more fruit.

PAULA: But I haven't told you the best part of my dream.

AUBREY: Tell me.

PAULA: Well, although we had been married only such a few years, I seemed to know by the look on their faces that none of our guests had ever heard anything – anything – anything peculiar about the fascinating hostess.

AUBREY: That's just how it will be, Paula. The world moves so quickly. That's just how it will be.

PAULA: (*with a little grimace*) I wonder! (*glancing at the fire*) Ugh! do throw another log on.

AUBREY: (*mending the fire*) There. But you mustn't be here long.

PAULA: Hospitable wretch! I've something important to tell you. No, stay where you are. (*turning from him, her face averted*) Look here, that was my dream, Aubrey; but the fire went out while I was dozing, and I woke up with a regular fit of the shivers. And the result of it all was that I ran upstairs and scribbled you a letter.

AUBREY: Dear baby!

PAULA: Remain where you are. (*taking a letter from her pocket*) This is it. I've given you an account of myself, furnished you with a list of my adventures since I – you know. (*weighing the letter in her hand*) I wonder if it would go for a penny. Most of it you're acquainted with; *I've* told you a good deal, haven't I?

AUBREY: Oh, Paula!

PAULA: What I haven't told you I daresay you've heard from others. But in case they've omitted anything – the dears – it's all here.

AUBREY: Why in Heaven's name must you talk like this to-night?

PAULA: It may save discussion by and by, don't you think? (*holding out the letter*) There you are.

AUBREY: No, dear, no. (*He takes the letter.*)

PAULA: Take it. Read it through after I've gone, and then – read it again, and turn the matter over in your mind finally. And if, even at the very last moment, you feel you – oughtn't to go to church with me, send a messenger to Pont Street, any time before eleven to-morrow, telling me that you're afraid, and I – I'll take the blow.

AUBREY: Why, what – what do you think I am?

PAULA: That's it. It's because I know you're such a dear good fellow that I want to save you the chance of ever feeling sorry you married me. I really love you so much, Aubrey, that to save you that I'd rather you treated me as – as the others have done.

AUBREY: (*turning from her with a cry*) Oh!

PAULA: (*after a slight pause*). I suppose I've shocked you. I can't help it if I have.
(*She sits, with assumed languor and indifference. He turns to her, advances and kneels by her.*)

AUBREY: My dearest, you don't understrand me. I – I can't bear to hear you always talking about – what's done with. I tell you I'll never remember it; Paula, can't you dismiss it? Try. Darling, if we promise each other to forget, to forget, we're bound to be happy. After all, it's a mechanical matter; the moment a wretched thought enters your head, you quickly think of something bright – it depends on one's will. (*referring to the letter he holds in his hand*) Shall I burn this, dear? Let me, let me!

PAULA: (*with a shrug of the shoulders*) I don't suppose there's much that's new to you in it – just as you like.
(*He goes to the fire and burns the letter.*)

AUBREY: There's an end of it. (*returning to her*) What's the matter?

PAULA: (*rising, coldly*) Oh, nothing! I'll go and put my cloak on.

AUBREY: (*detaining her*). What *is* the matter?

PAULA: Well, I think you might have said, 'You're very generous, Paula', or at least, 'Thank you, dear', when I offered to set you free.

AUBREY: (*catching her in his arms*) Ah!

PAULA: Ah! ah! Ha, Ha! It's all very well, but you don't know what it cost me to make such an offer. I do so want to be married.

AUBREY: But you never imagined – ?

PAULA: Perhaps not. And yet I *did* think of what I'd do at the end of our acquaintance if you preferred to behave like the rest. (*taking a flower from her bodice*)

AUBREY: Hush!

PAULA: Oh, I forgot!

AUBREY: What would you have done when we parted?

PAULA: Why, killed myself.

AUBREY: Paula, dear!

PAULA: It's true. (*putting the flower in his buttonhole*) Do you know I feel certain I should make away with myself if anything serious happened to me.

AUBREY: Anything serious! What, has nothing ever been serious to you, Paula?

PAULA: Not lately; not since a long while ago. I made up my mind then to have done with taking things seriously. If I hadn't, I – However, we won't talk about that.

AUBREY: But now, now, life will be different to you, won't it – quite different? Eh, dear?

PAULA: Oh yes, now. Only, Aubrey, mind you keep me always happy.

AUBREY: I will try to.

PAULA: I know I couldn't swallow a second big dose of misery. I know that if ever I felt wretched again – truly wretched – I should take a leaf out of Connie Tirlemont's book. You remember? They found her – (*with a look of horror*)

AUBREY: For God's sake, don't let your thoughts run on such things!

PAULA: (*laughingly*) Ha, ha, how scared you look! There, think of the time! Dearest, what will my coachman say! My cloak!

> (*She runs off, gaily, by the upper door.* AUBREY *looks after her for a moment, then he walks up to the fire and stands warming his feet at the bars. As he does so he raises his head and observes the letters upon the mantelpiece. He takes one down quickly.*)

AUBREY: Ah! Ellean! (*Opening the letter and reading.*) 'My dear father, – A great change has come over me. I believe my mother in Heaven has spoken to me, and counselled me to turn to you in your loneliness. At any rate, your words have reached my heart, and I no longer feel fitted for this solemn life. I am ready to take my place by you. Dear father, will you receive me? – ELLEAN.'

> (PAULA *re-enters, dressed in a handsome cloak. He stares at her as if he hardly realised her presence.*)

PAULA: What are you staring at? Don't you admire my cloak?

AUBREY: Yes.

PAULA: Couldn't you wait till I'd gone before reading your letters?

AUBREY: (*putting the letter away*) I beg your pardon.

PAULA: Take me downstairs to the carriage. (*slipping her arm through his*) How I tease you! To-morrow! I'm so happy!

> (*They go out.*)
> END OF THE FIRST ACT

THE SECOND ACT

A morning room in AUBREY TANQUERAY's *house, 'Highercoombe', near Willowmere, Surrey – a bright and prettily furnished apartment of irregular shape, with double doors opening into a small hall at the back, another door on the left, and a large recessed window through which is obtained a view of extensive grounds. Everything about the room is charming and graceful. The fire is burning in the grate, and a small table is tastefully laid for breakfast. It is a morning in early Spring, and the sun is streaming through the window.*

AUBREY *and* PAULA *are seated at breakfast, and* AUBREY *is silently reading his letters. Two servants, a man and a woman, hand dishes and then retire. After a while* AUBREY *puts his letters aside and looks across to the window.*

AUBREY: Sunshine! Spring!

PAULA: (*glancing at the clock*) Exactly six minutes.

AUBREY: Six minutes?

PAULA: Six minutes, Aubrey dear, since you made your last remark.

AUBREY: I beg your pardon; I was reading my letters. Have you seen Ellean this morning?

PAULA: (*coldly*) Your last observation but one was about Ellean.

AUBREY: Dearest, what *shall* I talk about?

PAULA: Ellean breakfasted two hours ago, Morgan tells me, and then went out
    walking with her dog.
AUBREY: She wraps up warmly, I hope; this sunshine is deceptive.
PAULA: I ran about the lawn last night, after dinner, in satin shoes. Were you
    anxious about me?
AUBREY: Certainly.
PAULA: (*melting*) Really?
AUBREY: You make me wretchedly anxious; you delight in doing incautious things.
    You are incurable.
PAULA: Ah, what a beast I am! (*going to him and kissing him, then glancing at the
    letters by his side*) A letter from Cayley?
AUBREY: He is staying very near here, with Mrs – Very near here.
PAULA: With the lady whose chimneys we have the honour of contemplating from
    our windows?
AUBREY: With Mrs Cortelyon – yes.
PAULA: Mrs Cortelyon! The woman who might have set the example of calling on
    me when we first threw out roots in this deadly–lively soil! Deuce take Mrs
    Cortelyon!
AUBREY: Hush! my dear girl!
PAULA: (*returning to her seat*) Oh, I know she's an old acquaintance of yours – and of
    the first Mrs Tanqueray. And she joins the rest of 'em in slapping the second
    Mrs Tanqueray in the face. However, I have my revenge – she's six-and-forty,
    and I wish nothing worse to happen to any woman.
AUBREY: Well, she's going to town, Cayley says here, and his visit's at an end. He's
    coming over this morning to call on you. Shall we ask him to transfer himself to
    us? Do say yes.
PAULA: Yes.
AUBREY: (*gladly*) Ah, ha! old Cayley!
PAULA: (*coldly*) He'll amuse *you*.
AUBREY: And you too.
PAULA: Because *you* find a companion, shall I be boisterously hilarious?*
AUBREY: Come, come! He talks London, and you know you like that.
PAULA: London! London or Heaven! which is farther from me!
AUBREY: Paula!
PAULA: Oh! Oh, I am so bored, Aubrey!
AUBREY: (*gathering up his letters, looking at her puzzled and going to her, leaning
    over her shoulder*) Baby, what can I do for you?
PAULA: I suppose, nothing. You have done all you can for me.
AUBREY: What do you mean?
PAULA: You have married me.
        (*He walks away from her thoughtfully, to the writing-table. As he places*

---

*MS adds:
AUBREY: You'll meet him at dinner.
PAULA: Yes, he can try his luck at getting a smile out of Ellean at dinner.
AUBREY: Come, come ...

*his letters on the table he sees an addressed letter, stamped for the post,
lying on the blotting-book; he picks it up.*)

AUBREY: (*in an altered tone*) You've been writing this morning before breakfast?

PAULA: (*looking at him quickly, then away again*) Er – that letter.

AUBREY: (*coming towards her with the letter in his hand*) To Lady Orreyed. Why?

PAULA: Why not? Mabel's an old friend of mine.

AUBREY: Are you – corresponding?

PAULA: I heard from her yesterday. They've just returned from the Riviera. She
seems happy.

AUBREY: (*sarcastically*) That's good news.

PAULA: Why are you always so cutting about Mabel? She's a good kind-hearted girl.
Everything's altered; she even thinks of letting her hair go back to brown. She's
Lady Orreyed. She's married to George. What's the matter with her?

AUBREY: (*turning away*) Oh!

PAULA: You drive me mad sometimes with the tone you take about things! Great
goodness, if you come to that, George Orreyed's wife isn't a bit worse than
yours! (*He faces her suddenly*) I suppose I needn't have made that observation.

AUBREY: No, there was scarcely a necessity.

(*He throws the letter on the table, and takes up the newspaper.*)

PAULA: I am sorry.

AUBREY: All right, dear.

PAULA: (*trifling with the letter*) I – I'd better tell you what I've written. I meant to do
so, of course. I – I've asked the Orreyeds to come and stay with us. (*He looks at
her and lets the paper fall to the ground in a helpless way*.) George was a great
friend of Cayley's. (*with rising anger*) I'm sure *he* would be delighted to meet
them here.

AUBREY: (*laughing mirthlessly*) Ha, ha, ha! They say Orreyed has taken to tippling
at dinner. Heavens above!

PAULA: Oh! I've no patience with you! You'll kill me with this life! (*She selects some
flowers from the vase on the table, cuts and arranges them, and fastens them in her
bodice*.) What is my existence Sunday to Saturday? In the morning, a drive
down to the village with the groom, to give my orders to the tradespeople. At
lunch, you and Ellean. In the afternoon, a novel, the newspapers; if fine,
another drive – *if* fine! Tea – you and Ellean. Then two hours of dusk; then
dinner – you and Ellean. Then a game of Bésique, you and I, while Ellean reads
a religious book in a dull corner. Then a yawn from me, another from you, a sigh
from Ellean; three figures suddenly rise – 'Good night, good night, good night!'
(*imitating a kiss*) 'God bless you!' *Ah!*

AUBREY: Yes, yes, Paula – yes, dearest – that's what it is *now*. But, by and by, if
people begin to come round us –

PAULA: Hah! That's where we've made the mistake, my friend Aubrey! (*pointing to
the window*) Do you believe these people will *ever* come round us? Your former
crony, Mrs Cortelyon? Or the grim old vicar, or that wife of his whose huge nose
is positively indecent? Or the Ullathornes, or the Gollans, or Lady William

---

Bésique: 'a game of cards in which the name "Bézique" is applied to the occurrence in one hand
of the knave of diamonds and queen of spades' (*OED*).

Petres? I know better! And when the young ones gradually take the place of the old, there will still remain the sacred tradition that the dreadful person who lives at the top of the hill is never, under any circumstances, to be called upon! And so we shall go on here, year in and year out, until the sap is run out of our lives, and we're stale and dry and withered from sheer, solitary respectability. Upon my word, I wonder we didn't see that we should have been happier if we'd gone in for the devil-may-care, *café*-living sort of life in town! After all, *I* have a set and you might have joined it. It's true I did want dearly, dearly, to be a married woman, but where's the pride in being a married woman among married women who are – married! If – (*seeing that* AUBREY's *head has sunk into his hands*) Aubrey! My dear boy! You're not – crying?

> (*He looks up, with a flushed face.* ELLEAN *enters, dressed very simply for walking. She is a low-voiced grave girl of about nineteen, with a face somewhat resembling a Madonna. Towards* PAULA *her manner is cold and distant.*)

AUBREY: (*in an undertone*) Ellean!

ELLEAN: Good morning, Papa. Good morning, Paula.

> (PAULA *puts her arms round* ELLEAN *and kisses her.* ELLEAN *makes little response.*)

PAULA: Good morning. (*brightly*) We've been breakfasting this side of the house, to get the sun.

> (*She sits at the piano and rattles at a gay melody. Seeing that* PAULA's *back is turned to them,* ELLEAN *goes to* AUBREY *and kisses him; he returns the kiss almost furtively. As they separate, the servants re-enter and proceed to carry out the breakfast-table.*)

AUBREY: (*to* ELLEAN) I guess where you've been: there's some gorse clinging to your frock.

ELLEAN: (*removing a sprig of gorse from her skirt*) Rover and I walked nearly as far as Black Moor.* The poor fellow has a thorn in his pad; I am going upstairs for my tweezers.

AUBREY: Ellean! (*She returns to him.*) Paula is a little depressed – out of sorts. She complains that she has no companion.

ELLEAN: I am with Paula nearly all the day, Papa.

AUBREY: Ah, but you're such a little mouse. Paula likes cheerful people about her.

ELLEAN: I'm afraid I am naturally rather silent; and it's so difficult to seem to be what one is not.

AUBREY: I don't wish that, Ellean.

ELLEAN: I will offer to go down to the village with Paula this morning – shall I?

AUBREY: (*touching her hand gently*) Thank you – do.

ELLEAN: When I've looked after Rover, I'll come back to her.

> (*She goes out;* PAULA *ceases playing, and turns on the music-stool looking at* AUBREY.)

PAULA: Well, have you and Ellean had your little confidence?

AUBREY: Confidence?

---

*MS adds: We shall never be as fine at walking as you, Papa.

PAULA: Do you think I couldn't feel it, like a pain between my shoulders?

AUBREY: Ellean is coming back in a few minutes to be with you.* (*bending over her*) Paula, Paula dear, is this how you keep your promise?

PAULA: (*rising impatiently and crossing swiftly to the settee where she sits, moving restlessly*) I *can't* keep my promise; I *am* jealous; it won't be smothered. I see you looking at her, watching her; your voice drops when you speak to her. I know how fond you are of that girl, Aubrey.

AUBREY: What would you have? I've no other home for her. She is my daughter.

PAULA: She is your saint. Saint Ellean!

AUBREY: You have often told me how good and sweet you think her.

PAULA: Good! – yes. Do you imagine *that* makes me less jealous?† (*going to him and clinging to his arm*) Aubrey, there are two sorts of affection – the love for a woman you respect, and the love for a woman you – love. She gets the first from you: I never can.

AUBREY: Hush, hush! you don't realise what you say.

PAULA: If Ellean cared for me only a little, it would be different. I shouldn't be jealous then. Why doesn't she care for me?

AUBREY: She – she – she will, in time.

PAULA: You can't say that without stuttering.

AUBREY: Her disposition seems a little unresponsive; she resembles her mother in many ways; I can see it every day.

PAULA: She's marble. It's a shame. There's not the slightest excuse; for all she knows, I'm as much a saint as she – only married. Dearest, help me to win her over!

AUBREY: Help you?

PAULA: You can. Teach her that it is her duty to love me; she hangs on to every word you speak. I'm sure, Aubrey, that the love of a nice woman who believed me to be like herself would do me a world of good. You'd get the benefit of it as well as I. It would soothe me; it would make me less horribly restless; it would take this – this – mischievous feeling from me. (*coaxingly*) Aubrey!

AUBREY: Have patience; everything will come right.

PAULA: Yes, if you help me.

AUBREY: In the meantime you will tear up your letter to Lady Orreyed, won't you?

PAULA: (*kissing his hand*) Of course I will – anything!

AUBREY: Ah, thank you, dearest! (*laughing*) Just imagine 'Saint Ellean' and that woman side by side!

PAULA: (*looking back with a cry*) Ah!

AUBREY: What?

PAULA: (*passionately*) It's Ellean you're considering, not me! It's all Ellean with you! Ellean! Ellean!

(ELLEAN *re-enters*.)

ELLEAN: Did you call me, Paula? (*Clenching his hands,* AUBREY *turns away and goes out*.) Is Papa angry?

---

*MS adds: For heaven's sake, Paula, try to get rid of this jealousy.

†MS adds: AUBREY: Do be considerate. My heart holds you both – first my wife, then my child. PAULA: (*going to him . . .*

PAULA: (*shrugging her shoulders*) I drive him distracted sometimes. There, I confess it!

ELLEAN: (*advancing*) Do you? Oh, why do you?

PAULA: Because I – because I'm jealous.

ELLEAN: Jealous?

PAULA: Yes – of you. (ELLEAN *is silent.*) Well, what do you think of that?

ELLEAN: I knew it; I've seen it. It hurts me dreadfully. What do you wish me to do? Go away?

PAULA: Leave us! (*beckoning her with a motion of the head*) Look here! (ELLEAN *goes to* PAULA *slowly and unresponsively.*) You could cure me of my jealousy very easily. Why don't you – like me?

ELLEAN: What do you mean by – like you? I don't understand.

PAULA: Love me.

ELLEAN: Love is not a feeling that is under one's control. I shall alter as times goes on, perhaps. I didn't begin to love my father deeply till a few months ago, and then I obeyed my mother.

PAULA: (*dryly*) Ah, yes you dream things, don't you – see them in your sleep? You fancy your mother speaks to you?

ELLEAN: When you have lost your mother it is a comfort to believe that she is dead only to this life, that she still watches over her child. I do believe that of my mother.

PAULA: (*slowly*) Well, and so you haven't been bidden to love *me*?

ELLEAN: (*after a pause, almost inaudibly*) No.

PAULA: Dreams are only a hash-up of one's day-thoughts, I suppose you know. Think intently of anything, and it's bound to come back to you at night. I don't cultivate dreams myself.

ELLEAN: Ah, I knew you would only sneer!

PAULA: I'm not sneering; I'm speaking the truth. I say that if you cared for me in the daytime I should soon make friends with those nightmares of yours. Ellean, why don't you try to look on me as your second mother? Of course there are not many years between us, but I'm ever so much older than you – in experience. I shall have no children of my own, I know that; it would be a real comfort to me if you would make me feel we belonged to each other. Won't you? Perhaps you think I'm odd – not nice. Well, the fact is I've two sides to my nature, and I've let the one almost smother the other. A few years ago I went through some trouble, and since then I haven't shed a tear. I believe if you put your arms round me just once I should run upstairs and have a good cry. There, I've talked to you as I've never talked to a woman in my life. Ellean, you seem to fear me. Don't! Kiss me!

> (*With a cry, almost of despair,* ELLEAN *turns from* PAULA, *and sinks on to the settee, covering her face with her hands.*)

(*indignantly*) Oh! Why is it? How dare you treat me like this? What do you mean by it? What do you mean?

> (*A* SERVANT *enters.*)

SERVANT: Mr Drummle, ma'am.

> (CAYLEY DRUMMLE, *in riding dress, enters briskly. The* SERVANT *retires.*)

PAULA: (*recovering herself*) Well, Cayley!

DRUMMLE: (*shaking hands with her cordially*) How are you? (*shaking hands with* ELLEAN, *who rises*) I saw you in the distance an hour ago, in the gorse near Stapleton's.

ELLEAN: I didn't see you, Mr Drummle.

DRUMMLE: My dear Ellean, it is my experience that no charming young lady of nineteen ever does see a man of forty-five. (*laughing*) Ha, ha!

ELLEAN: (*going to the door*). Paula, Papa wishes me to drive down to the village with you this morning. Do you care to take me?

PAULA: (*coldly*) Oh, by all means. Pray tell Watts to balance the cart for three.
> (ELLEAN *goes out.*)

DRUMMLE: How's Aubrey?

PAULA: Very well – when Ellean's about the house.

DRUMMLE: And you? I needn't ask.

PAULA: (*walking away to the window*) Oh, a dog's life, my dear Cayley, mine.

DRUMMLE: Eh?

PAULA: Doesn't that define a happy marriage? I'm sleek, well-kept, well-fed, never without a bone to gnaw and fresh straw to lie upon. (*gazing out of the window*) Oh, dear me!

DRUMMLE: H'm. Well, I heartily congratulate you on your kennel. The view from the terrace here is superb.

PAULA: Yes, I can see London.

DRUMMLE: London! Not quite so far, surely?

PAULA: I can. Also the Mediterranean, on a fine day. I wonder what Algiers looks like this morning from the sea! (*impulsively.*) Oh, Cayley, do you remember those jolly times on board Peter Jarman's yacht when we lay off – ? (*stopping suddenly, seeing* DRUMMLE *staring at her*) Good gracious! What are we talking about!
> (AUBREY *enters.*)

AUBREY: (*to* DRUMMLE) Dear old chap! Has Paula asked you?

PAULA: Not yet.

AUBREY: We want you to come to us, now that you're leaving Mrs Cortelyon – at once, to-day. Stay a month, as long as you please – eh, Paula?

PAULA: As long as you can possibly endure it – do, Cayley.

DRUMMLE: (*looking at* AUBREY) Delighted. (*to* PAULA) Charming of you to have me.

PAULA: My dear man, you're a blessing. I must telegraph to London for more fish! A strange appetite to cater for! Something to do, to do, to do!
> (*She goes out in a mood of almost childish delight.*)

DRUMMLE: (*eyeing* AUBREY) Well?

AUBREY: (*with a wearied, anxious look*) Well, Cayley?

DRUMMLE: How are you getting on?

AUBREY: My position doesn't grow less difficult. I told you, when I met you last week, of this feverish, jealous attachment of Paula's for Ellean?

---

the cart, i.e. dog-cart, a two-wheeled horse-drawn vehicle with cross-seats back to back.

DRUMMLE: Yes. I hardly know why, but I came to the conclusion that you don't consider it an altogether fortunate attachment.

AUBREY: Ellean doesn't respond to it.

DRUMMLE: These are early days. Ellean will warm towards your wife by and by.

AUBREY: Ah, but there's the question, Cayley!

DRUMMLE: What question?

AUBREY: The question which positively distracts me. Ellean is so different from – most women: I don't believe a purer creature exists out of heaven. And I – I ask myself am I doing right in exposing her to the influence of poor Paula's light, careless nature?

DRUMMLE: My dear Aubrey!

AUBREY: That shocks you! So it does me. I assure you I long to urge my girl to break down the reserve which keeps her apart from Paula, but somehow I can't do it – well, I don't do it. How can I make you understand? But when you come to us you'll understand quickly enough. Cayley, there's hardly a subject you can broach on which poor Paula hasn't some strange, out-of-the-way thought to give utterance to; some curious, warped notion. They are not mere worldly thoughts – unless, good God! they belong to the little hellish world which our blackguardism has created: no, her ideas have too little calculation in them to be called worldly. But it makes it the more dreadful that such thoughts should be ready, spontaneous; that expressing them has become a perfectly natural process; that her words, acts even, have almost lost their proper significance for her, and seem beyond her control. Ah, the pain of listening to it all from the woman one loves, the woman one hoped to make happy and contented, who is really and truly a good woman, as it were, maimed! Well, this is my burden, and I shouldn't speak to you of it but for my anxiety about Ellean. Ellean! What is to be her future? It is in my hands; what am I to do? Cayley, when I remember how Ellean comes to me, from another world I always think, when I realise the charge that's laid on me, I find myself wishing, in a sort of terror, that my child were safe under the ground!

DRUMMLE: My dear Aubrey, aren't you making a mistake?

AUBREY: Very likely. What is it?

DRUMMLE: A mistake, not in regarding your Ellean as an angel, but in believing that under any circumstances, it would be possible for her to go through life without getting her white robe – shall we say, a little dusty at the hem? Don't take me for a cynic. I am sure there are many women upon earth who are almost divinely innocent; but being on earth, they must send their robes to the laundry occasionally. Ah, and it's right that they should have to do so, for what can they learn from the checking of their little washing-bills but lessons of charity? Now I see but two courses open to you for the disposal of your angel.

AUBREY: Yes?

DRUMMLE: You must either restrict her to a paradise which is, like every earthly paradise, necessarily somewhat imperfect, or treat her as an ordinary flesh-and-blood young woman, and give her the advantage of that society to which she properly belongs.

AUBREY: Advantages?

DRUMMLE: My dear Aubrey, of all forms of innocence mere ignorance is the least admirable. Take my advice, let her walk and talk and suffer and be healed with the great crowd. Do it, and hope that she'll some day meet a good, honest fellow who'll make her life complete, happy, secure. Now you see what I'm driving at.

AUBREY: A sanguine programme, my dear Cayley! Oh, I'm not pooh-poohing it. Putting sentiment aside, of course I know that a fortunate marriage for Ellean would be the best – perhaps the only – solution of my difficulty. But you forget the danger of the course you suggest.

DRUMMLE: Danger?

AUBREY: If Ellean goes among men and women, how can she escape from learning, sooner or later, the history of – poor Paula's – old life?

DRUMMLE: H'm! You remember the episode of the Jeweller's Son in the Arabian Nights? Of course you don't. Well, if your daughter lives, she *can't* escape – what you're afraid of. (AUBREY *gives a half-stifled exclamation of pain.*) And when she does hear the story, surely it would be better that she should have some knowledge of the world to help her to understand it.

AUBREY: To understand!

DRUMMLE: To understand, to – to philosophise.

AUBREY: To philosophise?

DRUMMLE: Philosophy is toleration, and it is only one step from toleration to forgiveness.

AUBREY: You're right, Cayley; I believe you always are. Yes, yes. But, even if I had the courage to attempt to solve the problem of Ellean's future in this way, I – I'm helpless.

DRUMMLE: How?

AUBREY: What means have I now of placing my daughter in the world I've left?

DRUMMLE: Oh, some friend – some woman friend.

AUBREY: I have none; they're gone.

DRUMMLE: You're wrong there; I know one –

AUBREY: (*listening*) That's Paula's cart. Let's discuss this again.

DRUMMLE: (*going up to the window and looking out*) It isn't the dog-cart (*turning to* AUBREY) I hope you'll forgive me, old chap.

AUBREY: What for?

DRUMMLE: Whose wheels do you think have been cutting ruts in your immaculate drive?

> (*A* SERVANT *enters.*)

SERVANT: (*to* AUBREY) Mrs Cortelyon, sir.

AUBREY: Mrs Cortelyon! (*after a short pause*) Very well. (*The* SERVANT *withdraws.*) What on earth is the meaning of this?

DRUMMLE: Ahem! While I've been our old friend's guest, Aubrey, we have very naturally talked a good deal about you and yours.

AUBREY: Indeed, have you?

DRUMMLE: Yes, and Alice Cortelyon has arrived at the conclusion that it would

---

the Jeweller's Son: in 'The Story of Mohammed, Alee the Jeweller, or The False Khaleefeh', Mohammed Alee, son of a wealthy jeweller, marries the Lady Dunya, sister of the Vizir of the Khaleefeh. While she is away he responds to the advances of the Lady Zubeydeh, and upon her return Dunya has him beaten and driven out of her home.

have been far kinder had she called on Mrs Tanqueray long ago. She's going abroad for Easter before settling down in London for the season, and I believe she has come over this morning to ask for Ellean's companionship.

AUBREY: Oh, I see! (*frowning*) Quite a friendly little conspiracy, my dear Cayley!

DRUMMLE: Conspiracy! Not at all, I assure you. (*laughing*) Ha, ha!

> (ELLEAN *enters from the hall with* MRS CORTELYON, *a handsome, good-humoured, spirited woman of about forty-five.*)

ELLEAN: Papa –

MRS CORTELYON: (*to* AUBREY, *shaking hands with him heartily*) Well, Aubrey, how are you? I've just been telling this great girl of yours that I knew her when she was a sad-faced, pale baby. How is Mrs Tanqueray? I have been a bad neighbour, and I'm here to beg her forgiveness. Is she indoors?

AUBREY: She's upstairs putting on a hat, I believe.

MRS CORTELYON: (*sitting comfortably*) Ah! (*She looks round.*) We used to be very frank with each other, Aubrey. I suppose the old footing is no longer possible, eh?

AUBREY: If so, I'm not entirely to blame, Mrs Cortelyon.

MRS CORTELYON: Mrs Cortelyon? H'm! No, I admit it. But you must make some little allowance for me, *Mr Tanqueray*. Your first wife and I, as girls, were like two cherries on one stalk, and then I was the confidential friend of your married life. That post, perhaps, wasn't altogether a sinecure. And now – well, when a woman gets to my age I suppose she's a stupid, prejudiced, conventional creature. However, I've got over it and – (*giving him her hand*) – I hope you'll be enormously happy and let me be a friend once more.

AUBREY: Thank you, Alice.

MRS CORTELYON: That's right. I feel more cheerful than I've done for weeks. But I suppose it would serve me right if the second Mrs Tanqueray showed me the door. Do you think she will?

AUBREY: (*listening*) Here is my wife. (MRS CORTELYON *rises and* PAULA *enters dressed for driving; she stops abruptly on seeing* MRS CORTELYON.) Paula dear, Mrs Cortelyon has called to see you.

> (PAULA *starts, looks at* MRS CORTELYON *irresolutely, then after a slight pause barely touches* MRS CORTELYON'*s extended hand.*)

PAULA: (*whose manner now alternates between deliberate insolence and assumed sweetness*) Mrs – ? What name, Aubrey?

AUBREY: Mrs Cortelyon.

PAULA: Cortelyon? Oh, yes. Cortelyon.

MRS CORTELYON: (*carefully guarding herself throughout against any expression of resentment*) Aubrey ought to have told you that Alice Cortelyon and he are very old friends.

PAULA: Oh, very likely he has mentioned the circumstances. I have quite a wretched memory.

MRS CORTELYON: You know we are neighbours, Mrs Tanqueray.

---

two cherries on one stalk: Mrs Cortelyon may be referring to *A Midsummer Night's Dream*, III.ii: 'Like to a double cherry . . ./. . . moulded on one stem'.

PAULA: Neighbours? Are we really? Won't you sit down? (*They both sit.*) Neighbours! That's most interesting!

MRS CORTELYON: Very near neighbours. You can see my roof from your windows.

PAULA: I fancy I *have* observed a roof. But you have been away from home; you have only just returned.

MRS CORTELYON: I? What makes you think that?

PAULA: Why, because it is two months since we came to Highercoombe, and I don't remember your having called.

MRS CORTELYON: Your memory is now terribly accurate. No, I've not been away from home, and it is to explain my neglect that I am here, rather unceremoniously, this morning.

PAULA: Oh, to explain – quite so. (*with mock solicitude*) Ah, you've been very ill; I ought to have seen that before.

MRS CORTELYON: Ill!

PAULA: You look dreadfully pulled down. We poor women show illness so plainly in our faces, don't we?

AUBREY: (*anxiously*) Paula dear, Mrs Cortelyon is the picture of health.

MRS CORTELYON: (*with some asperity*) I have never *felt* better in my life.

PAULA: (*looking round innocently*) Have I said anything awkward? (*turning to AUBREY*) Aubrey, tell Mrs Cortelyon how stupid and thoughtless I always am!

MRS CORTELYON: (*to DRUMMLE, who is now standing close to her*) Really, Cayley –

> (*He soothes her with a nod and a smile and a motion of his finger to his lip.*)

Mrs Tanqueray, I am afraid my explanation will not be quite so satisfactory as either of those you have just helped me to. You may have heard – but, if you have heard, you have doubtless forgotten – that twenty years ago, when your husband first lived here, I was a constant visitor at Highercoombe.

PAULA: Twenty years ago – fancy! I was a naughty little child then.

MRS CORTELYON: Possibly. Well, at that time, and till the end of her life, my affections were centred upon the lady of this house.

PAULA: Were they? That was very sweet of you.

> (ELLEAN *creeps down quietly to* MRS CORTELYON, *listening intently to her.*)

MRS CORTELYON: I will say no more on that score, but I must add this: when, two months ago, you came here, I realised, perhaps for the first time, that I was a middle-aged woman, and that it had become impossible for me to accept without some effort a breaking-upon many tender associations. There, Mrs Tanqueray, that is my confession. Will you try to understand it and pardon me?

PAULA: (*watching ELLEAN – sneeringly*) Ellean dear, you appear to be very interested in Mrs Cortelyon's reminiscences; I don't think I can do better than make you my mouthpiece – there is such sympathy between us. What do you say – can we bring ourselves to forgive Mrs Cortelyon for neglecting us for two weary months?

MRS CORTELYON: (*to ELLEAN, pleasantly*). Well, Ellean? (*With a little cry of tenderness* ELLEAN *impulsively sits beside* MRS CORTELYON *and takes her hand.*) My dear child!

PAULA: (*in an undertone to* AUBREY) Ellean isn't so very slow in taking to Mrs Cortelyon!

MRS CORTELYON: (*to* PAULA *and* AUBREY) Come, this encourages me to broach my scheme. Mrs Tanqueray, it strikes me that you two good people are just now excellent company for each other, while Ellean would perhaps be glad of a little peep into the world you are anxious to avoid. Now I'm going to Paris to-morrow for a week or two before settling down in Chester Square, so – don't gasp, both of you! – if this girl is willing, and you have made no other arrangements for her, will you let her come with me to Paris, and afterwards remain with me in town during the Season?

    (ELLEAN *utters an exclamation of surprise.* PAULA *is silent.*)
What do you say?

AUBREY: Paula – Paula dear. (*hesitatingly*) My dear Mrs Cortelyon, this is wonderfully kind of you; I am really at a loss to – eh, Cayley?

DRUMMLE: (*watching* PAULA *apprehensively*) Kind! Now I must say I don't think so! I begged Alice to take *me* to Paris, and she declined. I am thrown over for Ellean! Ha! ha!

MRS CORTELYON: (*laughing*) What nonsense you talk, Cayley!
    (*The laughter dies out.* PAULA *remains quite still.*)

AUBREY: Paula dear.

PAULA: (*slowly collecting herself*) One moment. I – I don't quite – (*to* MRS CORTELYON) You propose that Ellean leaves Highercoombe almost at once and remains with you some months?

MRS CORTELYON: It would be a mercy to me. You can afford to be generous to a desolate old widow. Come, Mrs Tanqueray, won't you spare her?

PAULA: Won't *I* spare her? (*suspiciously*) Have you mentioned your plan to Aubrey – before I came in?

MRS CORTELYON: No, I had no opportunity.

PAULA: Nor to Ellean?

MRS CORTELYON: Oh, no.

PAULA: (*looking about her, in suppressed excitement*) This hasn't been discussed at all, behind my back?

MRS CORTELYON: My dear Mrs Tanqueray!

PAULA: Ellean, let us hear your voice in the matter!

ELLEAN: I should like to go with Mrs Cortelyon –

PAULA: Ah!

ELLEAN: That is if – if –

PAULA: If – if what?

ELLEAN: (*looking towards* AUBREY, *appealingly*) Papa?

PAULA: (*in a hard voice*) Oh, of course – I forgot. (*to* AUBREY) My dear Aubrey, it rests with you, naturally, whether I am – to lose – Ellean.

AUBREY: (*brightly*) Lose Ellean! (*advancing to* PAULA) There is no question of

---

settling down: i.e. for the summer 'Season'. *Chester Square*: a fashionable London district.

losing Ellean. You would see Ellean in town constantly when she returned from Paris; isn't that so, Mrs Cortelyon?

MRS CORTELYON: Certainly.

PAULA: (*laughing softly*) Oh, I didn't know I should be allowed that privilege.

MRS CORTELYON: Privilege, my dear Mrs Tanqueray!

PAULA: Ha, ha! that makes all the difference, doesn't it?

AUBREY: (*with assumed gaiety*) All the difference? I should think so! (*to* ELLEAN, *laying his hand upon her head, tenderly*) And you are quite certain you wish to see what the world is like on the other side of Black Moor?

ELLEAN: If you are willing, Papa, I am quite certain.

AUBREY: (*looking at* PAULA *irresolutely, then speaking with an effort*) Then I – I am willing.

PAULA: (*rising and striking the table lightly with her clenched hand*) That decides it! (*There is a general movement.*) (*excitedly to* MRS CORTELYON, *who advances towards her*) When do you want her?

MRS CORTELYON: We go to town this afternoon at five o'clock, and sleep to-night at Bayliss's. There is barely time for her to make her preparations.

PAULA: I will undertake that she is ready.

MRS CORTELYON: I've a great deal to scramble through at home too, as you may guess. Good-bye!

PAULA: (*turning away*) Mrs Cortelyon is going.

   (PAULA *stands looking out of the window, with her back to those in the room.*)

MRS CORTELYON: (*to* DRUMMLE) Cayley –

DRUMMLE: (*to her*) Eh?

MRS CORTELYON: I've gone through it, for the sake of Aubrey and his child, but I – I feel a hundred. Is that a mad-woman?

DRUMMLE: Of course; all jealous women are mad.

   (*He goes out with* AUBREY.)

MRS CORTELYON: (*hesitatingly to* PAULA) Good-bye, Mrs Tanqueray.

   (PAULA *inclines her head with the slightest possible movement, then resumes her former position.* ELLEAN *comes from the hall and takes* MRS CORTELYON *out of the room. After a brief silence,* PAULA *turns with a fierce cry, and hurriedly takes off her coat and hat, almost tearing them from her, and tosses them upon the settee. Upon removing her hat, she stabs it viciously with a long fastener.*)

PAULA: Oh! Oh! Oh! (*She drops into the chair as* AUBREY *returns; he stands looking at her.*) Who's that?

AUBREY: I. You have altered your mind about going out?

PAULA: Yes. Please to ring the bell.

AUBREY: (*touching the bell*) You are angry about Mrs Cortelyon and Ellean. Let me try to explain my reasons –

PAULA: Be careful what you say to me just now! I have never felt like this – except

---

Bayliss's: i.e. Bayliss's Hotel.

once – in my life. Be careful what you say to me! (*A* SERVANT *enters.*) (*rising*) Is Watts at the door with the cart?

SERVANT: Yes, ma'am.

PAULA: (*picking up the letter which has been lying upon the table*) Tell him to drive down to the post office directly, with this.

AUBREY: With that?

PAULA: Yes. My letter to Lady Orreyed.

   (*She gives the letter to the* SERVANT, *who goes out.*)

AUBREY: Surely you don't wish me to countermand any order of yours to a servant? Call the man back – take the letter from him!

PAULA: I have not the slightest intention of doing so.

AUBREY: (*going to the door*) I must, then. (*She snatches up her hat and coat and follows him.*) What are you going to do?

PAULA: If you stop that letter, walk out of the house.

AUBREY: I am right in believing that to be the letter inviting George Orreyed and his wife to stay here, am I not?

PAULA: Oh yes – quite right.

AUBREY: Let it go; I'll write to him by and by.

PAULA: (*facing him*) You dare!

AUBREY: Hush, Paula!

PAULA: Insult me again and, upon my word, I'll go straight out of the house!

AUBREY: Insult you?

PAULA: Insult me! What else is it? My God! what else is it? What do you mean by taking Ellean from me?

AUBREY: Listen –!

PAULA: Listen to *me*. And how do you take her? You pack her off in the care of a woman who has deliberately held aloof from me, who's thrown mud at me! Yet this Cortelyon creature has only to put foot here once to be entrusted with the charge of the girl you know I dearly want to keep near me!

AUBREY: Paula dear! hear me –!

PAULA: Ah! of course, of course! I can't be so useful to your daughter as such people as this; and so I'm to be given the go-by for any town friend of yours who turns up and chooses to patronise us! Hah! Very well, at any rate, as you take Ellean from me you justify my looking for companions where I can most readily find 'em.

AUBREY: You wish me to fully appreciate your reason for sending that letter to Lady Orreyed?

PAULA: Precisely – I do.

AUBREY: And could you, after all, go back to associates of that order? It's not possible!

PAULA: (*mockingly*) What, not after the refining influence of these intensely respectable surroundings? (*going to the door*) We'll see!

AUBREY: Paula!

PAULA: (*violently*) We'll see!

   (*She goes out. He stands still looking after her.*)

END OF THE SECOND ACT

THE THIRD ACT

The drawing-room at 'Highercoombe'. Facing the spectator two large French windows, sheltered by a verandah, leading into the garden; on the right is a door opening into a small hall. The fireplace, with a large mirror above it, is on the left-hand side of the room, and higher up in the same wall are double doors recessed. The room is richly furnished, and everything betokens taste and luxury. The windows are open, and there is moonlight in the garden.

LADY ORREYED, *a pretty, affected doll of a woman with a mincing voice and flaxen hair, is sitting on the ottoman, her head resting against the drum, and her eyes closed.*
PAULA, *looking pale, worn, and thoroughly unhappy, is sitting at a table. Both are in sumptuous dinner-gowns.*

LADY ORREYED: (*opening her eyes*) Well, I never! I dropped off! (*feeling her hair*) Just fancy! Where are the men?
PAULA: (*icily*) Outside, smoking.
> (*A* SERVANT *enters with coffee, which he hands to* LADY ORREYED. SIR GEORGE ORREYED *comes in by the window. He is a man of about thirty-five, with a low forehead, a receding chin, a vacuous expression, and an ominous redness about the nose.*)
LADY ORREYED: (*taking coffee*) Here's Dodo.
SIR GEORGE: I say, the flies under the verandah make you swear.
> (*The* SERVANT *hands coffee to* PAULA, *who declines it, then to* SIR GEORGE, *who takes a cup.*)
Hi! wait a bit! (*He looks at the tray searchingly, then puts back his cup.*) Never mind. (*quietly to* LADY ORREYED) I say, they're dooced sparin' with their liqueur, ain't they?
> (*The* SERVANT *goes out at window.*)
PAULA: (*to* SIR GEORGE). Won't you take coffee, George?
SIR GEORGE: (*pulling his moustache*). No, thanks. It's gettin' near time for a whisky and potass. (*approaching* PAULA, *regarding* LADY ORREYED *admiringly*) I say, Birdie looks rippin' to-night, don't she?
PAULA: Your wife?
SIR GEORGE: Yaas – Birdie.
PAULA: Rippin'?
SIR GEORGE: Yaas.
PAULA: Quite – quite rippin'.
> (*He moves round to the settee.* PAULA *watches him with distaste, then rises and walks away.* SIR GEORGE *falls asleep on the settee by fireplace.*)
LADY ORREYED: Paula love, I fancied you and Aubrey were a little more friendly at dinner. You haven't made it up, have you?
PAULA: We? Oh, no. We speak before others, that's all.
LADY ORREYED: And how long do you intend to carry on this game, dear?
PAULA: (*turning away impatiently*) I really can't tell you.

---

potass: potassic potassium, 'an alkaline monad metal, the basis of Potash' (*OED*).

LADY ORREYED: Sit down, old girl; don't be so fidgety. (PAULA *sits on the upper seat of the ottoman with her back to* LADY ORREYED.) Of course, it's my duty, as an old friend, to give you a good talking to – (PAULA *glares at her suddenly and fiercely*) but really I've found one gets so many smacks in the face through interfering in matrimonial squabbles that I've determined to drop it.

PAULA: I think you're wise.

LADY ORREYED: However, I must say that I do wish you'd look at marriage in a more solemn light – just as I do, in fact. It is such a beautiful thing – marriage, and if people in our position don't respect it, and set a good example by living happily with their husbands, what can you expect from the middle classes? When did this sad state of affairs between you and Aubrey actually begin?

PAULA: Actually, a fortnight and three days ago; I haven't calculated the minutes.

LADY ORREYED: A day or two before Dodo and I turned up – arrived.

PAULA: Yes. One always remembers one thing by another; we left off speaking to each other the morning I wrote asking you to visit us.

LADY ORREYED: Lucky for you I was able to pop down, wasn't it, dear?

PAULA: (*glaring at her again*) Most fortunate.

LADY ORREYED: A serious split with your husband without a pal on the premises – I should say, without a friend in the house – would be most unpleasant.

PAULA: (*turning to her abruptly*). This place must be horribly doleful for you and George just now. At least you ought to consider him before me. Why don't you leave me to my difficulties?

LADY ORREYED: Oh, we're quite comfortable, dear, thank you – both of us. George and me are so wrapped up in each other, it doesn't matter where we are. I don't want to crow over you, old girl, but I've got a perfect husband.

(SIR GEORGE *is now fast asleep, his head thrown back and his mouth open, looking hideous.*)

PAULA: (*glancing at* SIR GEORGE) So you've given me to understand.

LADY ORREYED: Not that we don't have our little differences. Why, we fell out only this very morning. You remember the diamond and ruby tiara Charley Prestwick gave poor dear Connie Tirlemont years ago, don't you?

PAULA: (*emphatically*) No, I do not.

LADY ORREYED: No? Well, it's in the market. Benjamin of Piccadilly has got it in his shop-window, and I've set my heart on it.

PAULA: You consider it quite necessary?

LADY ORREYED: Yes, because what I say to Dodo is this – a lady of my station must smother herself with hair ornaments. It's different with you, love – people don't look for so much blaze from you, but I've got rank to keep up; haven't I?

PAULA: Yes.

LADY ORREYED: Well, that was the cause of this little set-to between I and Dodo this morning. He broke two chairs, he was in such a rage. I forgot, they're your chairs; do you mind?

PAULA: No.

LADY ORREYED: You know, poor Dodo can't lose his temper without smashing something; if it isn't a chair, it's a mirror; if it isn't that, it's china – a bit of Dresden for choice. Dear old pet! He loves a bit of Dresden when he's furious. He doesn't really throw things *at* me dear; he simply lifts them up and drops them, like a gentleman. I expect our room upstairs will look rather wrecky before I get that tiara.

PAULA: Excuse the suggestion, perhaps your husband can't afford it.

LADY ORREYED: Oh, how dreadfully changed you are, Paula! Dodo can always mortgage something, or borrow off his ma. What *is* coming to you!

PAULA: Ah! (*She sits at the piano and touches the keys.*)

LADY ORREYED: Oh, yes do play! That's the one thing I envy you for.

PAULA: What shall I play?

LADY ORREYED: What was that heavenly piece you gave us last night, dear?

PAULA: A bit of Schubert. Would you like to hear it again?

LADY ORREYED: You don't know any comic songs, do you?

PAULA: I'm afraid not.

LADY ORREYED: I leave it to you, then.

> (PAULA *plays.* AUBREY *and* CAYLEY DRUMMLE *appear outside the window; they look into the room.*)

AUBREY: (*to* DRUMMLE) You can see her face in that mirror. Poor girl, how ill and wretched she looks.

DRUMMLE: When are the Orreyeds going?

AUBREY: (*entering the room*) Heaven knows!

DRUMMLE: (*following* AUBREY) But *you're* entertaining them; what's it to do with Heaven?

AUBREY: Do you know, Cayley, that even the Orreyeds serve a useful purpose? My wife actually speaks to me before our guests – think of that! I've come to rejoice at the presence of the Orreyeds!

DRUMMLE: I daresay; we're taught that beetles are sent for a benign end.

AUBREY: Cayley, talk to Paula again to-night.

DRUMMLE: Certainly, if I get the chance.

AUBREY: Let's contrive it. George is asleep; perhaps I can get that doll out of the way. (*As they advance into the room,* PAULA *abruptly ceases playing and finds interest in a volume of music.* SIR GEORGE *is now nodding and snoring apoplectically.*) Lady Orreyed, whenever you feel inclined for a game of billiards I'm at your service.

LADY ORREYED: (*jumping up*) Charmed, I'm sure! I really thought you'd forgotten poor little me. Oh, look at Dodo!

AUBREY: No, no, don't wake him; he's tired.

LADY ORREYED: I must, he looks so plain. (*rousing* SIR GEORGE) Dodo! Dodo!

SIR GEORGE: (*stupidly*) 'Ullo!

LADY ORREYED: Dodo, dear, you were snoring.

SIR GEORGE: Oh, I say, you could 'a told me that by and by.

AUBREY: You want a cigar, George; come into the billiard-room. (*giving his arm to* LADY ORREYED) Cayley, bring Paula.

> (AUBREY *and* LADY ORREYED *go out.*)

SIR GEORGE: (*rising*) Hey, what! Billiard-room! (*looking at his watch*) How goes the –? Phew! 'Ullo, 'Ullo! Whisky and potass!

> (*He goes rapidly after* AUBREY *and* LADY ORREYED. PAULA *resumes playing.*)

PAULA: (*after a pause*) Don't moon about after me, Cayley; follow the others.

DRUMMLE: Thanks, by and by. (*sitting*) That's pretty.

PAULA: (*after another pause, still playing*) I wish you wouldn't stare so.

DRUMMLE: Was I staring? I'm sorry. (*She plays a little longer then stops suddenly, rises, and goes to the window, where she stands looking out.* DRUMMLE *moves from the ottoman to the settee.*) A lovely night.

PAULA: (*startled*) Oh! (*without turning to him*) Why do you hop about like a monkey?

DRUMMLE: Hot rooms play the deuce with the nerves. Now, it would have done you good to have walked in the garden with us after dinner and made merry. Why didn't you?

PAULA: You know why.

DRUMMLE: Ah, you're thinking of the – difference between you and Aubrey?

PAULA: Yes, I *am* thinking of it.

DRUMMLE: Well, so am I. How long –?

PAULA: Getting on for three weeks.

DRUMMLE: Bless me, it must be! And this would have been such a night to have healed it! Moonlight, the stars, the scent of flowers; and yet enough darkness to enable a kind woman to rest her hand for an instant on the arm of a good fellow who loves her. Ah, ha! it's a wonderful power, dear Mrs Aubrey, the power of an offended woman! Only realise it! Just that one touch – the mere tips of her fingers – and, for herself and another, she changes the colour of the whole world!

PAULA: (*turning to him, calmly*) Cayley, my dear man, you talk exactly like a very romantic old lady.

(*She leaves the window and sits playing with the knick-knacks on the table.*)

DRUMMLE: (*to himself*) H'm, that hasn't done it! Well – ha, ha! – I accept the suggestion. (*standing beside her*) An old woman, eh?

PAULA: Oh, I didn't intend –

DRUMMLE: But why not? I've every qualification – well, almost. And I confess it would have given this withered bosom a throb of grandmotherly satisfaction if I could have seen you and Aubrey at peace before I take my leave to-morrow.

PAULA: To-morrow, Cayley!

DRUMMLE: I must.

PAULA: Oh, this house is becoming unendurable.

DRUMMLE: You're very kind. But you've got the Orreyeds.

PAULA: (*fiercely*) The Orreyeds! I – I hate the Orreyeds! I lie awake at night, hating them!

DRUMMLE: Pardon me, I've understood that their visit is, in some degree, owing to – hem! – your suggestion.

PAULA: Heavens! that doesn't make me like them better. Somehow or another, I – I've outgrown these people. This woman – I used to think her 'jolly!' – sickens me. I can't breathe when she's near me: the whiff of her handkerchief turns me faint! And she patronises me by the hour, until I – I feel my nails growing longer with every word she speaks!

DRUMMLE: My dear lady, why on earth don't you say all this to Aubrey?

PAULA: Oh, I've been such an utter fool, Cayley!

DRUMMLE: (*soothingly*) Well, well, mention it to Aubrey!

PAULA: No, no, you don't understand. What do you think I've done?

DRUMMLE: Done! What, *since* you invited the Orreyeds?

PAULA: Yes; I must tell you –

DRUMMLE: (*disturbed*) Perhaps you'd better not.

PAULA: Look here. I've intercepted some letters from Mrs Cortelyon and Ellean to – him. (*producing three unopened letters from the bodice of her dress*) There are the accursed things! From Paris – two from the Cortelyon woman, the other from Ellean!

DRUMMLE: But why – why?

PAULA: I don't know. Yes, I do! I saw letters coming from Ellean to her father; not a line to me – not a line. And one morning it happened I was downstairs before he was, and I spied this one lying with his heap on the breakfast-table, and I slipped it into my pocket – out of malice, Cayley, pure devilry! And a day or two afterwards I met Elwes the postman at the Lodge, and took the letters from him, and found these others amongst 'em. I felt simply fiendish when I saw them – fiendish! (*returning the letters to her bodice*) And now I carry them about with me, and they're scorching me like a mustard plaster!

DRUMMLE: Oh, this accounts for Aubrey not hearing from Paris lately!

PAULA: That's an ingenious conclusion to arrive at! Of course it does! (*with an hysterical laugh*) Ha, ha!

DRUMMLE: Well, well! (*laughing*) Ha, ha, ha!

PAULA: (*turning upon him*) I suppose it *is* amusing!

DRUMMLE: I beg pardon.

PAULA: Heaven knows I've little enough to brag about! I'm a bad lot, but not in mean tricks of this sort. In all my life this is the most caddish thing I've done. How am I to get rid of these letters – that's what I want to know? How am I to get rid of them?

DRUMMLE: If I were you I should take Aubrey aside and put them into his hands as soon as possible.

PAULA: What! and tell him to his face that I – ! No, thank you. I suppose *you* wouldn't like to –

DRUMMLE: No, no; I won't touch 'em!

PAULA: And you call yourself my friend?

DRUMMLE: (*good-humouredly*) No, I don't!

PAULA: Perhaps I'll tie them together and give them to his man in the morning.

DRUMMLE: That won't avoid an explanation.

PAULA: (*recklessly*) Oh, then he must miss them –

DRUMMLE: And trace them.

PAULA: (*throwing herself upon the ottoman*) I don't care!

DRUMMLE: I know you don't; but let me send him to you now, may I?

PAULA: Now! What do you think a woman's made of? I couldn't stand it, Cayley. I haven't slept for nights; and last night there was thunder, too! I believe I got the horrors.

DRUMMLE: (*taking the little hand-mirror from the table*) You'll sleep well enough when you deliver those letters. Come, come, Mrs Aubrey – a good night's rest! (*holding the mirror before her face*) It's quite time.

      (*She looks at herself for a moment, then snatches the mirror from him.*)

PAULA: You brute, Cayley, to show me that!

DRUMMLE: Then – may I? Be guided by a fr – a poor old woman! May I?

PAULA: You'll kill me, amongst you!

DRUMMLE: What do you say?

PAULA: (*after a pause*) Very well. (*He nods his head and goes out rapidly. She looks after him for a moment, and calls, 'Cayley! Cayley!' Then she again produces the letters, deliberately, one by one, fingering them with aversion. Suddenly she starts, turning her head towards the door.*) Ah!

      (AUBREY *enters quickly.*)

AUBREY: Paula!

PAULA: (*handing him the letters, her face averted*) There! (*He examines the letters, puzzled, and looks at her inquiringly.*) They are many days old. I stole them, I suppose to make you anxious and unhappy.

      (*He looks at the letters again, then lays them aside on the table.*)

AUBREY: (*gently*) Paula, dear, it doesn't matter.

PAULA: (*after a short pause*) Why – why do you take it like this?

AUBREY: What did you expect?

PAULA: Oh, but I suppose silent reproaches are really the severest. And then, naturally, you are itching to open your letters.

      (*She crosses the room as if to go.*)

AUBREY: Paula! (*She pauses.*) Surely, surely it's all over now?

PAULA: All over! (*mockingly*) Has my stepdaughter returned then? When did she arrive? I haven't heard of it!

AUBREY: You can be very cruel.

PAULA: That word's always on a man's lips; he uses it if his soup's cold. (*with another movement as if to go*) Need we –

AUBREY: I know I've wounded you, Paula. But isn't there any way out of this?

PAULA: When does Ellean return? To-morrow? Next week?

AUBREY: (*wearily*) Oh! Why should we grudge Ellean the little pleasure she is likely to find in Paris and in London.

PAULA: I grudge her nothing, if that's a hit at me. But with that woman – !

AUBREY: It must be that woman or another. You know that at present we are unable to give Ellean the opportunity of – of –

PAULA: Of mixing with respectable people.

AUBREY: The opportunity of gaining friends, experience, ordinary knowledge of the world. If you are interested in Ellean, can't you see how useful Mrs Cortelyon's good offices are?

PAULA: May I put one question? At the end of the London season, when Mrs Cortelyon has done with Ellean, is it understood that the girl comes back to us? (AUBREY *is silent.*) Is it? Is it?

AUBREY: Let us wait till the end of the season –

PAULA: Oh! I knew it. You're only fooling me; you put me off with any trash. I believe you've sent Ellean away, not for the reasons you give, but because you don't consider me a decent companion for her, because you're afraid she might get a little of her innocence rubbed off in my company. Come, isn't that the truth? Be honest! Isn't that it?

AUBREY: Yes.

(*There is a moment's silence on both sides.*)

PAULA: (*with uplifted hands as if to strike him*) Oh!

AUBREY: (*taking her by the wrists*) Sit down. Sit down. (*He puts her into a chair; she shakes herself free with a cry.*) Now listen to me. Fond as you are, Paula, of harking back to your past, there's one chapter of it you always let alone. I've never asked you to speak of it; you never offered to speak of it. I mean the chapter that relates to the time when you were – like Ellean. (*She attempts to rise; he restrains her.*) No, no.

PAULA: I don't choose to talk about that time. I won't satisfy your curiosity.

AUBREY: My dear Paula, I have no curiosity – I know what you were at Ellean's age. I'll tell you. You hadn't a thought that wasn't a wholesome one, you hadn't an impulse that didn't tend towards good, you never harboured a notion you couldn't have gossiped about to a parcel of children. (*She makes another effort to rise: he lays his hand lightly on her shoulder.*) And this was a very few years back – there are days now when you look like a schoolgirl – but think of the difference between the two Paulas. You'll have to think hard, because after a cruel life one's perceptions grow a thick skin. But, for God's sake, do think till you get these two images clearly in your mind, and then ask yourself what sort of a friend such a woman as you are to-day would have been for the girl of seven or eight years ago.

PAULA: (*rising*) How dare you? I could be almost as good a friend to Ellean as her own mother would have been had she lived. I know what you mean. How dare you?

AUBREY: You say that; very likely you believe it. But you're blind, Paula; you're blind. You! Every belief that a young, pure-minded girl holds sacred – that you once held sacred – you now make a target for a jest, a sneer, a paltry cynicism. I tell you, you're not mistress any longer of your thoughts or your tongue. Why, how often sitting between you and Ellean, have I seen her cheeks turn scarlet as you've rattled off some tale that belongs by right to the club or the smoking-room! Have you noticed the blush? If you have, has the cause of it ever struck you? And this is the girl you say you love, I admit that you *do* love, whose love you expect in return! Oh, Paula, I make the best, the only, excuse for you when I tell you you're blind!

PAULA: Ellean – Ellean blushes easily.

AUBREY: You blushed as easily a few years ago.

PAULA: (*after a short pause*). Well! Have you finished your sermon?

AUBREY: (*with a gesture of despair*) Oh Paula! (*going up to the window and standing with his back to the room*)

PAULA: (*to herself*) A few – years ago! (*She walks slowly towards the door, then suddenly drops upon the ottoman in a paroxysm of weeping.*) O God! A few years ago!

---

the club or the smoking-room: i.e. male company only.

AUBREY: (*going to her*) Paula!

PAULA: (*sobbing*) Oh, don't touch me!

AUBREY: Paula!

PAULA: Oh, go away from me! (*He goes back a few steps, and after a little while she becomes calmer and rises unsteadily; then in an altered tone*) Look here –! (*He advances a step; she checks him with a quick gesture*.) Look here! Get rid of these people – Mabel and her husband – as soon as possible! I – I've done with them!

AUBREY: (*in a whisper*) Paula!

PAULA: And then – then – when the time comes for Ellean to leave Mrs Cortelyon, give me – give me another chance! (*He advances again, but she shrinks away*.) No, no!

> (*She goes out by the door on the right. He sinks on to the settee, covering his eyes with his hands. There is a brief silence, then a SERVANT enters*.)

SERVANT: Mrs Cortelyon, sir, with Miss Ellean.

> (*AUBREY rises to meet MRS CORTELYON, who enters, followed by ELLEAN, both being in travelling dresses. The SERVANT withdraws*.)

MRS CORTELYON: (*shaking hands with AUBREY*) Oh, my dear Aubrey!

AUBREY: Mrs Cortelyon! (*kissing ELLEAN*) Ellean dear!

ELLEAN: Papa, is all well at home?

MRS CORTELYON: We're shockingly anxious.

AUBREY: Yes, yes, all's well. This is quite unexpected. (*to* MRS CORTELYON) You've found Paris unsufferably hot?

MRS CORTELYON: Insufferably hot! Paris is pleasant enough. We've had no letter from you!

AUBREY: I wrote to Ellean a week ago.

MRS CORTELYON: Without alluding to the subject I had written to you upon.

AUBREY: (*thinking*) Ah, of course –

MRS CORTELYON: And since then we've both written and you've been absolutely silent. Oh, it's too bad!

AUBREY: (*picking up the letters from the table*) It isn't altogether my fault. Here are the letters –

ELLEAN: Papa!

MRS CORTELYON: They're unopened.

AUBREY: An accident delayed their reaching me till this evening. I'm afraid this has upset you very much.

MRS CORTELYON: Upset me!

ELLEAN: (*in an undertone to* MRS CORTELYON) Never mind. Not now, dear – not to-night.

AUBREY: Eh?

MRS CORTELYON: (*to* ELLEAN *aloud*) Child, run away and take your things off. She doesn't look as if she'd journeyed from Paris to-day.

AUBREY: I've never seen her with such a colour. (*taking* ELLEAN's *hands*)

ELLEAN: (*to* AUBREY, *in a faint voice*) Papa, Mrs Cortelyon has been so very, very kind to me, but I – I have come home.

> (*She goes out*.)

AUBREY: Come home! (*to* MRS CORTELYON, *puzzled*) Ellean returns to us, then?

MRS CORTELYON: That's the very point I put to you in my letters, and you oblige me to travel from Paris to Willowmere on a warm day to settle it. I think perhaps it's right that Ellean should be with you just now, although I – My dear friend, circumstances are a little altered.

AUBREY: Alice, you're in some trouble.

MRS CORTELYON: Well – yes, I *am* in trouble. You remember pretty little Mrs Brereton who was once Caroline Ardale?

AUBREY: Quite well.

MRS CORTELYON: She's a widow now, poor thing. She has the *entresol* of the house where we've been lodging in the Avenue de Friedland. Caroline's a dear chum of mine; she formed a great liking for Ellean.

AUBREY: I'm very glad.

MRS CORTELYON: Yes, it's nice for her to meet her mother's friends. Er – that young Hugh Ardale the papers were full of some time ago – he's Caroline Brereton's brother, you know.

AUBREY: No, I didn't know. What did he do? I forget.

MRS CORTELYON: Checked one of those horrid mutinies at some far-away station in India, marched down with a handful of his men and a few faithful natives, and held the place until he was relieved. They gave him his company and a V.C. for it.

AUBREY: And he's Mrs Brereton's brother?

MRS CORTELYON: Yes. He's with his sister – *was* rather – in Paris. He's home – invalided. Good gracious, Aubrey why don't you help me out? Can't you guess what has occurred?

AUBREY: Alice!

MRS CORTELYON: Young Ardale – Ellean!

AUBREY: An attachment?

MRS CORTELYON: Yes, Aubrey. (*after a little pause*) Well, I suppose I've got myself into sad disgrace. But really I didn't foresee anything of this kind. A serious, reserved child like Ellean, and a boyish, high-spirited soldier – it never struck me as being likely. (AUBREY *paces to and fro thoughtfully.*) I did all I could directly Captain Ardale spoke – wrote to you at once. Why on earth don't you receive your letters promptly, and when you do get them why can't you open them? I endured the anxiety till last night, and then made up my mind – home! Of course, it has worried me terribly. My head's bursting. Are there any salts about? (AUBREY *fetches a bottle from a cabinet and hands it to her.*) We've had one of those hateful smooth crossings that won't let you be properly indisposed.

---

entresol: 'a low storey placed between the ground floor and the first floor' (*OED*); cf. 'mezzanine'.
V.C. = Victoria Cross, the highest award for gallantry.

AUBREY: My dear Alice, I assure you I've no thought of blaming you.

MRS CORTELYON: That statement always precedes a quarrel.

AUBREY: I don't know whether this is the worst or the best luck. How will my wife regard it? Is Captain Ardale a good fellow?

MRS CORTELYON: My dear Aubrey, you'd better read up the accounts of his wonderful heroism. Face to face with death for a whole week; always with a smile and a cheering word for the poor helpless souls depending on him! Of course, it's that that has stirred the depths of your child's nature. I've watched her while we've been dragging the story out of him, and if angels look different from Ellean at that moment, I don't desire to meet any, that's all!

AUBREY: If you were in my position – ? But you can't judge.

MRS CORTELYON: Why, if I had a marriageable daughter of my own and Captain Ardale proposed for her, naturally I should cry my eyes out all night – but I should thank Heaven in the morning.

AUBREY: You believe so thoroughly in him?

MRS CORTELYON: Do you think I should have only a headache at this minute if I didn't! Look here, you've got to see me down the lane; that's the least you can do, my friend. Come into my house for a moment and shake hands with Hugh.

AUBREY: What, is he here?

MRS CORTELYON: He came through with us, to present himself formally to-morrow. Where are my gloves? (AUBREY *fetches them from the ottoman.*) Make my apologies to Mrs Tanqueray, please. She's well, I hope? (*going towards the door*) I can't feel sorry she hasn't seen me in this condition.
          (ELLEAN *enters.*)

ELLEAN: (*to* MRS CORTELYON) I've been waiting to wish you good night. I was afraid I'd missed you.

MRS CORTELYON: Good night, Ellean.

ELLEAN: (*in a low voice, embracing* MRS CORTELYON) I can't thank you. Dear Mrs Cortelyon!

MRS CORTELYON: (*her arms round* ELLEAN, *in a whisper to* AUBREY) Speak a word to her.
          (MRS CORTELYON *goes out.*)

AUBREY: (*to* ELLEAN) Ellean, I'm going to see Mrs Cortelyon home. (*going to the door*) Tell Paula where I am; explain, dear.

ELLEAN: (*her head drooping*) Yes. Father! You are angry with me – disappointed?

AUBREY: Angry? – no.

ELLEAN: Disappointed?

AUBREY: (*smiling and going to her and taking her hand*) If so, it's only because you've shaken by belief in my discernment. I thought you took after your poor mother a little, Ellean; (*looking into her face earnestly*) but there's a look on your face to-night, dear, that I never saw on hers – never, never.

ELLEAN: (*leaning her head on his shoulder*) Perhaps I ought not to have gone away?

AUBREY: Hush! You're quite happy?

ELLEAN: Yes.

AUBREY: That's right. Then, as you are quite happy there is something I particularly want you to do for me, Ellean.

ELLEAN: What is that?

AUBREY: Be very gentle with Paula. Will you?

ELLEAN: You think —I have been unkind.

AUBREY: (*kissing her upon the forehead*) Be very gentle with Paula.

> (*He goes out and she stands looking after him. A rose is thrown through the window and falls at her feet. She picks up the flower wonderingly and goes to the window.*)

ELLEAN: (*starting back*) Hugh!

> (HUGH ARDALE, *a handsome young man of about seven-and-twenty, with a boyish face and manner, appears outside the window.*)

HUGH: Nelly! Nelly dear!

ELLEAN: What's the matter?

HUGH: Hush! Nothing. It's only fun. (*laughing*) Ha, ha, ha! I've found out that Mrs Cortelyon's meadow runs up to your father's plantation; I've come through a gap in the hedge.

ELLEAN: Why, Hugh?

HUGH: I'm miserable at The Warren; it's so different from the Avenue de Friedland. Don't look like that! Upon my word I meant just to peep at your home and go back, but I saw figures moving about here, and came nearer, hoping to get a glimpse of you. Was that your father? (*entering the room*)

ELLEAN: Yes.

HUGH: Isn't this fun! A rabbit ran across my foot while I was hiding behind that old yew.

ELLEAN: You must go away; it's not *right* for you to be here like this.

HUGH: But it's only fun, I tell you. You take everything so seriously. Do wish me good night.

ELLEAN: We have said good night.

HUGH: In the hall at The Warren, before Mrs Cortelyon and a man-servant. Oh, it's so different from the Avenue de Friedland!

ELLEAN: (*giving him her hand hastily*) Good night, Hugh.

HUGH: Is that all? We might be the merest acquaintances.

> (*He momentarily embraces her, but she releases herself.*)

ELLEAN: It's when you're like this that you make me feel utterly miserable. (*throwing the rose from her angrily*) Oh!

HUGH: I've offended you now, I suppose?

ELLEAN: Yes.

HUGH: Forgive me, Nelly. Come into the garden for five minutes; we'll stroll down to the plantation.

ELLEAN: No, no.

HUGH: For two minutes – to tell me you forgive me.

ELLEAN: I forgive you.

HUGH: Evidently. I shan't sleep a wink to-night after this. What a fool I am! Come down to the plantation. Make it up with me.

ELLEAN: There is somebody coming into this room. Do you wish to be seen here?

HUGH: I shall wait for you behind that yew-tree. You *must* speak to me. Nelly!

> (*He disappears. PAULA enters.*)

PAULA: Ellean!

ELLEAN: You – you are very surprised to see me, Paula, of course.

PAULA: Why are you here? Why aren't you with – your friend?

ELLEAN: I've come home – if you'll have me. We left Paris this morning; Mrs Cortelyon brought me back. She was here a minute or two ago; Papa has just gone with her to The Warren. He asked me to tell you.

PAULA: There are some people staying with us that I'd rather you didn't meet. It was hardly worth your while to return for a few hours.

ELLEAN: A few hours?

PAULA: Well, when do you go to London?

ELLEAN: I don't think I go to London, after all.

PAULA: (*eagerly*) You – you've quarrelled with her?

ELLEAN: No, no, no, not that; but – Paula! (*in an altered tone*) Paula!

PAULA: (*startled*) Eh? (ELLEAN *goes deliberately to* PAULA *and kisses her.*) Ellean!

ELLEAN: Kiss *me*.

PAULA: What – what's come to you?

ELLEAN: I want to behave differently to you in the future. Is it too late?

PAULA: Too – late! (*impulsively kissing* ELLEAN *and crying*) No – no – no! No – no!

ELLEAN: Paula, don't cry

PAULA: (*wiping her eyes*) I'm a little shaky; I haven't been sleeping. It's all right – talk to me.

ELLEAN: (*hesitatingly*) There is something I want to tell you –

PAULA: Is there – is there?

> (*They sit together on the ottoman,* PAULA *taking* ELLEAN'*s hand.*)

ELLEAN: Paula, in our house in the Avenue de Friedland, on the floor below us, there was a Mrs Brereton. She used to be a friend of my mother's. Mrs Cortelyon and I spent a great deal of time with her.

PAULA: (*suspiciously*) Oh! (*letting* ELLEAN'*s hand fall*) Is this lady going to take you up in place of Mrs Cortelyon?

ELLEAN: No, no. Her brother is staying with her – *was* staying with her. Her brother – (*She breaks off in confusion.*)

PAULA: (*looking into her face*) Well?

ELLEAN: (*almost inaudibly*) Paula –

> (*She rises and walks away* PAULA *following her.*)

PAULA: Ellean! (*taking hold of her*) You're not in love! (ELLEAN *looks at* PAULA *appealingly.*) Oh! *You* in love! You! Oh, this is why you've come home! Of course, you can make friends with me now! You'll leave us for good soon, I suppose; so it doesn't much matter being civil to me for a little while!

ELLEAN: Oh, Paula!

PAULA: Why, how you have deceived us – all of us! We've taken you for a cold-blooded little saint. The fools you've made of us! Saint Ellean! Saint Ellean!

ELLEAN: Ah, I might have known you'd only mock me!

PAULA: (*her tone changing*) Eh?

ELLEAN: I – I can't talk to you. (*sitting on the settee*) You do nothing else but mock and sneer, nothing else.

PAULA: Ellean dear! Ellean! I didn't mean it. I'm so horribly jealous, it's a sort of curse on me. (*kneeling beside* ELLEAN *and embracing her*) My tongue runs away with me. I'm going to alter, I swear I am. I've made some good resolutions, and as God's above me, I'll keep them! If you *are* in love, if you *do* ever marry, that's no reason why we shouldn't be fond of each other. Come you've kissed me of your own accord – you can't take it back. Now we're friends again, aren't we? Ellean dear! I want to know everything, everything. Ellean dear, Ellean!

ELLEAN: Paula, Hugh has done something that makes me very angry. He came with us from Paris to-day, to see Papa. He is staying with Mrs Cortelyon and – I ought to tell you –

PAULA: Yes, yes. What?

ELLEAN: He has found his way by The Warren meadow through the plantation up to this house. He is waiting to bid me good night. (*glancing towards the garden*) He is – out there.

PAULA: Oh!

ELLEAN: What shall I do?

PAULA: Bring him to see me! Will you?

ELLEAN: No, no.

PAULA: But I'm dying to know him. Oh, yes, you must. I shall meet him before Aubrey does. (*excitedly running her hands over her hair*) I'm so glad. (ELLEAN *goes out by the window.*) The mirror – mirror. What a fright I must look! (*Not finding the hand-glass on the table, she jumps on to the settee, and surveys herself in the mirror over the mantelpiece, then sits quietly down and waits.*) Ellean! Just fancy! Ellean!

(*After a pause* ELLEAN *enters by the window with* HUGH.)

ELLEAN: Paula, this Captain Ardale – Mrs Tanqueray.

(PAULA *rises and turns, and she and* HUGH *stand staring blankly at each other for a moment or two; then* PAULA *advances and gives him her hand.*)

PAULA: (*in a strange voice, but calmly*) How do you do?

HUGH: How do you do?

PAULA: (*to* ELLEAN) Mr Ardale and I have met in London, Ellean. Er – Captain Ardale, now?

HUGH: Yes.

ELLEAN: In London?

PAULA: They say the world's very small don't they?

HUGH: Yes.

PAULA: Ellean, dear, I want to have a little talk about you to Mr Ardale – Captain Ardale – alone. (*putting her arms round* ELLEAN, *and leading her to the door*) Come back in a little while. (ELLEAN *nods to* PAULA *with a smile and goes out, while* PAULA *stands watching her at the open door.*) In a little while – in a little – (*closing the door and taking a seat facing* HUGH, *who has not moved.*) Be quick! Mr Tanqueray has only gone down to The Warren with Mrs Cortelyon. What is to be done?

HUGH: (*blankly*) Done?

PAULA: Done – done. Something must be done.

HUGH: I understood that Mr Tanqueray had married a Mrs – Mrs –

PAULA: Jarman?

HUGH: Yes.

PAULA: I'd been going by that name. You didn't follow my doings after we
separated.

HUGH: No.

PAULA: (*sneeringly*) No.

HUGH: I went out to India.

PAULA: What's to be done?

HUGH: Damn this chance!

PAULA: Oh, my God!

HUGH: Your husband doesn't know, does he?

PAULA: That you and I – ?

HUGH: Yes.

PAULA: No. He knows about others.

HUGH: Not about me. How long were we – ?

PAULA: I don't remember, exactly.*

HUGH: Do you – do you think it matters?

PAULA: His – his daughter. (*With a muttered exclamation he turns away and sits with
his head in his hands.*) What's to be done?

HUGH: I wish I could think.

PAULA: Oh! Oh! What happened to that flat of ours in Ethelbert Street?

HUGH: I let it.

PAULA: All that pretty furniture?

HUGH: Sold it.

PAULA: I came across the key of the escritoire the other day in an old purse!
(*suddenly realising the horror and hopelessness of her position, and starting to her
feet with an hysterical cry of rage*) What am I maundering about?

HUGH: For God's sake, be quiet! Do let me think.

PAULA: This will send me mad! (*suddenly turning and standing over him*) You – you
beast, to crop up in my life again like this!

HUGH: I always treated you fairly.

PAULA: (*weakly*) Oh! I beg your pardon – I know you did – I –
(*She sinks on to the settee crying hysterically.*)

HUGH: Hush!

PAULA: She kissed me to-night! I'd won her over! I've had such a fight to make her
love me! And now – just as she's beginning to love me, to bring this on her!

HUGH: Hush, hush! Don't break down!

PAULA: (*sobbing*) You don't know! I – I haven't been getting on well in my
marriage. It's been my fault. The life I used to lead spoilt me completely. But I'd
made up my mind to turn over a new life from to-night. From to-night!

HUGH: Paula –

PAULA: Don't you call me that!

HUGH: Mrs Tanqueray, there is no cause for you to despair in this way. It's all right, I
tell you – it *shall* be all right.

---

*MS and PP add:
HUGH: It was only a little while.
PAULA: (*rocking herself to and fro, moaning*) Oh! Oh! Oh!
HUGH: Do you – do you think . . .

PAULA: (*shivering*) What are we to do?

HUGH: Hold our tongues.

PAULA: (*staring vacantly*) Eh?

HUGH: The chances are a hundred to one against any one ever turning up who knew us when we were together. Besides, no one would be such a brute as to split on us. If anybody did do such a thing we should have to lie! What are we upsetting ourselves like this for, when we've simply got to hold our tongues?

PAULA: You're as mad as I am!

HUGH: Can you think of a better plan?

PAULA: There's only one plan possible – let's come to our senses! Mr Tanqueray must be told.

HUGH: Your husband! What, and I lose Ellean! I lose Ellean!

PAULA: You've *got* to lose her.

HUGH: I *won't* lose her! I *can't* lose her!

PAULA: Didn't I read of your doing any number of brave things in India? Why, you seem to be an awful coward!

HUGH: That's another sort of pluck altogether – I haven't this sort of pluck.

PAULA: Oh, I don't ask *you* to tell Mr Tanqueray. That's my job.

HUGH: (*standing over her*) You – you – you'd better! You –

PAULA: (*rising*) Don't bully me! I intend to.

HUGH: (*taking hold of her; she wrenches herself free*) Look here, Paula! I never treated you badly – you've owned it. Why should you want to pay me out like this? You don't know how I love Ellean!

PAULA: Yes, that's just what I *do* know.

HUGH: I say you don't! She's as good as my own mother. I've been downright honest with her too. I told her, in Paris, that I'd been a bit wild at one time, and after a damned wretched day, she promised to forgive me because of what I'd done since in India. She's behaved like an angel to me! Surely I oughtn't to lose her, after all, just because I've been like other fellows! No; I haven't been half as rackety as a hundred men we could think of. Paula, don't pay me out for nothing; be fair to me, there's a good girl – be fair to me!

PAULA: Oh, I'm not considering you at all! I advise you not to stay here any longer; Mr Tanqueray is sure to be back soon.

HUGH: (*taking up his hat*) What's the understanding between us then? What have we arranged to do?

PAULA: I don't know what you're going to do. I've got to tell Mr Tanqueray.

HUGH: (*approaching her fiercely*) By God, you shall do nothing of the sort!

PAULA: You shocking coward!

HUGH: If you dare! (*going up to the window*) Mind! If you dare!

PAULA: (*following him*) Why, what would you do?

HUGH: (*after a short pause, sullenly*) Nothing. I'd shoot myself – that's nothing. Good night.

PAULA: Good night.

> (*He disappears. She walks unsteadily to the ottoman, and sits; and as she does so her hand falls upon the little silver mirror, which she takes up, staring at her own reflection.*)
> END OF ACT THREE

THE FOURTH ACT

The drawing-room at 'Highercoombe', the same evening.
PAULA *is still seated on the ottoman, looking vacantly before her, with the little mirror in her hand.* LADY ORREYED *enters.*
LADY ORREYED: There you are! You never came into the billiard-room. Isn't it maddening – Cayley Drummle gives me sixty out of a hundred and beats me. I must be out of form, because I know I play remarkably well for a lady. Only last month – (PAULA *rises.*) Whatever is the matter with you, old girl?
PAULA: Why?
LADY ORREYED: (*staring*) It's the light, I suppose. (PAULA *replaces the mirror on the table.*) By Aubrey's bolting from the billiard-table in that fashion I thought perhaps –
PAULA: Yes; it's all right.
LADY ORREYED: You've patched it up? (PAULA *nods*). Oh, I am jolly glad – ! (*Kisses her.*) I mean –
PAULA: Yes, I know what you mean. Thanks, Mabel.
LADY ORREYED: Now take my advice; for the future –
PAULA: Mabel, if I've been disagreeable to you while you've been staying here, I – I beg your pardon. (*She walks away and sits.*)
LADY ORREYED: You disagreeable, my dear? I haven't noticed it. Dodo and me both consider you make a first-class hostess, but then you've had such practice, haven't you? (*dropping on to the ottoman and gaping*) Oh, talk about being sleepy – !
PAULA: Why don't you – !
LADY ORREYED: Why, dear, I must hang about for Dodo. You may as well know it; he's in one of his moods.
PAULA: (*under her breath*) Oh – !
LADY ORREYED: Now, it's not his fault; it was deadly dull for him while we were playing billiards. Cayley Drummle did ask him to mark, but I stopped that; it's so easy to make a gentleman look like a billiard-marker. This is just how it always is; if poor old Dodo has nothing to do, he loses count, as you may say.
PAULA: Hark!
          (SIR GEORGE ORREYED *enters, walking slowly and deliberately; he looks pale and watery-eyed.*)
SIR GEORGE: (*with mournful indistinctness*) I'm 'fraid we've lef' you a grea' deal to yourself to-night, Mrs Tanqueray. Attra'tions of billiards. I apol'gise. I say, where's ol' Aubrey?
PAULA: My husband has been obliged to go out to a neighbour's house.
SIR GEORGE: I want his advice on a rather pressing matter connected with my family – my family. (*sitting*) To-morrow will do just as well.
LADY ORREYED: (*to* PAULA) This is the mood I hate so – drivelling about his precious family.
SIR GEORGE: The fact is, Mrs Tanqueray, I am not easy in my min' 'bout the way I am treatin' my poor ol' mother.
LADY ORREYED: (*to* PAULA) Do you hear that? That's *his* mother, but *my* mother he won't so much as look at!

SIR GEORGE: I shall write to Bruton Street firs' thing in the morning.

LADY ORREYED: (*to* PAULA) Mamma has stuck to me through everything – well, you know!

SIR GEORGE: I'll get ol' Aubrey to figure out a letter. I'll drop a line to Uncle Fitz too – dooced shame of the ol' feller to chuck me over in this manner. (*wiping his eyes*) All my family have chucked me over.

LADY ORREYED: (*rising*) Dodo!

SIR GEORGE: Jus' because I've married beneath me, to be chucked over! Aunt Lydia, the General, Hooky Whitgrave, Lady Sugnall – my own dear sister! – all turn their backs on me. It's more than I can stan'!

LADY ORREYED: (*approaching nearer to him with dignity*) Sir George, wish Mrs Tanqueray good night at once and come upstairs. Do you hear me?

SIR GEORGE: (*rising angrily*) Wha' –

LADY ORREYED: Be quiet.

SIR GEORGE: You presoom to order me about!

LADY ORREYED: You're making an exhibition of yourself!

SIR GEORGE: Look 'ere – !

LADY ORREYED: Come along, I tell you!

> (*He hesitates, utters a few inarticulate sounds, then snatches up a fragile ornament from the table, and is about to dash it on to the ground.* LADY ORREYED *retreats, and* PAULA *goes to him.*)

PAULA: George!

> (*He replaces the ornament.*)

SIR GEORGE: (*shaking* PAULA's *hand*) Good ni', Mrs Tanqueray.

LADY ORREYED: (*to* PAULA) Good night, darling. Wish Aubrey good night for me. Now, Dodo?

> (*She goes out.*)

SIR GEORGE: (*to* PAULA) I say, are you goin' to sit up for ol' Aubrey?

PAULA: Yes.

SIR GEORGE: Shall I keep you comp'ny?

PAULA: No, thank you, George.

SIR GEORGE: Sure?

PAULA: Yes, sure.

SIR GEORGE: (*shaking hands*). Good night again.

PAULA: Good night.

> (*She turns away. He goes out, steadying himself carefully.* DRUMMLE *appears outside the window with a cap on his head and smoking.*)

DRUMMLE: (*looking into the room, and seeing* PAULA) My last cigar. Where's Aubrey?

PAULA: Gone down to The Warren, to see Mrs Cortelyon home.

DRUMMLE: (*entering the room*). Eh? Did you say Mrs Cortelyon?

PAULA: Yes. She has brought Ellean back.

DRUMMLE: Bless my soul! Why?

PAULA: I – I'm too tired to tell you, Cayley. If you stroll along the lane you'll meet Aubrey. Get the news from him.

DRUMMLE: (*going to the window*) Yes, yes. (*returning to* PAULA) I don't want to bother you, only – the anxious old woman, you know. Are you and Aubrey – ?

PAULA: Good friends again?
DRUMMLE: (*nodding*) Um.
PAULA: (*giving him her hand*) Quite, Cayley, quite.
DRUMMLE: (*retaining her hand*) That's capital. As I'm off so early to-morrow
morning, let me say now – thank you for your hospitality.
(*He bends over her hand gallantly, then goes out by the window.*)
PAULA: (*to herself*) 'Are you and Aubrey – ?' 'Good friends again?' 'Yes.' 'Quite,
Cayley, quite.'
(*There is a brief pause, then* AUBREY *enters hurriedly, wearing a light
overcoat and carrying a cap.*)
AUBREY: Paula dear! Have you seen Ellean?
PAULA: I found her here when I came down.
AUBREY: She – she's told you?
PAULA: Yes, Aubrey.
AUBREY: It's extraordinary, isn't it! Not that somebody should fall in love with
Ellean or that Ellean herself should fall in love. All that's natural enough and
was bound to happen, I suppose, sooner or later. But this young fellow! You
know his history?
PAULA: (*startled*) His history?
AUBREY: You remember the papers were full of his name a few months ago?
PAULA: Oh, yes.
AUBREY: The man's as brave as a lion, there's no doubt about that; and, at the same
time, he's like a big good-natured schoolboy, Mrs Cortelyon says. Have you
ever pictured the kind of man Ellean would marry some day?
PAULA: I can't say that I have.
AUBREY: A grave, sedate fellow I've thought about – hah! She has fallen in love
with the way in which Ardale practically laid down his life to save those poor
people shut up in the Residency. (*taking off his coat*) Well, I suppose if a man
can do that sort of thing, one ought to be content. And yet – (*throwing his coat
on the settee*) I should have met him to-night, but he'd gone out. Paula dear, tell
me how you look upon this business.
PAULA: Yes, I will – I must. To begin with, I – I've seen Mr Ardale.
AUBREY: Captain Ardale?
PAULA: Captain Ardale.
AUBREY: Seen him?
PAULA: While you were away he came up here, through our grounds, to try to get a
word with Ellean. I made her fetch him in and present him to me.
AUBREY: (*frowning*) Doesn't Captain Ardale know there's a lodge and a front door
to this place? Never mind! What is your impression of him?
PAULA: Aubrey, do you recollect my bringing you a letter – a letter giving you an
account of myself – to the Albany late one night – the night before we got
married?
AUBREY: A letter?
PAULA: You burnt it; don't you know?

Residency, i.e. the British Resident's official address.

AUBREY: Yes; I know.

PAULA: His name was in that letter.

AUBREY: (*going back from her slowly, and staring at her*) I don't understand.

PAULA: (*with forced calmness*) Well – Ardale and I once kept house together. (*He remains silent, not moving.*) Why don't you strike me? Hit me in the face – I'd rather you did! Hurt me! hurt me!

AUBREY: (*after a pause*) What did you – and this man – say to each other – just now?

PAULA: I – hardly – know.

AUBREY: Think!

PAULA: The end of it all was that I – I told him I must inform you of – what had happened . . . he didn't want me to do that . . . I declared I would . . . he dared me to. (*breaking down*) Let me alone! – oh!

AUBREY: Where was my daughter while this went on?

PAULA: I – I had sent her out of the room . . . that is all right.

AUBREY: Yes, yes – yes, yes.

(*He turns his head towards the door.*)

PAULA: (*nervously*) Who's that?

(*A* SERVANT *enters with a letter.*)

SERVANT: The coachman has just run up with this from The Warren, sir.

(AUBREY *takes the letter.*) It's for Mrs Tanqueray, sir; there's no answer.

(*The* SERVANT *withdraws.* AUBREY *goes to* PAULA *and drops the letter into her lap; she opens it with uncertain hands.*)

PAULA: (*reading it to herself*) It's from – him. He's going away – or gone – I think. (*rising in a weak way*) What does it say? I never could make out his writing.

(*She gives the letter to* AUBREY *and stands near him looking at the letter over his shoulder as he reads.*)

AUBREY: (*reading*) 'I shall be in Paris by to-morrow evening. Shall wait there, at Meurice's, for a week, ready to receive any communication you or your husband may address to me. Please invent some explanation to Ellean. Mrs Tanqueray, for God's sake, do what you can for me.'

(PAULA *and* AUBREY *speak in low voices, both still looking at the letter.*)

PAULA: Has he left The Warren, I wonder, already?

AUBREY: That doesn't matter.

PAULA: No, but I can picture him going quietly off. Very likely he's walking on to Bridgeford or Cottering to-night, to get the first train in the morning. A pleasant stroll for him.

AUBREY: We'll reckon he's gone, that's enough.

PAULA: That isn't to be answered in any way?

AUBREY: Silence will answer that.

PAULA: He'll soon recover his spirits, I know.

AUBREY: You know. (*offering her the letter*) You don't want this, I suppose?

PAULA: No.

AUBREY: It's done with – done with.

(*He tears the letter into small pieces. She has dropped the envelope; she searches for it, finds it, and gives it to him.*)

PAULA: Here!

AUBREY: (*looking at the remnants of the letter*) This is no good; I must burn it.
PAULA: Burn it in your room.
AUBREY: Yes.
PAULA: Put it in your pocket for now.
AUBREY: Yes.
>   (*He does so.* ELLEAN *enters and they both turn, guiltily, and stare at her.*)
ELLEAN: (*after a short silence, wonderingly*) Papa –
AUBREY: What do you want, Ellean?
ELLEAN: I heard from Willis that you had come in; I only want to wish you good-night. (PAULA *steals away without looking back.*) What's the matter? Ah! Of course, Paula has told you about Captain Ardale?
AUBREY: Well?
ELLEAN: Have you and he met?
AUBREY: No.
ELLEAN: You are angry with him; so was I. But to-morrow when he calls and expresses his regret – to-morrow –
AUBREY: Ellean – Ellean!
ELLEAN: Yes, Papa?
AUBREY: I – I can't let you see this man again. (*He walks away from her in a paroxysm of distress, then, after a moment or two, he returns to her and takes her to his arms.*) Ellean! my child!
ELLEAN: (*releasing herself*) What has happened, Papa? What is it?
AUBREY: (*thinking out his words deliberately*) Something has occurred, something has come to my knowledge, in relation to Captain Ardale, which puts any further acquaintanceship between you two out of the question.
ELLEAN: Any further acquaintanceship . . . out of the question?
AUBREY: Yes.
>   (*He advances to her quickly, but she shrinks from him.*)
ELLEAN: No, no – I am quite well. (*after a short pause*) It's not an hour ago since Mrs Cortelyon left you and me together here; you had nothing to urge against Captain Ardale then.
AUBREY: No.
ELLEAN: You don't know each other; you haven't even seen him this evening. Father!
AUBREY: I have told you he and I have not met.
ELLEAN: Mrs Cortelyon couldn't have spoken against him to you just now. No, no, no; she's too good a friend to both of us. Aren't you going to give me some explanation? You can't take this position towards me – towards Captain Ardale – without affording me the fullest explanation.
AUBREY: Ellean, there are circumstances connected with Captain Ardale's career which you had better remain ignorant of. It must be sufficient for you that I consider these circumstances render him unfit to be your husband
ELLEAN: Father!
AUBREY: You must trust me, Ellean; you must try to understand the depth of my love for you and the – the agony it gives me to hurt you. You must trust me.

ELLEAN: I will, Father; but you must trust me a little too. Circumstances connected with Captain Ardale's career?

AUBREY: Yes.

ELLEAN: When he presents himself here to-morrow of course you will see him and let him defend himself?

AUBREY: Captain Ardale will not be here tomorrow.

ELLEAN: Not! You have stopped his coming here?

AUBREY: Indirectly – yes.

ELLEAN: But just now he was talking to me at that window! Nothing had taken place then! And since then nothing can have – ! Oh! Why – you have heard something against him from Paula.

AUBREY: From – Paula!

ELLEAN: She knows him.

AUBREY: She has told you so?

ELLEAN: When I introduced Captain Ardale to her she said she had met him in London. Of course! It is Paula who has done this!

AUBREY: (*in a hard voice*) I – I hope you – you'll refrain from rushing at conclusions. There's nothing to be gained by trying to avoid the main point, which is that you must drive Captain Ardale out of your thoughts. Understand that! You're able to obtain comfort from your religion, aren't you? I'm glad to think that's so. I talk to you in a harsh way, Ellean, but I feel your pain almost as acutely as you do. (*going to the door*) I – I can't say anything more to you to-night.

ELLEAN: Father! (*He pauses at the door.*) Father, I'm obliged to ask you this; there's no help for it – I've no mother to go to. Does what you have heard about Captain Ardale concern the time when he led a wild, a dissolute life in London?

AUBREY: (*returning to her slowly and staring at her*) Explain yourself!

ELLEAN: He has been quite honest with me. One day – in Paris – he confessed to me – what a man's life is – what his life had been –

AUBREY: (*under his breath*) Oh!

ELLEAN: He offered to go away, not to approach me again.

AUBREY: And you – you accepted his view of what a man's life is!*

ELLEAN: As far as *I* could forgive him, I forgave him.

AUBREY: (*with a groan*) Why, when was it you left us? It hasn't taken you long to get your robe 'just a little dusty at the hem'!

ELLEAN: What do you mean?

AUBREY: Hah! A few weeks ago my one great desire was to keep you ignorant of evil.

ELLEAN: Father, it is impossible to be ignorant of evil. Instinct, common instinct, teaches us what is good and bad. Surely I am none the worse for knowing what is wicked and detesting it!

AUBREY: *Detesting* it! Why, you *love* this fellow!

---

*MS and PP add: You accepted it without a murmur, with a smile perhaps?
ELLEAN: Father!
AUBREY: Well!

ELLEAN: Ah, you don't understand! I have simply judged Captain Ardale as we all pray to be judged. I have lived in imagination through that one week in India when he deliberately offered his life back to God to save those wretched, desperate people. In his whole career I see now nothing but that one week; those few hours bring him nearer the Saints, I believe, than fifty uneventful years of mere blamelessness would have done! And so, Father, if Paula has reported anything to Captain Ardale's discredit –

AUBREY: Paula – !

ELLEAN: It *must* be Paula; it can't be anybody else.

AUBREY: You – you'll please keep Paula out of the question. Finally, Ellean, understand me – I have made up my mind. (*again going to the door*)

ELLEAN: But wait – listen! I have made up my mind also.

AUBREY: Ah! I recognise your mother in you now!

ELLEAN: You need not speak against my mother because you are angry with me!

AUBREY: I – I hardly know what I'm saying to you. In the morning – in the morning – (*Moves to the door.*)

> (*He goes out. She remains standing and turns her head to listen. Then, after a moment's hesitation, she goes softly to the window and looks out under the verandah.*)

ELLEAN: (*in a whisper*) Paula! Paula!

> (PAULA *appears outside the window and steps into the room; her face is white and drawn, her hair is a little disordered.*)

PAULA: (*huskily*) Well?

ELLEAN: Have you been under the verandah all the while – listening?

PAULA: N – no.

ELLEAN: You *have* overheard us – I see you have. And it *is* you who have been speaking to my father against Captain Ardale. Isn't it? Paula, why don't you own it or deny it?

PAULA: Oh, I – I don't mind owning it; why should I?

ELLEAN: Ah! You seem to have been very, very eager to tell your tale.

PAULA: No, I wasn't eager, Ellean. I'd have given something not to have had to do it. I wasn't eager.

ELLEAN: Not! Oh, I think you might safely have spared us all for a little while.

PAULA: But, Ellean, you forget I – I am your stepmother. It was my – my duty – to tell your father what I – what I knew –

ELLEAN: What you knew! Why, after all, what can you know! You can only speak from gossip, report, hearsay! How is it possible that you – ! (*She stops abruptly. The two women stand staring at each other for a moment; then* ELLEAN *backs away from* PAULA *slowly.*) Paula!

PAULA: What – what's the matter?

ELLEAN: You – you knew Captain Ardale in London!

PAULA: Why – what do you mean?

ELLEAN: Oh!

> (*She makes for the door, but* PAULA *turns and catches her by the wrist.*)

PAULA: You shall tell me what you mean!

ELLEAN: Ah! (*suddenly looking fixedly in* PAULA's *face*) You *know* what I mean.

PAULA: You accuse me!

ELLEAN: It's in your face!

PAULA: (*hoarsely*) You – you think I'm – that sort of creature, do you?

ELLEAN: Let me go!

PAULA: Answer me! You've always hated me! (*shaking her*) Out with it!

ELLEAN: You hurt me!

PAULA: You've always hated me! You shall answer me!

ELLEAN: Well, then, I have always – always –

PAULA: What?

ELLEAN: I have always known what you were!

PAULA: Ah! Who – who told you?

ELLEAN: Nobody but yourself. From the first moment I saw you I knew you were altogether unlike the good women I'd left; directly I saw you I knew what my father had done. You've wondered why I've turned from you! There – that's the reason! Oh, but this is a horrible way for the truth to come home to every one! Oh!

PAULA: It's a lie! It's all a lie! (*forcing* ELLEAN *down upon her knees*) You shall beg my pardon for it. (ELLEAN *utters a loud shriek of terror.*) Ellean, I'm a good woman! I swear I am! I've always been a good woman! You dare to say I've ever been anything else! (*throwing her off violently*) It's a lie!

(AUBREY *re-enters.*)

AUBREY: Paula! (PAULA *staggers back as* AUBREY *advances. Raising* ELLEAN) What's this? What's this?

ELLEAN: (*faintly*) Nothing. (*She goes round the ottoman and leans upon it.*) It – it's my fault. Father, I – I don't wish to see Captain Ardale again.

(*She goes out,* AUBREY *slowly following her to the door.*)

PAULA: Aubrey, she – she guesses.

AUBREY: Guesses?

PAULA: About me – and Ardale.

AUBREY: About you – and Ardale?

PAULA: She says she suspected my character from the beginning . . . that's why she's always kept me at a distance . . . and now she sees through –

(*She falters; he helps her to the ottoman where she sits.*)

AUBREY: (*bending over her*) Paula, you must have said something – admitted something –

PAULA: I don't think so.* It – it's in my face.

AUBREY: What?

PAULA: She tells me so. She's right! I'm tainted through and through; anybody can see it, anybody can find it out. You said much the same to me to-night.

MS reads:

PAULA: I don't think so. Only – my face!

AUBREY: What?

PAULA: It's in my face, she says – in my face!

AUBREY: (*half to himself, as if dazed*) We – we must take steps to – what shall we do? We can't let matters remain as they are. If she has got this idea in her head, we had better – better – what – what?

PAULA: Ellean! So meek . . . [as on p. 128]

AUBREY: (*partly to himself, as if dazed*) If she has got this idea into her head we must drive it out, that's all. We must take steps to – What shall we do? We had better – better – (*sitting and staring before him*) What – what?

PAULA: Ellean! So meek, so demure! You've often said she reminded you of her mother. Yes, I know now what your first marriage was like.

AUBREY: We must drive this idea out of her head. We'll do something. What shall we do?

PAULA: She's a regular woman too. She could forgive *him* easily enough – but *me*! That's just a woman!

AUBREY: What *can* we do?

PAULA: Why, nothing! She'd have no difficulty in following up her suspicions. Suspicions! You should have seen how she looked at me!(*He buries his head in his hands. There is silence for a time, then she rises slowly and sits beside him.*) Aubrey!

AUBREY: Yes.

(*She looks at him pityingly.*)

PAULA: (*moving slightly*) I'm very sorry.

(*Without meeting her eyes, he lays his hands on her arm for a moment.*)

AUBREY: Well, we must look things straight in the face. At any rate, we've done with this.

PAULA: I suppose so. (*after a brief pause*) Of course, she and I can't live under the same roof any more. You know she kissed me to-night, of her own accord.

AUBREY: I asked her to alter towards you.

PAULA: That was it, then.

AUBREY: I – I'm sorry I sent her away.

PAULA: It was my fault; I made it necessary.

AUBREY: Perhaps now she'll propose to return to the convent, – well, she must.

PAULA: Would you like to keep her with you and – and leave me?

AUBREY: Paula – !

PAULA: You needn't be afraid I'd go back to – what I was. I couldn't.

AUBREY: Sssh, for God's sake! We – you and I – we'll get out of this place . . . what a fool I was to come here again!

PAULA: You lived here with your first wife!

AUBREY: We'll get out of this place and go abroad again, and begin afresh.

PAULA: Begin afresh?

AUBREY: There's no reason why the future shouldn't be happy for us – no reason that I can see –

PAULA: Aubrey!

AUBREY: Yes?

PAULA: You'll never forget this, you know.

AUBREY: This?

PAULA: To-night, and everything that's led up to it. Our coming here, Ellean, our quarrels – cat and dog! Mrs Cortelyon, the Orreyeds, this man! What an everlasting nightmare for you!

AUBREY: Oh, we can forget it, if we choose.

PAULA: That was always your cry. How *can* one do it?

AUBREY: We'll make our calculations solely for the future, talk, about the future, think about the future.

PAULA: I believe the future is only the past again, entered through another gate.

AUBREY: That's an awful belief.

PAULA: To-night proves it. You must see now that, do what we will, go where we will, you'll be continually reminded of – what I was. I see it.

AUBREY: You're frightened to-night; meeting this man has frightened you. But that sort of thing isn't likely to recur. The world isn't quite so small as all that.

PAULA: Isn't it! The only great distances it contains are those we carry within ourselves – the distances that separate husbands and wives, for instance. And so it'll be with us. You'll do your best – oh, I know that – you're a good fellow. But the circumstances will be too strong for you in the end, mark my words.

AUBREY: Paula – !

PAULA: Of course I'm pretty now – I'm pretty still – and a pretty woman, whatever else she may be, is always – well, endurable. But even now I notice that the lines of my face are getting deeper; so are the hollows about my eyes. Yes, my face is covered with little shadows that usen't to be there. Oh, I know I'm 'going off'. I hate paint and dye and those messes, but, by and by, I shall drift the way of the others; I shan't be able to help myself. And then, some day – perhaps very suddenly, under a queer, fantastic light at night or in the glare of the morning – that horrid, irresistible truth that physical repulsion forces on men and women will come to you, and you'll sicken at me.

AUBREY: I – !

PAULA: *You'll see me then, at last, with other people's eyes; you'll see me just as your daughter does now, as all wholesome folks see women like me. And I shall have no weapon to fight with – not one serviceable little bit of prettiness left me to defend myself with!† A worn out creature – broken up, very likely, some time before I ought to be – my hair bright, my eyes dull, my body too thin or too stout, my cheeks raddled and ruddled – a ghost, a wreck, a caricature, a candle that gutters, call such an end what you like! Oh, Aubrey, what shall I be able to say to you then? And this is the future you talk about! I know it – I know it! (*He is still sitting staring forward; she rocks herself to and fro as if in pain.*) Oh, Aubrey! Oh! Oh!

AUBREY: Paula – ! (*trying to comfort her*)

PAULA: (*with a moan*). Oh, and I wanted so much to sleep to-night! (*laying her head upon his shoulder. From the distance, in the garden, there comes the sound of* DRUMMLE's *voice; he is singing as he approaches the house.*) That's Cayley, coming back from The Warren. (*starting up*) He doesn't know, evidently. I – I won't see him!

---

*MS adds: You'll see a worn-out creature – broken up very likely, some time before she ought to be – her hair too bright, her eyes too dull, her body too thin or too stout, her cheeks raddled and ruddled. You'll see me then . . .

†MS reads: And it's an end that must come to women who've led my life – there's no dignity in old age for us. We may thank our stars if it's no worse than I've just pictured it. Aubrey – Aubrey – that is my future! Oh, Aubrey . . .

(*She goes out quickly.* DRUMMLE's *voice comes nearer.* AUBREY *rouses himself and snatches up a book from the table, making a pretence of reading. After a moment or two,* DRUMMLE *appears at the window and looks in.*)

DRUMMLE: Aha! my dear chap!

AUBREY: Cayley?

DRUMMLE: (*coming into the room*) I went down to The Warren after you.

AUBREY: Yes?

DRUMMLE: Missed you. Well? I've been gossiping with Mrs Cortelyon. Confound you, I've heard the news!

AUBREY: What have you heard?

DRUMMLE: What have I heard! Why – Ellean and young Ardale! (*looking at* AUBREY *keenly*) My dear Aubrey! Alice is under the impression that you are inclined to look on the affair favourably.

AUBREY: (*rising and advancing to* DRUMMLE) You've not – met Captain Ardale?

DRUMMLE: No. Why do you ask? By and by, I don't know that I need tell you – but it's rather strange. He's not at The Warren to-night.

AUBREY: No?

DRUMMLE: He left the house half an hour ago to stroll about the lanes; just now a note came from him, a scribble in pencil, simply telling Alice that she would receive a letter from him to-morrow. What's the matter? There's nothing very wrong, is there? My dear chap, pray forgive me if I'm asking too much.

AUBREY: Cayley, you – you urged me to send her away!

DRUMMLE: Ellean! Yes, yes. But – but – by all accounts this is quite an eligible young fellow. Alice has been giving me the history –

AUBREY: Curse him! (*hurling his book to the floor*) Curse him! Yes, I do curse him – him and his class! Perhaps I curse myself too in doing it. He has only led 'a man's life' – just as I, how many of us, have done! The misery he has brought on me and mine it's likely enough we, in our time, have helped to bring on others by this leading 'a man's life'! But I do curse him for all that. My God, *I've* nothing more to fear – I've paid *my* fine! And so I can curse him in safety. Curse him! Curse him!

DRUMMLE: In Heaven's name, tell me what's happened?

AUBREY: (*gripping* DRUMMLE's *arm*) Paula! Paula!

DRUMMLE: What?

AUBREY: They met to-night here. They – they – they're not strangers to each other.

DRUMMLE: Aubrey!

AUBREY: Curse him! My poor, wretched wife! My poor, wretched wife!

(*The door opens and* ELLEAN *appears. The two men turn to her. There is a moment's silence.*)

ELLEAN: Father . . . father . . .!

AUBREY: Ellean?

ELLEAN: I – I want you. (*He goes to her.*) Father . . . go to Paula! (*He looks into her face, startled.*) Quickly – quickly! (*He passes her to go out, she seizes his arm, with a cry.*) No, no; don't go!

(*He shakes her off and goes.* ELLEAN *staggers back towards* DRUMMLE.)

DRUMMLE: (*to* ELLEAN) What do you mean? What do you mean?

ELLEAN: I – I went to her room – to tell her I was sorry for something I had said to
 her. And I *was* sorry – I *was* sorry. I heard the fall. I – I've seen her. It's
 horrible.

DRUMMLE: She – she has – !

ELLEAN: Killed – herself? Yes – yes. So everybody will say. But I know – I helped to
 kill her. If I had only been merciful! (*She beats her breast.*)

  (**She faints upon the ottoman. He pauses for a moment irresolutely –
  then he goes to the door, opens it, and stands looking out.*)†
  THE END

---

*MS reads: She faints; he catches her and places her upon the ottoman. He pauses for a moment
irresolutely – then he goes to the bell and rings it.*
PP reads: *She faints upon the ottoman. He pauses for a moment irresolutely – then he goes to the
door, opens it, and stands looking out.*
†MS and PP add: DRUMMLE: (*as he does so*) And I – I've been hard on this woman! Good
God, men are hard on all women!

TRELAWNY OF THE 'WELLS'

An original comedietta in four acts

First produced at the Royal Court Theatre, London, on 20 January 1898, with the following cast:

Theatrical Folk

JAMES TELFER			Mr Athol Forde
AUGUSTUS COLPOYS			Mr E. M. Robson
FERDINAND GADD	(of the		Mr G. du Maurier
TOM WRENCH	Bagnigge-		Mr Paul Arthur
MRS TELFER (MISS VIOLET SYLVESTER)	Wells Theatre)		Mrs E. Saker
AVONIA BUNN			Miss Pattie Browne
ROSE TRELAWNY			Miss Irene Vanbrugh

IMOGEN PARROTT (of the Royal Olympic
Theatre)   Miss Hilda Spong
O'DWYER (Prompter at the Pantheon Theatre)   Mr Richard Purdon

MEMBERS OF THE COMPANY OF THE
PANTHEON THEATRE   Mr Vernon, Mr Foster, Mr Mellon and Miss Baird

HALL-KEEPER AT THE PANTHEON   Mr W. H. Quinton

Non-theatrical Folk

VICE-CHANCELLOR SIR WILLIAM
GOWER, KNT   Mr Dion Boucicault
ARTHUR GOWER   (his grandchildren)   Mr James Erskine
CLARA DE FŒNIX   Miss Eva Williams
MISS TRAFALGAR GOWER (Sir William's
sister)   Miss Isabel Bateman
CAPTAIN DE FŒNIX (Clara's husband)   Mr Sam Sothern
MRS MOSSOP   Miss Le Thière
MR ABLETT   Mr Fred Thorne
CHARLES   Mr Aubrey Fitzgerald
SARAH   Miss Polly Emery

'Oh, my dears – ! let us – get on with the rehearsal – !'

III *Trelawny of the 'Wells'*, 1898. The closing moment of the play. This shows Pinero's original view for Act IV: 'The stage of a theatre, with the proscenium arch and the dark and empty auditorium in the

A DIRECTION TO THE STAGE MANAGER

The costumes and scenic decoration of this little play should follow, to the closest detail, the mode of the early 'sixties – the period, in dress, of crinoline and the peg-top trouser; in furniture, of horsehair and mahogany, and the abominable 'walnut-and-rep'. No attempt should be made to modify such fashions in illustration, to render them less strange, even less grotesque, to the modern eye. On the contrary, there should be an endeavour to reproduce, perhaps to accentuate, any feature which may now seem particularly quaint and bizarre. Thus, lovely youth should be shown decked uncompromisingly at it was at the time indicated, at the risk (which the author believes to be a slight one) of pointing the chastening moral that, while beauty fades assuredly in its own time, it may appear to succeeding generations not to have been beauty at all.

NOTE

On the occasion of the revival of the Old Vic* I struck out all mention of Bagnigge-Wells from the programme and frankly described the Company of the 'Wells' as 'of Sadler's-Wells Theatre'. Also, in Act I, I further gave up disguise by making Mrs Mossop speak of Rose Trelawny as 'the best juvenile-lady the "Wells" has known since Mr Phelps's management'.

A. P.

---

*Opening on 1 June 1925

THE FIRST ACT

The scene represents a sitting-room on the first floor of a respectable lodging-house. On the right are two sash-windows, having Venetian blinds and giving a view of houses on the other side of the street. The grate of the fireplace is hidden by an ornament composed of shavings and paper roses. Over the fireplace is a mirror, and on each side of the fireplace a sideboard-cupboard. On the left is a door; a landing is seen outside. Between the windows stand a cottage-piano and a piano-stool. On the wall, above the piano, hangs a small looking-glass. Above the sofa on the left stands a large black trunk, the lid bulging with its contents, and displaying some soiled theatrical finery. On the front of the trunk, in faded lettering, appear the words 'Miss Violet Sylvester, Theatre Royal, Drury Lane'. Under the sofa there are two or three pairs of ladies' satin shoes, much the worse for wear, and on the sofa a white-satin bodice, yellow with age, a heap of dog-eared playbooks, and some other litter of a like character. On the top of the piano there is a wig-block with a man's wig upon it, and in the corners of the room there stand some walking-sticks and a few theatrical swords. In the centre of the stage is a large circular table. There is a clean cover upon it, and on the top of the sideboard-cupboards are knives and forks, with black handles, plate, glass, cruet-stands, and some gaudy flowers in vases – all suggesting preparations for festivity.

The woodwork of the room is grained, the ceiling plainly white-washed, and the wallpaper is of a neutral tint and much faded. The pictures are engravings in maple frames, and a portrait or two in oil, framed in gilt. The furniture, curtains, and carpet are worn, but everything is clean and well kept.

The light is that of afternoon in early summer.

MRS MOSSOP – *a portly, middle-aged Jewish lady, elaborately attired – is left of the table laying the tablecloth.* ABLETT *enters hastily left, divesting himself of his coat as he does so. He is dressed in rusty black for 'waiting'.*

MRS MOSSOP: (*in a fluster*) Oh, here you are, Mr Ablett – !

ABLETT: Good day, Mrs Mossop.

MRS MOSSOP: (*bringing the cruet-stands*) I declare I thought you'd forgotten me.

ABLETT: (*hanging his coat upon a curtain-knob, and turning up his shirt-sleeves*) I'd begun to fear I should never escape from the shop, ma'am. Jest as I was preparing' to clean myself, the 'ole universe seemed to cry aloud for pertaters. (*relieving* MRS MOSSOP *of the cruet-stands, and satisfying himself as to the contents of the various bottles*) Now, you take a seat, Mrs Mossop. You 'ave but to say 'Mr Ablett, lay for so many', and the exact number shall be laid for.

MRS MOSSOP: (*sinking into the armchair*) I hope the affliction of short breath may be spared you, Ablett. Ten is the number.

ABLETT: (*whipping-up the mustard energetically*) Short-breathed you may be, ma'am, but not short-sighted. That gal of yours is no ordinary gal, but to 'ave set 'er to wait on ten persons would 'ave been to 'ave caught disaster. (*bringing knives and forks, glasses etc., and glancing round the room*) I am in Mr and Mrs Telfer's setting-room, I believe, ma'am?

MRS MOSSOP: (*surveying the apartment complacently*) And what a handsomely proportioned room it is, to be sure!

ABLETT: May I h'ask if I am to 'ave the honour of includin' my triflin' fee for this job in their weekly book?

MRS MOSSOP: No, Ablett – a separate bill, please. The Telfers kindly give the use of their apartment, to save the cost of holding the ceremony at the 'Clown' Tavern; but share and share alike over the expenses is to be the order of the day.

ABLETT: I thank you, ma'am. (*rubbing up the knives with a napkin*) You let fall the word 'ceremony', ma'am –

MRS MOSSOP: Ah, Ablett, and a sad one – a farewell cold collation to Miss Trelawny.

ABLETT: Lor' bless me! I 'eard a rumour –

MRS MOSSOP: A true rumour. She's taking her leave of us, the dear.

ABLETT: This will be a blow to the 'Wells', ma'am.

MRS MOSSOP: The best juvenile-lady the 'Wells' has known since Mr Phelps's management.

ABLETT: Report 'as it, a love affair, ma'am.

MRS MOSSOP: A love affair, indeed! And a poem into the bargain, Ablett, if poet was at hand to write it.

ABLETT. Reelly, Mrs Mossop! (*polishing a tumbler*) Is the beer to be bottled or draught, ma'am, on this occasion?

MRS MOSSOP: Draught for Miss Trelawny, invariably.

ABLETT: Then draught it must be all round, out of compliment. Jest fancy! nevermore to 'ear customers speak of Trelawny of the 'Wells', except as a pleasin' memory! A non-professional gentleman they give out, ma'am.

MRS MOSSOP: Yes.

ABLETT: Name of Glover.

MRS MOSSOP: Gower, Grandson of Vice-Chancellor Sir William Gower, Mr Ablett.

ABLETT: You don't say, ma'am!

MRS MOSSOP: No father nor mother, and lives in Cavendish Square with the old judge and a great aunt.

ABLETT: Then Miss Trelawny quits the Profession, ma'am, for good and all, I presoom?

MRS MOSSOP: Yes, Ablett* She played last night for the last time – the last time on the stage. (*rising and going to the sideboard-cupboard*)†

ABLETT: And when is the weddin' to be, ma'am?

MRS MOSSOP: It's not yet decided, Mr Ablett. In point of fact, before the Gower family positively say Yes to the union, Miss Trelawny is to make her home in Cavendish Square for a short term – 'short term' is the Gower family's own

---

Mr Phelps: Samuel Phelps, leading Victorian actor, was manager of Sadler's Wells from 1843 to 1862.

Vice-Chancellor: 'One of the higher judges in the former Court of Chancery (merged with the Supreme Court in 1876)'. (*OED*)

*Heinemann (1899) (H) adds:
Yes, Ablett, she's at the theaytre at this moment, distributing some of her little ornaments and fallals among the ballet. She played last night . . .

†H adds:
And without so much as a line in the bill to announce it. What a benefit she might have taken!
ABLETT: I know one who was good for two box tickets, Mrs Mossop.
MRS MOSSOP: But no. 'No fuss', said the Gower family, 'no publicity. Withdraw quietly' – that was the Gower family's injunctions – 'withdraw quietly, and have done with it'.
ABLETT: And when is the weddin' to be . . .

expression – in order to habituate herself to the West End. They're sending their carriage for her at two o'clock this afternoon, Mr Ablett – their carriage and pair of bay horses.

ABLETT: Well, I dessay a West End life has sooperior advantages over the Profession in some respecks, Mrs Mossop.

MRS MOSSOP: When accompanied by wealth, Mr Ablett. Here's Miss Trelawny but nineteen, and in a month-or-two's time she'll be ordering about her own powdered footman, and playing on her grand piano. How many actresses do *that*, I should like to know!

(TOM WRENCH's *voice is heard.*)

TOM: (*outside the door*) Rebecca! Rebecca, my loved one!

MRS MOSSOP: Oh, go along with you, Mr Wrench!

(TOM *enters, with a pair of scissors in his hand. He is a shabbily dressed, ungraceful man of about thirty, with a clean-shaven face, curly hair, and eyes full of good-humour.*)

TOM: My own, especial Rebecca!

MRS MOSSOP: Don't be a fool, Mr Wrench! Now, I've no time to waste. I know you want somethin –

TOM: Everything, adorable. But most desperately do I stand in need of a little skilful trimming at your fair hands.

MRS MOSSOP: (*taking the scissors from him and clipping the frayed edges of his shirt-cuffs and collar*) First it's patching a coat, and then it's binding an Inverness – ! Sometimes I wish that top room of mine was empty.

TOM: And sometimes I wish my heart was empty, cruel Rebecca.

MRS MOSSOP: (*giving him a thump*) Now, I really will tell Mossop of you, when he comes home! (*She turns* TOM *round to trim the back of his collar.*) I've often threatened it –

TOM (*to* ABLETT) Whom do I see! No – it can't be – but yes – I believe I have the privilege of addressing Mr Ablett, the eminent greengrocer, of Rosoman Street?

ABLETT: (*sulkily*) Well, Mr Wrench, and wot of it?

TOM: You possess a cart, good Ablett, which may be hired by persons of character and responsibility. 'By the hour or job' – so runs the legend. I will charter it, one of these Sundays, for a drive to Epping.

ABLETT: I dunno so much about that, Mr Wrench.

TOM: Look to the springs, good Ablett, for this comely lady will be my companion.

MRS MOSSOP: Dooce take your impudence! Give me your other hand. Haven't you been to rehearsal this morning with the rest of 'em?

TOM: I have, and have left my companions still toiling. My share in the interpretation of Sheridan Knowles's immortal work did not necessitate my remaining after the first act.

MRS MOSSOP: Another poor part, I suppose, Mr Wrench?

TOM: Another, and to-morrow yet another, and on Saturday two others – all equally, damnably rotten.

MRS MOSSOP: Ah, well, well! *somebody* must play the bad parts in this world, on

---

Sheridan Knowles: prominent early nineteenth-century playwright. The 'immortal work' is presumably *The Hunchback* (see p. 143)

and off the stage. There (*returning the scissors*) there's no more edge left to
fray; we've come to the soft. (*as he points the scissors at his breast*) Ah! don't do
that!

TOM: You are right, sweet Mossop. I won't perish on an empty stomach. (*taking her
aside*) But tell me, shall I disgrace the feast, eh? Is my appearance too
scandalously seedy?

MRS MOSSOP: Not *it*, my dear.

TOM: Miss Trelawny – do you think she'll regard me as a blot on the banquet?
(*wistfully*) Do you, Beccy?

MRS MOSSOP: She! la! don't distress yourself. She'll be too excited to notice *you*.

TOM: H'm, yes! Now I recollect, she has always been that. Thanks, Beccy.

> (*A knock, at the front door, is heard.* MRS MOSSOP *hurries to the
> window.*)

MRS MOSSOP: Who's that? (*opening the window and looking out*) It's Miss Parrott!
Miss Parrott's arrived!

TOM: Jenny Parrott? Has Jenny condescended – ?

MRS MOSSOP: *Jenny!* Where are your manners, Mr Wrench?

TOM: (*grandiloquently*) Miss Imogen Parrott, of the Olympic Theatre.

MRS MOSSOP: (*at the door, to* ABLETT) Put your coat on, Ablett. We are not
selling cabbages. (*She disappears, and is heard speaking in the distance.*) Step
up, Miss Parrott! Tell Miss Parrott to mind that mat, Sarah – !

TOM: Be quick, Ablett, be quick! The *élite* is below! More despatch, good Ablett!

ABLETT: (*struggling into his coat – to* TOM, *spitefully*) Miss Trelawny's leavin' will
make all the difference to the old 'Wells'. The season'll terminate abrupt, and
then the comp'ny'll be h'out, Mr Wrench – h'out, sir! (*He produces gloves and
puts on the left one.*)

TOM: (*adjusting his necktie, at the mirror over the piano*) Which will lighten the
demand for the spongy turnip and the watery marrow, my poor Ablett.

ABLETT: (*under his breath*) Presumpshus! (*He makes a horrifying discovery*) Two
lefts! That's Mrs Ablett all over!

> (*During the rest of the act, he is continually in difficulties, through his
> efforts to wear one of the gloves upon his right hand.* MRS MOSSOP
> *now re-enters, with* IMOGEN PARROTT. IMOGEN *is a pretty, light-
> hearted young woman, of about seven-and-twenty, daintily dressed and
> carrying a parcel.*)

MRS MOSSOP: (*outside, to* IMOGEN) There, it might be only yesterday you lodged
in my house, to see you gliding up those stairs! And this the very room you
shared with poor Miss Brooker – !

IMOGEN: (*advancing to* TOM) Well, Wrench, and how are you?

TOM: (*bringing her a chair, and demonstratively dusting the seat of it with his pocket-
handkerchief*) Thank you, much the same as when you used to call me Tom.

IMOGEN: Oh, but I have turned over a new leaf, you know, since I have been at the
Olympic.

MRS MOSSOP: I am sure my chairs don't require dusting, Mr Wrench.

Olympic Theatre, Wych Street, Strand; especially successful under the management of Madame
Vestris (1831–7) and Alfred Wigan (1853–7).

TOM: (*placing the chair below the table, and blowing his nose with his handkerchief, with a flourish*) My way of showing homage, Mossop.

MRS MOSSOP: Miss Parrott has sat on them often enough, when she was an honoured member of the 'Wells' – haven't you, Miss Parrott?

IMOGEN: (*sitting with playful dignity*) I suppose I must have done so. Don't remind me of it. I sit on nothing nowadays but down pillows covered with cloth of gold.

        (MRS MOSSOP *and* ABLETT *prepare to withdraw.* TOM *crosses up to fireplace.*)

MRS MOSSOP: (*at the door, to* IMOGEN) Ha, ha! ha! I could fancy I'm looking at Undine again – Undine, the Spirit of the Waters. She's not the least changed since she appeared as Undine – is she, Mr Ablett?

ABLETT: (*joining* MRS MOSSOP) No – or as Prince Cammyralzyman in the pantomine. *I* never 'ope to see a pair o' prettier limbs –

MRS MOSSOP: (*sharply*) Now then!

        (*She pushes him out; they disappear.*)

IMOGEN: (*after a shiver at* ABLETT'*s remark*) In my present exalted station I don't hear much of what goes on at the 'Wells', Wrench. Are your abilities still –
still – ?

TOM: Still unrecognised, still confined within the almost boundless and yet repressive limits of Utility – General Utility? (*nodding*) H'm, still.

IMOGEN: Dear me! a thousand pities! I positively mean it.

TOM: Thanks.

IMOGEN: What do you think! You were mixed up in a funny dream I dreamt one night lately.

TOM: (*bowing*) Highly complimented.

IMOGEN: It was after a supper which rather – well, I'd had some strawberries sent me from Hertfordshire.

TOM: Indigestion levels all ranks.

IMOGEN: It was a nightmare. I found myself on the stage of the Olympic in that wig you – oh, gracious! You used to play your very serious little parts in it –

TOM: The wig with the ringlets?

IMOGEN: Ugh! yes.

TOM: I wear it to-night, for the second time this week, in a part which is very serious – and very little.

IMOGEN: Heavens! it *is* in existence then!

TOM: And long will be, I hope. I've only three wigs, and this one accommodates itself to so many periods.

IMOGEN: Oh, how it used to amuse the gallery-boys!

TOM: They still enjoy it. If you looked in this evening at half-past seven – I'm done at a quarter to eight – if you looked in at half-past seven, you would hear the same glad, rapturous murmur in the gallery when the presence of that wig is

---

Undine: a number of musical pieces in the Victorian period made use of this figure, first introduced by E. T. A. Hoffman. The only such entitled *Undine, the Spirit of the Waters*, by E. L. Blanchard, was first produced at the Marylebone in 1852.
Prince Cammyralzyman: Not precisely identifiable but a typical Victorian *dramatis persona*.
General Utility: the humblest of 'lines' – categories of part – in the Victorian theatrical company.

discovered. Not that they fail to laugh at my other wigs, at every article of adornment I possess, in fact! Good God, Jenny – !

IMOGEN: (*wincing*) Ssssh!

TOM: Miss Parrott – if they gave up laughing at me now, I believe I – I believe I should – *miss it*. I believe I couldn't spout my few lines now in silence; my unaccompanied voice would sound so strange to me. Besides, I often think those gallery-boys are really fond of me, at heart. You can't laugh as they do – rock with laughter sometimes! – at what you dislike.

IMOGEN: Of course not. *Of course* they like you, Wrench. You cheer them, make their lives happier –

TOM: And to-night, by-the-by, I also assume that beast of a felt hat – the grey hat with the broad brim, and the imitation wool feathers. You remember it?

IMOGEN: Y–y–yes.

TOM: I see you do. Well, that hat still persists in falling off, when I most wish it to stick on. It will tilt and tumble to-night – during one of Telfer's pet speeches; I feel it will.

IMOGEN: Ha, ha, ha!

TOM: And those yellow boots; I wear *them* to-night –

IMOGEN: No!

TOM: Yes!

IMOGEN: Ho, ho, ho, ho!

TOM: (*with forced hilarity*) Ho, ho! ha, ha! And the spurs – the spurs that once tore your satin petticoat! You recollect – ?

IMOGEN: (*her mirth suddenly checked*) Recollect!

TOM: You would see those spurs to-night too, if you patronised us – *and* the red-worsted tights. The worsted tights are a little thinner, a little more faded and discoloured, a little more darned – Oh, yes, thank you, I am still, as you put it, still – still – still –

> (*He walks away, going to the mantelpiece and turning his back upon her.*)

IMOGEN: (*after a brief pause*) I'm sure I didn't intend to hurt your feelings, Wrench.

TOM: (*turning with some violence*) You! you hurt my feelings! Nobody can hurt my feelings! I have no feelings – !

> (ABLETT *re-enters, carrying three chairs of odd patterns.* TOM *seizes the chairs and places them about the table, noisily.*)

ABLETT: (*put out*) Look here, Mr Wrench! if I'm to be 'ampered in performin' my dooties – (*He places the remaining chair below the table.*)

TOM: More chairs, Ablett! In my apartment, the chamber nearest heaven, you will find one with a loose leg. We will seat Mrs Telfer upon that. She dislikes me, and she is, in every sense, a heavy woman.

ABLETT: (*moving towards the door – dropping his glove*) My opinion, you are meanin' to 'arrass me, Mr Wrench –

TOM: (*picking up the glove, and throwing it to* ABLETT – *singing*) 'Take back thy glove, thou faithless fair!' Your glove, Ablett.

'*Take back thy glove, thou faithless fair!*' – presumably a line from a Victorian ballad.

ABLETT: Thank you, sir, it *is* my glove and you are no gentleman.

       (*He withdraws.*)

TOM: True, Ablett – not even a Walking Gentleman.

IMOGEN: Don't go on so, Wrench. What about your plays? Aren't you trying to write any plays just now?

TOM: Trying! I am doing more than trying to write plays. I am writing plays. I have written plays.

IMOGEN: Well?

TOM: My cupboard upstairs is choked with 'em.

IMOGEN: Won't anyone take a fancy – ?

TOM: Not a sufficiently violent fancy.

IMOGEN: You know, the speeches were so short, and had such ordinary words in them, in the plays you used to read to me – no big opportunity for the leading lady, Wrench.

TOM: M' yes. I strive to make my people talk and behave like live people, don't I – ?

IMOGEN: (*vaguely*) I suppose you do.

TOM: To fashion heroes out of actual, dull, everyday men – the sort of men you see smoking cheroots in the club windows in St James's Street; and heroines from simple maidens in muslin frocks. Naturally, the managers won't stand that.

IMOGEN: Why, of course not.

TOM: If *they* did, the public wouldn't.

IMOGEN: Is it likely?

TOM: Is it likely? I wonder!

IMOGEN: Wonder – what?

TOM: Whether they would

IMOGEN: The public!

TOM: The public. Jenny, I wonder about it sometimes so hard that that little bedroom of mine becomes a banqueting-hall, and this lodging-house a castle.

       (*There is a loud and prolonged knocking at the front door.*)

IMOGEN: Here they are, I suppose.

TOM: (*pulling himself together*) Good lord! have I become dishevelled? (*He goes up as if to look in glass.*)

IMOGEN: (*slyly*) Why, are you anxious to make an impression, even down to the last, Wrench?

TOM: (*angrily*) Stop that!

IMOGEN: It's no good your being sweet on her any longer, surely?

TOM: (*glaring at her*) What cats you all are, you girls!

IMOGEN: (*holding up her hands*) Oh! oh, dear! How vulgar – after the Olympic!

       (ABLETT *returns, carrying three more chairs.*)

ABLETT: (*arranging these chairs on the left of the table*) They're all 'ome! they're all 'ome! (TOM *places the four chairs belonging to the room at the table.*) (*to* IMOGEN) She looks 'eavenly, Miss Trelawny does. I was jest takin' in the ale when she floated down the Crescent on her lover's arm. (*wagging his head at* IMOGEN *admiringly*) There, I don't know which of you two is the –

Walking Gentleman: after General Utility the next humblest of acting 'lines' (see above, p. 140).

IMOGEN: (*haughtily*) Man, keep your place!

ABLETT: (*hurt*) H'as you please, miss – but you apperently forget I used to serve you with vegetables.

> (*He takes up a position at the door as* TELFER *and* GADD *enter. TELFER is a thick-set, elderly man, with a worn, clean-shaven face, and iron-grey hair 'clubbed' in the theatrical fashion of the time. Sonorous, if somewhat husky, in speech, and elaborately dignified in bearing, he is at the same time a little uncertain about his H's.* GADD *is a flashily dressed young man of seven-and-twenty, with brown hair arranged à la Byron, and moustache of a deeper tone.*)

TELFER: (*advancing to* IMOGEN, *and kissing her, paternally*) Ha, my dear child! I heard you were 'ere. Kind of you to visit us. Welcome! I'll just put my 'at down –

> (*He places his hat on the top of the piano, and inspects the table.*)

GADD: (*coming to* IMOGEN, *in an elegant, languishing way*) Imogen, my darling. (*kissing her*) Kiss Ferdy!

IMOGEN: Well, Gadd, how goes it? – I mean how are you?

GADD: (*earnestly*) I'm hitting them hard this season, my darling. To-night, Sir Thomas Clifford. They're simply waiting for my Clifford.

IMOGEN: But who on earth is your Julia?

GADD: Ha! Mrs Telfer *goes on* for it – a venerable stop-gap. Absurd, of course; but we daren't keep my Clifford from them any longer.

IMOGEN: You'll miss Rose Trelawny in business pretty badly, I expect, Gadd?

GADD: (*with a shrug of the shoulders*) She was to have done Rosalind for my benefit. Miss Fitzhugh joins on Monday; I must pull *her* through it somehow. I would reconsider my bill, but they're waiting for my Orlando, waiting for it –

> (COLPOYS *enters – an insignificant, wizen little fellow who is unable to forget that he is a low-comedian. He stands at the door, squinting hideously at* IMOGEN *and indulging in extravagant gestures of endearment.*)

COLPOYS: (*failing to attract her attention*) My love! my life!

IMOGEN: (*nodding to him, indifferently*) Good afternoon, Augustus.

COLPOYS: (*ridiculously*) She speaks! she hears me!

ABLETT: (*holding his glove before his mouth, convulsed with laughter*) Ho, ho! oh, Mr Colpoys! oh, reelly, sir! ho, dear!

GADD: (*to* IMOGEN, *darkly*) Colpoys is not nearly as funny as he was last year. Everybody's saying so. We want a low-comedian badly.

> (*He retires, deposits his hat on the wig-block, and joins* TELFER *and* TOM.)

COLPOYS: (*staggering to* IMOGEN *and throwing his arms about her neck*) Ah – h – h! after all these years!

IMOGEN: (*pushing him away*) Do be careful of my things, Colpoys!

ABLETT: (*going out, blind with mirth*) Ha, ha, ha! ho, ho!

> (*He collides with* MRS TELFER, *who is entering at this moment.*

Sir Thomas Clifford: in *The Hunchback* by Sheridan Knowles, a standard play in the early Victorian theatre.

MRS TELFER *is a tall, massive lady of middle age – a faded queen of tragedy.*)

(*as he disappears*) I'm sure I beg your pardon, Mrs Telfer, ma'am.

MRS TELFER: Violent fellow! (*advancing to* IMOGEN *and kissing her solemnly*) How is it with you, Jenny Parrott?

IMOGEN: Thank you, Mrs Telfer, as well as can be. And you?

MRS TELFER: (*waving away the inquiry*) I am obliged to you for this response to my invitation. It struck me as fitting that at such a time you should return for a brief hour or two to the company of your old associates – (*becoming conscious of* COLPOYS *behind her, making grimaces at* IMOGEN) Eh – h – h? (*turning to* COLPOYS *and surprising him*) Oh – h – h! Yes, Augustus Colpoys, you are extremely humorous *off.*

COLPOYS: (*stung*) Miss Sylvester – Mrs Telfer!

MRS TELFER: *On* the stage, sir, you are enough to make a cat weep.

COLPOYS: Madam! from one artist to another! well, I – ! 'Pon my soul! (*retreating and talking under his breath*) Popular favourite! draw more money than all the – old guys –

MRS TELFER: (*following him*) What do you say, sir? Do you mutter?

> (*They explain mutually.* AVONIA BUNN *enters – an untidy, tawdrily dressed young woman of about three-and-twenty, with the airs of a suburban soubrette.*)

AVONIA: (*embracing* IMOGEN) Dear old girl!

IMOGEN: Well, Avonia?

AVONIA: This is jolly, seeing you again. My eye, what a rig-out! She'll be up directly. (*with a gulp*) She's taking a last look-round at our room.

IMOGEN: You've been crying, 'Vonia.

AVONIA: No, I haven't. (*breaking down*) If I have I can't help it. Rose and I have chummed together – all this season – and part of last – and – it's a hateful profession! The moment you make a friend – ! (*looking towards the door*) There! isn't she a dream? I dressed her –

> (*She moves away, as* ROSE TRELAWNY *and* ARTHUR GOWER *enter.* ROSE *is nineteen, wears washed muslin, and looks divine. She has much of the extravagance of gesture, over-emphasis in speech, and freedom of manner engendered by the theatre, but is graceful and charming nevertheless.* ARTHUR *is a handsome, boyish young man – 'all eyes' for* ROSE.)

ROSE: (*meeting* IMOGEN) Dear Imogen!

IMOGEN: (*kissing her*) Rose dear!

ROSE: To think of your journeying from the West to see me make my exit from Brydon Crescent. But you're a good sort; you always were. Do sit down and tell me – oh – ! Let me introduce Mr Gower. Mr Arthur Gower – Miss Imogen Parrott. *The* Miss Parrott, of the Olympic.

ARTHUR: (*reverentially*) I know. I've seen Miss Parrott as Jupiter, and as – I forget the name – in the new comedy –

> (IMOGEN *and* ROSE *sit, below the table.*)

ROSE: He forgets everything but the parts *I* play, and the pieces *I* play in – poor child! Don't you, Arthur?

ARTHUR: (*standing by* ROSE, *looking down upon her*) Yes – no. Well, of course I do! How can I help it, Miss Parrott? Miss Parrott won't think the worse of me for that – will you, Miss Parrott?

MRS TELFER: I am going to remove my bonnet. Imogen Parrott – ?

IMOGEN: Thank you, I'll keep my hat on, Mrs Telfer – take care!

> (MRS TELFER, *in turning to go, encounters* ABLETT, *who is entering with two jugs of beer. Some of the beer is spilt.*)

ABLETT: I beg your pardon, ma'am.

MRS TELFER: (*examining her skirts*). Ruffian!

> (*She departs.*)

ROSE: (*to* ARTHUR) Go and talk to the boys. I haven't seen Miss Parrott for ages.

> (ARTHUR, *in backing away from them, comes against* ABLETT, *who comes down after putting jugs on sideboard.*)

ABLETT: I beg your pardon, sir.

ARTHUR: I beg yours.

ABLETT: (*grasping* ARTHUR's *hand*) Excuse the freedom, sir, if freedom you regard it as –

ARTHUR: Eh – ?

ABLETT: You 'ave plucked the flower, sir; you 'ave stole our ch'icest blossom.

ARTHUR: (*trying to get away*) Yes, yes, I know –

ABLETT: Cherish it, Mr Glover – !

ARTHUR: I will, I will. Thank you –

> (MRS MOSSOP's *voice is heard calling* 'Ablett!' ABLETT *releases* ARTHUR *and goes out.* ARTHUR *joins* COLPOYS *and* TOM.)

ROSE: (*to* IMOGEN) The carriage will be here in half an hour. I've so much to say to you. Imogen, the brilliant hits you've made! How lucky you have been!

IMOGEN: *My* luck! What about *yours*?

ROSE: Yes, isn't this a wonderful stroke of fortune for me! Fate, Jenny! that's what it is – Fate! Fate ordains that I shall be a well-to-do fashionable lady, instead of a popular but toiling actress. Mother often used to stare into my face, when I was little, and whisper, 'Rosie, I wonder what is to be your – fate.' Poor mother! I hope she *sees*.

IMOGEN: Your Arthur seems nice.

ROSE: Oh, he's a dear. Very young, of course – not much more than a year older than me – than I. But he'll grow manly in time, and have moustaches, and whiskers out to here, he says.

IMOGEN: How did you – ?

ROSE: He saw me act Blanche in 'The Pedlar of Marseilles', and fell in love.

IMOGEN: Do you prefer Blanche – ?

ROSE: To Celestine? Oh, yes. You see, I got leave to introduce a song – where Blanche is waiting for Raphael on the bridge. (*singing, dramatically but in low tones*) 'Ever of thee I'm fondly dreaming –'

IMOGEN: I know –

'*The Pedlar of Marseilles*'. No such title appears in Allardyce Nicoll's 'Handlist of Plays' (*A History of English Drama*, Vol. v) and the piece seems to be imaginary. 'Ever of thee I'm fondly dreaming', however, is an authentic ballad (see Appendix B, below, pp. 200–1).

(*They sing together.*)

ROSE *and* IMOGEN: 'Thy gentle voice my spirit can cheer.'

ROSE: It was singing that song that sealed my destiny, Arthur declares. At any rate, the next thing was he began sending bouquets and coming to the stage-door. Of course, I never spoke to him, never glanced at him. Poor Mother brought me up in that way, not to speak to anybody, nor look.

IMOGEN: Quite right.

ROSE: I do hope she sees.

IMOGEN: And then – ?

ROSE: Then Arthur managed to get acquainted with the Telfers, and Mrs Telfer presented him to me. Mrs Telfer has kept an eye on me all through. Not that it was necessary, brought up as I was – but she's a kind old soul.

IMOGEN: And now you're going to live with his people for a time, aren't you?

ROSE: Yes – on approval.

IMOGEN: Ha, ha, ha! you don't mean that!

ROSE: Well, in a way – just to reassure them, as they put it. The Gowers have such odd ideas about theatres, and actors and actresses.

IMOGEN: Do you think you'll like the arrangement?

ROSE: It'll only be for a little while. I fancy they're prepared to take to me, especially Miss Trafalgar Gower –

IMOGEN: Trafalgar!

ROSE: Sir William's sister; she was born Trafalgar year, and christened after it –

        (MRS MOSSOP *and* ABLETT *enter, carrying trays on which are a pile of plates and various dishes of cold food – a joint, a chicken and tongue, a ham, a pigeon pie, etc. They proceed to set out the dishes on the table.*)

AVONIA: Here comes the food! Oh, we are going to have a jolly time (*General chatter.* COLPOYS *takes the pigeon pie and, putting it on his head, trots round in front of table*) Now, Gus, you'll drop it – don't be silly! Put it down!

        (COLPOYS *puts it on the table, and* AVONIA *brings bread to table.* ARTHUR *takes joints and vegetables from* MRS MOSSOP *and places them on table.* ABLETT *goes up and, assisted by* TELFER *and others, places ham, tongue, vegetables, etc., on table.* MRS MOSSOP *cuts bread.* ABLETT *pours out beer.*)

IMOGEN: (*cheefully*) Well, God bless you, my dear. I'm afraid *I* couldn't give up the stage though, not for all the Arthurs –

ROSE: Ah, your mother wasn't an actress.

IMOGEN: No.

ROSE: Mine was, and I remember her saying to me once, 'Rose, if ever you have the chance, get out of it.'

IMOGEN: The Profession?

ROSE: Yes. 'Get out of it'; Mother said, 'if ever a good man comes along, and offers to marry you and to take you off the stage, seize the chance – get out of it.'

IMOGEN: Your mother was never popular, was she?

ROSE: Yes, indeed she was, most popular – till she grew oldish and lost her looks.

Trafalgar: i.e. the naval Battle of Trafalgar (1805) in which Nelson lost his life.

IMOGEN: Oh, *that's* what she meant then?

ROSE: Yes, that's what she meant.

IMOGEN: (*shivering*) Oh, lor', doesn't it make one feel depressed!

ROSE: Poor Mother! Well, I hope she sees.

MRS MOSSOP: Now, ladies and gentlemen, everything is prepared – (*a general murmur of satisfaction*) – and I do trust to your pleasure and satisfaction.

TELFER: Ladies and gentlemen, I beg you to be seated. (*There is a general movement.*) Miss Trelawny will sit 'ere, on my right. On my left, my friend Mr Gower will sit. Next to Miss Trelawny – who will sit beside Miss Trelawny?

GADD *and* COLPOYS: I will.

AVONIA: No, do let me! (*She is pushed up stage by* COLPOYS.)

>   (GADD, COLPOYS *and* AVONIA *gather round* ROSE *and wrangle for the vacant place.*)

ROSE: (*standing by her chair*) It must be a gentleman, 'Vonia – Now, if you two boys quarrel – !

GADD: Please don't push me, Colpoys!

COLPOYS: 'Pon my soul, Gadd – !

ROSE: I know how to settle it. Tom Wrench – !

TOM: (*coming to her*) Yes?

>   (COLPOYS *and* GADD *move away, arguing.*)

IMOGEN: (*seating herself*) Mr Gadd and Mr Colpoys shall sit by me, one on each side.

>   (COLPOYS *sits on* IMOGEN's *right*, GADD *on her left,* AVONIA *sits between* TOM *and* GADD; MRS MOSSOP *on the right of* COLPOYS. *Amid much chatter, the viands are carved by* MRS MOSSOP, TELFER *and* TOM. *Some plates of chicken, etc., are handed round by* ABLETT, *while others are passed about by those at the table.*)

TELFER: (*handing plate to* ARTHUR) Mr Gower –

GADD: (*quietly to* IMOGEN, *during a pause in the hubbub*) Telfer takes the chair, you observe. Why *he* – more than myself, for instance?

IMOGEN: (*to* GADD) The Telfers have lent their room –

GADD: Their stuffy room! That's no excuse. I repeat, Telfer has thrust himself into this position.

IMOGEN: He's the oldest man present.

GADD: True. And he begins to age in his acting too. His H's! scarce as pearls!

IMOGEN: Yes, that's shocking. Now, at the Olympic, slip an H and you're damned for ever.

GADD: And he's losing all his teeth. To act with him, it makes the house seem half empty.

>   (ABLETT *is now going about pouring out the ale. Occasionally he drops his glove, misses it, and recovers it.*)

TELFER: (*to* IMOGEN) Miss Parrott, my dear, follow the counsel of one who has sat at many a 'good man's feast' – have a little 'am.

'*good man's feast*': Telfer may have an imperfect recollection of *As You Like It*, ii.vii: 'True is it that we have seen better days . . . And sat at good men's feasts'.

IMOGEN: Thanks, Mr Telfer.
        (MRS TELFER *returns.*)
MRS TELFER: Sitting down to table in my absence! (*to* TELFER) How is this,
    James?
TELFER: We are pressed for time, Violet, my love.
ROSE: Very sorry, Mrs Telfer.
MRS TELFER: (*taking her place between* ARTHUR *and* MRS MOSSOP – *gloomily*)
    A strange proceeding.
ROSE: Rehearsal was over so late. (*to* TELFER) You didn't get to the last act till a
    quarter to one, did you?
AVONIA: (*taking off her hat and flinging it across the table to* COLPOYS) Gus! catch!
    Put it on the sofa, there's a dear boy. (COLPOYS *perches the hat upon his head,*
    and behaves in a ridiculous, mincing way. ABLETT *is again convulsed with*
    laughter. Some of the others are amused also, but more moderately.) Take that
    off, Gus! Mr Colpoys, you just take my hat off! Put it down! You'll spoil the
    feathers. Gus!
        (COLPOYS *rises, imitating the manners of a woman, and deposits the*
        hat on the sofa.)
ABLETT: Ho, ho, ho! oh, don't, Mr Colpoys! oh, don't, sir!
        (COLPOYS *returns to the table.*)
GADD (*aside to* IMOGEN) It makes me sick to watch Colpoys in private life. He'd
    stand on his head in the street, if he could get a ragged infant to laugh at him.
    (*picking the leg of a fowl furiously*) What I say is this. Why can't an actor,
    in private life, be simply a gentleman? (*loudly and haughtily*) More tongue
    here!
ABLETT: (*hurrying to him*) Yessir, certainly, sir. (*again discomposed by some antic*
    on the part of COLPOYS) Oh, don't, Mr Colpoys! (*going to* TELFER *with*
    GADD'*s plate – speaking to* TELFER *while* TELFER *carves a slice of tongue*) I
    shan't easily forget this afternoon, Mr Telfer. (*exhausted*) This'll be something
    to tell Mrs Ablett. Ho, ho! oh, dear, oh dear!
        (ABLETT, *averting his face from* COLPOYS, *brings back* GADD'*s*
        plate. By an unfortunate chance, ABLETT'*s glove has found its way to*
        the plate and is handed to GADD *by* ABLETT.)
GADD: (*picking up the glove in disgust*) Merciful powers! What's this!
ABLETT: (*taking the glove*) I beg your pardon, sir – my error, entirely.
        (*A firm rat-tat-tat at the front door is heard. There is a general*
        exclamation. At the same moment SARAH, *a diminutive servant, in a*
        crinoline, appears in the doorway.)
SARAH: (*breathlessly*) The kerridge has just drove up!
ALL: The carriage! The carriage!
        (IMOGEN *and* GADD *go to lower window.* COLPOYS *and*
        AVONIA *go to upper window.* MRS MOSSOP *hurries away, pushing*
        SARAH *before her.*)
TELFER: Dear me, dear me! before a single speech has been made.
AVONIA: (*at the window*) Rose, do look!
IMOGEN: (*at the other window*) Come here, Rose!
ROSE: (*shaking her head*) Ha, ha! I'm in no hurry; I shall see it often enough.

(*turning to* TOM.) Well, the time has arrived. (*laying down her knife and fork*) Oh, I'm so sorry, now.

TOM: (*brusquely*) Are you? I'm glad.

ROSE: Glad! That *is* hateful of you, Tom Wrench!

ARTHUR: (*looking at his watch*) The carriage is certainly two or three minutes before its time, Mr Telfer

TELFER: Two or three – ! The speeches, my dear sir, the speeches!

> (MRS MOSSOP *returns, panting.*)

MRS MOSSOP: The footman, a nice-looking young man with hazel eyes, says the carriage and pair can wait for a little bit. They must be back by three, to take their lady into the Park –

TELFER: (*rising*) Ahem! Resume your seats, I beg. Ladies and gentlemen –

AVONIA: Wait, wait! We're not ready!

> (IMOGEN, GADD, COLPOYS *and* AVONIA *return to their places.*
> ABLETT *stands by the door.*)

TELFER: (*producing a paper from his breast-pocket*) Ladies and gentlemen, I devoted some time this morning to the preparation of a list of toasts. I now 'old that list in my hand. The first toast – (*He pauses, to assume a pair of spectacles.*)

GADD: (*aside to* IMOGEN) *He* arranges the toast-list! *He!*

IMOGEN: (*to* GADD) Hush!

> (GADD *turns to table and eats.*)

TELFER: The first toast that figures 'ere is, naturally, that of The Queen. (*laying his hand on* ARTHUR's *shoulder*) With my young friend's chariot at the door, his horses pawing restlessly and fretfully upon the stones, I am prevented from enlarging upon the merits of this toast. Suffice it, both Mrs Telfer and I have had the honour of acting before Her Majesty upon no less than two occasions.

GADD: (*to* IMOGEN) Tsch, tsch, tsch! an old story!

TELFER: Ladies and gentlemen, I give you – (*to* COLPOYS) – the malt is with you, Mr Colpoys.

COLPOYS: Here you are, Telfer.

TELFER: I give you The Queen, coupling with that toast the name of Miss Violet Sylvester – Mrs Telfer.* Miss Sylvester has so frequently impersonated the various queens of tragedy that I cannot but feel she is a fitting person to acknowledge our expression of loyalty. (*raising his glass*) The Queen! And Miss Violet Sylvester!

ALL: The Queen! The Queen! And Miss Violet Sylvester!

> (*All rise, except* MRS TELFER, *and drink the toast. After drinking,*
> MRS MOSSOP *passes her tumbler to* ABLETT.)

ABLETT: The Queen! Miss Vi'lent Sylvester!

> (*He drinks and returns the glass to* MRS MOSSOP. *The company being
> re-seated,* MRS TELFER *rises. Her reception is a polite one.*)

---

the Park: i.e. Hyde Park.
*H reads:
. . . Mrs Telfer – formerly as you are aware, of the Theatre Royal, Drury Lane. Miss Sylvester has so frequently and, if I may say so, so nobly impersonated . . .

MRS TELFER: (*heavily*) Ladies and gentlemen, I have played fourteen or fifteen queens in my time –

TELFER: Thirteen, my love, to be exact; I was calculating this morning.

MRS TELFER: Very well, I have played thirteen of 'em. And, as parts, they are not worth a tinker's oath. I thank you for the favour with which you have received me.

> (*She sits; the applause is heartier. During the demonstration* SARAH *appears in the doorway, with a kitchen chair.*)

ABLETT: (*to* SARAH) Wot's all this?

SARAH: (*to* ABLETT) Is the speeches on?

ABLETT: H'on! Yes, and you be h'off!

> (SARAH *places the chair against the open door –* ABLETT *trying to stop her – and sits, full of determination. At intervals* ABLETT *vainly represents to her the impropriety of her proceeding.*)

TELFER: (*again rising*) Ladies and gentlemen. Bumpers, I charge ye! The toast I 'ad next intended to propose was Our Immortal Bard, Shakespeare, and I had meant, myself, to 'ave offered a few remarks in response –

GADD: (*to* IMOGEN, *bitterly*) Ha!

TELFER: But with our friend's horses champing their bits, I am compelled – nay, forced – to postpone this toast to a later period of the day, and to give you now what we may justly designate the toast of the afternoon. Ladies and gentlemen, we are about to lose, to part with, one of our companions.*

AVONIA: (*with a sob*) I detested her at first

COLPOYS: Order!

IMOGEN: Be quiet, 'Vonia!

TELFER: Her late mother an actress, herself made familiar with the stage from childhood if not from infancy, Miss Rose Trelawny – for I will no longer conceal from you that it is to Miss Trelawny I refer – (*loud applause*) Miss Trelawny is the stuff of which great actresses are made.

ALL: Hear, hear!

ABLETT: (*softly*) 'Ear, 'ear!

TELFER: So much for the actress. Now for the young lady – nay, the woman, the gyirl. Rose is a good girl – (*loud applause, to which* ABLETT *and* SARAH *contribute largely.* AVONIA *rises, and impulsively embraces* ROSE. IMOGEN *rises and brings her back to her seat, then returns to her own.*) A good girl –

MRS TELFER: (*clutching a knife*) Yes, and I should like to hear anybody, man or woman –!

TELFER: She is a good girl, and will be long remembered by us as much for her private virtues as for the commanding authority of her genius. (*more applause, during which there is a sharp altercation between* ABLETT *and* SARAH)

---

*H adds:

... one of our companions, a young comrade who came amongst us many months ago, who in fact joined the company of the 'Wells' last February twelvemonth, after a considerable experience in the provinces of this great country.

COLPOYS: Hear, hear!

AVONIA: (*tearfully*). Hear, hear! (*with a sob*) ...

And now, what has happened to 'the expectancy and Rose of the fair
state'?

IMOGEN: Good, Telfer! good!

GADD: (*to* IMOGEN) Tsch, tsch! forced! forced!

TELFER: I will tell you – (*impressively*) a man has crossed her path.

ABLETT: (*in a low voice*) Shame!

MRS MOSSOP: (*turning to him*) Mr Ablett!

TELFER: A man – ah, but also a gentle-man.* (*applause*) That gentleman, with the
modesty of youth – for I may tell you at once that 'e is not an old man – comes to
us and asks us to give him this gyirl to wife. And friends, we have done so.†
Riches this youthful pair will possess – but what is gold? May they be rich in each
other's society, in each other's love! May they – I can wish them no greater joy –
be as happy in their married life – as‡ Miss Sylvester and I 'ave been in ours!
(*raising his glass*) Miss Rose Trelawny – Mr Arthur Gower!
            (*The toast is drunk by the company, upstanding.*)

THE COMPANY: (*heartily*) Rose! dear Rose! Miss Rose Trelawny – Rose dear! (*in
polite manner*) Mr Arthur Gower! Mr Gower!
            (*Three cheers are called for by* COLPOYS, *and given. Those who have
            risen, then sit.*)

TELFER: Miss Trelawny.

ROSE: (*weeping*) No, no, Mr Telfer.

MRS TELFER: (*to* TELFER, *softly*) Let her be for a minute, James.

TELFER: Mr Gower.
            (ARTHUR *rises and is well received.*)

ARTHUR: Ladies and gentleman, I – I would I were endowed with Mr Telfer's flow
of – of – of splendid eloquence.

TELFER: No, no!

ARTHUR: But I am no orator, no speaker, and therefore cannot tell you how highly –
how – how deeply I appreciate the – the compliment –

ABLETT: You deserve it, Mr Glover!

ALL: Hush!

ARTHUR: All I can say is that I regard Miss Trelawny in the light of a – a solemn
charge, and I – I trust that, if ever I have the pleasure of – of meeting any of you
again, I shall be able to render a good – a – a – satisfactory – satisfactory –

TOM: (*in an audible whisper*) Account.

ARTHUR: Account of the way – of the way – in which I – in which – (*loud applause*)
Before I bring these observations to a conclusion, let me assure you that it has
been a great privilege to me to meet – to have been thrown with – a band of
artists – whose talents – whose striking talents – whose talents –

'*the expectancy . . . fair state*': *Hamlet*, III.i.

*H adds:

A gentleman of probity, a gentleman of honour, and a gentleman of wealth and standing.

†H adds:

A few preliminaries 'ave, I believe, still to be conducted between Mr. Gower and his family, and
then the bond will be signed, the compact entered upon, the mutual trust accepted.

‡H adds:

as – my – as Miss Sylvester and I . . .

TOM: (*kindly, behind his hand*) Sit down.

ARTHUR: (*helplessly*) Whose talents not only interest and instruct the – the more refined residents of this district, but whose talents –

IMOGEN: (*aside to* COLPOYS) Get him to sit down.

ARTHUR: The fame of whose talents, I should say –

COLPOYS: (*aside to* MRS MOSSOP) He's to sit down. Tell Mother Telfer.

ARTHUR: The fame of whose talents has spread to – to regions –

MRS MOSSOP: (*pushing her chair back – aside to* MRS TELFER) They say he's to sit down.

ARTHUR: To – to quarters of the town – to quarters –

MRS TELFER: (*to* ARTHUR) Sit down!

ARTHUR: Eh?

MRS TELFER: You finished long ago. Sit down.

ARTHUR: Thank you. I'm exceedingly sorry. Great heavens, how wretchedly I've done it!

> (*He sits, burying his head in his hands. More applause.*)

TELFER: Rose, my child.

> (ROSE *starts to her feet. The rest rise with her, and cheer again, and wave handkerchiefs. She goes from one to the other, round the table, embracing and kissing and crying over them all excitedly.* SARAH *is kissed, but upon* ABLETT *is bestowed only a handshake, to his evident dissatisfaction. After being kissed,* IMOGEN *runs to the piano and strikes up the air of 'Ever of Thee'. When* ROSE *gets back to the place she mounts her chair, with the aid of* TOM *and* TELFER, *and faces them with flashing eyes. They pull the flowers out of the vases and throw them at her.*)

ROSE: Mr Telfer, Mrs Telfer! My friends! Boys! Ladies and gentlemen! No, don't stop, Jenny! Go on!

> (IMOGEN *plays again.*)

(*singing, her arms stretched out to them*) 'Ever of thee I'm fondly dreaming. Thy gentle voice –' You remember! The song I sang in 'The Pedlar of Marseilles' – which made Arthur fall in love with me! Well, I know I shall dream of *you* – of all of you, very often, as the song says. Don't believe (*wiping away her tears*) oh, don't believe that, because I shall have married a swell, you and the old 'Wells' – the dear old 'Wells'! – (*cheers*) You and the old 'Wells' will have become nothing to me! No, many and many a night you will see me in the house, looking down at you from the Circle – me and my husband –

ARTHUR: Yes, yes, certainly!

ROSE: And if you send for me I'll come behind the curtain to you, and sit with you and talk of bygone times, these times that end to-day. And shall I tell you the moments which will be the happiest to me in my life, however happy I may be with Arthur? Why, whenever I find that I am recognised by people, and pointed out – people in the pit of a theatre, in the street, no matter where; and when I can fancy they're saying to each other, 'Look! that was Miss Trelawny! You remember – Trelawny! Trelawny of the "Wells!"' –

> (*They cry* 'Trelawny!' *and* 'Trelawny of the "Wells!"' *and again* 'Trelawny!' *wildly. Then there is the sound of a sharp rat-tat at the front door.* IMOGEN *leaves the piano and looks out of the window.*)

IMOGEN (*to somebody below*) What is it?

A VOICE: Miss Trelawny, ma'am. We can't wait.

ROSE: (*weakly*) Oh, help me down –

> (*They assist her, and gather round her finally, bidding her farewell.*)
> END OF THE FIRST ACT

THE SECOND ACT

The scene represents a spacious drawing-room in a house in Cavendish Square. The walls are sombre in tone, the ceiling dingy, the hangings, though rich, are faded, and altogether the appearance of the room is solemn, formal and depressing. On the right are folding-doors admitting to a further drawing-room. Beyond these is a single door. The wall on the left is mainly occupied by three sash-windows. The wall facing the spectators is divided by two pilasters into three panels. On the centre panel is a large mirror, reflecting the fireplace; on the right hangs a large oil-painting – a portrait of Sir William Gower in his judicial wig and robes. On the left hangs a companion picture – a portrait of Miss Gower. In the corners of the room there are marble columns supporting classical busts, and between the doors stands another marble column, upon which is an oil lamp. Against the lower window there are two chairs and a card-table. Behind a further table supporting a lamp stands a threefold screen.

The lamps are lighted, but the curtains are not drawn, and outside the window it is twilight.

SIR WILLIAM GOWER *is seated, near a table, asleep, with a newspaper over his head, concealing his face.* MISS TRAFALGAR GOWER *is sitting at the further end of a couch, also asleep, and with a newspaper over her head. At the lower end of this couch sits* MRS DE FŒNIX – CLARA – *a young lady of nineteen, with a 'married' air. She is engaged upon some crochet-work. On the other side of the room, near a table,* ROSE *is seated, wearing the look of boredom which has reached the stony stage. On another couch* ARTHUR *sits, gazing at his boots, his hands in his pockets. On the right of this couch stands* CAPTAIN DE FŒNIX, *leaning against the wall, his mouth open, his head thrown back and his eyes closed.* DE FŒNIX *is a young man of seven-and-twenty – an example of the heavily whiskered 'swell' of the period. Everybody is in dinner-dress. After a moment or two* ARTHUR *rises and tiptoes down to* ROSE. CLARA *raises a warning finger and says 'Hush!'. He nods to her, in assent.*

ARTHUR: (*on* ROSE's *left – in a whisper*) Quiet, isn't it?

ROSE: (*to him, in a whisper*) Quiet! Arthur – ! (*clutching his arm*) Oh, this dreadful
half-hour after dinner, every, *every* evening!

ARTHUR: (*creeping across to the right of the table, looking cautiously at sleepers, and
sitting there*) Grandfather and Aunt Trafalgar must wake up soon. They're
longer than usual to-night.

ROSE: (*to him, across the table*) Your sister Clara, over there, and Captain de Fœnix –
when they were courting, did they have to go through this?

ARTHUR: Yes.

ROSE: And now that they are married, they still endure it!

ARTHUR: Yes.

ROSE: And we, when *we* are married, Arthur, shall *we* – ?

ARTHUR: Yes. I suppose so.

ROSE: (*passing her hand across her brow*) Phe–ew!

(DE FŒNIX, *fast asleep, is now swaying, and in danger of toppling over.* CLARA *grasps the situation and rises.*)

CLARA: (*in a guttural whisper*) Ah, Frederick! no, no, no!

ROSE *and* ARTHUR: (*turning in their chairs*) Eh – what – ? ah – h – h – h!

    (*As* CLARA *reaches her husband, he lurches forward into her arms.*)

DE FŒNIX: (*his eyes bolting*) Oh! who – ?

CLARA: Frederick dear, wake!

DE FŒNIX: (*dazed*) How did this occur?

CLARA: You were tottering, and I caught you.

DE FŒNIX: (*collecting his senses*) I wemember. I placed myself in an upwight position, dearwest, to prewent myself dozing.

CLARA: (*sinking on to the couch*) How you alarmed me!

    (*Seeing that* ROSE *is laughing,* DE FŒNIX *comes down to her.*)

DE FŒNIX: (*in a low voice*) Might have been a vevy serwious accident, Miss Trelawny.

ROSE: (*seating herself on the footstool*) Never mind. (*pointing to the chair she has vacated*) Sit down and talk. (*He glances at the old people and shakes his head.*) Oh, do, do, do! do sit down, and let us all have a jolly whisper. (*He sits.*) Thank you, Captain Fred. Go on! tell me something – anything; something about the military –

DE FŒNIX: (*again looking at the old people, then wagging his finger at* ROSE) I know; you want to get me into a wow. (*settling himself into his chair*) Howwid girl!

ROSE: (*despairingly*) Oh–h–h! (*There is a brief pause and then the sound of a street-organ, playing in the distance, is heard. The air is 'Ever of Thee'.*) Hark! (*excitedly*) Hark!

CLARA, ARTHUR *and* DE FŒNIX: Hush!

ROSE: (*heedlessly*) The song I sang in 'The Pedlar' – 'The Pedlar of Marseilles'! The song that used to make you cry, Arthur – !

    (*They attempt vainly to hush her down.*)

    (*dramatically, in hoarse whispers*) And then Raphael enters – comes on to the bridge. The music continues, softly. 'Raphael, why have you kept me waiting? Man, do you wish to break my heart – (*thumping her breast*) a woman's hear–r–rt, Raphael?'

    (SIR WILLIAM *and* MISS GOWER *suddenly whip off their newspapers and sit erect.* SIR WILLIAM *is a grim, bullet-headed old gentleman of about seventy;* MISS GOWER *a spare, prim lady, of gentle manners, verging upon sixty. They stare at each other for a moment, silently.*)

SIR WILLIAM: What a hideous riot, Trafalgar!

MISS GOWER: Rose dear, I hope I have been mistaken – but through my sleep I fancied I could hear you shrieking at the top of your voice.

    (SIR WILLIAM *gets on to his feet; all rise, except* ROSE, *who remains seated sullenly.*)

SIR WILLIAM: (*emphatically*) Trafalgar, it is becoming impossible for you and me to obtain repose. (*turning his head sharply*) Ha! is not that a street-organ? (*to* MISS GOWER) An organ?

MISS GOWER: Undoubtedly. An organ in the Square, at this hour of the evening – singularly out of place!

SIR WILLIAM: (*looking round*) Well, well, well, does no one stir?

ROSE: (*under her breath*) Oh, don't stop it! (*She clasps her hands.*)

> (CLARA *goes out quickly. With a great show of activity,* ARTHUR *and* DE FŒNIX *hurry across the room and, when there, do nothing.*)

SIR WILLIAM: (*coming upon* ROSE *and peering down at her*) What are ye upon the floor for, my dear? (*He looks around.*) Have we no cheers? (*to* MISS GOWER – *producing his snuff-box*) Do we lack cheers here, Trafalgar?

MISS GOWER: (*crossing to* ROSE) My dear Rose! (*raising her*) Come, come, come, this is quite out of place! Young ladies do not crouch and huddle upon the ground – do they, William?

SIR WILLIAM: (*taking snuff*) A moment ago I should have hazarded the opinion that they do not. (*chuckling unpleasantly*) He, he, he!

> (CLARA *returns. The organ-music ceases abruptly.*)

CLARA: (*coming to* SIR WILLIAM) Charles was just running out to stop the organ when I reached the hall, Grand-pa.

SIR WILLIAM: (*going up to her and looking her full in the face*) Ye'd surely no intention, Clara, of venturing, yourself, into the public street – the open Square – ?

CLARA: (*faintly*) I meant only to wave at the man from the door –

MISS GOWER: Oh, Clara, that would hardly have been in place!

SIR WILLIAM: (*raising his hands*) In mercy's name, Trafalgar, what *is* befalling my household?

MISS GOWER: (*bursting into tears*) Oh, William – !

> (ROSE *and* CLARA *exchange looks and creep away and join the others.* MISS GOWER *totters to* SIR WILLIAM *and drops her head upon his breast.*)

SIR WILLIAM: Tut, tut, tut, tut!

MISS GOWER: (*aside to him, between her sobs*) I – I – I – I know what is in your mind.

SIR WILLIAM: (*drawing a long breath*) Ah–h–h–h!

MISS GOWER: Oh, my dear brother, be patient!

SIR WILLIAM: Patient!

MISS GOWER: Forgive me; I should have said hopeful. Be hopeful that I shall yet succeed in ameliorating the disturbing conditions which are affecting us so cruelly.

SIR WILLIAM: Ye never will, Trafalgar; *I've* tried.

MISS GOWER: Oh, do not despond already! I feel sure there are good ingredients in Rose's character. (*clinging to him*) In time, William, we shall shape her to be a fitting wife for our rash and unfortunate Arthur – (*He shakes his head.*) In time, William, in time!

SIR WILLIAM: (*soothing her*) Well, well, well! There, there, there! (*Turns to her.*) At least, my dear sister, I am perfectly aweer that I possess in you the woman above all others whose example should compel such a transformation.

MISS GOWER: (*throwing her arms about his neck*) Oh, brother, what a compliment – !

SIR WILLIAM: Tut, tut, tut! And now, before Charles sets the card-table, don't you think we had better – eh Trafalgar?

MISS GOWER: Yes, yes – our disagreeable duty. Let us discharge it. (SIR WILLIAM *crosses to right, taking snuff.*) Rose dear, be seated. The Vice-Chancellor has something to say to us. Let us all be seated.

    (*There is consternation among the young people. All sit.*)

SIR WILLIAM: (*peering about him*) Are ye seated?

EVERYBODY: Yes.

SIR WILLIAM: What I desire to say is this. When Miss Trelawny took up her residence here, it was thought proper, in the peculiar circumstances of the case, that you, Arthur – (*pointing a finger at* ARTHUR) you –

ARTHUR: Yes, sir.

SIR WILLIAM: That you should remove yourself to the establishment of your sister Clara and her husband in Holles Street, round the corner –

ARTHUR: Yes Sir.

CLARA: Yes, Grand-pa.

DE FŒNIX: Certainly, Sir William.

SIR WILLIAM: Taking your food in this house, and spending other certain hours here, under the surveillance of your great-aunt Trafalgar.

MISS GOWER: Yes, William.

SIR WILLIAM: This was considered to be decorous, and, towards Miss Trelawny, a highly respectful, course to pursue.

ARTHUR: Yes, sir.

MISS GOWER: Any other course would have been out of place.

SIR WILLIAM: And yet – (*again extending a finger at* ARTHUR) what is this that is reported to me?

ARTHUR: I don't know, sir.

SIR WILLIAM: I hear that ye have on several occasions, at night, after having quitted this house with Captain and Mrs de Fœnix, been seen on the other side of the way, your back against the railings, gazing up at Miss Trelawny's window; and that you have remained in that position for a considerable space of time. Is this true, sir?

ROSE: (*boldly*) Yes, Sir William.

SIR WILLIAM: I venture to put a question to my grandson, Miss Trelawny.

ARTHUR: Yes, sir, it is quite true.

SIR WILLIAM: Then, sir, let me acqueent you that these are not the manners, nor the practices, of a gentleman.

ARTHUR: No, sir?

SIR WILLIAM: No, sir, they are the manners, and the practices, of a troubadour.

MISS GOWER: A troubadour in Cavendish Square! Quite out of place!

ARTHUR: I – I'm very sorry, sir; I – I never looked at it in that light.

SIR WILLIAM: (*snuffing*) Ah–h–h–h! ho! pi–i–i—sh!

ARTHUR: But at the same time, sir, I daresay – of course I don't speak from precise knowledge – but I daresay there were a good many – a good many –

SIR WILLIAM: Good many – what, sir?

ARTHUR: A good many very respectable troubadours, sir –

ROSE: (*starting to her feet, heroically and defiantly*) And what I wish to say, Sir

William, is this. I wish to avow, to declare before the world, that Arthur and I have had many lengthy interviews while he has been stationed against those railings over there; murmuring to him softly from my bedroom window, he responding in tremulous whispers –

(SIR WILLIAM *struggles to his feet.*)

SIR WILLIAM: You – you tell me such things – !

(*All rise.*)

MISS GOWER: The Square, in which we have resided for years – ! Our neighbours – !

SIR WILLIAM: (*shaking a trembling hand at* ARTHUR) The – the character of my house – !

ARTHUR: Again I am extremely sorry, sir – but these are the only confidential conversations Rose and I now enjoy.

SIR WILLIAM: (*turning upon* CLARA *and* DE FŒNIX) And you, Captain de Fœnix – an officer and a gentleman! And you, Clara! This could scarcely have been without your cognizance, without, perhaps, your approval – !

(CHARLES *enters, carrying two branch candlesticks with lighted candles.* CHARLES *is in plush and powder and wears luxuriant whiskers.*)

CHARLES: The cawd-table, Sir William?

MISS GOWER: (*agitatedly*) Yes, yes, by all means, Charles; the card-table, as usual.

(CHARLES *carries the candlesticks to the table.*)

(*to* SIR WILLIAM) A rubber will comfort you, soothe you –

(SIR WILLIAM *and* MISS GOWER *seat themselves upon a couch, she with her arm through his, affectionately.* CLARA *and* DE FŒNIX *get behind the screen; their scared faces are seen occasionally over the top of it.* CHARLES *brings the card-table opens it and arranges it, placing four chairs, which he collects from different parts of the room, round the table.* ROSE *and* ARTHUR *talk in rapid undertones.*)

ROSE: Infamous! Infamous!

ARTHUR: Be calm, Rose dear, be calm!

ROSE: Tyrannical! diabolical! I cannot endure it.

(*She throws herself into a chair. He stands behind her, apprehensively, endeavouring to calm her.*)

ARTHUR: (*over her shoulder*) They mean well, dearest –

ROSE: (*hysterically*) Well! ha, ha, ha!

ARTHUR: But they are rather old-fashioned people –

ROSE: Old-fashioned! – they belong to the time when men and women were put to the torture. I am being tortured – mentally tortured –

ARTHUR: They have not many more years in this world –

ROSE: Nor I, at this rate, many more months. They are killing me – like Agnes in *The Spectre of St Ives*. She expires, in the fourth act, as I shall die in Cavendish Square, painfully, of no recognised disorder –

ARTHUR: And anything we can do to make them happy –

ROSE: To make the Vice-Chancellor happy! I won't try! I will not! He's a fiend, a vampire – !

The Spectre of St Ives: apparently another imaginary piece.

ARTHUR: Oh, hush!

ROSE: (*snatching up* SIR WILLIAM's *snuff-box which he has left upon the table*) His snuff-box! I wish I could poison his snuff, as Lucrezia Borgia would have done. *She* would have removed him within two hours of my arrival – I mean, her arrival. (*opening the snuff-box and mimicking* SIR WILLIAM) And here he sits and lectures me, and dictates to me! to Miss Trelawny! 'I venture to put a question to my grandson, Miss Trelawny!' Ha, ha! (*taking a pinch of snuff thoughtlessly but vigorously*) 'Yah–h–h–h! pish!' 'Have we no cheers? Do we lack cheers here, Trafalgar?' (*suddenly*) Oh – !

ARTHUR: What have you done?

ROSE: (*in suspense, replacing the snuff-box*) The snuff – !

ARTHUR: Rose dear!

ROSE: (*putting her handkerchief to her nose, and rising*) Ah – !

> (CHARLES, *having prepared the card-table, and arranged the candlesticks upon it, has withdrawn.* MISS GOWER *and* SIR WILLIAM *now rise.*)

MISS GOWER: The table is prepared, William. Arthur, I assume you would prefer to sit and contemplate Rose – ?

ARTHUR: Thank you, Aunt.

> (ROSE *sneezes violently, and is led away, helplessly, by* ARTHUR. SIR WILLIAM *looks surprised and annoyed.*)

MISS GOWER: (*to* ROSE) Oh, my dear child! (*looking round*) Where are Frederick and Clara?

CLARA *and* DE FŒNIX: (*appearing from behind the screen, shamefacedly*) Here.

> (*The intending players cut the pack, and seat themselves.* SIR WILLIAM *sits up the stage,* CAPTAIN DE FŒNIX *facing him,* MISS GOWER *on the right of the table, and* CLARA *on the left.*)

ARTHUR: (*while this is going on, to* ROSE) Are you in pain, dearest? Rose!

ROSE: Agony!

ARTHUR: Pinch your upper lip –

> (*She sneezes twice, loudly, and sinks back upon the couch.*)

SIR WILLIAM: (*testily*) Sssh! sssh!sssh! This is to be whist, I hope.

MISS GOWER: Rose, Rose! young ladies do not sneeze quite so continuously.

> (DE FŒNIX *is dealing.*)

SIR WILLIAM: (*with gusto*) I will thank you, Captain de Fœnix, to exercise your intelligence this evening to its furthest limit.

DE FŒNIX: I'll twy, sir.

SIR WILLIAM: (*laughing unpleasantly*) He, he, he! Last night, sir –

CLARA: Poor Frederick had toothache last night, Grand-pa.

SIR WILLIAM: (*tartly*) Whist is whist, Clara, and toothache is toothache. We will endeavour to keep the two things distinct, if you please. He, he!

MISS GOWER: Your interruption was hardly in place, Clara dear – ah!

DE FŒNIX: Hey! What – ?

MISS GOWER: A misdeal.

CLARA: (*faintly*) Oh, Frederick!

SIR WILLIAM: (*partly rising*) Captain de Fœnix!

DE FŒNIX: I – I'm fwightfully gwieved, sir –

(*The cards are re-dealt by* MISS GOWER. ROSE *now gives way to a violent paroxysm of sneezing.* SIR WILLIAM *rises.*)

MISS GOWER: William –
      (*The players rise.*)

SIR WILLIAM: (*to the players*) Is this whist, may I ask?
      (*They sit.*)

ROSE: (*weakly*) I – I think I had better – what d'ye call it? – withdraw for a few moments.

SIR WILLIAM: (*sitting again*) Do so.
      (ROSE *disappears.* ARTHUR *is leaving the room with her.*)

MISS GOWER: (*sharply*) Arthur! where are you going?

ARTHUR: (*returning promptly*) I beg your pardon, Aunt.

MISS GOWER: Really, Arthur – !

SIR WILLIAM: (*rapping upon the table*) Tsch, tsch, tsch!

MISS GOWER: Forgive me, William.
      (*They play.*)

SIR WILLIAM: (*intent upon his cards*) My snuff-box, Arthur; be so obleeging as to search for it.

ARTHUR: (*brightly*) I'll bring it to you, sir. It is on the –

SIR WILLIAM: Keep your voice down, sir. We are playing – (*emphatically throwing down a card, as fourth player*) whist. Mine.

MISS GOWER: (*picking up the trick*) No, William.

SIR WILLIAM: (*glaring*). No!

MISS GOWER*: I played a trump.

DE FŒNIX: Yes, sir, Aunt Trafalgar played a trump – the seven –

SIR WILLIAM: I will not trouble you, Captain de Fœnix, to echo Miss Gower's information.

DE FŒNIX: Vevy sowwy, sir.

MISS GOWER: (*gently*) It *was* a *little* out of place, Frederick.

SIR WILLIAM: Sssh! whist.
      (MISS GOWER *leads.* ARTHUR *is now on* SIR WILLIAM'*s right, with the snuff-box.*)

    (*to* ARTHUR) Eh? what? (*taking the snuff-box*) Oh, thank ye. Much obleeged, much obleeged.
      (ARTHUR *walks away and picks up a book.* SIR WILLIAM *turns in his chair, watching* ARTHUR.)

MISS GOWER: You to play, William. (*a pause*) William, dear – ?
      (*She also turns, following the direction of his gaze. Laying down his cards, he leaves the card-table and goes over to* ARTHUR *slowly. Those at the card-table look on apprehensively.*)

SIR WILLIAM: (*in a queer voice*) Arthur.

ARTHUR: (*shutting his book*) Excuse me, Grandfather.

SIR WILLIAM: Ye – ye're a troublesome young man, Arthur.

---

*H has:
MISS GOWER: Clara played a trump.
DE FOENIX: Yes, sir, Clara played a trump . . .

ARTHUR: I – I don't mean to be one, sir.

SIR WILLIAM: As your poor father was, before ye. And if you are fool enough to marry, and to beget children, doubtless your son will follow the same course. (*taking snuff*) Y–y–yes, but I shall be dead 'n' gone by that time, it's likely. Ah–h–h–h! pi–i–i–sh I shall be sitting in the Court Above by that time –
>(*From the adjoining room comes the sound of* ROSE's *voice singing 'Ever of Thee' to the piano. There is great consternation at the card-table. They all rise.* ARTHUR *is moving towards the folding-doors.*)

(*detaining him – quietly*) No, no, let her go on, I beg. Let her continue. (*returning to the card-table, with deadly calmness*) We will suspend our game while this young lady performs her operas.

MISS GOWER: (*taking his arm*) William – !

SIR WILLIAM: (*in the same tone*) I fear this is no longer a comfortable home for ye, Trafalgar; no longer the home for a gentlewoman. I apprehend that in these days my house approaches somewhat closely to a Pandemonium. (*suddenly taking up the cards, in a fury, and flinging them across the room over his head*) And this is whist – whist – !
>(CLARA *and* DE FŒNIX *rise and stand together.* ARTHUR *pushes open the upper part of the folding-doors.*)

ARTHUR: Rose! stop! Rose!
>(*The song ceases and* ROSE *appears.*)

ROSE: (*at the folding-doors*). Did anyone call?

ARTHUR: You have upset my grandfather.

MISS GOWER: Miss Trelawny, how – how dare you do anything so – so out of place?

ROSE: There's a piano in there, Miss Gower.

MISS GOWER: You are acquainted with the rule of this household – no music when the Vice-Chancellor is within doors.

ROSE: But there are so many rules. One of them is that you may not sneeze.

MISS GOWER: Ha! you must never answer –

ROSE: No, that's another rule.

MISS GOWER: Oh, for shame!

ARTHUR: You see, Aunt, Rose is young, and – and – you make no allowance for her, give her no chance –

MISS GOWER: Great heaven! what is this you are charging me with?

ARTHUR: I don't think the 'rules' of this house are fair to Rose! Oh, I must say it – they are horribly unfair!

MISS GOWER: (*clinging to* SIR WILLIAM) Brother!

SIR WILLIAM: Trafalgar! (*putting her aside and advancing to* ARTHUR) Oh, indeed, sir! And so you deliberately accuse your great-aunt of acting towards ye and Miss Trelawny *malâ fide* –

ARTHUR: Grandfather, what I intended to –

SIR WILLIAM: I will afford ye the opportunity of explaining what ye intended to convey, downstairs, at once, in the library. (*A general shudder*) Obleege me by following me, sir. (*to* CLARA *and* DE FŒNIX) Captain de Fœnix – I see no

---

malâ fide: 'in bad faith' (legal term).

prospect of any further social relaxation this evening. You and Clara will do me the favour of attending in the hall, in readiness to take this young man back to Holles Street. (*giving his arm to* MISS GOWER) My dear sister – (*to* ARTHUR) Now, sir.

       (SIR WILLIAM *and* MISS GOWER *go out.* ARTHUR *comes to* ROSE *and kisses her.*)

ARTHUR: Good night, dearest. Oh, good night! Oh, Rose – !

SIR WILLIAM: (*outside the door*) Mr Arthur Gower!

ARTHUR: I am coming, sir –

       (*He goes out quickly.*)

DE FŒNIX: (*approaching* ROSE *and taking her hand sympathetically*) Haw – ! I – weally – haw ! –

ROSE: Yes, I know what you would say. Thank you, Captain Fred.

CLARA: (*embracing* ROSE) Never mind! We will continue to let Arthur out at night as usual. I am a married woman! (*joining* DE FŒNIX) and a married woman will turn, if you tread upon her often enough – !

       (DE FŒNIX *and* CLARA *depart.*)

ROSE: (*pacing the room, shaking her hands in the air desperately*) Oh–h–h! ah–h–h!

       (*The upper part of the folding-doors opens, and* CHARLES *appears.*)

CHARLES: (*mysteriously*) Miss Rose –

ROSE: What – ?

CHARLES: (*advancing*) I see Sir William h'and the rest descend the stairs. I 'ave been awaitin' the chawnce of 'andin' you this, Miss Rose.

       (*He produces a dirty scrap of paper, wet and limp, with writing upon it, and gives it to her.*)

ROSE: (*handling it daintily*) Oh, it's damp! –

CHARLES: Yes, miss; a little gentle shower 'ave been takin' place h'outside – 'eat spots, cook says.

ROSE: (*reading*) Ah! from some of my friends.

CHARLES: (*behind his hand*) Perfesshunnal, Miss Rose?

ROSE: (*intent upon the note*) Yes – Yes –

CHARLES: I was reprimandin' the organ, miss, when I observed them lollin' against the square railin's examinin' h'our premises, and they wentured for to beckon me. An egstremely h'affable party, miss. (*hiding his face*) Ho! one of them caused me to laff!

ROSE: (*excitedly*) They want to speak to me – (*referring to the note*) to impart something to me, of an important nature. Oh, Charles, I know not what to do.

CHARLES: (*languishingly*) Whatever friends may loll against them railin's h'opposite, Miss Rose, you 'ave one true friend in this 'ouse – Chawles Gibbons –

ROSE: (*nodding*) Thank you, Charles. Mr Briggs, the butler, is sleeping out to-night, isn't he?

CHARLES: Yes, miss, he 'ave leave to sleep at his sister's. I 'appen to know he 'ave gone to Cremorne.

Cremorne: Cremorne Gardens, Chelsea, a popular resort of Londoners in the nineteenth century.

ROSE: Then, when Sir William and Miss Gower have retired, do you think you could
let me go forth; and wait at the front door while I run across and grant my
friends a hurried interview?

CHARLES: Suttingly, miss.

ROSE: If it reached the ears of Sir William, or Miss Gower, you would lose your place,
Charles!

CHARLES: (*haughtily*) I'm aweer, miss; but Sir William was egstremely rood to me
dooring dinner, over that mis'ap to the ontray – (*A bell rings violently.*)
S'william!

> (*He goes out. The rain is heard pattering against the window-panes.*
> ROSE *goes from one window to another, looking out. It is now almost*
> *black outside the windows.*)

ROSE: (*discovering her friends*) Ah! yes, yes! ah–h–h–h! (*She snatches an antimacassar*
from a chair and, jumping on to the couch, waves it frantically to those outside.)
The dears! the darlings! the faithful creatures – ! (*listening*) Oh – !

> (*She descends, in a hurry, and flings the antimacassar under the couch,*
> *as* MISS GOWER *enters. At the same moment there is a vivid flash of*
> *lightning.*)

MISS GOWER: (*startled*) Oh, how dreadful! (*to* ROSE, *frigidly*) The Vice-Chancellor
has *felt* the few words he has addressed to Arthur, and has retired for the night.

> (*There is a roll of thunder.* ROSE *is alarmed.*)

(*clinging to a chair*) Mercy on us! Go to bed, child, directly. We will all go to our
beds, hoping to awake to-morrow in a meeker and more submissive spirit.
(*kissing* ROSE *upon the brow*) Good night. (*another flash of lightning*) Oh – !
Don't omit to say your prayers, Rose – and in a simple manner. I always fear
that, from your peculiar training, you may declaim them. That is so out of place –
oh – !

> (*Another roll of thunder.* ROSE *goes across the room, meeting*
> CHARLES, *who enters carrying a lantern. They exchange significant*
> *glances, and she disappears.*)

CHARLES: (*coming to* MISS GOWER) I am now at liberty to accompany you round
the 'ouse, ma'am –

> (*A flash of lightning.*)

MISS GOWER: Ah – ! (*her hand to her heart*) Thank you, Charles – but to-night I must
ask you to see that everything is secure, alone. This storm – so very seasonable;
but, from girlhood, I could never – (*a roll of thunder*) Oh, good night.

> (*She flutters away. The rain beats still more violently upon the window-*
> *panes.*)

CHARLES: (*glancing at the window*) Ph–e–e–w! Great 'evans!

> (*He is dropping the curtains at the window, when* ROSE *appears at the*
> *folding-doors.*)

ROSE: (*in a whisper*) Charles!

CHARLES: Miss?

ROSE: (*coming into the room, distractedly*) Miss Gower has gone to bed.

CHARLES: Yes, miss – oh – !

> (*A flash of lightning*)

ROSE: Oh! my friends! my poor friends!

CHARLES: *H'and* Mr Briggs at Cremorne! Reelly, I should 'ardly advise you to wenture h'out, miss –

ROSE: Out! No! Oh, but get them in!

CHARLES: *In*, Miss Rose! indoors!

ROSE: Under cover – (*a roll of thunder*) Oh! (*wringing her hands*) They are my friends! Is it a rule that I am never to see a friend, that I mayn't even give a friend shelter in a violent storm? (*to* CHARLES) Are you the only one up?

CHARLES: I b'lieve so, miss. Any'ow the wimming-servants is quite h'under my control.

ROSE: Then tell my friends to be deathly quiet, and to creep – to tiptoe – (*The rain strikes the window again. She picks up the lantern, which* CHARLES *has deposited upon the floor, and gives it to him.*) Make haste! I'll draw the curtains –
> (*He hurries out. She goes from window to window, dropping the curtains, talking to herself excitedly as she does so.*)

My friends! my own friends! ha! I'm not to sneeze in this house! nor to sing! or breathe, next! wretches! oh my! wretches! (*blowing out the candles and removing the candlesticks to the table – singing, under her breath, wildly*) 'Ever of thee I'm fondly dreaming –' (*mimicking* SIR WILLIAM *again*) 'What are ye upon the floor for, my dear? Have we no cheers? Do we lack cheers here, Trafalgar –?'
> (CHARLES *returns.*)

CHARLES: (*to those who follow him*) Hush! (*to* ROSE) I discovered 'em clustered in the doorway –
> (*There is a final peal of thunder as* AVONIA, GADD, COLPOYS *and* TOM WRENCH *enter, somewhat diffidently. They are apparently soaked to their skins, and are altogether in a deplorable condition. AVONIA alone has an umbrella, which she allows to drip upon the carpet, but her dress and petticoats are bedraggled, her finery limp, her hair lank and loose.*)

ROSE: 'Vonia!

AVONIA: (*coming to her, and embracing her fervently*) Oh, ducky, ducky, ducky! Oh, but what a storm!

ROSE: Hush! How wet you are! (*shaking hands with* GADD) Ferdinand – (*crossing to* COLPOYS *and shaking hands with him*) Augustus – (*shaking hands with* TOM) Tom Wrench –

AVONIA: (*to* CHARLES) Be so kind as to put my umbrella on the landing, will you? Oh, thank you very much, I'm sure.
> (CHARLES *withdraws with the umbrella.* GADD *and* COLPOYS *shake the rain from their hats on to the carpet and furniture.*)

TOM: (*quietly, to* ROSE) It's a shame to come down on you in this way. But they would do it, and I thought I'd better stick to 'em.

GADD: (*who is a little flushed and unsteady*) Ha! I shall remember this accursed evening.

AVONIA: Oh, Ferdy –!

ROSE: Hush! you must be quiet. Everybody has gone to bed, and I – I'm not sure I'm allowed to receive visitors –

AVONIA: Oh!

GADD: Then we are intruders?

ROSE: I mean, such late visitors.

(COLPOYS *has taken off his coat, and is shaking it vigorously.*)

AVONIA: Stop it, Augustus! Ain't I wet enough? (*to* ROSE) Yes, it is latish, but I so wanted to inform you – here (*bringing* GADD *forward*) – allow me to introduce – my husband.

ROSE: Oh, no!

AVONIA: (*laughing merrily*) Yes, ha, ha, ha!

ROSE: Sssh, sssh, sssh!

AVONIA: I forgot. (*to* GADD) Oh, darling Ferdy, you're positively soaked! (*to* ROSE) Do let him take his coat off, like Gussy –

GADD: (*jealously*) 'Vonia, not so much of the Gussy!

AVONIA: There you are, flying out again! As if Mr Colpoys wasn't an old friend!

GADD: Old friend or no old friend –

ROSE: (*diplomatically*) Certainly, take your coat off, Ferdinand.

(GADD *joins* COLPOYS; *they spread out their coats upon the couch*) (*feeling* TOM'*s coat-sleeve*) And you?

TOM: (*after glancing at the others – quietly*) No, thank you.

AVONIA: (*sitting*) Yes, dearie, Ferdy and I were married yesterday.

ROSE: (*sitting*) Yesterday!

AVONIA: Yesterday morning. We're on our honeymoon now. You know, the 'Wells' shut a fortnight after you left us, and neither Ferdy nor me could fix anything, just for the present, elsewhere; and as we hadn't put-by during the season – you know it never struck us to put-by during the season – we thought we'd get married.

ROSE: Oh, yes.

AVONIA: You see, a man and his wife can live almost on what keeps one, rent *and* ceterer; and so, being deeply attached, as I tell you, we went off to church and did the deed. Oh, it will be such a save. (*looking up at* GADD *coyly*) Oh, Ferdy – !

GADD: (*laying his hand upon her head, dreamily*) Yes, child, I confess I love you –

COLPOYS: (*behind* ROSE, *imitating* GADD) Child, I confess I adore you.

TOM: (*taking* COLPOYS *by the arm and swinging him away from* ROSE) Enough of that, Colpoys!

COLPOYS: What!

ROSE: (*rising*) Hush!

TOM: (*under his breath*) If you've never learnt how to behave –

COLPOYS: Don't you teach behaviour, sir, to a gentleman who plays a superior line of business to yourself! (*muttering*) 'Pon my soul! rum start – !

AVONIA: (*going to* ROSE) Of course I ought to have written to you, dear, properly, but you remember the weeks it takes me to write a letter –

(GADD *sits in the chair* AVONIA *has just quitted. She returns and seats herself upon his knee.*)

And so I said to Ferdy, over tea, 'Ferdy, let's spend a bit of our honeymoon in doing the West End thoroughly, and going and seeing where Rose Trelawny lives.' And we thought it only nice and polite to invite Tom Wrench and Gussy –

GADD: 'Vonia, much less of the Gussy!

AVONIA: (*kissing* GADD) Jealous boy! (*beaming*) Oh, and we *have* done the West
    End thoroughly. There, I've never done the West End so thoroughly in my life!
    And when we got outside your house I couldn't resist – (*her hand on* GADD'*s
    shirt-sleeve*) Oh, gracious! I'm sure you'll catch your death, my darling – !
ROSE: I think I can get him some wine. (*to* GADD) Will you take some wine,
    Ferdinand?
             (GADD *rises, nearly upsetting* AVONIA.)
AVONIA: Ferdy!
GADD: I thank you. (*with a wave of the hand*) Anything, anything –
AVONIA: (*to* ROSE) Anything that goes with stout, dear.
ROSE: (*at the door, turning to them*) 'Vonia – boys – be very still.
AVONIA: Trust *us*!
             (ROSE *tiptoes out.* COLPOYS *is now at the card-table, cutting a pack
             of cards which remains there.*)
COLPOYS: (*to* GADD) Gadd, I'll see you for pennies.
GADD: (*loftily*) Done, sir, with you!
             (*They seat themselves at the table and cut for coppers.* TOM *is walking
             about, surveying the room.*)
AVONIA: (*taking off her hat and wiping it with her handkerchief*) Well, Thomas,
    what do you think of it?
TOM: *This* is the kind of chamber I want for the second act of my comedy –
AVONIA: Oh, lor', your head's continually running on your comedy. Half this
    blessed evening –
TOM: I tell you, I won't have doors stuck here, there, and everywhere; no, nor
    windows in all sorts of impossible places!
AVONIA: Oh, really! Well, when you do get your play accepted, mind you see that
    Mr Manager gives you exactly what you ask for – won't you?
TOM: You needn't be satirical, if you *are* wet. Yes, I will! (*pointing to the left*)
    Windows on the one side (*pointing to the right*) doors on the other – just where
    they should be, architecturally. And locks on the doors, *real locks*, to work;
    and handles – to turn! (*rubbing his hands together gleefully*) Ha, ha! you wait!
    wait – !
             (ROSE *re-enters, a plate of biscuits in her hand, followed by
             CHARLES, *who carries a decanter of sherry and some wine-glasses.*)
ROSE: Here, Charles –
             (CHARLES *places the decanter and the glasses on the table.*)
GADD: (*whose luck has been against him, throwing himself, sulkily, on to the couch*)
    Bah! I'll risk no further stake.
COLPOYS: Just because you lose sevenpence in coppers you go on like this!
             (CHARLES, *turning from the table, faces* COLPOYS.)
    (*tearing his hair, and glaring at* CHARLES *wildly*) Ah–h–h, I am ruined! I have
    lost my all! my children are beggars – !
CHARLES: Ho, ho, ho!, he, he, he!
ROSE: Hush, hush!
             (CHARLES *goes out, laughing, quietly.*)
    (*to everybody*) Sherry?
GADD: (*rising*) Sherry.

(AVONIA, COLPOYS *and* GADD *gather round the table and help themselves to sherry and biscuits.*)

ROSE: (*to* TOM) Tom, won't you – ?

TOM: (*watching* GADD *anxiously*) No, thank you. The fact is, we – we have already partaken of refreshments, once or twice during the evening –

(COLPOYS *and* AVONIA, *each carrying a glass of wine and munching a biscuit, go to the couch where they sit.*)

GADD: (*pouring out sherry – singing*) 'And let me the canakin clink, clink – and let me the canakin –'

ROSE: (*coming to him*) Be quiet, Gadd!

COLPOYS: (*raising his glass*) The Bride!

ROSE: (*turning, kissing her hand to* AVONIA) Yes, yes – (GADD *hands* ROSE *his glass; she puts her lips to it.*) The Bride! (*She returns the glass to* GADD.)

GADD: (*sitting*) My Bride!

(TOM, *from behind the table, unperceived, takes the decanter and hides it under the table; then sits.* GADD, *missing the decanter, sits and contents himself with the biscuits.*)

AVONIA: Well, Rose, my darling, we've been talking about nothing but ourselves. How are you getting alone here?

ROSE: Getting along? Oh, I – I don't fancy I'm getting along very well, thank you.

COLPOYS *and* AVONIA: Not – !

GADD: (*his mouth full of biscuit*) Not –!

ROSE: (*sitting by the card-table*) No, boys; no 'Vonia. The truth is, it isn't as nice as you'd think it. I suppose the Profession had its drawbacks – Mother used to say so – but (*raising her arms*) one could fly. Yes, in Brydon Crescent one was a dirty little London sparrow perhaps; but here, in this grand square – ! Oh, it's the story of the caged bird, over again.

AVONIA: A love-bird, though.

ROSE: Poor Arthur? Yes, he's a dear. (*rising*) But the Gowers – the old Gowers! the Gowers! the Gowers!

AVONIA *and* COLPOYS: The Gowers! What does she mean by 'the Gowers'?

(ROSE *paces the room, beating her hands together. In her excitement, she ceases to whisper, and gradually becomes loud and voluble. The others, following her lead, chatter noisily – excepting* TOM, *who sits, thoughtfully, looking before him.*)

ROSE: The ancient Gowers! the venerable Gowers!

AVONIA: You mean, the grandfather – ?

ROSE: And the aunt – the great-aunt – the great bore of a great-aunt! The very mention of 'em makes something to 'tap, tap, tap, tap' at the top of my head.

AVONIA: Oh, I *am* sorry to hear this. Well, upon my word – !

ROSE: Would you believe it? 'Vonia – boys – you'll never believe it! I mayn't walk out with Arthur alone, nor see him here alone. I mayn't sing; no, nor sneeze even –

AVONIA: (*shrilly*) Not sing or sneeze!

COLPOYS: (*indignantly*) Not sneeze!

'And let . . . canakin': Othello II.iii.

ROSE: No, nor sit on the floor – the *floor*!

AVONIA: Why, when we shared rooms together, you were always on the floor!

GADD: (*producing a pipe, and knocking out the ashes on the heel of his boot*) In heaven's name, what kind of house can this be!

AVONIA: I wouldn't stand it, would you, Ferdinand?

GADD: (*loading his pipe*) Gad, no!

AVONIA: (*to* COLPOYS) Would you, Gus dear?

GADD: (*under his breath*) Here! not so much of the Gus dear –

AVONIA: (*to* COLPOYS) Would you?

COLPOYS: No, I'm blessed if I would, my darling.

GADD: (*his pipe in his mouth*) Mr Colpoys! less of the darling!

AVONIA: (*rising*) Rose, don't you put up with it! (*striking the top of the card-table vigorously*) I say, don't you stand it! (*embracing* ROSE) You're an independent girl, dear; they came to you, these people, not you to them, remember.

ROSE: (*sitting on the couch*) Oh, what can I do? I can't do anything.

AVONIA: Can't you! (*coming to* GADD) Ferdinand, advise her. You tell her how to –

GADD: (*who has risen*) Miss Bunn – Mrs Gadd, you have been all over Mr Colpoys this evening, ever since we –

AVONIA: (*angrily, pushing him back into his chair*) Oh, don't be a silly!

GADD: Madam!

AVONIA: (*returning to* COLPOYS) Gus, Ferdinand's foolish. Come and talk to Rose, and advise her, there's a dear boy –

(COLPOYS *rises; she takes his arm, to lead him to* ROSE. *At that moment* GADD *advances to* COLPOYS *and slaps his face violently.*)

COLPOYS: Hey – !

GADD: Miserable viper!

(*The two men close.* TOM *runs to separate them.* ROSE *rises with a cry of terror. There is a struggle and general uproar. The card-table is overturned, with a crash, and* AVONIA *utters a long and piercing shriek. Then the house-bells are heard ringing violently.*)

ROSE: Oh – !

(*The combatants part; all look scared.*)

(*at the door, listening*) They are moving – coming! Turn out the – (*She shuts the door and goes to the table.*)

(*She turns out the light at the table. The room is in half-light as* SIR WILLIAM *enters cautiously, closely followed by* MISS GOWER. *They are both in dressing-gowns and slippers;* SIR WILLIAM *carries a thick stick and his bedroom candle.* ROSE *is standing by a chair,* GADD, AVONIA, COLPOYS *and* TOM *are together.*)

SIR WILLIAM: Miss Trelawny – !

MISS GOWER: Rose – ! (*running behind the screen*) Men!

SIR WILLIAM: Who are these people?

ROSE: (*advancing a step or two*) Some friends of mine, who used to be at the 'Wells', have called upon me, to inquire how I am getting on.

(ARTHUR *enters quickly.*)

ARTHUR: (*looking round*) Oh! Rose – !

SIR WILLIAM: (*turning upon him*) Ah–h–h–h! How come you here?

ARTHUR: I was outside the house. Charles let me in, knowing something was wrong.

SIR WILLIAM: (*peering into his face*) Troubadouring – ?

ARTHUR: Troubadouring; yes, sir. (*to* ROSE) Rose, what is this?

SIR WILLIAM: (*fiercely*) No, sir, this is my affair. (*placing his candlestick on the table*) Stand aside! (*raising his stick furiously*) Stand aside!

> (ARTHUR *moves to the right.*)

MISS GOWER: (*over the screen*) William –

SIR WILLIAM: Hey?

MISS GOWER: Your ankles –

SIR WILLIAM: (*adjusting his dressing-gown*) I beg your pardon. (*to* ARTHUR) Yes, I can answer your question. (*pointing his stick, first at* ROSE, *then at the group*) Some friends of that young woman's, connected with – the play-house, have favoured us with a visit, for the purpose of ascertaining how she is – getting on. (*touching* GADD'*s pipe, which is lying at his feet, with the end of his stick*) A filthy tobacco-pipe. To whom does it belong? Whose is it?

> (ROSE *picks it up and passes it to* GADD, *bravely.*)

ROSE: It belongs to one of my friends.

SIR WILLIAM: (*taking* GADD'*s empty wine-glass and holding it to his nose*) Phu, yes! In brief, a drunken debauch. (*to the group*) So ye see, gentlemen – (*to* AVONIA) and you, madam; (*to* ARTHUR) and you, sir; you see, all of ye (*sinking into chair, coughing from exhaustion*), exactly how Miss Trelawny is getting on.

MISS GOWER: (*over the screen*) William –

SIR WILLIAM: What is it?

MISS GOWER: Your ankles –

SIR WILLIAM: (*leaping to his feet, in a frenzy*) Bah!

MISS GOWER: Oh, they seem so out of place!

SIR WILLIAM: (*flourishing his stick*) Begone! A set of garish, dissolute gipsies! Begone!

> (GADD, AVONIA, COLPOYS *and* WRENCH *gather together, the men hastily putting on their coats, etc.*)

AVONIA: Where is my umbrella?

GADD: A hand with my coat here!

COLPOYS: 'Pon my soul! London artists – !

AVONIA: We don't want to remain where we're not heartily welcome, I can assure everybody.

SIR WILLIAM: Open windows! Let in the air!

AVONIA: (*to* ROSE, *who is standing above the wreck of the card-table*) Good-bye, my dear –

ROSE: No, no, 'Vonia. Oh, don't leave me behind you!

ARTHUR: Rose – !

ROSE: Oh, I'm very sorry, Arthur. (*to* SIR WILLIAM) Indeed I am very sorry, Sir William. But you are right – gipsies – gipsies! (*to* ARTHUR) Yes, Arthur, if you were a gipsy, as I am – as these friends o'mine are, we might be happy together. But I've seen enough of your life, my dear boy, to know that I'm no wife for you. I should only be wretched, and would make you wretched; and the end, when it arrived, as it very soon would, would be much as it is to-night – !

ARTHUR: (*distractedly*) You'll let me see you, talk to you, to-morrow, Rose?

ROSE: No, never!

SIR WILLIAM: (*sharply*) You mean that?

ROSE: (*facing him*) Oh, don't be afraid. I give you my word.

SIR WILLIAM: (*gripping her hand*) Thank ye. Thank ye.

TOM: (*quietly – to* ARTHUR) Mr Gower, come and see *me* to-morrow – (*He moves away to the door.*)

ROSE: (*turning to* AVONIA, GADD, *and* COLPOYS) I'm ready –

MISS GOWER: (*coming from behind the screen to the back of the couch*) Not to-night, child, not to-night! Where will you go?

AVONIA: (*holding* ROSE) To her old quarters in Brydon Crescent. Send her things after her, if you please.

MISS GOWER: And then – ?

ROSE: Then back to the 'Wells' again, Miss Gower! – back to the 'Wells' – !

        END OF THE SECOND ACT

    THE THIRD ACT

The scene represents an apartment on the second floor of MRS MOSSOP's *house. The room is of a humbler character than that shown in the First Act; but, though shabby, it is neat. On the right is a door, outside which is supposed to be the landing. In a wall at the back is another door, presumably admitting to a further chamber. On the left there is a fireplace, with a fire burning, and over the mantelpiece a mirror. In the left-hand corner of the room is a small bedstead with a tidily made bed, which can be hidden by a pair of curtains of some common and faded material, hanging from a cord slung from wall to wall. At the foot of the bedstead stands a large theatrical dress-basket. On the wall, by the head of the bed, are some pegs on which hang a skirt or two and other articles of attire. On the right, against the back wall, there is a chest of drawers, the top of which is used as a washstand. In front of this is a small screen, and close by there are some more pegs with things hanging upon them. On the right wall, above the sofa, is a hanging bookcase with a few books. A small circular table, with a somewhat shabby cover upon it, stands near the fireplace. The walls are papered, the doors painted stone-colour. An old felt carpet is on the floor. The light is that of morning.*

(MRS MOSSOP, *now dressed in a workaday gown, has just finished making the bed. There is a knock at the centre door.*)

AVONIA: (*from the adjoining room*) Rose!

MRS MOSSOP: (*giving a final touch to the quilt*) Eh?

AVONIA: Is Miss Trelawny in her room?

MRS MOSSOP: No, Mrs Gadd; she's at rehearsal.

AVONIA: Oh –

    (MRS MOSSOP *draws the curtains, hiding the bed from view.*
    AVONIA *enters by the door on the right, in a morning wrapper which has seen its best days. She carries a pair of curling-tongs, and her hair is evidently in process of being dressed in ringlets.*)

Of course she is; I forgot. There's a call for 'The Pedlar of Marseilles'. Thank

Gawd, *I'm* not in it. (*singing*) 'I'm a great guerilla chief, I'm a robber and a thief – (MRS MOSSOP *laughs.*) I can either kill a foe or prig a pocket-handkerchief – '.

MRS MOSSOP: (*dusting the ornaments on the mantelpiece*) Bless your heart, you're very gay this morning!

AVONIA: It's the pantomime. I'm always stark mad as the pantomime approaches. I don't grudge letting the rest of the company have their fling at other times – but with the panto comes *my* turn. (*throwing herself full length upon the sofa gleefully*) Ha, ha, ha! the turn of Avonia Bunn! (*with a change of tone*) I hope Miss Trelawny won't take a walk up to Highbury, or anywhere, after rehearsal. I want to borrow her gilt belt. My dress has arrived.

MRS MOSSOP: (*much interested*) No! has it?

AVONIA: Yes, Mrs Burroughs is coming down from the theatre at twelve-thirty to see me in it. (*singing*) 'Any kind of villainy cometh natural to me, So it endeth with a combat and a one, two, three – ! ' *

MRS MOSSOP: (*surveying the room*) Well, that's as cheerful as I can make things look, poor dear!

AVONIA: (*taking a look round, seriously*) It's pretty bright – if it wasn't for the idea of Rose Trelawny having to economise!

MRS MOSSOP: Ah–h!

AVONIA: (*rising*) That's what I can't swallow. (*sticking her irons in the fire angrily*) One room! and on the second floor! (*turning to* MRS MOSSOP) Of course, Gadd and me are one-room people too – and on the same floor; but then Gadd is so popular *out* of the theatre, Mrs Mossop – he's obliged to spend such a load of money at the 'Clown' –

MRS MOSSOP: (*who has been dusting the bookcase, coming to the table*) Mrs Gadd, dearie, I'm sure I'm not in the least inquisitive; no one could accuse me of it – but I should like to know just one thing.

AVONIA: (*testing her irons upon a sheet of paper which she takes from the table*) What's that?

MRS MOSSOP: Why *have* they been and cut down Miss Trelawny's salary at the 'Wells'?

AVONIA: (*hesitatingly*) H'm, everybody's chattering about it; you could get to hear easily enough –

MRS MOSSOP: Oh, I daresay.

AVONIA: So I don't mind. Poor Rose! They tell her she can't act now, Mrs Mossop.

MRS MOSSOP: Can't act!

AVONIA: (*turning to* MRS MOSSOP) No, dear old girl, she's lost it; it's gone from her – the trick of it –

> (TOM *enters by the door on the right, carrying a table-cover of a bright pattern.*)

TOM: (*coming upon* MRS MOSSOP, *disconcerted*) Oh – !

MRS MOSSOP: My first floor table-cover!

TOM: Y–y–yes. (*exchanging the table-covers*) I thought, as the Telfers have departed,

---

*These snatches of song are from 'The Miller and His Men', a burlesque mealy-drama, by Francis Talfourd and Henry J. Byron, produced at the Strand Theatre, April 9th, 1860. [*Pinero's note*]

and as their late sitting-room is at present vacant, that Miss Trelawny might
enjoy the benefit – hey?

MRS MOSSOP: Well, I never –!

      (*She goes out.*)

AVONIA: (*curling her hair, at the mirror over the mantelpiece*) I say, Tom, I wonder if
I've done wrong–

TOM: It all depends upon whether you've had the chance.

AVONIA: I've told Mrs Mossop the reason they've reduced Rose's salary.

TOM: You needn't.

AVONIA: She had only to ask any other member of the company –

TOM: To have found one who could have kept silent.

AVONIA: (*remorsefully*) Oh, I could burn myself!

TOM: Besides, it isn't true.

AVONIA: What –?

TOM: That Rose Trelawny is no longer up to her work.

AVONIA: (*sadly*) Oh, Tom!

TOM: It isn't the fact, I say!

AVONIA: Isn't it the fact that ever since Rose returned from Cavendish Square – ?

TOM: She has been reserved, subdued, lady-like –

AVONIA: (*shrilly*) She was always lady-like!

TOM: I'm aware of that!

AVONIA: Well, then, what do you mean by – ?

TOM: (*in a rage, turning away*) Oh –!

AVONIA: (*heating her irons again*) The idea!

TOM: (*cooling down*) She was always a lady-like *actress*, on the stage and off it, but
now she has developed into a – (*at a loss*) into a–

AVONIA: (*scornfully*) Ha!

TOM: Into a lady-like human being. These fools at the 'Wells'! Can't act, can't she!
No, she can no longer *spout*, she can no longer *ladle*, the vapid trash, the – the –
the turgid rodomontade –

AVONIA (*doubtfully*) You'd better be careful of your language, Wrench.

TOM: (*with a twinkle in his eye – mopping his brow*) You're a married woman,
'Vonia –

AVONIA: (*holding her irons to her cheek, modestly*) I know, but still –

TOM: Yes, deep down in the well of that girl's nature there has been lying a little,
bright, clear pool of genuine refinement, girlish simplicity. And now the bucket
has been lowered by love; experience has turned the handle; and up comes the
crystal to the top, pure and sparkling. Why, her broken engagement to poor
young Gower has really been the making of her! It has transformed her! Can't
act, can't she! (*drawing a long breath*) How she would play Dora in my comedy!

AVONIA: Ho, that comedy!

TOM: How she would murmur those love-scenes!

AVONIA: Murder –!

TOM: (*testily*) Murmur. (*partly to himself*) Do you know, 'Vonia, I had Rose in my
mind when I imagined Dora – ?

AVONIA: Ha, ha! you astonish me.

TOM: And Arthur Gower when I wrote the character of Gerald, Dora's lover. (*in a low voice*) Gerald and Dora – Rose and Arthur – (*he sits*) Gerald and Dora – (*suddenly*) 'Vonia – !

AVONIA: (*singeing her hair*) Ah – ! Oh, lor'! What now?

TOM: I wish you could keep a secret.

AVONIA: Why, can't I?

TOM: Haven't you just been gossiping with Mother Mossop?

AVONIA: (*behind his chair, breathlessly, her eyes bolting*) A secret, Tom?

TOM: (*nodding*) I should like to share it with you, because – you are fond of her too –

AVONIA: Ah – !

TOM: And because the possession of it is worrying me. But there, I can't trust you.

AVONIA: Mr Wrench!

TOM: No, you're a warm-hearted woman, 'Vonia, but you're a sieve.

AVONIA: (*going down upon her knees beside him*) I swear! By all my hopes, Tom Wrench, of hitting 'em as Prince Charming in the coming pantomime, I swear I will not divulge, leave alone tell a living soul, any secret you may entrust to me, or let me know of, concerning Rose Trelawny of the 'Wells'. Amen!

TOM: (*in her ear*) 'Vonia, *I know where Arthur Gower is.*

AVONIA: *Is*! Isn't he still in London.?

TOM: (*producing a letter mysteriously*) No. When Rose stuck to her refusal to see him – listen – mind, not a word – !

AVONIA: By all my hopes – !

TOM: (*checking her*) All right, all right! (*reading*) 'Theatre Royal, Bristol. Friday – '

AVONIA: Theatre Royal, Br– !

TOM: Be quiet! (*reading*) 'My dear Mr Wrench. A whole week and not a line from you to tell me how Miss Trelawny is. When you are silent I am sleepless at night and a haggard wretch during the day. Young Mr Kirby, our Walking Gentleman, has been unwell, and the management has given me temporarily some of his business to play – '

AVONIA: Arthur Gower – !

TOM: Will you – ? (*reading*) 'Last night I was allowed to appear as Careless in "The School for Scandal". Miss Mason, the Lady Teazle, complimented me, but the men said I lacked vigour' – the old cry! – 'and so this morning I am greatly depressed'. (*He half turns away, and leans his elbow on the table; she comes a little nearer to look over the letter.*) 'But I will still persevere, as long as you can assure me that no presuming fellow is paying attention to Miss Trelawny. Oh, how badly she treated me! – '

AVONIA: (*following the reading of the letter*) 'How badly she treated me – !'

TOM: 'I will never forgive her – only love her – '

AVONIA: 'Only love her – '

TOM: 'Only love her, and hope I may some day become a great actor, and, like herself, a gipsy. Yours very gratefully, Arthur Gordon.'

AVONIA: In the Profession!

Prince Charming: usually 'principal boy' (the *travestie* rôle) in *Cinderella*, but perhaps another pantomime is intended here.

Theatre Royal, Bristol: built 1766. At this time under the management of the Macready-Chute family (relatives of W. C. Macready). Now the home of the Bristol Old Vic Company.

TOM: Bolted from Cavendish Square – went down to Bristol –

AVONIA: How did he manage it all? (TOM *taps his breast proudly.*) But isn't Rose to be told? Why shouldn't she be told?

TOM: She has hurt the boy, stung him to the quick, and he's proud.

AVONIA: But she loves him now that she believes he has forgotten her. She only half-loved him before. She loves him!

TOM: Serve her right.

AVONIA: Oh, Tom, is she never to know?

TOM: (*folding the letter carefully*) Some day, when he begins to make strides.

AVONIA: Strides! He's nothing but General Utility at present?

TOM: (*putting the letter in his pocket*) No.

AVONIA: And how long have you been that?

TOM: Ten years.

AVONIA: (*with a little screech*) Ah–h–h! She ought to be told!

TOM: (*seizing her wrist*) Woman, you won't – !

AVONIA: (*raising her disengaged hand*) By all my hopes of hitting 'em – !

TOM: All right, I believe you – (*listening*) Sssh!

> (*They rise and separate, he moving to the fire, she to the right, as* ROSE *enters.* ROSE *is now a grave, dignified, somewhat dreamy young woman.*)

ROSE: (*looking from* TOM *to* AVONIA) Ah – ?

TOM *and* AVONIA: Good morning.

ROSE: (*kissing* AVONIA) Visitors!

AVONIA: My fire's so black; (*showing her irons*) I thought you wouldn't mind –

ROSE: (*removing her gloves*) Of course not. (*seeing the table-cover*) Oh – !

TOM: Mrs Mossop asked me to bring that upstairs. It was in the Telfers' room, you know, and she fancied –

ROSE: How good of her! Thanks, Tom. (*taking off her hat and mantle*) Poor Mr and Mrs Telfer! They still wander mournfully about the 'Wells'; they can get nothing to do.

> (*Carrying her hat and umbrella, she disappears through the curtains.*)

TOM: (*to* AVONIA, *in a whisper, across the room*) The Telfers – !

AVONIA: Eh?

TOM: She's been giving 'em money.

AVONIA: Yes.

TOM: Damn!

ROSE: (*reappearing*) What are you saying about me?

AVONIA: I was wondering whether you'd lend me that belt you bought for Ophelia; to wear during the first two or three weeks of the pantomime –

ROSE: Certainly, 'Vonia, to wear throughout –

AVONIA: (*embracing her*) No, it's too good; I'd rather fake one for the rest of the time. (*looking into her face*) What's the matter?

ROSE: I will make you a present of the belt, 'Vonia, if you will accept it. I bought it when I came back to the 'Wells', thinking everything would go on as before. But – it's of no use; they tell me I cannot act effectively any longer –

TOM: (*indignantly*) Effectively – !

ROSE: First, as you know, they reduce my salary –

TOM *and* AVONIA (*with clenched hands*) Yes!
ROSE: And now, this morning – you can guess –
AVONIA: (*hoarsely*) Got your notice?
ROSE: Yes.
TOM *and* AVONIA: Oh–h–h–h!
ROSE: (*after a little pause*) Poor Mother! I hope she doesn't see. (*Overwhelmed, AVONIA and TOM sit.*) I was running through Blanche, my old part in 'The Pedlar of Marseilles', when Mr Burroughs spoke to me. It is true I was doing it tamely, but – it is such nonsense.
TOM: Hear, hear!
ROSE: And then, the poor little song I used to sing on the bridge –
AVONIA: (*singing, softly*) 'Ever of thee I'm fondly dreaming –'
TOM *and* AVONIA: (*singing*) 'Thy gentle voice my spirit can cheer.'
ROSE: I told Mr Burroughs I should cut it out. So ridiculously inappropriate!
TOM: And that – did it?
ROSE: (*smiling at him*) That did it.
AVONIA: (*kneeling beside her, and embracing her tearfully*) My ducky! Oh, but there are other theatres besides the 'Wells' –
ROSE: For me? – only where the same trash is acted.
AVONIA (*with a sob*) But a few months ago you l–l–liked your work.
ROSE: Yes (*dreamily*), and then I went to Cavendish Square, engaged to Arthur – (TOM *rises and leans upon the mantelpiece, looking into the fire.*) How badly I behaved in Cavendish Square! How unlike a young lady! What if the old folks *were* overbearing and tyrannical, Arthur could be gentle with them. 'They have not many more years in this world', he said – dear boy! – 'and anything we can do to make them happy –' And what *did* I do? *There* was a chance for me – to be patient, and womanly; and I proved to them that I was nothing but – an actress.
AVONIA: (*rising, hurt but still tearful*) It doesn't follow, because one is a –
ROSE: Yes, 'Vonia, it does! We are only dolls, partly human, with mechanical limbs that *will* fall into stagey postures, and heads stuffed with sayings out of rubbishy plays. (*She rises and goes to* AVONIA.) It isn't *the* world we live in, merely *a* world – such a queer little one! I was less than a month in Cavendish Square, and very few people came there; but they were *real* people – *real*! For a month I lost the smell of gas and oranges, and the hurry and noise, and the dirt and the slang, and the clownish joking, at the 'Wells'. I didn't realise at the time the change that was going on in me; I didn't realize it till I came back. And then, by degrees, I discovered what had happened –
> (TOM *is now near her. She takes his hand and drops her head upon* AVONIA's *shoulder.*)
(*wearily*) Oh, Tom! Oh, 'Vonia –!
> (*From the next room comes the sound of the throwing about of heavy objects, and of* GADD's *voice uttering loud imprecations.*)
(*alarmed*) Oh –!
AVONIA: (*listening attentively*) Sounds like Ferdy.
> (*She goes to the centre door*).
(*at the keyhole*) Ferdy! ain't you well, darling?
GADD: (*on the other side of the door*) Avonia!

AVONIA: I'm in Miss Trelawny's room.

GADD: Ah – ?

AVONIA: (*to* ROSE *and* TOM) Now, what's put Ferdy out? (GADD *enters with a wild look.*) Ferdinand!

TOM: Anything wrong, Gadd?

GADD: Wrong! Wrong! (*sitting*) What d'ye think?

AVONIA: Tell us!

GADD: I have been asked to appear in the pantomime.

AVONIA: (*shocked*) Oh, Ferdy! – you!

GADD: I, a serious actor, if ever there was one; a poetic actor – !

AVONIA: What part, Ferdy?

GADD: The insult, the bitter, insult! the gross indignity!

AVONIA: What part, Ferdy?

GADD: I who have not been seen in pantomime for years, not since I shook the dust of the T.R. Stockton from my feet.

AVONIA: Ferdy, what part?

GADD: I simply looked at Burroughs, when he preferred his request, and swept from the theatre.

AVONIA: What part, Ferdy?

GADD: A part, too, which is seen for a moment at the opening of the pantomime, and not again till its close.

AVONIA: Ferdy.

GADD: Eh?

AVONIA: What part?

GADD: A character called the Demon of Discontent.

> (ROSE *turns away to the fireplace;* TOM *curls himself up on the sofa and is seen to shake with laughter.*)

AVONIA: (*walking about indignantly*) Oh! (*returning to* GADD) Oh, it's a rotten part! Rose dear, I assure you, as artist to artist, that part is absolutely rotten. (*to* GADD) You won't play it, darling?

GADD: (*rising*) Play it! I would see the 'Wells' in ashes first.

AVONIA: We shall lose our engagements, Ferdy. I know Burroughs; we shall be out, both of us

GADD: Of course we shall. D'ye think I have not counted the cost?

AVONIA: (*putting her hand in his*) I don't mind, dear – for the sake of your position – (*struck by a sudden thought*) Oh – !

GADD: What – ?

AVONIA: There now – we haven't put-by!

> (*There is a knock at the door.*)

ROSE: Who is that?

COLPOYS: (*outside the door*) Is Gadd here, Miss Trelawny?

ROSE: Yes.

COLPOYS: I want to see him.

GADD: Wrench, I'll trouble you. Ask Mr Colpoys whether he approaches me as a

---

T.R. Stockton: for Theatre Royal, Stockton-on-Tees.

friend, an acquaintance, or in his capacity of stage-manager at the 'Wells' – the tool of Burroughs.

TOM: (*at the door, solemnly*) Colpoys, are you here as Gadd's bosom friend, or as a mere tool of Burroughs?

> (*An inaudible colloquy follows between* TOM *and* COLPOYS. TOM*'s head is outside the door; his legs are seen to move convulsively, and the sound of suppressed laughter is heard.*)

GADD: (*turning*) Well, well?

TOM: (*closing the door sharply, and facing* GADD *with great seriousness*) He is here as the tool of Burroughs.

GADD: I will receive him.

> (TOM *admits* COLPOYS, *who carries a mean-looking 'part', and a letter.*)

COLPOYS: (*after formally bowing to the ladies*) Oh, Gadd, Mr Burroughs instructs me to offer you this part in the pantomime. (*handing the part to* GADD) Demon of Discontent. (GADD *takes the part and flings it to the ground.* AVONIA *picks it up and reads it.*) You refuse it?

GADD: I do. (*with dignity*) Acquaint Mr Burroughs with my decision, and add that I hope his pantomime will prove an utterly mirthless one. May Boxing-night, to those unfortunate enough to find themselves in the theatre, long remain a dismal memory; and may succeeding audiences, scanty and dissatisfied – ! (COLPOYS *presents* GADD *with the letter.* GADD *opens it and reads.*) I leave. The Romeo, the Orlando, the Clifford – leaves!

AVONIA: (*coming to* GADD, *indicating some lines in the part*) Ferdy, this ain't so bad – (*reading*)

> 'I'm Discontent! from Orkney's isle to Dover
> To make men's bile bile-over I endover – '

GADD: 'Vonia! (*taking the part from* AVONIA, *with mingled surprise and pleasure*) Ho, ho! no, that's not bad. (*reading*)

> 'Tempers, though sweet, I whip up to a lather,
> Make wives hate husbands, sons wish fathers farther.'

'Vonia, there's something to lay hold of here! I'll think this over. (*rising, addressing* COLPOYS) Gus, I have thought this over. I play it.

> (*They all gather round him, and congratulate him.* AVONIA *embraces and kisses him.*)

TOM *and* COLPOYS: That's right!

ROSE: I'm very pleased, Ferdinand.

AVONIA: (*tearfully*) Oh, Ferdy!

GADD: (*in high spirits*) Egad, I play it! Gus, I'll stroll back with you to the 'Wells'.

> (AVONIA *accompanies* COLPOYS *and* GADD *to the door, clinging to* GADD

---

a mean-looking 'part': No member of a Victorian company could expect to rehearse from a complete text. His own lines (with the barest indication of cues) were written down and constituted a 'part'. His importance was judged by the length of this MS.

Boxing-night: i.e. 26 December, the traditional opening night for a Christmas pantomime.

Clifford: in *The Hunchback* by Knowles (see above, p. 143).

'*I'm . . . endover –* ': apparently imaginary (but entirely typical) lines for a pantomime demon.

who is shaking hands with ROSE) Miss Trelawny – ! (*flourishing the part*)
'Vonia, I see myself in this! (*kissing her*) Steak for dinner!
    (GADD *and* COLPOYS *go out.* TOM *shrieks with laughter.*)
AVONIA: (*turning upon him, angrily and volubly*) Yes, I heard you with Colpoys
    outside that door, if Gadd didn't. It's a pity, Mr Wrench, you can't find
    something better to do – !
ROSE: (*pacifically*) Hush, hush, 'Vonia! Tom, assist me with my basket; I'll give
    'Vonia her belt –
        (TOM *and* ROSE *go behind the curtains and presently emerge carrying
        the dress-basket which they deposit near the sofa.*)
AVONIA: (*flouncing across the room*) Making fun of Gadd! – an artist to the roots of
    his hair! There's more talent in Gadd's little finger – !
ROSE: (*rummaging among the contents of the basket*) 'Vonia, 'Vonia!
AVONIA: And if Gadd *is* to play a demon in the pantomime, what do *you* figure as,
    Tom Wrench, among half a dozen other things? Why, as part of a dragon! Yes,
    and *which end* – ?
ROSE: (*quietly to* TOM) Apologise to 'Vonia at once, Tom.
TOM: (*meekly*) Mrs Gadd, I beg your pardon.
AVONIA: (*coming to him and kissing him*) Granted, Tom; but you should be a little
    more considerate –
ROSE: (*holding up the belt*) Here – !
AVONIA: (*taking the belt, ecstatically*) Oh, isn't it lovely! Rose, you dear! you sweet
    thing! (*Singing a few bars of the Jewel song from 'Faust' then rushing at* ROSE
    and embracing her) I'm going to try my dress on, to show Mrs Burroughs. Come
    and help me into it. I'll unlock my door on my side – (TOM *politely opens the
    door for her to pass out.* ROSE *crosses to fire.*) Thank you, Tom – (*kissing him
    again*) only you should be more considerate towards Gadd –
        (*She disappears.*)
TOM: (*calling after her*) I will be; I will – (*shutting the door*) Ha, ha, ha!
ROSE: (*smiling*) Hush! Poor 'Vonia! (*mending the fire*) Excuse me, Tom – have you a
    fire upstairs in your room, to-day?
TOM: Er–n–not to-day – (*inspired*) it's Saturday. I never have a fire on a Saturday.
ROSE: (*coming to him*) Why not?
TOM: (*looking away from her*) Don't know – creatures of habit –
ROSE: (*gently touching his coat-sleeve*) Because if you would like to smoke your pipe
    by my fire while I'm with 'Vonia –
        (*The key is heard to turn in the lock of the further room.*)
AVONIA: (*from the further room*) It's unlocked.
ROSE: I'm coming.
        (*She unbolts the door on her side, and goes into* AVONIA's *room,
        shutting the door behind her. The lid of the dress-basket is open,
        showing the contents; a pair of little satin shoes lie at the top.* TOM *takes
        up one of the shoes and presses it to his lips. There is a knock at the door
        on the right. He returns the shoe to the basket, closes the lid, and walks
        away.*)

---

which end: c.f. the two 'ends' of a pantomime horse.

TOM: Yes?
> (*The door opens slightly and* IMOGEN *is heard.*)

IMOGEN: (*outside*) Is that you, Wrench?

TOM: (*brightening up*) Hullo!
> (IMOGEN, *in out-of-door costume, enters breathlessly.*)

IMOGEN: (*closing the door – speaking rapidly and excitedly*) Mossop said you were in Rose's room –

TOM: (*shaking hands with her*) She'll be here in a few minutes.

IMOGEN: It's you I want. Let me sit down.

TOM: (*going to the armchair*) Here –

IMOGEN: (*sitting on the right of the table, panting*) Not near the fire –

TOM: What's up?

IMOGEN: Oh, Wrench! p'r'aps my fortune's made!

TOM: (*quite calmly*) Congratulate you, Jenny.

IMOGEN: Do be quiet; don't make such a racket. You see, things haven't been going at all satisfactorily at the Olympic lately. There's Miss Puddifant –

TOM: I know – no lady.

IMOGEN: *How* do you know?

TOM: Guessed.

IMOGEN: Quite right; and a thousand other annoyances. And at last I took it into my head to consult Mr Clandon, who married an aunt of mine and lives at Streatham, and he'll lend me five hundred pounds.

TOM: What for?

IMOGEN: Towards taking a theatre.

TOM: (*dubiously*) Five hundred –

IMOGEN: It's all he's good for, and he won't advance that unless I can get a *further* five, or eight, hundred from some other quarter.

TOM: What theatre?

IMOGEN: The *Pantheon* happens to be empty.

TOM: Yes; it's been *that* for the last twenty years.

IMOGEN: Don't throw wet blankets – I mean – (*referring to her tablets, which she carries in her muff*) I've got it all worked out in black and white. There's a deposit required on account of rent – two hundred pounds. Cleaning the theatre – (*looking at* TOM) what do *you* say?

TOM: Cleaning *that* theatre!

IMOGEN: I say, another two hundred.

TOM: That would remove the top layer –

IMOGEN: Cost of producing the opening play, five hundred pounds. Balance for emergencies, three hundred. You generally have a balance for emergencies.

TOM: You generally have the emergencies, if not the balance!

IMOGEN: Now the question is, will five hundred produce the play?

TOM: What play?

IMOGEN: Your play.

Pantheon: a theatre of this name (with variations) operated in Oxford Street between 1772 and 1814, but it is evidently used here for the Queen's Theatre, Charlotte Street, which Marie Wilton renamed the Prince of Wales's and opened in 1865.

TOM: (*quietly*) My –
IMOGEN: Your comedy.
TOM: (*turning to the fire – in a low voice*) Rubbish!
IMOGEN: Well, Mr Clandon thinks it *isn't*. I gave it to him to read, and he – well, he's quite taken with it.
TOM: (*walking about, his hands in his pockets, his head down, agitatedly*) Clandon – Landon – what's his name – ?
IMOGEN: Tony Clandon – Anthony Clandon –
TOM: (*choking*) He's a – he's a –
IMOGEN: He's a hop-merchant.
TOM: No he's not – (*sitting on the sofa, leaning his head on his hands*) he's a stunner.
IMOGEN: (*rising*) So you grasp the position. Theatre – manageress – author – play, found; and eight hundred pounds *wanted*!
TOM: Oh, lord!
IMOGEN: Who's got it?
TOM: (*rising – wildly*) The Queen's got it! Miss Burdett-Coutts has got it!
IMOGEN: Don't be a fool, Wrench. Do you remember old Mr Morfew, of Duncan Terrace? He used to take great interest in us all at the 'Wells'. *He* has money.
TOM: He has gout; we don't see him now.
IMOGEN: Gout! – how lucky! That means he's at home. Will you run round to Duncan Terrace – ?
TOM: (*looking down at his clothes*) I!
IMOGEN: Nonsense, Wrench; we're not asking him to advance money on your clothes.
TOM: The clothes are the man, Jenny.
IMOGEN: And the woman – ?
TOM: The face is the woman.
IMOGEN: I'll go! Is my face good enough?
TOM: (*enthusiastically*) I should say so!
IMOGEN: (*taking his hands*) Ha, ha! it has been in my possession longer than you have had your oldest coat, Tom!
TOM: Make haste, Jenny!
IMOGEN: (*running up to the door*) Oh, it will last till I get to Duncan Terrace. (*turning*) Tom, you may have to read your play to Mr Morfew. Have you another copy? Uncle Clandon has mine.
TOM: (*holding his head*) I think I have – I don't know –
IMOGEN: Look for it! find it! If Morfew wants to hear it, we must strike while the iron's hot.
TOM: While the gold's hot!
IMOGEN *and* TOM: Ha, ha, ha!
(MRS MOSSOP *enters, showing some signs of excitement.*)

---

stunner: i.e. a wonder (because he likes Tom's play).
Miss Burdett-Coutts: Angelina Georgina Burdett-Coutts (1814–1906), daughter of Francis Burdett, Radical politician, and Sophia Coutts. She inherited great wealth in 1837 on the death of Harriet, Duchess of St Albans, the widow of Thomas Coutts, and supported many philanthropic causes. She was created a baroness in 1871.

IMOGEN: (*pushing her aside*) Oh, get out of the way, Mrs Mossop –
(IMOGEN *departs.*)
MRS MOSSOP: Upon my – ! (*to* TOM) A visitor for Miss Trelawny! Where's Miss
Trelawny?
TOM: With Mrs Gadd. Mossop!
MRS MOSSOP: Don't bother me now –
TOM: Mossop, the apartments vacated by the Telfers! Dare to let 'em without giving
me the preference.
MRS MOSSOP: You!
TOM: (*seizing her hands and swinging her round*) I may be wealthy, sweet Rebecca!
(*embracing her*) I may be rich and honoured!
MRS MOSSOP: Oh, have done! (*releasing herself*) My lodgers do take such liberties –
TOM: (*at the door, grandly*) Beccy, half a scuttle of coal, to start with.
(*He goes out, leaving the door slightly open.*)
MRS MOSSOP: (*knocking at the door of the further room*) Miss Trelawny, my dear!
Miss Trelawny!
(*The door opens, a few inches.*)
ROSE: (*looking out*) Why, what a clatter you and Mr Wrench have been
making – !
MRS MOSSOP: (*beckoning her mysteriously*) Come here, dear.
ROSE: (*closing the door, and entering the room wonderingly*) Eh?
MRS MOSSOP: (*in awe*) Sir William Gower!
ROSE: Sir William!
MRS MOSSOP: Don't be vexed with me. 'I'll see if she's at home', I said. 'Oh yes,
woman, Miss Trelawny's at home', said he, and hobbled straight in. I've shut
him in the Telfers' room –
(*There are three distinct raps, with a stock, at the right-hand door.*)
ROSE *and* MRS MOSSOP: Oh–h!
ROSE: (*faintly*) Open it.
(MRS MOSSOP *opens the door, and* SIR WILLIAM *enters. He is
feebler, more decrepit, than when last seen. He wears a plaid about his
shoulders and walks with the aid of a stick.*)
MRS MOSSOP: (*at the door*) Ah, and a sweet thing Miss Trelawny is – !
SIR WILLIAM: (*turning to her*) Are you a relative?
MRS MOSSOP: No, I am *not* a relative –
SIR WILLIAM: Go.
(*She departs; he closes the door with the end of his stick.*)
(*facing* ROSE) My mind is not commonly a wavering one, Miss Trelawny, but it
has taken me some time – months – to decide upon calling on ye.
ROSE: Won't you sit down?
SIR WILLIAM: (*after a pause of hesitation, sitting upon the dress-basket*) Ugh!
ROSE: (*with quiet dignity*) Have we no chairs? Do we lack chairs here, Sir William?
(*He gives her a quick, keen look, then rises and walks to the fire.*)
SIR WILLIAM: (*turning suddenly, bringing his stick down upon the table with
violence*) My grandson! my grandson! Where is he?
ROSE: Arthur – !
SIR WILLIAM: I had but one.

ROSE: Isn't he – in Cavendish Square – ?
SIR WILLIAM: Isn't he in Cavendish Square! No, he is not in Cavendish Square, as you know well.
ROSE: Oh, I *don't* know –
SIR WILLIAM: Tsch!
ROSE: When did he leave you?
SIR WILLIAM: Tsch!
ROSE: When?
SIR WILLIAM: He made his escape during the night, twenty-second of August last – (*pointing his finger at her*) as you know well.
ROSE: Sir William, I assure you –
SIR WILLIAM: Tsch! (*taking off his gloves*) How often does he write to ye?
ROSE: He does not write to me. He did write day after day, two or three times a day, for about a week. That was in June, when I came back here. (*with drooping head*) He never writes now.
SIR WILLIAM: Visits ye – ?
ROSE: No.
SIR WILLIAM: Comes troubadouring – ?
ROSE: No, no, no. I have not seen him since that night. I refused to see him – (*with a catch in her breath*) Why, he may be – !
SIR WILLIAM: (*fumbling in his pocket*) Ah, but he's not. He's alive; (*producing a small packet of letters*) Arthur's alive (*advancing to her*) and full of his tricks still. His great-aunt Trafalgar receives a letter from him once a fortnight, posted in London –
ROSE: (*holding out her hand for the letters*) Oh – !
SIR WILLIAM: (*putting them behind his back*) Hey!
ROSE: (*faintly*) I thought you wished me to read them.
        (*He yields them to her grudgingly.*)
        (*taking his hand and bending over it*) Ah, thank you.
SIR WILLIAM: (*withdrawing his hand with a look of disrelish*) What are ye doing, madam? What are ye doing?
        (*He sits, producing his snuff-box; she sits, upon the basket, facing him, and opens the packet of letters.*)
ROSE: (*reading a letter*) 'To reassure you as to my well-being, I cause this to be posted in London by a friend – '
SIR WILLIAM: (*pointing a finger at her again, accusingly*) A friend!
ROSE: (*looking up, with simple pride*) He would never call me *that*. (*reading*) 'I am in good bodily health, and as contented as a man can be who has lost the woman he loves, and will love till his dying day – ' Ah – !
SIR WILLIAM: Read no more! Return them to me! Give them to me, ma'am!
        (*Rising, she restores the letters, meekly.*)
        (*peering up into her face*) What's come to ye? You are not so much of a vixen as you were.
ROSE: (*shaking her head*) No.
SIR WILLIAM: (*suspiciously*) Less of the devil – ?
ROSE: Sir William, I am sorry for having been a vixen, and for all my unruly conduct, in Cavendish Square. I humbly beg your, and Miss Gower's, forgiveness.

SIR WILLIAM: (*taking snuff, uncomfortably*) Pi–i–i–sh! extraordinary change.
ROSE: Aren't *you* changed, Sir William, now that you have lost him?
SIR WILLIAM: I!
ROSE: Don't you love him now, the more? (*His head droops a little, and his hands wander to the brooch which secures his plaid.*) Let me take your shawl from you. You would catch cold when you go out –
    (*He allows her to remove the plaid, protesting during the process.*)
SIR WILLIAM: I'll not trouble ye, ma'am. Much obleeged to ye, but I'll not trouble ye. (*Rising*) I'll not trouble ye –
    (*He walks away to the fireplace. She folds the plaid and lays it upon the sofa.*)
    (*looking round – in an altered tone*) My dear, gipsying doesn't seem to be such a good trade with ye, as it used to be by all accounts –
    (*The door of the further room opens and* AVONIA *enters boldly, in the dress of a burlesque prince – cotton-velvet shirt, edged with bullion trimming, a cap, white tights, ankle boots, etc.*)
AVONIA: (*unconsciously*) How's this, Rose – ?
SIR WILLIAM: Ah–h–h–h!
ROSE: Oh, go away, 'Vonia!
AVONIA: Sir Gower! (*to* SIR WILLIAM) Good morning.
    (*She withdraws.*)
SIR WILLIAM: (*pacing the room – again very violent*) Yes! and these are the associates you would have tempted my boy – my grandson – to herd with! (*flourishing his stick*) Ah–h–h–h!
ROSE: (*sitting upon the basket – weakly*) That young lady doesn't live in that attire. She is preparing for the pantomime –
SIR WILLIAM: (*standing over her*) And now he's gone; lured away, I suspect, by one of ye – (*pointing to the door of* AVONIA's *room*)
    (AVONIA *reappears defiantly.*)
AVONIA: Look here, Sir Gower –
ROSE: (*rising*) Go, 'Vonia!
AVONIA: (*to* SIR WILLIAM) We've met before, if you remember, in Cavendish Square –
ROSE: (*sitting again, helplessly*) Oh, Mrs Gadd – !
SIR WILLIAM: Mistress! a married lady!
AVONIA: Yes, I spent some of my honeymoon at your house –
SIR WILLIAM: What!
AVONIA: Excuse my dress; it's all in the way of my business. Just one word about Rose.
ROSE: Please, 'Vonia – !
AVONIA: (*to* SIR WILLIAM, *who is glaring at her in horror*) Now, there's nothing to stare at, Sir Gower. If you must look anywhere in particular, look at that poor thing. A nice predicament you've brought her to!
SIR WILLIAM: Sir – ! (*correcting himself*) Madam!

---

bullion trimming: 'a fringe of gold and silver thread twists' (*OED*).

AVONIA: You've brought her to beggary, amongst you! You've broken her heart; and, what's worse, you've made her genteel. She can't act, since she left your mansion; she can only mope about the stage with her eyes fixed, like a person in a dream – dreaming of him, I suppose, and of what it is to be a lady. And first she's put upon half-salary; and then, to-day, she gets the sack – the entire sack, Sir Gower! So there's nothing left for her but to starve, or to make artificial flowers. Miss Trelawny I'm speaking of! (*crossing to* ROSE *and embracing her.*) Our Rose! Our Trelawny! (*to* ROSE, *breaking down*) Excuse me for interfering, ducky. (*retiring, in tears*) Good day, Sir Gower.
> (*She goes out.*)
SIR WILLIAM: (*after a pause, to* ROSE) Is this – the case?
ROSE: (*standing, and speaking in a low voice*) Yes. As you have noticed, fortune has turned against me, rather.
SIR WILLIAM: (*penitently*) I – I'm sorry, ma'am. I – I believe ye've kept your word to us concerning Arthur. I – I –
ROSE: (*not heeding him, looking before her, dreamily*) My mother knew how fickle fortune could be to us gipsies. One of the greatest actors that ever lived warned her of that –
SIR WILLIAM: Miss Gower will also feel extremely – extremely –
ROSE: Kean once warned mother of that.
SIR WILLIAM: (*in an altered tone*) Kean? Which Kean?
ROSE: Edmund Kean. My mother acted with Edmund Kean, when she was a girl.
SIR WILLIAM: (*approaching her slowly, speaking in a queer voice*) With Kean? with Kean!
ROSE: Yes.
SIR WILLIAM: (*at her side, in a whisper*) My dear, I – *I've* seen Edmund Kean.
ROSE: Yes?
SIR WILLIAM: A young man then, I was; quite different from the man I am now – impulsive, excitable. Kean! (*Drawing a deep breath*) Ah, he was a *splendid* gipsy!
ROSE: (*looking down at the dress-basket*) I've a little fillet in there that my mother wore as Cordelia to Kean's Lear –
SIR WILLIAM: I may have seen your mother also. I was somewhat different in those days –
ROSE: (*kneeling at the basket and opening it*) And the Order and chain, and the sword, he wore in Richard. He gave them to my father; I've always prized them.
> (*She drags to the surface a chain with an Order attached to it, and a sword-belt and sword – all very theatrical and tawdry – and a little gold fillet.*)
(*handing him the chain*) That's the Order.

Kean: Edmund Kean, the outstanding English tragic actor in the nineteenth century. His powers began to fail from about 1825, and Pinero's notes for this play date the performance of *Richard III* referred to as 1820. His son Charles was also a leading actor-manager, hence the question: 'Which Kean?'
fillet: 'a headband; a ribbon, string, or any narrow material used for binding the hair' (*OED*).
Richard: i.e. *Richard III*.

SIR WILLIAM: (*handling it tenderly*) Kean! God bless me!

ROSE: (*holding up the fillet*) My poor mother's fillet.

SIR WILLIAM: (*looking at it*) I may have seen her. (*thoughfully, gazing in front*) I was a young man then. (*looking at ROSE steadily*) Put it on, my dear.

    (*She goes to the mirror and puts on the fillet.*)

    (*examining the Order*) Lord bless us! How he stirred me! how he – !

    (*He puts the chain over his shoulders. ROSE turns to him.*)

ROSE: (*advancing to him*) There!

SIR WILLIAM: (*looking at her*) Cordelia! Cordelia! – With Kean!

ROSE: (*adjusting the chain upon him*) This should hang so. (*returning to the basket and taking up the sword-belt and sword*) Look!

SIR WILLIAM: (*handling them*) Kean! (*to her, in a whisper*) I'll tell ye! I'll tell ye! When I saw him as Richard – I was young and a fool – (*He goes a step or two, then returns to her.*) I'll tell ye – he almost fired me with an ambition to – to – (*fumbling with the belt*) How did he carry this?

ROSE: (*fastening the belt, with the sword, round him*) In this way –

SIR WILLIAM: Ah! (*He paces the stage, growling and muttering, and walking with a limp and one shoulder hunched. She watches hims, seriously.*) Ah! he was a little man too! I remember him, as if it were last night! I remember – (*pausing and looking at her fixedly*) My dear, your prospects in life have been injured by your unhappy acquaintanceship with my grandson.

ROSE: (*gazing into the fire*) Poor Arthur's prospects in life – what of them?

SIR WILLIAM: (*testily*) Tsch, tsch, tsch!

ROSE: If I knew where he is – !

SIR WILLIAM: Miss Trelawny, if you cannot act, you cannot earn your living.

ROSE: How is he earning *his* living?

SIR WILLIAM: And if you cannot earn your living, you must be provided for.

ROSE: (*turning to him*) Provided for?

SIR WILLIAM: Miss Gower was kind enough to bring me here in a cab. She and I will discuss plans for making provision for ye, while driving home.

ROSE: (*advancing to him*) Oh, I beg you will do no such thing, Sir William.

SIR WILLIAM: Hey!

ROSE: I could not accept any help from you or Miss Gower.

SIR WILLIAM: You must! You shall!

ROSE: I will not.

SIR WILLIAM: (*touching the Order and the sword*) Ah – ! Yes, I – I'll buy these of ye, my dear –

ROSE: Oh, no, no! not for hundreds of pounds! Please take them off!

    (*There is a hurried knocking at the door.*)

SIR WILLIAM: (*startled*) Who's that? (*struggling with the chain and belt*) Remove these – !

    (*The handle is heard to rattle. SIR WILLIAM disappears behind the curtains. IMOGEN opens the door and looks in.*)

IMOGEN: (*seeing only ROSE, and coming to her and embracing her*) Rose darling, where is Tom Wrench?

ROSE: He was here not long since –

IMOGEN: (*going to the door and calling, desperately*) Tom! Tom Wrench! Mr
    Wrench!

ROSE: Is anything amiss?

IMOGEN: (*shrilly*) Tom!

ROSE: Imogen!

IMOGEN: (*returning to* ROSE) Oh, my dear, forgive my agitation – !
                (TOM *enters, buoyantly, flourishing the manuscript of his play.*)

TOM: I've found it! At the bottom of a box – 'deeper than did ever plummet
    sound – '! (*to* IMOGEN) Eh? What's the matter?

IMOGEN: Oh, Tom, old Mr Morfew – !

TOM: (*blankly*) Isn't he willing – ?

IMOGEN: (*with a gesture of despair*) I don't know. He's dead.

TOM: No!

IMOGEN: Three weeks ago. Oh, what a chance he has missed!
                (TOM *bangs his manuscript down upon the table savagely.*)

ROSE: What is it, Tom? Imogen, what is it?

IMOGEN: (*pacing the stage*) I can think of no one else –

TOM: Done again!

IMOGEN: We shall lose it, of course –

ROSE: Lose what?

TOM: The opportunity – her opportunity, *my* opportunity, *your* opportunity, Rose.

ROSE: (*coming to him*) My Opportunity, Tom?

TOM: (*pointing to the manuscript*) My play – my comedy – my youngest born! Jenny
    has a theatre – could have one – has five hundred towards it, put down by a man
    who believes in my comedy, God bless him – ! the only fellow who has ever
    believed – !

ROSE: Oh Tom! (*turning to* IMOGEN) oh, Imogen!

IMOGEN: My dear, five hundred! We want another five, at least.

ROSE: Another five!

IMOGEN: Or eight.

TOM: And you are to play the part of Dora. Isn't she Jenny – I mean, wasn't she?

IMOGEN: Certainly. Just the sort of simple little Miss you *could* play now, Rose. And
    we thought that old Mr Morfew would help us in the speculation. Speculation! –
    it's a dead certainty!

TOM: *Dead* certainty? Poor Morfew!

IMOGEN: And here we are, stuck fast – !

TOM: (*sitting upon the dress-basket dejectedly*) And they'll expect me to rehearse that
    dragon to-morrow with enthusiasm.

ROSE: (*putting her arm round his shoulder*) Never mind, Tom.

TOM: No, I won't – (*taking her hand*) Oh, Rose – ! (*looking up at her*) oh, Dora – !
                (SIR WILLIAM, *divested of his theatrical trappings, comes from
                behind the curtain.*)

IMOGEN: Oh – !

'*deeper . . . sound*': *The Tempest*, v.i.

TOM: (*rising*) Eh?

ROSE: (*retreating*) Sir William Gower, Tom.

SIR WILLIAM: (*to* TOM) I had no wish to be disturbed, sir, and I withdrew (*bowing to* IMOGEN) when that lady entered the room. I have been a party, it appears, to a consultation upon a matter of business. (*to* TOM) Do I understand, sir, that you have been defeated in some project which would have served the interests of Miss Trelawny?

TOM: Y–y–yes, sir.

SIR WILLIAM: Mr Wicks –

TOM: Wrench –

SIR WILLIAM: Tsch! Sir, it would give me pleasure – it would give my grandson, Mr Arthur Gower, pleasure – to be able to aid Miss Trelawny at the present moment.

TOM: S–s–sir William, w–w–would you like to hear my play – ?

SIR WILLIAM: (*sharply*) Hey! (*looking round*) Ho, ho!

TOM: My comedy?

SIR WILLIAM: (*cunningly*) So ye think I might be induced to fill the office ye designed for the late Mr – Mr –

IMOGEN: Morfew.

SIR WILLIAM: Morfew, eh?

TOM: N–n–no, sir.

SIR WILLIAM: No! no!

IMOGEN: (*shrilly*) Yes!

SIR WILLIAM: (*after a short pause, quietly*) Read your play, sir. (*pointing to a chair at the table*) Sit down. (*to* ROSE *and* IMOGEN) Sit down.

> (TOM *goes to the chair indicated.* MISS GOWER'*s voice is heard outside the door.*)

MISS GOWER: (*outside*) William! (ROSE *opens the door;* MISS GOWER *enters.*) Oh, William, what has become of you? Has anything dreadful happened?

SIR WILLIAM: Sit down, Trafalgar. This gentleman is about to read a comedy. A cheer! (*testily*) Are there no cheers here? (ROSE *brings the chair and places it for* MISS GOWER *beside* SIR WILLIAM'*s chair.*) Sit down.

MISS GOWER: (*sitting, bewildered*) William, is all this – quite – ?

SIR WILLIAM: Yes, Trafalgar, quite in place – quite in place –

> (IMOGEN *sits as* COLPOYS *and* GADD *swagger in, at the door,* COLPOYS *smoking a pipe,* GADD *a large cigar.*)

> (*to* TOM, *referring to* GADD *and* COLPOYS) Friends of yours?

TOM: Yes, Sir William.

SIR WILLIAM: (*to* GADD *and* COLPOYS) Sit down. (*imperatively*) Sit down and be silent!

> (GADD *and* COLPOYS *seat themselves upon the sofa, like men in a dream.* ROSE *sits on the dress-basket.*)

AVONIA: (*opening her door slightly – in an anxious voice*) Rose – !

SIR WILLIAM: Come in, ma'am, come in! (AVONIA – *still in her pantomime dress – enters, coming down to* ROSE.) Sit down, sit down, ma'am.

> (AVONIA *sits beside* ROSE, *next to* MISS GOWER.)

MISS GOWER: (*in horror*) Oh–h–h–h!

SIR WILLIAM: (*restraining her*). Quite in place, Trafalgar; quite in place. (*to* TOM)
    Now, sir!
TOM: (*opening his manuscript and reading*) 'Life, a comedy, by Thomas Wrench – '
    END OF THE THIRD ACT

THE FOURTH ACT

(*As altered for the revival of the play at the Victoria Theatre – the 'Old Vic' – in 1925.*)
*The scene represents the stage of a theatre, the footlights and proscenium arch of the
actual stage being the proscenium arch and the footlights of the mimic stage. At the back
is an old and worn pair of flats dimly picturing a baronial hall. Some odd pieces of
scenery are piled against the flats. On the left runs a brick wall in which is a doorway
admitting to the Green-room. Down left, set obliquely to face the stage, is the prompt-
table. A chair is on either side of it. Down right, not far from the proscenium arch,
stands a large throne-chair with a gilt frame and red velvet seat, now much dilapidated,
and close to the flats at the back, there are a 'property' stool, a table and a chair, all of a
similar style to the throne-chair and in like condition. In the middle of the stage, as if
placed there for the purpose of rehearsal, are another table and chair. On this table is a
work-basket containing a ball of wool and a couple of knitting-needles; and on the
prompt-table there is a book. A faded and ragged carpet of green baize covers the floor
of the stage.*
*The wings and borders, and any other scenic appointments which may be shown, should
suggest by their shabbiness a theatre fallen into decay. The light is a dismal one, but it is
relieved by a shaft of sunlight entering through a window in the flies.*
*Down left in front of the proscenium arch, there is a flight of wooden steps, fixed
temporarily to enable the stage-manager to leave the stage at certain times and direct the
rehearsal from the stalls.*
(MRS TELFER *is seated upon the throne-chair in an attitude of dejection.* TELFER
enters from the Green-room.)
TELFER: (*coming to her*) Is that you, Violet?
MRS TELFER: Is the reading over?
TELFER: Almost. My part is confined to the latter 'alf of the second act; so being
    close to the Green-room door, (*with a sigh*) I stole away.
MRS TELFER: It affords you no opportunity, James?
TELFER: (*shaking his head*) A mere fragment.
MRS TELFER: (*rising*) Well, but a few good speeches to a man of your stamp –
TELFER: Yes, but this is so line-y, Violet; so very line-y. And what d'ye think the
    character is described as?
MRS TELFER: What?
TELFER: 'An old, stagey, out-of-date actor.'
        (*They stand looking at each other for a moment, silently.*)
MRS TELFER: (*falteringly*) Will you – be able – to get near it, James?
TELFER: (*looking away from her*) I daresay –

---

the reading: since none of the members of a Victorian 'stock' company received a complete text
(see above, p. 176), their knowledge of a new play derived from a reading either by the author or
the manager.

MRS TELFER: (*laying a hand upon his shoulder*) That's all right, then.

TELFER: And you – what have they called you for, if you're not in the play? They 'ave not dared to suggest understudy?

MRS TELFER: (*playing with her fingers*) They don't ask me to act at all, James.

TELFER: Don't ask you – !

MRS TELFER: Miss Parrott offers me the position of Wardrobe-mistress.

TELFER: Violet – !

MRS TELFER: Hush!

TELFER: Let us both go home.

MRS TELFER: (*restraining him*) No, let us remain. We've been idle six months, and I can't bear to see you without your watch and all your comforts about you.

TELFER: (*pointing towards the Green-room*) And so this new-fangled stuff, and these dandified people, are to push us, and such as us, from our stools!

MRS TELFER: Yes, James, just as some other new fashion will, in course of time, push *them* from their stools.

> (*From the Green-room comes the sound of a slight clapping of hands, followed by a murmur of voices. IMOGEN, elaborately dressed, enters from the Green-room and goes leisurely to the prompt-table. She is followed by TOM, manuscript in hand, smarter than usual in appearance; and he by O'DYWER – an excitable Irishman of about forty, with an extravagant head of hair – who carries a small bundle of 'parts' in brown-paper covers. TOM and O'DWYER join IMOGEN.*)

O'DWYER: (*to TOM*) Mr Wrench, I congratulate ye; I have that honour, sir. Your piece will do, sir; it will take the town, mark me.

TOM: Thank you, O'Dwyer.

IMOGEN: Look at the sunshine! There's a good omen, at any rate.

O'DWYER: Oh, sunshine's nothing. (*to TOM*) But did ye observe the gloom on their faces whilst ye were readin'?

IMOGEN: (*anxiously*) Yes, they did look glum.

O'DWYER: Glum! – it might have been a funeral! There's a healthy prognostication for ye, if ye loike! It's infallible.

> (*A keen-faced gentleman and a lady enter, from the Green-room, and stroll across the stage to the right, where they lean against the wings and talk. Then two young gentlemen enter and loiter about at the back. ROSE follows.*
> *Note – The actors and the actress appearing for the first time in this act, as members of the Pantheon Company, are outwardly greatly superior to the GADDS, the TELFERS and COLPOYS.*)

ROSE: (*shaking hands with TELFER*) Why didn't you sit near me, Mr Telfer? (*crossing to MRS TELFER and kissing her*) Fancy our being together again, and at the West End! (*to TELFER*) Do you like the play?

TELFER: Like it! There's not a speech in it, my dear – not a real *speech*; nothing to dig your teeth into –

O'DWYER: (*allotting the parts, under the direction of TOM and IMOGEN*) Mr

---

'*parts*': see above, p. 176.

Mortimer! (*One of the young gentlemen advances and receives his part from* O'DWYER, *and retires, reading it.*) Mr Denzil!
(*The keen-faced gentleman takes his part, then joins* IMOGEN *on her left and talks to her. The lady now has something to say to the solitary young gentleman at the back.*)

TOM: (*to* O'DWYER, *quietly, handing him a part*) Miss Brewster.

O'DWYER: (*beckoning to the lady, who does not observe him*) Come here, my love.

TOM: (*to* O'DWYER) No, no, O'Dwyer – not your 'love'.

O'DWYER: (*perplexed*) Not?

TOM: No.

O'DWYER: No?

TOM: Why, you are meeting her this morning for the first time.

O'DWYER: That's true enough. (*approaching the lady and handing her the part*) Miss Brewster.

THE LADY: Much obliged.

O'DWYER: (*quietly to her*) It'll fit ye like a glove, darlin'.
(*The lady sits conning her part.* O'DWYER *returns to the prompt-table.*)

TELFER: (*to* ROSE) Your lover in the play? Which of these young sparks plays your lover – Harold or Gerald – ?

ROSE: Gerald. I don't know. There are some people not here to-day, I believe.

O'DWYER: Mr Hunston!
(*The second young gentleman advances, receives his part, and rejoins the other young gentleman.*)

ROSE: Not that young man, I hope. Isn't he a little bandy?

TELFER: One of the finest Macduffs I ever fought with was bow-legged.

O'DWYER: Mr Kelfer!

TOM: (*to* O'DWYER) No, no – Telfer.

O'DWYER: Telfer.
(TELFER *draws himself erect, puts his hand in his breast, but otherwise remains stationary.*)

MRS TELFER: (*anxiously*) That's you, James.

O'DWYER: Come on, Mr Telfer! Look alive, sir!

TOM: (*to* O'DWYER) Sssh, sssh, sssh! don't, don't – !
(TELFER *advances to the prompt-table, slowly. He receives his part from* O'DWYER)
(*to* TELFER, *awkwardly*) I – I hope the little part of Poggs appeals to you, Mr Telfer. Only a sketch, of course; but there was nothing else – quite – in your –

TELFER: Nothing? To whose share does the Earl fall?

TOM: Oh, Mr Denzil plays Lord Parracourt.

TELFER: Denzil? I've never 'eard of 'im. Will you get to me to-day?

TOM: We – we expect to do so.

TELFER: Very well. (*stiffly*) Let me be called in the street.
(*He stalks away.*)

MRS TELFER: (*relieved*) Thank heaven! I was afraid James would break out.

ROSE: (*to* MRS TELFER) But you, dear Mrs Telfer – you weren't at the reading – what are *you* cast for?

MRS TELFER: I? (*wiping away a tear*) I am the Wardrobe-mistress of this theatre.

ROSE: You! (*embracing her*) Oh! oh!

MRS TELFER: (*composing herself*) Miss Trelawny – Rose – my child, if we are set to scrub a floor – and we may come to that yet – let us make up our minds to scrub it legitimately – with dignity –

(*She disappears and is seen no more.*)

O'DWYER: Miss Trelawny! Come here, my de –

TOM: (*to* O'DWYER) Hush!

O'DWYER: Miss Trelawny!

(ROSE *receives her part from* O'DWYER *and, after a word or two with* TOM *and* IMOGEN, *joins the two young gentlemen. The lady who has been seated at the back now rises and meets the keen-faced gentleman who has finished his conversation with* IMOGEN.)

THE LADY: (*to the keen-faced gentleman*) I say, Mr Denzil, who plays Gerald?

THE GENTLEMAN: Gerald?

THE LADY: The man I have my scene with in the third act – the hero –

THE GENTLEMAN: Oh, a young gentleman from the country, I understand.

THE LADY: From the country!

THE GENTLEMAN: He is coming up by train this morning, Miss Parrott tells me; from Bath or somewhere –

THE LADY: Well, whoever he is, if he can't play that scene with me decently, my part's not worth rags.

TOM: (*to* IMOGEN, *who is sitting at the prompt-table*) Er – h'm – shall we begin, Miss Parrott?

IMOGEN: Certainly, Mr Wrench.

TOM: We'll begin, O'Dwyer.

(*The lady titters at some remark from the keen-faced gentleman.*)

O'DWYER: (*coming down the stage, violently*) Clear the stage there! I'll not have it! Upon my honour, this is the noisiest theatre I've ever set foot in! (*The stage is cleared, the characters, other than* O'DWYER, IMOGEN *and* TOM, *disappearing into the Green-room.*) I can't hear myself speak for all the riot and confusion!

TOM: (*to* O'DWYER:) My dear O'Dwyer, there is *no* riot, there is *no* confusion –

IMOGEN: (*to* O'DWYER) Except the riot and confusion *you* are making.

TOM: You know, you're admirably earnest, O'Dwyer, but a little excitable.

O'DWYER: (*calming himself*) Oh, I beg your pardon, I'm sure. (*emphatically*) My system is, begin as ye mean to go on.

IMOGEN: But we *don't* mean to go on like that.

TOM: Of course not; of course not. Now, let me see – (*pointing to the table in the centre*) we shall want another chair here.

O'DWYER: Another chair?

TOM: A garden chair.

O'DWYER: (*excitably*) Another chair! Now then, another chair! Properties! where are ye? do ye hear me callin'? must I raise my voice to ye – ?

(*He rushes away*)

IMOGEN: (*to* TOM) Phew! where did you get *him* from?

TOM: (*wiping his brow*) Known Michael for years – most capable, invaluable fellow –

IMOGEN: (*simply*) I wish he was dead.

TOM: So do I. (O'DWYER *returns, carrying a light chair.*) Well, where's the property man?

O'DWYER: (*pleasantly*) It's all right, now. He's gone to dinner.

TOM: (*placing the chair in position*) Ah, then he'll be back some time during the afternoon. (*looking about him*) That will do. (*taking up his manuscript*) Call – haven't you engaged a call-boy yet, O'Dwyer?

O'DWYER: I have, sir, and the best in London.

IMOGEN: Where is he?

O'DWYER: He has sint an apology for his non-attindance.

IMOGEN: Oh – !

O'DWYER: A sad case, ma'am! He's buryin' his wife.

TOM: Wife!

IMOGEN: The call-boy!

TOM: What's his age?

O'DWYER: Ye see, he happens to be an elder brother of my own –

IMOGEN *and* TOM: Oh, lord!

TOM: Never mind! Let's get on! Call Miss – (*looking towards the right*) is that the Hall-Keeper?

        (*A man, suggesting by his appearance that he is the* HALL-KEEPER, *presents himself, with a card in his hand.*)

O'DWYER: (*furiously*) Now then! Are we to be continually interrupted in this fashion? Have I, or have I not, given strict orders that nobody whatever – ?

TOM: Hush, hush! see whose card it is; give me the card –

O'DWYER: (*handing the card to* TOM) Ah, I'll make rules here. In a week's time you'll not know this for the same theatre –

        (TOM *has passed the card to* IMOGEN *without looking at it.*)

IMOGEN: (*staring at it blankly*) Oh – !

TOM: (*to her*) Eh?

IMOGEN: Sir William!

TOM: Sir William!

IMOGEN: What can he want? what shall we do?

TOM: (*after referring to his watch – to the* HALL-KEEPER) Bring this gentleman on to the stage.

        (*The* HALL-KEEPER *withdraws.*)

        (*to* O'DWYER) Make yourself scarce for a few moments, O'Dwyer. Some private business –

O'DWYER: All right. I've plenty to occupy me. I'll begin to frame those rules –

        (*He disappears.*)

IMOGEN: (*to* TOM) Not here –

TOM: (*to* IMOGEN) The boy can't arrive for another twenty minutes. Besides, we must, sooner or later, accept responsibility for our act.

IMOGEN: (*leaning upon his arm*) Heavens! I foretold this!

TOM: (*grimly*) I know – 'said so all along'.

Hall-Keeper: apparently an alternative name for the stage doorkeeper.

IMOGEN: If he should withdraw his capital!

TOM: (*with clenched hands*) At least, that would enable me to write a melodrama.

IMOGEN: Why?

TOM: I should then understand the motives and the springs of Crime!

>   (*The* HALL-KEEPER *reappears, showing the way to* SIR WILLIAM
>   GOWER. SIR WILLIAM'*s hat is drawn down over his eyes, and the
>   rest of his face is almost entirely concealed by his plaid. The* HALL-
>   KEEPER *withdraws.*)

>   (*receiving* SIR WILLIAM) How d'ye do, Sir William?

SIR WILLIAM: (*giving him two fingers – with a grunt*) Ugh!

TOM: These are odd surroundings for you to find yourself in – (IMOGEN *advances.*)
Miss Parrott –

SIR WILLIAM: (*advancing to her – giving her two fingers*) Good morning, ma'am.

IMOGEN: This is perfectly delightful.

SIR WILLIAM: What is?

IMOGEN: (*faintly*) Your visit.

SIR WILLIAM: Ugh! (*weakly*) Give me a cheer. (*looking about him*) Have ye no
cheers here?

TOM: Yes.

>   (TOM *places the throne-chair nearer to* SIR WILLIAM, *who sinks into
>   it.*)

SIR WILLIAM: Thank ye; much obleeged. (*to* IMOGEN) Sit.

>   (IMOGEN *hurriedly fetches the stool and seats herself beside the
>   throne-chair.*)

>   (*producing his snuff-box*) You are astonished at seeing me here, I daresay?

TOM: Not at all.

SIR WILLIAM: (*glancing at* TOM) Addressing the lady. (*to* IMOGEN) You are
surprised to see me?

IMOGEN: Very.

SIR WILLIAM: (*to* TOM) Ah! (TOM *retreats, getting behind* SIR WILLIAM'*s chair
and looking down upon him.*) The truth is, I am beginning to regret my
association with ye.

IMOGEN: (*her hand to her heart*) Oh–h–h–h!

TOM: (*under his breath*) Oh! (*holding his fist over* SIR WILLIAM'*s head*) Oh–h–h–h!

IMOGEN: (*piteously*) You – you don't propose to withdraw your capital, Sir William?

SIR WILLIAM: That would be a breach of faith, ma'am –

IMOGEN: Ah!

TOM: (*walking about, jauntily*) Ha!

IMOGEN: (*seizing* SIR WILLIAM'*s hand*) Friend!

SIR WILLIAM: (*withdrawing his hand sharply*) I'll thank ye not to repeat that action,
ma'am. But I – I have been slightly indisposed since I made your acqueentance
in Clerkenwell; I find myself unable to sleep at night. (*to* TOM) That comedy of
yours – it buzzes continually in my head, sir.

TOM: It was written with such an intention, Sir William – to buzz in people's heads.

SIR WILLIAM: Ah, I'll take care ye don't read me another, Mr Wicks; at any rate,
another which contains a character resembling a member of my family – a *late*
member of my family. I don't relish being reminded of late members of my

family in this way, and being kept awake at night, thinking – turning over in my mind –

IMOGEN: (*soothingly*) Of course not.

SIR WILLIAM: (*taking snuff*) Pa–a–a–h! pi–i–i–sh! When I saw Kean, as Richard, he reminded me of no member of my family. Shakespeare knew better than that, Mr Wicks. (*to* IMOGEN) And therefore, ma'am, upon receiving your letter last night , acqueenting me with your intention to commence rehearsing your comedy – (*glancing at* TOM) *his* comedy –

IMOGEN: (*softly*) *Our* comedy –

SIR WILLIAM: Ugh! – to-day at noon, I determined to present myself here and request to be allowed to – to –

TOM: (*sharply*) To watch the rehearsal?

SIR WILLIAM: The rehearsal of those episodes in your comedy which remind me of a member of my family – a *late* member.

IMOGEN: (*constrainedly*) Oh, certainly –

TOM: (*firmly*) By all means.

SIR WILLIAM: (*rising, assisted by* TOM) I don't wish to be steered at by any of your – what d'ye call 'em? – your gipsy crew –

TOM: Ladies and Gentlemen of the Company, we call 'em.

SIR WILLIAM: (*tartly*) I don't care what ye call 'em. (TOM *restores the throne-chair to its former position.*) Put me into a curtained box, where I can hear, and see, and not be seen; and when I've heard and seen enough, I'll return home – and – and obtain a little sleep; and to-morrow I shall be well enough to sit in Court again.

TOM: (*calling*) Mr O'Dwyer –

    (O'DWYER *appears;* TOM *speaks a word or two to him, and hands him the manuscript of the play.*)

IMOGEN: (*to* SIR WILLIAM, *falteringly*) And if you are pleased with what you see this morning, perhaps you will attend another –?

SIR WILLIAM: (*angrily*) Not I. After to-day I wash my hands of ye. What do plays and players do, coming into my head, disturbing my repose! (*more composedly, to* TOM, *who has returned to his side*) Your comedy has merit, sir. You call it *Life.* There is a character in it – a young man – not unlike life – not unlike a late member of my family. Obleege me with your arm.* My box, sir – my box –

    (TOM *leads* SIR WILLIAM *to down left.*)

TOM: (*to* O'DWYER) Begin rehearsal. Begin rehearsal! Call Miss Trelawny!

    (TOM *and* SIR WILLIAM *disappear down left.*)

O'DWYER: Miss Trelawny! Miss Trelawny! (*rushing to the left*) Miss Trelawny! how long am I to stand here shoutin' myself hoarse – ?

    (ROSE *appears.*)

ROSE: (*gently*) Am I called?

O'DWYER: (*instantly calm*) You are, darlin'. (O'DWYER *stands book in hand.*

---

*H adds:

Madam (*to* IMOGEN), I have arrived at the conclusion that Miss Trelawny belongs to a set of curious people who in other paths might have been useful members of society. But after today I've done with ye. (*to* TOM) My box, sir . . .

IMOGEN *and* ROSE *stand together near prompt-table. The other members of the company come from the Green-room and stand watching the rehearsal.*) Now then! (*reading from the manuscript*) 'At the opening of the play Peggy and Dora are discovered – ' Who's Peggy? (*excitedly*) Where's Peggy? Am I to – ?

IMOGEN: Here I am! here I am! I am Peggy.

O'DWYER: (*calm*) Of course ye are, lovey – ma'am, I should say –

IMOGEN: Yes, you should.

O'DWYER: 'Peggy is seated upon the Right, Dora on the Left – '

    (ROSE *and* IMOGEN *seat themselves accordingly.*)

(*in a difficulty*) No – Peggy on the Left, Dora on the Right. (*violently*) This is the worst written scrip I've ever held in my hand – (ROSE *and* IMOGEN *change places.*) So horribly scrawled over, and interlined, and – no – I was quite correct. Peggy is on the Right, and Dora is on the Left.

    (IMOGEN *and* ROSE *again change seats.*)

(*reading from the manuscript*) 'Peggy is engaged in – in – ' I can't decipher it. A scrip like this is a disgrace to any well-conducted theatre. (*to* IMOGEN) I don't know what you're doin'. 'Dora is – is – ' (*to* ROSE) You are also doin' something or another. Now then! When the curtain rises, you are discovered, both of ye, employed in the way described – (TOM *returns.*) Ah, here ye are! (*resigning the manuscript to* TOM, *and pointing out a passage*) I've got it smooth as far as there.

TOM: Thank you.

O'DWYER: (*seating himself at prompt-table*) You're welcome.

TOM: (*to* ROSE *and* IMOGEN) Ah, you're not in your right positions. Change places, please.

    (IMOGEN *and* ROSE *change seats once more.* O'DWYER *rises and goes off left.*)

O'DWYER: (*out of sight, violently*) A scrip like that's a scandal! If there's a livin' soul that can read bad handwriting, I am that man! But of all the – !

TOM: Hush, hush! Mr O'Dwyer!

O'DWYER: (*returning to his chair*) Here.

TOM: (*taking the book from the prompt-table and handing it to* IMOGEN) You are reading.

O'DWYER: (*sotto voce*) I thought so.

TOM: (*to* ROSE) You are working.

O'DWYER: Working.

TOM: (*pointing to the basket on the table*) There are your needles and wool.

    (ROSE *takes the wool and the needles out of the basket.*)

(*taking the ball of wool from her and placing it on the ground in the centre of the stage*) You have allowed the ball of wool to roll from your lap on to the grass.*

(*Hurrying down the wooden steps and directing the rehearsal from the front row of the stalls*) The curtain rises. (*to* IMOGEN) Miss Parrott –

---

*H adds:
You will see the reason for that presently.
ROSE: I remember it, Mr Wrench.
TOM: The curtain rises . . .

IMOGEN: (*referring to her part*) What do I say?
TOM: Nothing – you yawn.
IMOGEN: (*yawning, in a perfunctory way*) Oh–h!
TOM: As if you meant it, of course.
IMOGEN: Well, of course.*
O'DWYER: (*jumping up*) This sort of thing. (*yawning extravagantly*) He – oh!
TOM: (*irritably*) Thank you, O'Dwyer; thank you.
O'DWYER: (*sitting again*) You're welcome.
TOM: (*to* ROSE) You speak.
ROSE: (*reading from her part – retaining the needles at the end of the wool*) 'What are
    you reading, Miss Chaffinch?'
IMOGEN: (*reading from her part*) 'A novel.'
ROSE: 'And what is the name of it?'
IMOGEN: '*The Seasons.*'
ROSE: 'Why is it called that?'
IMOGEN: 'Because all the people in it do seasonable things.'
ROSE: 'For instance – ?'
IMOGEN: 'In the Spring, fall in love.'
ROSE: 'In the Summer?'
IMOGEN: 'Become engaged. Delightful!'
ROSE: 'Autumn?'
IMOGEN: 'Marry. Heavenly!'
ROSE: 'Winter?'
IMOGEN: 'Quarrel. Ha, ha, ha!'
TOM : (*to* IMOGEN) Close the book – with a bang –
                (*During all the above* TOM, *manuscript in hand, moves from one side
                of the stalls to the other, gesticulating in the manner of a conductor of an
                orchestra.*)
O'DWYER: (*bringing his hands together sharply by way of suggestion*) Bang!
TOM: (*irritably*) Yes, yes, O'Dwyer. (*to* IMOGEN) Now rise –
O'DWYER: Up ye get!†
TOM: And walk about, discontentedly.
IMOGEN: (*walking about*) 'I've nothing to do; let's tell each other our ages.'
ROSE: 'I am nineteen.'
TOM: (*to* IMOGEN) In a loud whisper –
IMOGEN: 'I am twenty-two.'

---

*H adds:
TOM: Your yawn must tell the audience that you are a young lady who is driven by boredom to
almost any extreme.
†H adds:
TOM: And cross to Dora.
IMOGEN: (*going to* ROSE) 'Miss Harrington, don't you wish occasionally that you were
engaged to be married?'
ROSE: 'No.'
IMOGEN: 'Not on wet afternoons?'
ROSE: 'I am perfectly satisfied with this busy little life of mine, as your aunt's companion.'
TOM: (*to* IMOGEN) Walk about discontentedly . . .

O'DWYER: (*rising, and speaking to* TOM *across the footlights*) Now, hadn't ye better make that *six*-and-twenty?

IMOGEN: (*coming forward with asperity*) Why? why?

TOM: No, no, certainly not. Go on.

IMOGEN: (*angrily*) Not till Mr O'Dwyer retires into his corner.

TOM: O'Dwyer –

(O'DWYER, *with the air of martyrdom, disappears down left.*)

(*at the prompt-table, to* ROSE) You speak.

ROSE: 'I shall think, and feel, the same when I am twenty-two, I am sure. I shall never wish to marry.'*

TOM: (*returning to the stage and summoning the keen-faced gentleman*) Mr Denzil.

O'DWYER: (*putting his head round the corner*) Mr Denzil!

(*The keen-faced gentleman comes forward, reading his part, and meets* IMOGEN.)

THE GENTLEMAN: (*speaking in the tones of an old man*) 'Ah, Miss Peggy!'

TOM: (*to* ROSE) Rise, Miss Trelawny.

O'DWYER: (*his head again appearing*) Rise, darlin'!

(ROSE *rises.*)

THE GENTLEMAN: (*to* IMOGEN) 'Your bravura has just arrived from London. Lady McArchie wishes you to try it over.'†

IMOGEN: (*taking his arm*) 'Delighted, Lord Parracourt. (*to* ROSE) Miss Harrington, bring your work indoors and hear me squall.'‡

(IMOGEN *and the keen-faced gentleman indicate that they go off left. He rejoins his companions; she returns to the prompt-table.*)

---

*H adds:
TOM: (*to* IMOGEN) Sit on the stump of the tree.
IMOGEN: Where's that?
TOM: (*pointing to the stool down the stage*) Where that stool is.
IMOGEN: (*sitting on the stool*) 'Miss Harrington, who is the Mr Gerald Leigh who is expected down today?'
ROSE: 'Lord Parracourt's secretary.'
IMOGEN: 'Old and poor!'
ROSE: 'Neither, I believe. He is the son of a college chum of Lord Parracourt's – so I heard his lordship tell Lady McArchie – and is destined for public life.'
IMOGEN: 'Then he's young?'
ROSE: 'Extremely, I understand.'
IMOGEN: (*jumping up, in obedience to a sign from* TOM) 'Oh, how can you be so spiteful!'
ROSE: 'I!'
IMOGEN: 'You mean he's too young!'
ROSE: 'Too young for what?'
IMOGEN: 'Too young for – oh, bother!'
TOM: (*looking at the keen-faced gentleman*) Mr Denzil . . .
bravura: 'passage of music requiring exceptional powers' (*OED*), but the context suggests the music for a complete song.
†H adds:
' . . . try it over, and if I may add my entreaties – '
‡H adds:
(*to the* GENTLEMAN) 'Why, you must have telegraphed to Town!'
THE GENTLEMAN: (*as they cross the stage*) 'Yes, but even telegraphy is too sluggish in executing your smallest command.'

ROSE: 'Why do Miss Chaffinch and her girl-friends talk of nothing, think of nothing apparently, but marriage? Ought a woman to make marriage the great object of life? Can there be no other? I wonder – '
> (*She goes off left, the wool trailing after her, and disappears into the Green-room. The ball of wool remains in the centre of the stage.*)

TOM: (*reading from his manuscript*) 'The piano is heard; and Peggy's voice singing. Gerald enters – '

IMOGEN: (*clutching* TOM's *arm*) There – !

TOM: Ah, yes, here is Mr Gordon. (ARTHUR *appears in a travelling coat.* TOM *and* IMOGEN *hasten to him and shake hands with him vigorously.*) How are you?

IMOGEN: (*nervously*) How are you?

ARTHUR: (*breathlessly, getting between the two*) Miss Parrott! Mr Wrench! forgive me if I am late; my cab-horse galloped from the station –

TOM: We had just reached your entrance. Have your read your part over?

ARTHUR: Read it (*taking it from his pocket*) I know every word of it! It has made my journey from Bristol like a flight through the air! Why, Mr Wrench (*turning over the leaves of his part*) some of this is almost *me*!

TOM *and* IMOGEN: (*nervously*) Ha, ha, ha!

TOM: Come! you enter! (*pointing to the right*) There! (*running down the wooden steps*) You stroll on, looking about you! (*in the stalls again*) Now, Mr Gordon!

ARTHUR: (*advancing to the centre of the stage, occasionally glancing at his part*) 'A pretty place. I am glad I left the carriage at the lodge and walked through the grounds.'
> (*There is an exclamation, proceeding from* SIR WILLIAM, *who, seated behind a curtain, is in the stage-box in the auditorium, and the sound of the overturning of a chair.*)

IMOGEN: Oh!

O'DWYER: (*appearing, looking into the auditorium*) What's that? This is the noisiest theatre I've ever set foot in – !

TOM: Don't heed it! (*to* ARTHUR) Go on, Mr Gordon.

ARTHUR: 'Somebody singing. A girl's voice. Lord Parracourt made no mention of anybody but his hostess – the dry, Scotch widow. (*picking up the ball of wool*) This is Lady McArchie's, I'll be bound. The very colour suggests spectacles and iron-grey curls – '

TOM: Dora returns. (*calling*) Dora!

O'DWYER: Dora! where are ye?

THE GENTLEMAN: (*going towards the Green-room door*) Dora! Dora!
> (ROSE *appears in the wings.*)

ROSE: (*to* TOM) I'm sorry.

TOM: Go on, please!
> (*There is another sound, nearer the stage, of the overturning of some object.*)

O'DWYER: What – ?

TOM: Don't heed it!

ROSE: (*coming face to face with* ARTHUR) Oh – !

ARTHUR: Rose!

TOM: Go on, Mr Gordon!

ARTHUR: (*to* ROSE, *holding out the ball of wool*) 'I beg your pardon – are you
     looking for this?'
ROSE: 'Yes, I – I – I – ' Oh, Mr Gower, why are you here?
ARTHUR: Don't you know?
ROSE: No.
ARTHUR: Why, Miss Trelawny, I am trying to be – what you are.
ROSE: What I am – ?
ARTHUR: Yes – a gipsy.
ROSE: A gipsy – a gip – (*dropping her head upon his breast*) Oh, Arthur!
          (SIR WILLIAM *totters on from down left.*)
SIR WILLIAM: Arthur!
ARTHUR: (*going to him*) Grandfather!
O'DWYER: (*indignantly*) Upon my soul – !
TOM: Leave the stage, O'Dwyer!
          (O'DWYER *vanishes.* IMOGEN *goes to the members of the company
          at the back and talks to them; gradually they withdraw into the Green-
          room.* ROSE *retreats as* TOM *hurriedly returns to the stage.*)
SIR WILLIAM: What's this? What is it – ?
ARTHUR: (*bewildered*) Sir, I – I – you – and – and Rose – are the last persons I
     expected to meet here –
SIR WILLIAM: Ah–h–h–h!
ARTHUR: Perhaps you have both already learnt, from Mr Wrench or Miss Parrott,
     that I have – become – a gipsy, sir?*
SIR WILLIAM: Not *I*; (*pointing to* TOM *and* IMOGEN) these – these people have
     thought it decent to allow me to make the discovery for myself.
          (*He sinks into the throne-chair.* TOM *crosses to him.* ROSE *goes to*
          ARTHUR.)
TOM: (*to* SIR WILLIAM) Sir William, the secret of your grandson's choice of a
     profession –
SIR WILLIAM: (*scornfully*) Profession!
TOM: Was one that I was pledged to keep as long as it was possible to do so. And pray
     remember that your attendance here this morning is entirely your own act. It
     was our intention –
SIR WILLIAM: (*struggling to his feet*) Where is the door? the way to the door?
TOM: And let me beg you to understand this, Sir William – that Miss Trelawny was,
     till a moment ago, as ignorant as yourself of Mr Arthur Gower's doings, of his
     movements, of his whereabouts. She would never have thrown herself in his
     way, in this manner. Whatever conspiracy –
SIR WILLIAM: Conspiracy! The right word – conspiracy!
TOM: Whatever conspiracy there has been is my own – to bring these two young
     people together again, to make them happy –
          (ROSE *holds out her hand to* TOM; *he takes it. They are joined by*
          IMOGEN.)
SIR WILLIAM: (*looking about him*) The door! the door!

---

*H reads:
ARTHUR: . . . that I have – become – an actor, sir?

ARTHUR: (*going to* SIR WILLIAM) Grandfather, may I, when rehearsal is over, venture to call in Cavendish Square – ?

SIR WILLIAM: Call – !

ARTHUR: Just to see Aunt Trafalgar, sir? I hope Aunt Trafalgar is well, sir.

SIR WILLIAM: (*with a slight change of tone*) Your Great-Aunt Trafalgar? Ugh, yes, I suppose she will consent to see ye –

ARTHUR: Ah, sir – !

SIR WILLIAM: But *I* shall be out; *I* shall not be within doors.

ARTHUR: Then, if Aunt Trafalgar will receive me, sir, do you think I may be allowed to – to bring Miss Trelawny with me – ?

SIR WILLIAM: What! ha, I perceive you have already acquired the impudence of your vagabond class, sir; the brazen effrontery of a set of – !

ROSE: (*facing him*) Forgive him! forgive him! Oh, Sir William, why may not Arthur become, some day, a *splendid* gipsy?

SIR WILLIAM: Eh?

ROSE: Like –

SIR WILLIAM: (*peering into her face*) Like – ?

ROSE: Like –

TOM: Yes, sir, a gipsy, though of a different order from the old order which is departing – a gipsy of the new school!

SIR WILLIAM: (*to* ROSE) Well, Miss Gower is a weak, foolish lady; for aught I know she may allow this young man to – to – take ye –

IMOGEN: I would accompany Rose, of course, Sir William.

SIR WILLIAM: (*tartly*) Thank ye, ma'am. (*turning*) I'll go to my carriage.

ARTHUR: Sir, if you have the carriage here, and if you would have the patience to sit out the rest of the rehearsal, we might return with you to Cavendish Square.

SIR WILLIAM: (*choking*) Oh–h–h–h!

ARTHUR: Grandfather, we are not rich people, and a cab to us –

SIR WILLIAM: (*exhausted*) Arthur – !

TOM: Sir William will return to his box! (*going to the left*) O'Dwyer!

SIR WILLIAM: (*protesting weakly*) No, sir! no!

　　　　　(O'DWYER *appears.*)

TOM: Mr O'Dwyer, escort Sir William Gower to his box.

　　　　　(ARTHUR *leads* SIR WILLIAM *to* O'DWYER, SIR WILLIAM *still uttering protests.* ROSE *and* IMOGEN *embrace.*)

O'DWYER: (*giving an arm to* SIR WILLIAM) Lean on me, sir! heavily, sir – !

TOM: Shall we proceed with the rehearsal, Sir William, or wait till you are seated?

SIR WILLIAM (*violently*) Wait! Confound ye, d'ye think I want to remain here all day!

　　　　　(SIR WILLIAM *and* O'DWYER *disappear down left.*)

TOM: (*coming to centre, with* ARTHUR *on his left – wildly*) Go on with the rehearsal! Mr Gordon and Miss Rose Trelawny! Miss Trelawny! (ROSE *goes to him, on his right.*) Trelawny – late of the 'Wells'! Let us – let – (*Gripping* ARTHUR's *hand tightly, he bows his head upon* ROSE's *shoulder.*) Oh, my dears – ! let us – get on with the rehearsal – !

　　　　　(SIR WILLIAM *shows himself in the front of the stage-box as the* CURTAIN *falls.*)

　　　　　THE END

APPENDIX B

'Ever of Thee' by George Linley and Foley Hall

Ev - er of thee, I'm fond - ly dreaming, Thy gen-tle voice, my
Ev - er of thee, when sad ___ and lone-ly, Wand'-ring a-far, my

spir - it can cheer; Thou wert the star that mild - ly beam-ing,
soul joy'd to dwell; Ah! then I felt I loved ___ thee on - ly

Shone o'er my path, when all was dark and drear.
All seem'd to fade be - fore af-fec-tion's spell.

Still in my heart, thy form I ___ cher - ish, Ev'-ry kind thought like a
Years have not chill'd the love I ___ cher - ish, True as the stars, hath my

THE THUNDERBOLT

An episode in the history of a provincial family, in four acts.

First produced at the St James's Theatre, London, on 9 May 1908, with the following cast:

JAMES MORTIMORE	Mr Louis Calvert
ANN (his Wife)	Miss Kate Bishop
STEPHEN MORTIMORE	Mr Norman Forbes
LOUISA (his Wife)	Miss Alice Beet
THADDEUS MORTIMORE	Mr George Alexander
PHYLLIS (his Wife)	Miss Mabel Hackney
JOYCE } (the Thaddeus	Miss Mignon Clifford
CYRIL } Mortimores' children)	Master Cyril Bruce
COLONEL PONTING	Mr Wilfred Draycott
ROSE (his Wife, née Mortimore)	Miss May Palfrey
HELEN THORNHILL	Miss Stella Campbell
THE REV. GEORGE TRIST	Mr Reginald Owen
MR VALLANCE (Solicitor, of	
Singlehampton)	Mr Julian Royce
MR ELKIN (Solicitor, of Linchpool)	Mr J. D. Beveridge
MR DENYER (a House agent)	Mr F. J. Arlton
HEATH (a Manservant)	Mr Richard Haigh
A SERVANT GIRL at Nelson Villas	Miss Gladys Dale
TWO OTHERS at "Ivanhoe"	Miss Sybil Maurisse
	Miss Vere Sinclair

The scene of the First Act is laid at Linchpool, a city in the Midlands. The rest of the action takes place, a month later, in the town of Singlehampton.

'You leave my wife out of it – !'

IV *The Thunderbolt*, 1908. Act III: Thaddeus Mortimore (George Alexander) faces his family.

THE FIRST ACT

The scene represents a large, oblong room, situated on the ground floor and furnished as a library. At the back, facing the spectator, are three sash windows, slightly recessed, with venetian blinds. There is a chair in each recess. At the further end of the right-hand wall a door opens from the hall, the remaining part of the wall – that nearer to the audience – being occupied by a long dwarf-bookcase. This bookcase finishes at each end with a cupboard, and on the top of each cupboard stands a lamp. The keys of the cupboards are in their locks.

On the left-hand side of the room, in the middle of the wall, is a fireplace with a fender-stool before it, and on either side of the fireplace there is a tall bookcase with glazed doors. A high-backed armchair faces the fireplace at the further end. A smoking-table with the usual accessories, a chair and a settee stand at the nearer end of the fireplace, a few feet from the wall.

Almost in the centre of the room, facing the spectator, there is a big knee-hole writing-table with a lamp upon it. On the further side of the table is a writing-chair. Another chair stands beside the table.

On the right, near the dwarf-bookcase, there is a circular library-table on which are strewn books, newspapers and magazines. Round this table a settee and three chairs are arranged.

The furniture and decorations, without exhibiting any special refinement of taste, are rich and massive.

The venetian blinds are down and the room is in semi-darkness. What light there is proceeds from the bright sunshine visible through the slats.

[Note: Throughout, 'right' and 'left' are the spectators' right and left, not the actor's.]

Seated about the room, as if waiting for somebody to arrive, are JAMES *and* ANN MORTIMORE, STEPHEN *and* LOUISA, THADDEUS *and* PHYLLIS, *and* COLONEL PONTING *and* ROSE. *The ladies are wearing their hats and gloves.*

Everybody is in the sort of black which people hurriedly muster while regular mourning is in the making – in the case of the MORTIMORES, *the black being added to apparel of a less sombre kind. All speak in subdued voices.*

ROSE: (*a lady of forty-four, fashionably dressed and coiffured and with a suspiciously blooming complexion – on the settee on the left, fanning herself*) Oh, the heat! I'm stifled.

LOUISA: (*on the right – forty-six, a spare, thin-voiced woman*) Mayn't we have a window open?

ANN: (*beside the writing-table – a stolid, corpulent woman of fifty*) I don't think we *ought* to have a window open.

JAMES: (*at the writing-table – a burly, thick-set man, a little older than his wife, with iron-gray hair and beard and a crape band round his sleeve*) Phew! Why not, mother?

ANN: It isn't usual in a house of mourning – except in the room where the –

PONTING: (*In the arm-chair before the fireplace – fifty-five, short, stout, apoplectic.*) Rubbish! (*dabbing his brow.*) I beg your pardon – it's like the Black Hole of Calcutta.

THADDEUS: (*rising from the settee on the right, where he is sitting with* PHYLLIS *– a meek, care-worn man of two-and-forty*) Shall I open one a little way?

STEPHEN: (*on the further side of the library-table – forty-nine, bald, stooping, with red rims to his eyes, wearing spectacles*) Do, Tad.

        (THADDEUS *goes to the window on the right and opens it.*)

THADDEUS: (*from behind the venetian blind*) Here's a fly.

JAMES: (*taking out his watch as he rises*) That'll be Crake. Half-past eleven. He's in good time.

THADDEUS: (*looking into the street*) It isn't Crake. It's a young fellow.

JAMES: Young fellow?

THADDEUS: (*emerging*) It's Crake's partner.

JAMES: His partner?

STEPHEN: Crake has sent Vallance.

JAMES: What's he done that for? Why hasn't he come himself? This young man doesn't know anything about our family.

ANN: He'll know the law, James.

JAMES: Oh, the law's clear enough, mother.

        (*After a short silence,* HEATH, *a middle-aged man-servant, appears, followed by* VALLANCE. VALLANCE *is a young man of about five-and-thirty.*)

HEATH: Mr Vallance.

JAMES: (*advancing to* VALLANCE *as* HEATH *retires*) Good morning.

VALLANCE: Good morning. (*inquiringly*) Mr Mortimore?

JAMES: James Mortimore.

VALLANCE: Mr Crake had your telegram yesterday evening.

JAMES: Yes, he answered it, telling us to expect him.

VALLANCE: He's obliged to go to London on business. He's very sorry. He thought I'd better run through.

JAMES: Oh, well – glad to see you (*introducing the others*) My wife. My sister Rose – Mrs Ponting. My sister-in-law, Mrs Stephen Mortimore. My sister-in-law, Mrs Thaddeus. My brother Stephen.

STEPHEN: (*rising*) Mr Vallance was pointed out to me at the Institute the other night. (*shaking hands with* VALLANCE) You left by the eight forty-seven?

VALLANCE: Yes, I changed at Mirtlesfield.

JAMES: Colonel Ponting – my brother-in-law. (PONTING, *who has risen, nods to* VALLANCE *and joins* ROSE.) My younger brother, Thaddeus.

THADDEUS: (*who has moved away to the left*) How d'ye do?

JAMES: (*putting* VALLANCE *into the chair before the writing-table and switching on the light of the lamp*) You sit yourself down there. (*to everybody*) Who's to be spokesman?

STEPHEN: (*joining* LOUISA) Oh, you explain matters, Jim.

        (LOUISA *makes way for* STEPHEN, *transferring herself to another chair so that her husband may be nearer* VALLANCE.)

JAMES: (*to* PONTING) Colonel?

PONTING: (*sitting by* ROSE) Certainly; you do the talking, Mortimore.

JAMES: (*sitting, in the middle of the room, astride a chair which he fetches from the*

---

fly: 'any one-horse covered carriage, as a cab or hansom, let out on hire. Perhaps short for 'Fly-by-Night'.(*OED*).

window on the right) Well, Mr Vallance, the reason we wired you yesterday – wired Mr Crake, rather – asking him to meet us here this morning, is this. Something has happened here in Linchpool, which makes it necessary for us to obtain a little legal assistance.

VALLANCE: Yes?

JAMES: Not that we anticipate legal difficulties, whichever way the affair shapes. At the same time, we consider it advisable that we should be represented by our own solicitor – a solicitor who has our interests at heart, and nobody's interests but ours. (*looking round*) Isn't that it?

STEPHEN: We want our interests watched – our interests exclusively.

PONTING: Watched – that's it. I'm speaking for my wife, of course.

ROSE: (*with a languid drawl*) Yes, watched. We should like our interests watched.

JAMES: (*to* VALLANCE) These are the facts. I'll start with a bit of history. We Mortimores are one of the oldest, and, I'm bold enough to say, one of the most respected, families in Singlehampton. You're a newcomer to the town; so I'm obliged to tell you things I shouldn't have to tell Crake, who's been the family's solicitor for years. Four generations of Mortimores – I'm not counting our youngsters, who make a fifth – four generations of Mortimores have been born in Singlehampton, and the majority of 'em have earned their daily bread there.

VALLANCE: Indeed?

JAMES: Yes, sir, indeed. Now, then. (*pointing to the writing-table*) Writing-paper's in the middle drawer. (VALLANCE *takes a sheet of paper from the drawer and arranges it before him*.) My dear father and mother – both passed away – had five children, four sons and a daughter. I'm the second son; then comes Stephen; then Rose – Mrs Colonel Ponting; then Thaddeus. You see us all round you.

VALLANCE: (*selecting a pen*) Five children, you said?

JAMES: Five. The eldest of us was Ned – Edward –

STEPHEN: Edward Thomas Mortimore.

JAMES: Edward cut himself adrift from Singlehampton six-and-twenty years ago. He died at a quarter-past three yesterday morning.

STEPHEN: Upstairs.

JAMES: We're in his house.

STEPHEN: We lay him to rest in the cemetery here on Monday.

VALLANCE: (*sympathetically*) I was reading in the train, in one of the Linchpool papers –

JAMES: Oh, they've got it in all the papers.

VALLANCE: Mr Mortimore, the brewer?

JAMES: The same. Aye, he was a big man in Linchpool.

STEPHEN: A very big man.

JAMES: And, what's more, a very wealthy one; there's no doubt about that. Well, we can't find a will, Mr Vallance.

VALLANCE: Really?

JAMES: To all appearances, my brother's left no will – died intestate.

VALLANCE: Unmarried?

JAMES: Unmarried; a bachelor. Now, then, sir – just to satisfy my good lady – in the event of no will cropping up, what becomes of my poor brother's property?

VALLANCE: It depends upon what the estate consists of. As much of it as is real estate would go to the heir-at-law – in this instance, the eldest surviving brother.

PONTING: (*impatiently*) Yes, yes, but it's all personal estate – personal estate, every bit of it.

JAMES: (*to* VALLANCE) The Colonel's right. It's personal estate entirely, so we gather. The Colonel and I were pumping Elkin's managing-clerk about it this morning.

VALLANCE: Elkin?

JAMES: Elkin, Son and Tullis.

STEPHEN: Mr Elkin has acted as my poor brother's solicitor for the last fifteen years.

JAMES: And *he's* never made a will for Ned.

STEPHEN: Nor heard my brother mention the existence of one.

JAMES: (*to* VALLANCE) Well? In the case of personal estate – ?

VALLANCE: In that case, equal division between next-of-kin.

JAMES: That's us – me, and my brothers, and my sister?

VALLANCE: Yes.

JAMES: (*to* ANN) What did I tell you, Ann? (*to the rest*) What did I tell everybody?

(STEPHEN *polishes his spectacles, and* PONTING *pulls at his moustache, vigorously.* ROSE, ANN *and* LOUISA *resettle themselves in their seats with great contentment.*)

VALLANCE: (*writing*) 'Edward' – (*looking up*) Thomas? (JAMES *nods.*) 'Thomas – Mortimore –'

JAMES: Of 3 Cannon Row and Horton Lane –

STEPHEN: Horton Lane is where the brewery is.

JAMES: Linchpool, brewer.

STEPHEN: 'Gentleman' is the more correct description. The business was converted into a company in nineteen-hundred and four.

LOUISA: Gentleman, ah! What a gentlemanly man he was!

ANN: A perfect gentleman in every respect.

ROSE: Most gentlemanlike, poor dear thing.

PONTING: Must have been. I never saw him – but must have been.

JAMES: (*to* VALLANCE) Gentleman, deceased –

STEPHEN: Died, June the twentieth –

JAMES: Aged fifty-three. Two years my senior.

VALLANCE: (*with due mournfulness*) No older? (*writing*) You are James –

JAMES: James Henry. 'Ivanhoe', Claybrook Road, and Victoria Yard. Singlehampton, builder and contractor.

ANN: My husband is a parish guardian and a rural-district councilman.

JAMES: Never mind that, mother.

ANN: Eight years treasurer of the Institute, and one of the founders of the Singlehampton and Claybrook Temperance League.

LOUISA: Stephen was one of the founders of the League too – weren't you, Stephen?

JAMES: (*to* VALLANCE) Stephen Philip Mortimore, 11 The Crescent, and 32 King Street, Singlehampton, printer and publisher; editor and proprietor of our Singlehampton *Times and Mirror*

LOUISA: Author of the History of Singlehampton and its Surroundings –

STEPHEN: All right, Lou.

LOUISA: With Ordnance Map.

JAMES: Rose Emily Rackstraw Ponting –

ROSE: My mother was a Rackstraw.

JAMES: Wife of Arthur Everard Ponting, West Sussex Regiment, Colonel, retired, 17a Coningsby Place, South Belgravia, London. That's the lot.

ANN: No –

JAMES: Oh, there's Tad. (*to* VALLANCE) Thaddeus John Mortimore –

THADDEUS: (*who is standing, looking on, with his elbows resting upon the back of the chair before the fireplace – smiling diffidently*) Don't forget me, Jim.

JAMES: 6 Nelson Villas, Singlehampton, professor of music. Any further particulars, Mr Vallance?

VALLANCE: (*finished writing and leaning back in his chair*) May I ask, Mr Mortimore, what terms you and your sister and brothers were on with the late Mr Mortimore?

JAMES: Terms?

VALLANCE: What I mean is, your late brother was a man of more than ordinary intelligence; he must have known who his estate would benefit, in the event of his dying intestate.

JAMES: (*with a nod*) Aye.

VALLANCE: My point is, was he on such terms with you as to make it reasonably probable that he should have desired his estate to pass to those who are here?

JAMES: (*Rubbing his beard*) Reasonably probable?

STEPHEN: Certainly.

PONTING: In my opinion, certainly.

JAMES: (*looking at the others*) He sent for us when he was near his end –

STEPHEN: Showing that old sores were healed – thoroughly healed – as far as he was concerned.

VALLANCE: Old sores?

JAMES: He wouldn't have done that if he hadn't had a fondness for his family – eh?

ANN: Of course not.

LOUISA: Of course he wouldn't.

PONTING: Quite so.

VALLANCE: Then, I take it, there had been – er – ?

STEPHEN: An estrangement. Yes, there *had*.

JAMES: Oh, I'm not one for keeping anything in the back-ground. Up to a day or two before his death, we hadn't been on what you'd call terms with my brother for many years, Mr Vallance.

STEPHEN: Unhappily.

JAMES: *De mortuis* – how's it go? –

STEPHEN: *De mortuis nil nisi bonum.*

JAMES: Well, plain English is good enough for me. (*to* VALLANCE) But I don't attempt to deny it – at one time of his life my poor brother Edward was a bit of a scamp, sir.

STEPHEN: A little rackety – a little wild. Young men will be young men.

ANN: (*shaking her head*) I've a grown-up son myself.

LOUISA: (*inconsequently*) And there are two sides to every question. I always say – don't I, Stephen? –

STEPHEN: Yes, yes, yes.

LOUISA: There are two sides to every question.

JAMES: (*to* VALLANCE) No, sir, after Edward cleared out of Singlehampton, we didn't see him again, any of us, till about fifteen years back. Then he came to settle here, in this city, and bought Cordingly's brewery.

LOUISA: Only forty miles away from his birthplace.

STEPHEN: Forty-two miles.

LOUISA: That was fate.

STEPHEN: Chance.

LOUISA: *I* don't know the difference between chance and fate.

STEPHEN: (*irritably*) No, you don't, Lou.

JAMES: Then some of us used to knock up against him occasionally – generally on the line, at Mirtlesfield junction. But it was only a nod, or a how-d'ye-do, we got from him; and it never struck us till last Tuesday morning that he kept a soft corner in his heart for us all.

VALLANCE: Tuesday – ?

ANN: First post.

JAMES: We had a letter from Elkin, telling us that poor Ned was seriously ill; and saying that he was willing to shake hands with the principal members of the family, if they chose to come through to Linchpool.

STEPHEN: Thank God we came.

JAMES: Aye, thank God.

ANN *and* LOUISA: Thank God.

ROSE: (*affectedly*) It will always be a sorrow to me that I didn't get down till it was too late. I shall never cease to reproach myself.

JAMES: (*indulgently*) Oh, well, you're a woman o' fashion, Rose.

ROSE: (*with a simper*) Still, if I had guessed the end was as near as it was, I'd have given up my social engagements without a murmur. (*appealing to* PONTING) Toby – !

PONTING: Without a murmur – without a murmur; both of us would.

VALLANCE: (*rising, putting his notes into his pocket-book as he speaks*) I think it would perhaps be as well that I should meet Mr Elkin.

STEPHEN: That's the plan.

JAMES: (*rising*) Just what I was going to propose.

STEPHEN: Elkin knows we have communicated with our solicitor.

JAMES: (*looking at his watch*) He's gone round to the Safe Deposit Company in Lemon Street.

STEPHEN: His latest idea is that my brother may have rented a safe there.

PONTING: (*who has risen with* JAMES) Preposterous. Never heard anything more grotesque.

JAMES: The old gentleman will want to drag the river Linch next.

PONTING: As if a man of wealth and position, with safes and strong-rooms of his own, would deposit his will in a place of that sort. 'Pon my word, it's outrageous of Elkin.

STEPHEN: It does seem rather extravagant.

ROSE: Absurd.

VALLANCE: (*coming forward*) We must remember that it's the duty of all concerned to use every possible means of discovery. (*to* JAMES) Your brother had an office at the brewery?

JAMES: Elkin and I turned that inside-out yesterday.

STEPHEN: In the presence of Mr Holt and Mr Friswell, two of the directors.

VALLANCE: And his bank – ?

JAMES: London City and Midland. Four tin boxes. We've been through 'em.

STEPHEN: The most likely place of deposit, I should have thought, was the safe in this room.

PONTING: Exactly. The will would have been there if there had been a will at all.

> (JAMES *switches on the light of the lamp which stands above the cupboard at the further end of the dwarf-bookcase.*)

JAMES: (*opening the cupboard and revealing a safe*) Yes, this is where my brother's private papers are.

STEPHEN: This was his library and sanctum.

JAMES: (*listening as he shuts the cupboard door*) Hallo! (*opening the room door a few inches and peering into the hall*) Here *is* Elkin.

> (*There is a slight general movement denoting intense interest and suspense.* ANN *gets to her feet.*)

JAMES: (*closing the door and coming forward a little – grimly*) Well! Hey! I wonder whether he's found anything in Lemon Street?

PONTING: (*clutching* ROSE'*s shoulder and dropping back into his chair – under his breath*) Good God!

ANN: (*staring at her husband*) James – !

JAMES: (*sternly*) Go and sit down, mother. (ANN *retreats and seats herself beside* ROSE) If he *has*, we ought to feel glad; that's how we ought to feel.

STEPHEN: (*resentfully*) Of course we ought. That's how we *shall* feel.

JAMES: Poor old Ned! It's his wishes we've got to consider – (*returning to the door*) his wishes (*opening the door again*) Come in, Mr Elkin. Waiting for you, sir.

> (*He admits* ELKIN, *a grey-haired, elderly man of sixty.*)

JAMES: (*presenting* VALLANCE) Mr Vallance – Crake and Vallance, Singlehampton, our solicitors. (ELKIN *advances and shakes hands with* VALLANCE.) Mr Vallance has just run over to see how we're getting on.

ELKIN: (*to* VALLANCE, *genially*) I don't go often to Singlehampton nowadays. I recollect the time, Mr Vallance, when the whole of the south side of the town was meadow-land. Would you believe it – meadow-land! And where they've built the new hospital, old Dicky Dunn, the farmer, used to graze his cattle. (*to* JAMES, *who is touching his sleeve*) Eh?

JAMES: (*rather huskily*) Excuse me. Any luck?

ELKIN: Luck?

JAMES: In Lemon Street. Find anything?

ELKIN: (*shaking his head*) No. There is nothing there in your brother's name. (*Again there is a general movement, but this time of relief.*) It was worth trying.

JAMES: Oh, it was worth trying.

STEPHEN: (*heartily*) Everything's worth trying.

PONTING: (*jumping up*) Everything. Mustn't leave a stone unturned.

> (*The strain being over,* ROSE *and* ANN *rise and go to the fireplace,*

where PONTING *joins them.* THADDEUS *moves away and seats*
    himself at the centre window.)

ELKIN: (*sitting beside the writing-table*) This is a puzzling state of affairs, Mr
    Vallance.

VALLANCE: Oh, come, Mr Elkin!

ELKIN: I don't want to appear uncivil to these ladies and gentlemen – very puzzling.

VALLANCE: Scarcely what one would have expected, perhaps; but what is there
    that's puzzling about it?

JAMES: (*standing by* ELKIN) People have died intestate before to-day, Mr Elkin.

STEPHEN: It's a common enough occurrence.

VALLANCE: (*to* ELKIN) I understand you acted for the late Mr Mortimore for a
    great many years?

ELKIN: Ever since he came to Linchpool.

VALLANCE: His most prosperous years.

        (ELKIN *assents silently.*)

JAMES: When he was making money to *leave*.

VALLANCE: (*to* ELKIN) And the subject of a will was never broached between
    you?

ELKIN: I won't say that. I've thrown out a hint or two at different times.

VALLANCE: Without any response on his part?

ELKIN: Without any practical response, I admit. (JAMES *and* STEPHEN *shrug their*
    shoulders.) But he must have employed other solicitors previous to my
    connection with him. I can't trace his having done so; but no commercial man
    gets to eight-and-thirty without having something to do with us chaps.

VALLANCE: (*sitting on the settee on the left*) Assuming a will of long standing, he
    may have destroyed it, may he not, recently?

ELKIN: Recently?

VALLANCE: Quite recently. Here we have a man at variance with his family and
    dangerously ill. What do we find him doing? We find him summoning his
    relatives to his bedside and becoming reconciled to them –

JAMES: Completely reconciled.

STEPHEN: Completely.

ELKIN: (*to* VALLANCE) At my persuasion. I put pressure on him to send for his
    belongings.

VALLANCE: Indeed? Granting that, isn't it reasonable to suppose that, subsequent
    to this reconciliation – ?

ELKIN: Oh, no; he destroyed no document of any description after he took to his
    bed. That I've ascertained.

VALLANCE: Well, theorising is of no use, is it? We have to deal with the simple fact,
    Mr Elkin.

JAMES: Yes, that's all we have to deal with.

STEPHEN: The simple fact.

ELKIN: No will.

PONTING: (*who, with the rest, has been following the conversation between* ELKIN
    and VALLANCE) No will.

---

belongings: 'persons related in any way' (*OED*).

ELKIN: (*after a pause*) Do you know, Mr Vallance, there is one thing I shouldn't have been unprepared for?

VALLANCE: What?

ELKIN: A will drawn by another solicitor, behind my back, *during* my association with Mr Mortimore.

VALLANCE: Behind your back?

ELKIN: He was a most attractive creature – one of the most engaging, and one of the ablest, I've ever come across; but he was remarkably secretive with me in matters relating to his private affairs – remarkably secretive.

VALLANCE: Secretive?

ELKIN: Reserved, if you like. Why, it wasn't till a few days before his death – last Saturday – it wasn't till last Saturday that he first spoke to me about this child of his.

VALLANCE: Child?

ELKIN: This young lady we are going to see presently.

VALLANCE: (*looking at* JAMES *and* STEPHEN) Oh, I – I haven't heard anything of her.

ELKIN: Bless me, haven't you been told?

JAMES: (*uncomfortably*) We hadn't got as far as that with Mr Vallance.

STEPHEN: (*clearing his throat*) Mr Elkin did not think fit to inform *us* of her existence till yesterday.

JAMES: (*looking at his watch*) Twelve o'clock she's due, isn't she?

ELKIN: (*to* JAMES) You fixed the hour. (*to* VALLANCE) I wrote to her at the same time that I communicated with his brothers. Unfortunately she was away, visiting.

STEPHEN: She's studying painting at one of these art-schools in Paris.

ELKIN: She arrived late late night. Mrs Elkin and I received her. Only four-and-twenty. A nice girl.

VALLANCE: Is the mother living?

ELKIN: No.

JAMES: The mother was a person of the name of Thornhill.

STEPHEN: Calling herself Thornhill – some woman in London. She died when the child was quite small.

JAMES: (*with a jerk of the head towards the safe*) There's a bundle of the mother's letters in the safe.

ELKIN: This meeting with the family is my arranging. As matters stand, Miss Thornhill is absolutely unprovided for, Mr Vallance. And there was the utmost affection between Mortimore and his daughter – as he acknowledged her to be – undoubtedly. Now you won't grumble at me for my use of the word 'puzzling'?

VALLANCE: (*looking round*) I am sure my clients, should the responsibility ultimately rest with them, will do what is just and fitting with regard to the young lady.

JAMES: More than just – more than just, if it's left to me.

STEPHEN: We should be only too anxious to behave in a liberal manner, Mr Vallance.

LOUISA: We're parents ourselves – all except Colonel and Mrs Ponting.

ANN: My own girl – my Cissy – is nearly four-and-twenty.

ROSE: (*seated upon the fender-stool*) I suppose we should have to make her an allowance of sorts, shouldn't we?

JAMES: A monthly allowance.

STEPHEN: Monthly or quarterly.

PONTING: Yes, but this art-school in Paris – you've no conception what that kind of fun runs into.

JAMES: Schooling doesn't go on for ever, Colonel.

PONTING: But it'll lead to an *atelier* – a studio – if you're not careful.

ROSE: The art-school could be dropped, surely?

STEPHEN: Perhaps the art-school isn't strictly necessary.

ROSE: And she has an address in a most expensive quarter of Paris – didn't you say, Jim?

JAMES: The Colonel says it's a swell locality.

PONTING: Most expensive. The father – if he *was* her father – seems to have squandered money on her.

STEPHEN: Well, well, we shall see what's to be done.

PONTING: Squandered money on her recklessly.

JAMES: Yes, yes, we'll see, Colonel; we'll see.

        (PHYLLIS, *who has taken no part in what has been going on, suddenly rises. She is a woman of thirty-five, white-faced and faded, but with decided traces of beauty. Everybody looks at her in surprise.*)

PHYLLIS: (*falteringly*) I – I beg your pardon –

LOUISA: (*startled*) Good gracious me, Phyllis!

PHYLLIS: (*gaining firmness as she proceeds*) I beg your pardon. With every respect for Rose and Colonel Ponting, if we must come into Edward Mortimore's money, we mustn't let it make an atom of difference to the child.

LOUISA: Really, Phyllis!

STEPHEN: (*stiffly*) My dear Phyllis –

JAMES: (*half amused, half contemptuously*) Oh, we mustn't, mustn't we, Phyllis?

PHYLLIS: He was awfully devoted to her in his lifetime, it turns out. Colonel Ponting and Rose ought to remember that.

PONTING: (*walking away in umbrage to the window on the left, followed by* ROSE) Thank you, Mrs Thaddeus.

THADDEUS: (*who has risen and come to the writing-table*) Phyl – Phyl –

PHYLLIS: (*to* JAMES *and* STEPHEN) Jim – Stephen – you couldn't stint the girl after pocketing your brother's money; you couldn't do it!

ANN: James –

JAMES: Eh, mother?

ANN: I don't think we need to be taught our duty by Phyllis.

STEPHEN: (*rising and going over to the fireplace*) Frankly, I don't think we need.

LOUISA: (*following him*) Before Mr Elkin and Mr Vallance!

THADDEUS: Stephen – Lou – you don't understand Phyl.

JAMES: It isn't for want of plain speaking. Tad.

THADDEUS: (*sitting at the writing-table*) No, but listen – Jim –

JAMES: (*joining those at the fireplace*) Blessed if I've ever been spoken to in this style in my life!

THADDEUS: Jim, listen. If we come into Ned's money, we come into his debts into the bargain. There are no assets without liabilities. The girl's a debt – a big debt, as it were. Well, what does she cost? Five hundred a year? Six – seven – eight hundred a year? What's it matter? What would a thousand a year matter? Whatever Ned could afford, *we* could, amongst us. Why he should have neglected to make Miss Thornhill independent is a mystery – I'm with you there, Mr Elkin. Perhaps his sending for us, and shaking hands with us as he did, was his way of giving her into our charge. Heaven knows what was in his mind. But this is certain – if it falls to our lot to administer Ned's estate, we administer, not only to the money, but to the girl, and the art-school, and her comfortable lodgings, and anything else in reason. There's nothing offensive in our saying this.

ELKIN: Not in the least.

THADDEUS: (*with a deprecating little laugh*) Ha! We don't often put our oar into family discussions, Phyl and I. Stephen – (*turning in his chair*) Rosie –

JAMES: (*looking down on* THADDEUS – *grinning*) Hallo, Tad! Why, I've always had the credit of being the speaker o' the family. You're developing all of a sudden.

        (HEATH *enters.*)

HEATH: (*looking round the room*) Mrs Thaddeus Mortimore – ?

THADDEUS: (*pointing to* PHYLLIS *who is now seated in a chair on the right*) Here she is.

HEATH: (*in a hushed voice*) Two young ladies from Roper's, to fit Mrs Thaddeus Mortimore with her mourning.

THADDEUS: (*rising*) They weren't ready for Phyllis at ten o'clock. (*over his shoulder, as he joins* PHYLLIS *at the door*) Hope you don't object to their waiting on her here.

HEATH: (*to* THADDEUS) On the first floor, sir.

        (PHYLLIS *and* THADDEUS *go out.* HEATH *is following them.*)

VALLANCE: (*to* HEATH, *rising*) Er – (*to* ELKIN) What's his name?

ELKIN: (*calling to* HEATH, *who returns*) Heath –

VALLANCE: (*going to* HEATH) Have you a room where Mr Elkin and I can be alone for a few minutes?

HEATH: There's the dining-room, sir.

VALLANCE: (*turning to* ELKIN) Shall we have a little talk together?

ELKIN: (*rising*) By all means.

VALLANCE: (*to the others*) Will you excuse us?

ELKIN: (*taking* VALLANCE'*s arm*) Come along. (*passing out with* VALLANCE – *regretfully*) Ah, Heath, the dining-room!

HEATH: (*as he disappears, closing the door*) Yes, Mr Elkin; that's over, sir.

JAMES: (*who has crossed over to the right, to watch the withdrawal of* ELKIN *and* VALLANCE) What have those two got to say to each other on the quiet in such a deuce of a hurry?

PONTING: (*coming forward*) My dear good friends, I beg you won't think me too presuming –

JAMES: (*sourly*) What is it, Colonel?

PONTING: But you mustn't, you really mustn't, allow yourselves to be dictated to – bullied –

JAMES: Bullied?

PONTING: Into doing anything that isn't perfectly agreeable to you.

STEPHEN: You consider we're being bullied, Colonel?

JAMES: If it comes to bullying –

PONTING: It *has* come to bullying, if I'm any judge of bullying. First, you have Mr Elkin, a meddlesome, obstructive –

STEPHEN: (*sitting at the writing-table*) Oh, he's obviously antagonistic to us – obviously.

PONTING: Of course he is. He sniffs a little job of work over this Miss Thornhill. It's his policy to cram Miss Thornhill down our throats. That's his game.

JAMES: (*between his teeth*) By George –

PONTING: And then you get Mr Vallance, your own lawyer. –

JAMES: (*sitting in a chair on the right*) Aye, I'm a bit disappointed with Vallance.

PONTING: Dogmatising about what is just and what is fitting –

STEPHEN: Hear, hear, Colonel! You don't pay a solicitor to take sides against you.

JAMES: As if we couldn't be trusted to do the fair thing of our own accord!

PONTING: The upshot being that Miss Thornhill, supported openly by the one, and tacitly by the other, will be marching in here and – and –

JAMES: Kicking up a rumpus.

PONTING: I shouldn't be surprised.

LOUISA: A rumpus! (*sitting upon the settee on the left*) She wouldn't dare.

ANN: (*rising*) That would be terrible – a rumpus –

ROSE: (*in the middle of the room*) I shouldn't be surprised either. You mustn't expect too much, you know, from a girl who's –

STEPHEN: (*interpreting* ROSE's *shrug*) Illegitimate.

ANN: No, I suppose we oughtn't to expect her to be the same as our children.

PONTING: And finally, to cap it all, you have your brother Thaddeus – your brother –

JAMES: Ha, yes! Tad obliged us with a pretty stiff lecture, didn't he?

LOUISA: So did Phyllis.

ANN: (*seating herself beside* LOUISA:) It was Phyllis who began it.

ROSE: (*swaying herself to and fro upon the back of the chair next to the writing-table*) Tad's wife! She's a suitable person to be lectured by, I must say.

STEPHEN: Poor old Tad! He was only trying to excuse her rudeness.

ROSE: Just fancy! The two Tads sharing equally with ourselves!

STEPHEN: It *is* curious, at first sight.

ROSE: Extraordinary.

STEPHEN: But, naturally, the law makes no distinctions.

ROSE: No. It was the lady's method of announcing that she's as good as we are.

JAMES: Tad and his wife with forty or fifty thousand pound, p'r'aps, to play with! So the world wags.

ROSE: Positively maddening.

LOUISA: We shall see Phyllis aping us now more than ever.

ANN: And making that boy and girl of hers still more conceited.

LOUISA: They needn't let apartments any longer; that's a mercy.

ANN: We shall be spared that disgrace.

JAMES: Strong language, mother.

STEPHEN: Hardly disgrace. You can't call the curate of their parish church a lodger in the ordinary sense of the term.

LOUISA: Phyllis's girl might make a match of it with Mr Trist in a couple of years' time. She's fifteen.

ANN: A forward fifteen.

ROSE: It's a fairy story. A woman who's brought nothing but the worst of luck to Tad from the day he married her!

JAMES: The devil's luck.

STEPHEN: Been his ruin – his ruin professionally – without the shadow of a doubt.

LOUISA: Such a good-looking fellow he used to be, too.

ANN: Handsome.

LOUISA: (*archly*) It was Tad I fell in love with, Stephen – not with you.

STEPHEN: And popular. *He'd* have had the conductorship of the choral societies but for his mistake; Rawlinson would never have had it. Councillor Pritchard admitted as much at a committee-meeting.

PONTING: (*seated upon the settee on the right*) Butcher – the wife's father – wasn't he?

ROSE: Just as bad. Old Burdock kept a grocer's shop at the corner of East Street.

STEPHEN: West Street.

ROSE: West Street, was it? She's the common or garden over-educated petty-tradesman's daughter.

JAMES: (*oratorically*) No, no; you can't *over*-educate, Rose. You can *wrongly* educate –

ROSE: Oh, don't start that, Jim. (*to* PONTING) She was a pupil of Tad's.

STEPHEN: (*holding up his hands*) Marriage – marriage – !

LOUISA: Stephen!

JAMES: If it isn't the right sort o' marriage – !

STEPHEN: Poor old Tad!

JAMES: *Rich* old Tad to-day, though! (*chuckling*) Ha, ha!

ROSE: (*glancing at the door*) Sssh – !

> (THADDEUS *returns. The others look down their noses or at distant objects.*)

THADDEUS: (*closing the door and advancing*) I – I hope you're not angry with Phyllis.

STEPHEN: (*resignedly*) Angry?

THADDEUS: Or with me.

ANN: Anger would be out of place in a house of mourning.

JAMES: Women's tongues, Tad!

STEPHEN: Yes; the ladies – they will make mischief.

LOUISA: Not every woman, Stephen.

THADDEUS: Phyllis hasn't the slightest desire to make mischief. Why on earth should Phyl want to make mischief? (*sitting in the chair in the middle of the room*) She's a little nervey – a little unstrung; that's what's the matter with Phyllis.

LOUISA: There's no cause for *her* to be specially upset that I can think of.

ANN: *She* didn't know Edward in the old days as we did.

THADDEUS: No, but being with him on Wednesday night, when the change came –

that's affected her very deeply, poor girl; bowled her over. (*to* ROSE) She helped to nurse him.

ROSE: (*indifferently*) One of the nurses cracked up, didn't she?

JAMES: The night-nurse.

THADDEUS: (*nodding*) Sent word late on Wednesday afternoon that she couldn't attend to her duties.

STEPHEN: The day-nurse knocking off at eight o'clock! Dreadful!

THADDEUS: There we were, rushing about all over the place – all over the place – to find a substitute.

JAMES: And no success.

THADDEUS: (*rubbing his knees*) There's where Phyllis came in handy; there's where Phyl came in handy.

LOUISA: Phyllis hadn't more than two or three hours of it, while Ann and I were resting, when all's said and done.

ANN: Not more than two or three hours alone, at the outside.

THADDEUS: No; but, as I say, it was during those two or three hours that the change set in. It's been a shock to her.

LOUISA: The truth is, Phyllis delights in making a fuss, Tad.

THADDEUS: Phyl!

ANN: She loves to make a martyr of herself.

THADDEUS: Phyl does!

LOUISA: *You* delight to make a martyr of her, then; perhaps that's it.

ANN: I suppose you do it to hide her faults.

LOUISA: It would be far more sensible of you, Tad, to strive to correct them –

ANN: If it's not too late – far more sensible.

LOUISA: And teach her a diffferent system of managing her home –

ANN: And how to bring up her children more in keeping with their position –

LOUISA: With less pride and display.

ANN: They treat their *cousins* precisely like dirt.

LOUISA: Dirt under the foot.

ANN: Why Phyllis can't be satisfied with a cook-general passes my comprehension –

ROSE: (*wearily*) Oh, shut up!

JAMES: Steady, mother!

THADDEUS: (*looking at them all*) Ah, you've never liked Phyllis from the beginning, any of you.

LOUISA: Never liked her!

THADDEUS: Never cottoned to her, never appreciated her. Oh, I know – old Mr Burdock's shop! (*simply*) Well, Ann; well, Lou; shop or no shop, there's no better wife – no better woman – breathing than Phyl.

LOUISA: One may like a person without being blind to shortcomings.

ANN: Nobody's flawless – nobody.

LOUISA: There are two sides to every person as well as to every question, I always maintain.

THADDEUS: However, maybe it won't matter so much in the future. It hasn't made things easier for us in the past. (*snapping his fingers softly*) But now –

STEPHEN:(*caustically*) Henceforth you and your wife will be above the critical opinion of others, eh, Tad?

JAMES: Aye, Tad's come into money now. Mind what you're at, mother! Be careful, Lou! Tad's come into money.

THADDEUS: (*in a quiet voice, but clenching his hands tightly*) My God, I hope I have! I'm not a hypocrite, Jim. My God, I hope I have!

(*The door opens and* ELKIN *appears.*)

ELKIN: Miss Thornhill is here.

(*There is a general movement.* THADDEUS *walks away to the fireplace.* JAMES, STEPHEN *and* PONTING *also rise and* ROSE *joins* PONTING *at the library-table.* ANN *and* LOUISA *shake out their skirts formidably, their husbands taking up a position near them.* HELEN THORNHILL *enters, followed by* VALLANCE *who closes the door.*)

ELKIN: (*presenting* HELEN) Miss Thornhill. (*to* HELEN, *pointing to the group on the left*) These gentlemen are the late Mr Mortimore's brothers. (*pointing to* ROSE) His sister.

HELEN: (*a graceful, brilliant-looking girl with perfectly refined manners, wearing an elegant travelling-dress – almost inaudibly*) Oh, yes.

ELKIN: (*with a wave of the hand towards the others*) Members of the family by marriage.

(*She sits, at* ELKIN's *invitation, in the chair beside the writing-table. The attitude of the* JAMES *and* STEPHEN MORTIMORES, *and of the* PONTINGS, *undergoes a marked change.*)

JAMES: (*after a pause, advancing a step or two.*) I'm the eldest brother. (*awkwardly*) James, I am.

STEPHEN: (*drawing attention to himself by an uneasy cough*) Stephen.

ANN: (*humbly*) I'm Mrs James.

LOUISA: (*in the same tone*) Mrs Stephen.

ROSE: (*seating herself on the left of the library-table*) Rose – Mrs Ponting. (*glancing at* PONTING) My husband.

THADDEUS: (*now standing behind the writing-table*) Thaddeus. My wife is upstairs, trying on her –

(*He checks himself and retreats, again sitting at the centre window.*)

JAMES: (*seating himself at the writing-table*) Tired, I daresay?

HELEN: (*who has received the various announcements with a dignified inclination of the head*) A little.

STEPHEN: (*bringing forward the arm-chair from the fireplace*) You weren't in Paris, Mr Elkin tells us, when his letter – ?

HELEN: No; I was nearly a nine hours' journey from Paris, staying with friends at St Etienne.

ROSE: A pity.

LOUISA: Great pity.

HELEN: Mr Elkin's letter was re-posted and reached me on Wednesday. I got back to Paris that night.

ELKIN: (*seating himself beside her*) And had a hard day's travelling again yesterday.

STEPHEN: (*sitting in the arm-chair*) She must be worn out.

ANN: Indeed she must.

PONTING: (*sitting by* ROSE) Hot weather, too. Most exhausting.

ELKIN: (*to* HELEN) And you were out and about this morning with Mrs Elkin before eight, I heard?

HELEN: She brought me round here.

ELKIN: (*sympathetically*) Ah, yes.

JAMES: Round here? (ELKIN *motions significantly towards the ceiling.*) Oh – aye. (*after another pause, to* HELEN) When did you see him last – alive?

HELEN: In April. He spent Easter with me. (*unobtrusively opening a little bag which she carries and taking out a handkerchief*) We always spent our holidays together. (*drying her eyes*) I was to have met him at Rouen on the fifteenth of next month; we were going to Etretat.

ELKIN: (*after a further silence*) Er – h'm! – the principal business we are here to discuss is, I presume, the question of Miss Thornhill's future.

HELEN: (*quickly*) Oh, no, please.

ELKIN: No?

HELEN: If you don't mind, I would rather my future were taken for granted, Mr Elkin, without any discussion.

ELKIN: Taken for granted?

HELEN: I am no worse off than thousands of other young women who are suddenly thrown upon their own resources. I'm a great deal better off than many, for there's a calling already open to me – art. My prospects don't daunt me in the least.

ELKIN: No, no; nobody wants to discourage you –

HELEN: (*interrupting* ELKIN) I confess – I confess I am disappointed – hurt – that father hasn't made even a slight provision for me – not for the money's sake, but because – because I meant so much to him, I've always believed. He *would* have made me secure if he had lived longer, I am convinced.

ELKIN: (*soothingly*) Not improbable; not improbable.

HELEN: But I don't intend to let my mind dwell on that. What I do intend to think is that, in leaving me with merely my education and the capacity for earning my living, he has done more for my happiness – my real happiness – than if he had left me every penny he possessed. With no incentive to work, I might have drifted by-and-by into an idle, aimless life. I *should* have done so.

STEPHEN: A very rational view to take of it.

PONTING: Admirable!

(*There is a nodding of heads and a murmur of approval from the ladies.*)

ELKIN: Very admirable and praiseworthy. (*to the others, diplomatically*) But we are not to conclude that Miss Thornhill declines to entertain the idea of some – some arrangement which would enable her to embark upon her artistic career –

HELEN: Yes, you are. I don't need assistance, and I couldn't accept it. (*flaring up*) I will accept nothing that hasn't come to me direct from my father – nothing. (*softening*) But I am none the less grateful to you, dear Mr Elkin – (*looking round*) to everybody – for this kindness.

STEPHEN: (*with a sigh*) So be it; so be it, if it must be so.

PONTING: We don't wish to *force* assistance upon Miss Thornhill.

STEPHEN: On the contrary; we respect her independence of character.

(ELKIN *shrugs his shoulders at* VALLANCE *who is now seated upon the settee on the right.*)

JAMES: (*stroking his beard*) Art – art. You've been studying painting, haven't you?

HELEN: At Julian's, in the Rue de Berri, for three years – for pleasure, I imagined.

JAMES: (*glancing furtively at* ANN) D'ye do oil portraits – family groups and so on?

HELEN: I'm not very successful as a colourist. Black and white is what I am best at.

JAMES: (*dubiously*) Black and white –

STEPHEN: Is there much demand for that form of art in Paris?

HELEN: Paris? Oh, I shall come to London.

JAMES: London, eh?

HELEN: My drawing isn't quite good enough for over there. It's only good enough for England. I shall sell my jewellery and furniture – I'm sharing a flat in the Avenue de Messine with an American girl – and that will carry me along excellently till I'm fairly started. Oh, I shall do very well.

ROSE: I live in London. My house will be somewhere for you to drop into, whenever you feel inclined.

HELEN: Thank you.

PONTING: (*pulling at his moustache*) Often as you like – often as you like –

ROSE: (*loftily*) As I am in 'society', as they call it, that will be nice for you.

JAMES: (*to* ANN) Now, then, mother, don't you be behind-hand –

ANN: I'm sure I shall be very pleased if Miss Thornton –

A MURMUR: Thornhill –

ANN: If she'll pay us a visit. We're homely people, but she and Cissy could play tennis all day long.

LOUISA: If she does come to Singlehampton, she mustn't go away without staying a day or two in the Crescent. (*to* HELEN) Do you play chess, dear? (HELEN *shakes her head.*) My husband will teach you – won't you Stephen?

STEPHEN: Honoured.

THADDEUS: (*who has risen and come forward*) I'm sorry my wife isn't here. We should be grieved if Miss Thornhill left us out in the cold.

HELEN: (*looking at him with interest*) You are father's musical brother, aren't you?

THADDEUS: Yes – Tad.

HELEN: (*with a faint smile*) I promise not to leave you out in the cold. (*to everybody*) I can only repeat, I am most grateful. (*to* ELKIN, *about to rise*) Mrs Elkin is waiting for me, to take me to the dressmaker –

ELKIN: (*detaining her*) One moment – one moment. (*to the others*) Gentlemen, Mr Vallance and I have had our little talk and we agree that the proper course to pursue in the matter of the late Mr Mortimore's estate is to proceed at once to insert an advertisement in the public journals.

JAMES: An advertisement?

ELKIN: With the object of obtaining information respecting any will which he may have made at any time.

JAMES: (*after a pause*) Oh – very good.

STEPHEN: (*coldly*) Does Mr Vallance really advise that this is the proper course?

(VALLANCE *rises and* THADDEUS *again retires.*)

VALLANCE: (*assentingly*) In the peculiar circumstances of the case.

ELKIN: We propose also to go a step further. We propose to circularise.

JAMES: Circularise?

PONTING: (*disturbed*) What the dev – what's that?

ELKIN: We propose to address a circular to every solicitor in the law-list asking for such information.

HELEN: (*to* ELKIN) Is this necessary?

ELKIN: Mr Vallance will tell us –

VALLANCE: It comes under the head of taking all reasonable measures to find a will.

HELEN: (*looking round*) I – I sincerely hope that no one will think that it is on my behalf that Mr Elkin –

ELKIN: (*checking her*) My dear, these are formal, and amicable, proceedings, to which *everybody*, we suggest, should be a party.

VALLANCE: Everybody.

ELKIN: (*invitingly*) Everybody.

JAMES: (*breaking a chilly silence*) All right. Go ahead, Mr Elkin. (to STEPHEN) We're willing?

STEPHEN: Why not; why not? Rose – ?

ROSE: (*hastily*) Oh, certainly.

VALLANCE: (*to* JAMES) I have your authority, Mr Mortimore, for acting with Mr Elkin in this matter?

JAMES: You have, sir.

ELKIN: (*to* VALLANCE, *rising*) Will you come round to my office with me?

> (HELEN *rises with* ELKIN, *whereupon the other men get to their feet.* ANN *and* LOUISA *also rise as* HELEN *comes to them and offers her hand.*)

ANN: (*shaking hands*) We're at the Grand Hotel –

LOUISA: (*shaking hands*) So am I and my husband.

HELEN: I'll call, if I may.

> (*She shakes hands with* STEPHEN *and* JAMES *and goes to* ROSE.)

ROSE: (*rising to shake hands with her*) We're at the Grand too. Colonel Ponting and I would be delighted –

PONTING: Delighted.

> (HELEN *merely bows to* PONTING; *then she shakes hands with* THADDEUS *and passes out into the hall.*)

ELKIN: (*who has opened the door for* HELEN – *to everybody, genially*) Good day; good day.

JAMES *and* STEPHEN: Good day, Mr Elkin. Good day.

> (ELKIN *follows* HELEN.)

VALLANCE: (*At the door* – *to* JAMES *and* STEPHEN) Where can I see you later?

JAMES: The Grand. Food at half-past one.

VALLANCE: Thank you very much.

> (*He bows to the ladies and withdraws, closing the door after him.*)

PONTING: (*pacing the room indignantly*) I wouldn't give the fellow so much as a dry biscuit!

> (*There is a general break up,* ANN *and* LOUISA *joining* ROSE *on the right.*)

JAMES: (*pacifically*) Oh, there's no occasion to upset yourself, Colonel.

PONTING: (*on the left*) I wouldn't! I wouldn't! He's against us on every point.

JAMES: Let 'em advertise, if it amuses 'em. (*in an outburst*) Let 'em advertise *and* circularise till they're blue in the face.

ROSE: (*with a shrill laugh*) Jim! Ha! ha! ha!

ANN *and* LOUISA: (*solemnly*) Hus–s–sh!

JAMES: (*dropping to a whisper*) Oh, I – I forgot.

STEPHEN: Yes, yes, yes; it's nothing more than a lawyer's trick, to swell their bill of costs.

JAMES: Of course it isn't; of course it isn't. (*passing his hand under his beard*) I want some air, mother. Get out o' this.

ANN: (*fastening her mantle*) You've an appointment at the tailor's, remember.

STEPHEN: (*looking at his watch*) So have I.

JAMES: Are you coming, Colonel? (*finding himself in the centre of a group – with a change of manner*) I say! What a beautiful girl, this girl of Ned's!

STEPHEN: Exceedingly.

PONTING: (*producing his cigarette-case*) Charming young woman.

ANN *and* LOUISA: Lovely. A lovely girl.

ROSE: Quite presentable.

JAMES: And she doesn't ask a shilling of us – not a bob.

STEPHEN: She impressed me enormously.

PONTING: (*an unlighted cigarette in his mouth*) Charming; charming.

JAMES: Ned ought to have left her a bit; he ought to have left her a bit. (*resolutely*) Mother – we'll have her down home.

STEPHEN: We must tell some fib or other as to who she is. Yes, we'll show her a little hospitality.

PONTING: And Rosie – in London. That'll make it up to her.

ROSE: Yes, that'll make it up to her.

(*The ladies move into the hall; the men follow.*)

JAMES: (*in the doorway – to THADDEUS, who is now seated at the writing-table*) Tad, I'll stand you and your wife a good lunch. One-thirty.

(THADDEUS *nods acceptance and* JAMES *goes after the others.* THADDEUS *rises, and, looking through the blind of the middle window, watches them depart. Presently* PHYLLIS *appears, putting on her gloves.*)

PHYLLIS: (*at the door, drawing a breath of relief*) They've gone.

THADDEUS: (*turning*) Is that you, Phyl?

PHYLLIS: (*coming further into the room*) I've been waiting on the landing.

THADDEUS: Why didn't you come back, dear? You've missed Miss Thornhill.

PHYLLIS: (*walking away to the left, working at the fingers of a glove*) Yes, I – I know

THADDEUS: The very person we were all here to meet.

PHYLLIS: I – I came over nervous. (*eagerly*) What is she like?

THADDEUS: Such an aristocratic-looking girl.

PHYLLIS: Is she – is she?

THADDEUS: I'll tell you all about her by-and-by. (*pushing the door to and coming to* PHYLLIS, *anxiously*) What do you think they're going to do now, Phyl?

PHYLLIS: Who?

THADDEUS: The lawyers. They're going to advertise.

PHYLLIS: Advertise?

THADDEUS: In the papers – to try to discover a will.

PHYLLIS: I – I suppose that's a mere matter of form?

THADDEUS: Elkin and Vallance say so. According to Stephen, it's simply a lawyer's dodge to run up costs. (*brightening*) Anyhow, we mustn't complain, where a big estate is involved –

PHYLLIS: Is it – such a – big estate?

THADDEUS: Guess.

PHYLLIS: I can't.

THADDEUS: (*coming closer to her*) I heard Elkin's managing-clerk tell Jim and the Colonel this morning that poor Ned may have died worth anything between a hundred-and-fifty and two hundred thousand pounds.

PHYLLIS: (*faintly*) Two hundred thousand – !

THADDEUS: Yes.

PHYLLIS: Oh, Tad – !

> (*She sits, on the settee on the left, leaning her head upon her hands.*)

THADDEUS: Splitting the difference, and allowing for death duties, our share would be close upon forty thousand. To be on the safe side, put it at thirty-nine thousand. Thirty-nine thousand pounds! (*moving about the room excitedly*) I've been reckoning. Invest that at four-per-cent. – one is justified in calculating upon a four-per-cent. basis – invest thirty-nine thousand at four-per-cent. and there you have an income of over fifteen hundred a year. Fifteen hundred a year! (*returning to her*) When we die, seven-hundred-and-fifty a year for Joyce, seven-hundred-and-fifty for Cyril! (*She rises quickly and clings to him, burying her head upon his shoulder and clutching at the lapel of his coat.*) Poor old lady! (*putting his arms round her*) Poor old lady! You've gone through such a lot, haven't you?

PHYLLIS: (*sobbing*) We both have.

THADDEUS: Sixteen years of it.

PHYLLIS: Sixteen years.

THADDEUS: Of struggle – struggle and failure.

PHYLLIS: Failure brought upon you by your wife – by me.

THADDEUS: Nonsense – nonsense –

PHYLLIS: You always call it nonsense; you know it's true. If you hadn't married me – if you'd married a girl of a better family – you wouldn't have lost caste in the town –

THADDEUS: Hush, hush! Don't cry, Phyl; don't cry, old lady.

PHYLLIS: You'd have had the choral societies, and the High School, and the organ at All Saints; you'd have been at the top of the tree long ago. You know you would!

THADDEUS: (*rallying her*) And if *you* hadn't married *me*, you might have captivated a gay young officer at Claybrook and got to London eventually. Rose did it, and you might have done it. So that makes us quits. Don't cry.

PHYLLIS: (*gradually regaining her composure*) There *was* a young fellow at the barracks who was after me.

THADDEUS: (*nodding*) You were prettier than Rose, a smarter girl altogether.

PHYLLIS: (*drying her eyes*) I'll be smart again now, dear. I'm only thirty-five. What's thirty-five!

THADDEUS: The children won't swallow up everything now, will they?

PHYLLIS: No; but Joyce shall look sweeter and daintier than ever, though.

THADDEUS: Cyril shall have a first-class, public-school education; that I'm
 determined upon. There's Rugby – Rugby's the nearest – or Malvern –
PHYLLIS: (*with a catch in her breath*) Oh, but – Tad – we'll leave Singlehampton,
 won't we?
THADDEUS: Permanently?
PHYLLIS: Yes – yes –
THADDEUS: Wouldn't that be rather a mistake?
PHYLLIS: A mistake!
THADDEUS: Just as we're able to hold up our heads in the town.
PHYLLIS: We should never be able to hold our heads in Singlehampton. If we were
 clothed in gold, we should still be lepers underneath; the curse would still rest on
 us.
THADDEUS: (*bewildered*) But where – where shall we – ?
PHYLLIS: I don't care – anywhere. (*passionately*) Anywhere where I'm not sneered
 at for bringing up my children decently, and for making my home more tasteful
 than my neighbours'; anywhere where it isn't known that I'm the daughter of a
 small shopkeeper – the daughter of 'old Burdock of West Street'! (*imploringly*)
 Oh, Tad – !
THADDEUS: You're right. Nothing is ever forgiven you in the place you're born in.
 We'll clear out.
PHYLLIS: (*slipping her arm through his*) When – when will you get me away?
THADDEUS: Directly, directly; as soon as the lawyers –
 (*He pauses, looking at her blankly.*)
PHYLLIS: (*frightened*) What's the matter?
THADDEUS: We – we're talking as if – as if Ned's money is already ours!
PHYLLIS: (*withdrawing her arm – steadily*) It will be.
THADDEUS: Will it, do you think – ?
PHYLLIS: (*with an expressionless face*) I prophesy – it will be.
 (HEATH *enters and, seeing* THADDEUS *and* PHYLLIS, *draws
 back.*)
HEATH: I'm sorry, sir. I thought the room was empty.
THADDEUS: We're going. (*as he and* PHYLLIS *pass out into the hall*) Don't come
 to the door.
HEATH: Thank you, sir.
 (HEATH *quickly and methodically replaces the chair at the window on
 the right. Then, after a last look round, he switches off the lights and
 leaves the room again in gloom.*)
 END OF THE FIRST ACT

 THE SECOND ACT

*The scene represents the drawing-room of a modern, cheaply-built villa. In the wall at
the back are two windows. One is a bay-window provided with a window-seat; the
other, the window on the right, opens to the ground into a small garden. At the bottom
of the garden a paling runs from left to right, and in the paling there is a gate which gives
access to a narrow lane. Beyond are the gardens and backs of other houses.
The fireplace is on the right of the room, the door on the left. A grand pianoforte, with*

its head towards the windows, and a music-stool occupy the middle of the room. On the right of the music-stool there is an arm-chair, and against the piano, facing the fireplace, there is a settee. Another settee faces the audience at the further end of the fireplace, and on the nearer side, opposite this settee, is an arm-chair. Also on the right hand, but nearer to the spectator, there is a round table. An ottoman, opposing the settee by the piano, stands close to the table.

At the end of the piano there is a small table with an arm-chair on its right and left, and on the extreme left of the room stands another arm-chair with a still smaller table beside it. On the left of the bay-window there is a writing-table, and in front of the writing-table, but turned to the window, a chair. Other articles of furniture fill spaces against the walls. There is a mirror over the fireplace and a clock on the mantelshelf, and lying upon the round table are a hat and a pair of gloves belonging to HELEN. *Some flowers in pots hide the empty grate.*

The room and everything in the room are eloquent of narrow means, if not of actual poverty. But the way in which the cheap furniture is dressed up, in the manner of its arrangement about the room, give evidence of taste and refinement.

The garden is full of the bright sunshine of a fine July afternoon.

THADDEUS *is at the piano accompanying a sentimental ballad which* TRIST, *standing beside him is singing.* PHYLLIS, *looking more haggard than when last seen, is on the settee by the fireplace. Her hands lie idly upon some needlework in her lap and she is deep in thought.* HELEN, *engaged in making a sketch of* JOYCE *and* CYRIL, *who are facing her, is sitting in the chair on the right of the table at the end of the piano. A drawing-block is on her knees and a box of crayons on the table at her elbow.*

HELEN *and the* THADDEUS MORTIMORES *are dressed in mourning, but not oppressively so.*

THADDEUS: (*taking his hands from the key-board – to* TRIST) No, no. fill your lungs, man, fill your lungs.

(PHYLLIS, *roused by the break in the music, picks up her work.*)

TRIST: (*a big, healthy-looking, curly-headed young fellow in somewhat shabby clerical clothes*) I'm afraid it's no good, my dear chap. The fact is, air will not keep in my lungs.

THADDEUS: (*starting afresh with the symphony*) Once more –

HELEN: (*to the children, softly*) Do you want a rest?

CYRIL: (*a handsome boy of fourteen, standing close to his sister*) No, thanks.

JOYCE: (*in the chair on the extreme left – a slim, serious child, a year older than* CYRIL) Oh, no; don't give us a rest.

(*As the symphony ends, the door opens a little way and* JAMES *pops his head in.*)

JAMES: Hallo!

THADDEUS: Hallo, Jim!

(JAMES *enters, followed by* STEPHEN; *both with an air of bustle and self-importance. They also are in mourning, are gloved and are wearing their hats which they remove on entering.*)

---

symphony: 'A passage for instruments alone (or, by extension, for a single instrument) occurring in a vocal composition as an introduction, interlude, or close to an accompaniment' (*OED*).

STEPHEN: May we come in?
JAMES: Good afternoon, Mr Trist.
STEPHEN: How do you do, Mr Trist?
TRIST: (*to* JAMES *and* STEPHEN) How are you; how are you?
JAMES: (*to the children, kissing* JOYCE) Well, kids! (*shaking hands with* HELEN) Well, my dear! (*crossing to* PHYLLIS, *who rises*) Don't get up, Phyllis. What's this? You're not very bobbish, I hear.
PHYLLIS: (*nervously*) It's nothing.
THADDEUS: (*tidying his music*) She's sleeping badly just now, poor old lady.
STEPHEN: (*who has greeted* HELEN *and the children* – *to* PHYLLIS) Oh, Phyllis, Louisa has discovered a wonderful cure for sleeplessness at the herbalists in Crown Street. A few dried leaves merely. You strew them under the bed and the effect is magical.
JAMES: Glass of warm milk's *my* remedy –
STEPHEN: Eighteen-pence an ounce, it costs.
JAMES: Not that sleeplessness bothers *me*.
PHYLLIS: (*sitting on the ottoman and resuming her work* – *to* STEPHEN) Thank you for telling me about it.
JAMES: (*to* HELEN) Making quite a long stay here.
HELEN: (*smiling*) Am I not?
STEPHEN: You and Phyllis, Tad, are more honoured than we were in the Crescent.
JAMES: Or we were at 'Ivanhoe'. She was only a couple o' nights with us.
STEPHEN: *Less* with us. She arrived one morning and left the next.
JAMES: (*to* HELEN) Been in Nelson Villas over a week, haven't you?
HELEN: (*touching her drawing*) Is it more than a week?
JAMES: (*looking at* HELEN'*s drawing*) Taking the youngsters' portraits, too.
STEPHEN: (*also looking at the drawing*) H'm! I suppose children *are* difficult subjects.
TRIST: (*moving towards the door* – *to* HELEN) Miss Thornhill, don't forget your engagement.
HELEN: (*to* JOYCE *and* CYRIL) Mr Trist is going to treat us to the flower-show by-and-by.
CYRIL. Good man!
JOYCE: Oh, Mr Trist!
STEPHEN: (*to* TRIST) Not driving you away, I hope?
TRIST: (*at the door*) No, no; I've some work to do.
          (*He withdraws.* STEPHEN *puts his hat on the top of the piano.*)
JAMES: (*after watching the door close*) Decent sort o' young man, that; nothing of the lodger about him.
STEPHEN: I've always said so. (*to* THADDEUS, *lowering his voice*) Mr Trist knows how – er – h'm – poor Edward left his affairs?
THADDEUS: Everybody does; it's all over the town.
STEPHEN: (*resignedly*) Yes; impossible to keep it to ourselves.
JAMES: Thanks to their precious advertisement. (*to* JOYCE *and* CYRIL, *loudly*) Now, then, children; be off with you! I want to talk to your father and mother.
JOYCE: (*to* HELEN) Will you excuse us?
CYRIL: Awfully sorry, Helen.

(*The children pass through the open window into the garden and disappear.* HELEN *rises, and, having laid her drawing-block aside, is following them.*)

JAMES: (*to* HELEN) Not you, my dear. You're welcome to hear our business.

HELEN: Oh, no; you mustn't let me intrude.

STEPHEN: I think Helen *ought* to hear it. (HELEN *pauses, standing by the table on the right.*) I think she ought to be made aware of what's going on.

JAMES: Tad –

THADDEUS: (*coming forward*) Eh?

JAMES: The meeting's to take place this afternoon.

(PHYLLIS *looks up from her work suddenly with parted lips.*)

THADDEUS: This afternoon?

STEPHEN: At four o'clock.

THADDEUS: (*glancing at the clock on the mantelpiece*) It's past three now.

JAMES: (*placing his hat on the table at the end of the piano and sitting at the left of the table*) It's been fixed up at last rather in a hurry.

STEPHEN: (*sitting in the chair on the extreme left*) We didn't get Elkin's letter, telling us he was coming through, till this morning.

THADDEUS: You might have notified us earlier, though, one of you. Just like you fellows!

STEPHEN: (*waving his arms*) On the day I go to press I've quite enough to remember.

JAMES: (*to* THADDEUS, *roughly*) It's your holiday-time; what have *you* got to do? An hour's notice is as good as a week's.

STEPHEN: (*to* HELEN) This is a meeting of the family, Helen, to be held at my brother's house, for the purpose of – er –

HELEN: (*advancing a little*) Winding matters up?

JAMES: For the purpose of receiving Elkin and Vallance's report.

HELEN: (*keenly*) And to – ?

JAMES: And to decide upon the administration of the estate on behalf of the next-of-kin.

HELEN: In my words – wind matters up. (*with an appearance of cheerfulness*) Which means an end to a month's suspense, doesn't it?

THADDEUS: (*apologetically*) A not very satisfactory end to yours.

HELEN: To mine? (*with an effort*) Oh, I – I've suffered no suspense, Mr Tad. Mr Elkin has kept me informed of the result of the advertising and the circularising from the beginning.

THADDEUS: But there has been no result.

HELEN: No result *is* the result.

STEPHEN: Exactly.

(*During the following talk,* HELEN *moves away and seats herself in the chair by the head of the piano.* PHYLLIS *has resumed her work again, bending over it so that her face is almost hidden.*)

THADDEUS: (*to* JAMES *and* STEPHEN) Will Rose and the Colonel be down?

JAMES: We're on our way to the station to meet 'em.

STEPHEN: (*bitterly*) Ha! Will they be down!

THADDEUS: You didn't overlook *them*, evidently.

JAMES: (*with a growl*) No; the gallant Colonel doesn't give us much chance of overlooking *him*.

STEPHEN: Colonel Ponting might be the only person interested, judging by the tone he adopts.

JAMES: A nice life he's been leading us lately.

STEPHEN: Elkin and Vallance are sick of him.

JAMES: Hasn't two penny pieces to clink together; that's the size of it.

STEPHEN: A man may be hard up and yet behave with dignity.

JAMES: I expect the decorators are asking for a bit on the nail.

THADDEUS: (*siting on the right of the table at the end of the piano*) Decorators?

STEPHEN: (*to* THADDEUS) Haven't you heard – ?

THADDEUS: No.

STEPHEN: The magnificent house they've taken in Carlos Place – ?

JAMES: Close to Berkeley Square.

STEPHEN: (*correcting* JAMES'*s pronunciation*) *Bark*eley Square.

JAMES: Stables and motor-garridge at the back.

STEPHEN: Oh, yes; they're decorating and furnishing most elaborately. Lou had a note from Rose a day or two since.

JAMES: He'll strip my sister of every penny she's come into, if she doesn't look out.

STEPHEN: The gross indelicacy of the thing is what offends me. *We* have been content to remain passive.

JAMES: And I fancy our plans and projects are as important as the Colonel's.

STEPHEN: I should assume so.

JAMES: (*to* STEPHEN, *with a jerk of the thumb towards* THADDEUS) Shall I – ?

STEPHEN: No harm in it *now*.

JAMES: (*to* THADDEUS, *leaning forward – impressively*) Tad –

THADDEUS: What?

JAMES: That land at the bottom of Gordon Street, where the allotment grounds are –

THADDEUS: Yes?

JAMES: It's mine.

THADDEUS: Yours, Jim?

JAMES: It belongs to me. I've signed the contract and paid a deposit.

THADDEUS:What do you intend to do with it?

JAMES: What should I intend to do with it – eat it? I intend to build there – build the finest avenue of houses in Singlehampton. (*rising and going to the piano, where he traces a plan on the lid with his finger*) Look here! (THADDEUS *joins him and watches the tracing of the plan.*) Here's Gordon Street. Here's the pub at the corner. I come along here – straight along here – to Albert Terrace. Opposite Albert Terrace I take in Clark's piano factory; and where Clark's factory stands I lay out an ornamental garden with a fountain in the middle of it. On I go at a curve, to avoid the playground of Fothergill's school, till I reach Bolton's store. He stops me, but I'll squeeze him out some day, as sure as my name's James Henry! (*to* THADDEUS) D'ye see?

THADDEUS: (*uncomfortably, eyeing* HELEN) Splendid; splendid.

JAMES: (*moving round the head of the piano to the right*) Poor old Ned! Ha! my brother won't have done so badly by his native town after all.

THADDEUS: (*under his breath, trying to remind* JAMES *of* HELEN's *presence*) Jim
    – Jim –

JAMES: (*obliviously, coming upon* HELEN) D'ye know the spot we're talking about,
    my dear?

HELEN: No.

JAMES: You must get 'em to walk you down there. (*to* PHYLLIS) You trot her down
    there, Phyllis.

PHYLLIS:(*without raising her eyes from her work*) I will.

STEPHEN: (*to* JAMES) You haven't told them *everything*, Jim.

JAMES: (*sitting upon the settee by the piano*) Haven't I? (*mopping his brow*) Oh, your
    offices –

STEPHEN: (*to everybody*) It isn't of the greatest importance, perhaps, but it's part of
    James's scheme to erect an exceptionally noble building in the new road to
    provide adequate printing and publishing offices for the *Times and Mirror*.

THADDEUS: What, you're not deserting King Street, Stephen?

STEPHEN: (*rising and walking to the fireplace*) Yes, I've had enough of those
    cramped, poky premises.

THADDEUS: They *are* inconvenient.

STEPHEN: (*on the hearthrug, facing the others*) And, to be perfectly frank, I've had
    enough of Mr Hammond and the *Courier*.

THADDEUS: I don't blame you there. The *Courier* is atrociously personal
    occasionally.

STEPHEN: (*pompously*) I don't say it because Hammond is, in a manner, my rival –
    I'm not so small-minded as that – but I do say that he is a vulgar man and that
    the *Courier* is a vulgar and mischievous journal.

JAMES: He's up-to-date, though, is Mister Freddy Hammond.

STEPHEN: His plant is slightly more modern than mine, I admit.

JAMES: (*chuckling*) Aye, you'll be able to present those antediluvian printing-presses
    of yours to the museum as curiosities.

STEPHEN: (*with a wave of the hand*) Anyhow, the construction of Jim's new road
    marks a new era in the life of the *Times and Mirror*. (*leaving the fireplace*) I'm
    putting no less than twelve thousand pounds into the dear old paper, Tad.

THADDEUS: (*standing by the table on the left*) Twelve thousand – !

STEPHEN: How will that agree with Mr Hammond's digestion, eh? Twelve thousand
    pounds! (*coming to* THADDEUS) And what are *your* plans for the future, if
    one may ask? You'll leave these wretched villas, of course?

THADDEUS: (*evasively*) Oh, I – I'm waiting till this law-business is absolutely
    settled.

STEPHEN: (*hastily*) Quite right; quite right. So am I; so am I, actually. But we may
    talk, I suppose, among ourselves –

JAMES: (*looking at his watch and rising*) By George! We shall miss Rose and the
    Colonel.

STEPHEN: (*fetching his hat*) Pish! the Colonel.

JAMES: (*shaking hands hurriedly with* HELEN *who rises*) Ta-ta, my dear. (*as he
    passes* PHYLLIS) See you at the meeting, Phyllis.

STEPHEN: (*to* HELEN, *across the piano*) Good-bye, Helen.

JAMES: (*who has picked up his hat, at the door*) Don't be late, Tad.

STEPHEN: (*at the door*) No, no; don't be late.

THADDEUS: Four o'clock.

STEPHEN: Sharp.

> (THADDEUS *follows* JAMES *and* STEPHEN *into the hall and returns immediately.*)

THADDEUS: (*closing the door*) My dear Helen, I apologise to you most humbly.

HELEN: (*coming forward*) For what?

THADDEUS: For Jim's bad taste, and Stephen's, in talking before you as they've been doing.

HELEN: Oh, it's of no consequence.

THADDEUS: I could have kicked Jim.

HELEN: (*impulsively*) Mr Tad – (*giving him her hand*) I congratulate you. (*going to* PHYLLIS *and kissing her lightly upon the cheek*) I congratulate you both heartily. No two people in the world deserve good fortune more than you do.

THADDEUS: It's extremely kind and gracious of you to take it in this way.

HELEN: Why, in what other way could I take it?

THADDEUS: At your age, you mayn't esteem money very highly. But – there are other considerations –

HELEN: (*turning away and seating herself upon the settee by the piano*) Yes, we won't speak of those.

THADDEUS: (*walking to the bay-window*) And there was just a chance that the inquiries might have brought a will to light – a will benefiting you. Though you were anxious not to appear unfriendly to the family, you must have realised that.

HELEN: Whether I did or not, it's all done with now finally – finally (*blowing the subject from her*) Phew!

THADDEUS: (*his elbows on the piano, speaking across it to* HELEN) Phyl and I are not altogether selfish and grasping. She has been worrying herself to death these last few days – haven't you, Phyl? – ever since we heard the meeting was near at hand.

PHYLLIS: (*in a low voice*) Yes.

THADDEUS: Ever since you came to us, in fact.

HELEN: (*jumping up*) Ah, what a nuisance I've been to you! (*sitting beside* PHYLLIS) How relieved you'll be to pack me off to-morrow!

THADDEUS: To-morrow?

> (*Uttering a little sound,* PHYLLIS *stops working and stares straight before her.*)

HELEN: (*slipping an arm round* PHYLLIS's *waist*) That letter I had while we were at lunch – it was from a girl who used to sit next to me at Julian's. She's found me some capital rooms, she says, close to Regent's Park, and I'm going to look at them. (THADDEUS *comes to her.*) In any event, the sooner I get out of Singlehampton the better.

THADDEUS: Why?

HELEN: Everybody in the town eyes me so queerly; I'm certain they suspect.

THADDEUS: It's your imagination.

HELEN: It isn't. (*hesitatingly*) I – I've confided in Mr Trist.

THADDEUS: (*surprised*) Confided in Trist?

HELEN: (*nodding*) I hated the idea of his thinking me – deceitful.

THADDEUS: (*sitting on the settee by the piano*) Trist would never have guessed.

HELEN: Oh, Mr Tad, who, in heaven's name, that wasn't born yesterday *could* believe the story of my being simply a *protégée* of father's, the daughter of an old business friend of his? Your brother Stephen may be an excellent editor, but his powers of invention are beneath contempt.

THADDEUS: (*laughing*) Ha, ha, ha! (*rubbing his knees*) that's one for Stephen; that's a rap for Stephen.

HELEN: And then, again, the other members of the family are becoming so horribly jealous.

THADDEUS: (*seriously*) Ah, yes.

HELEN: You noticed your brother's remarks? And Mrs James and Mrs Stephen almost cut me in East Street this morning.

THADDEUS: (*clenching his fists*) Thank God, we shall have done with that sort of thing directly we shake the dust of Singlehampton from our feet!

HELEN: Directly you –

THADDEUS: (*gaily*) There! Now I've let the cat out of the bag. Phyllis will tell you. You tell her, Phyl. (*rising*) I promised Rawlinson I'd help him index his madrigals this afternoon; I'll run round to him and explain. (*pausing on his way to the door*) Helen, you must be our first visitor in our new home, wherever we pitch our tent. Make that a bargain with her, Phyl. (*at the door, to* PHYLLIS) we'll start at ten minutes to, old lady. be ready.

    (*He disappears, closing the door after him.*)

HELEN: (*rising and walking away to the left*) Well! I do think it shabby of you, Phyllis. You and Mr Tad might have trusted me with your secret. (*facing her*) Phyllis, wouldn't it be glorious if you came to London to live – or near London? Wouldn't it!

PHYLLIS: (*in a strange, quiet voice, her hands lying quite still upon her lap*) Helen – Helen dear –

HELEN: Yes?

PHYLLIS: That morning, a month ago, in Linchpool – while we were all sitting in your poor father's library waiting for you –

HELEN: (*returning to her*) On the Friday morning –

PHYLLIS: There was a discussion as to making you an allowance, and – (*her eyes avoiding* HELEN's) and everybody was most anxious – most anxious – that you should be placed upon a proper footing.

HELEN: Mr Elkin broached the subject when I arrived. You were out of the room.

PHYLLIS: Yes. And you declined –

HELEN: Certainly. I gave them my reasons. Why do you bring this up?

    (PHYLLIS *rises, laying her work upon the table behind her.*)

PHYLLIS: (*drawing a deep breath*) Helen – I want you to reconsider your decision.

HELEN: Reconsider it?

PHYLLIS: I want you to reconsider your determination not to accept an allowance from the family.

HELEN: Impossible.

PHYLLIS: Oh, don't be so hasty. Listen first. This good fortune of ours – of Tad's and mine – that you've congratulated us upon – I shall never enjoy it –

HELEN: (*incredulously*) Oh, Phyllis!

PHYLLIS: I shall not. It will never bring me a moment's happiness unless you consent to receive an allowance from the family – (HELEN *seats herself in the chair on the extreme left with her back to* PHYLLIS) sufficient to give you a sense of independence –

HELEN: I couldn't

PHYLLIS: And to make your future perfectly safe.

HELEN: I couldn't

PHYLLIS: (*entreatingly*) Do – do –

HELEN: It's out of the question.

PHYLLIS: Please – for my sake – !

HELEN: (*turning to her*) I'm sorry to distress you, Phyllis; indeed I'm sorry. But when you see me gaining some little position in London, through my work, you'll cease to feel miserable about me.

PHYLLIS: Never – never –

HELEN: (*starting up and walking to the fireplace impetuously*) Oh, you don't understand me – my pride. A pensioner of the Mortimore family! I! How can you suggest it? I refused their help before I was fully acquainted with these, to me, uncongenial relations of father's – I don't include Mr Tad in that expression, of course; and now I *am* acquainted with them I would refuse it a thousand times. If I were starving, I wouldn't put myself under the smallest obligation to the Mortimores.

PHYLLIS: (*unsteadily*) Obligation – to – the – Mortimores – obligation – ! (*as if about to make some communication to* HELEN, *supporting herself by leaning upon the table on the right, her body bent forward – almost inaudibly*) Helen – Helen –

HELEN: What – ?

> (*There is a short silence, and then* PHYLLIS *drops back upon the settee by the piano.*)

PHYLLIS: (*rocking herself to and fro*) Oh – oh, dear – oh – !

HELEN: (*coming to her and standing over her*) You're quite ill, Phyllis; your bad nights are taking it out of you dreadfully. You ought to have the advice of a doctor.

PHYLLIS: (*weakly*) No – don't send for the doctor –

HELEN: Go up to your room, then, and keep quiet till Mr Tad calls you. (*glancing at the clock*) You've a quarter-of-an-hour –

PHYLLIS: (*clutching* HELEN's *skirt*) Helen – you're fond of me and Tad – you said yesterday how attached you'd grown to us –

HELEN: (*soothingly*) I am – I am – very fond of you.

PHYLLIS: And the children – ?

HELEN: Yes, yes.

PHYLLIS: My poor children!

HELEN: Hush! Why *poor* children? Pull yourself together. Go up to your room.

PHYLLIS: (*taking* HELEN's *hand and caressing it*) Helen – if you won't accept an allowance from the entire family, accept it from Tad and me.

HELEN: No, no, no.

PHYLLIS: Four – three hundred a year.

HELEN: No.

PHYLLIS: Two hundred.

HELEN: No.

PHYLLIS: We could spare it. We shouldn't miss it; we should never miss it.

HELEN: Not a penny.

PHYLLIS: (*rising and gripping* HELEN's *shoulders*) You shall – you shall accept it, Helen.

HELEN: Phyllis! (*releasing herself and drawing back*) Phyllis, you're very odd to-day. You've got this allowance idea on the brain. Look here; don't let's mention the subject again, or I – I shall be offended.

PHYLLIS: (*dully, hanging her head*) All right. Very well.

HELEN: Forgive me. It happens to be just the one point I'm sensitive upon. (*listening, then going to the open window*) Here are the children. Do go upstairs. (*calling into the garden*) Hallo! (PHYLLIS *leaves the room as* CYRIL *and* JOYCE *appear outside the window. The boy is carrying a few freshly cut roses.*) Now, then, children! Isn't it time we routed Mr Trist out of his study?

CYRIL: (*entering and going towards the door*) I'll stir the old chap up. (*remembering the nosegay*) Oh – (*presenting it to* HELEN *who comes forward with* JOYCE) Allow me –

HELEN: For me? How sweet of you! (*placing the flowers against her belt and then at her breast*) Where shall I wear them – here, or here?

CYRIL: Anywhere you like. (*awkwardly*) We sha'n't see anything nicer at the flower-show, I'm certain.

HELEN: No; they're beautiful.

CYRIL: (*his eyes on the carpet*) I don't mean the flowers –

HELEN: (*inclining her head*) Thank you. (*to* CYRIL, *who again makes for the door*) Don't disturb mother. (*moving away to the fireplace where, at the mirror over the mantelshelf, she fixes the roses in her belt*) She has to go to Claybrook Road with your father in a little while and I want her to rest.

CYRIL: (*pausing*) She *is* seedy, isn't she? (*puckering his brows*) Going to uncle Jim's, are they?

HELEN: Yes.

CYRIL: That's to do with our money, I expect.

HELEN: (*busy at the mirror*) With your money?

CYRIL: Father's come into a heap of money, you know.

JOYCE: (*reproachfully*) Cyril!

CYRIL: (*not heeding her*) So have uncle Jim and uncle Stephen and aunt Rose.

HELEN: I'm delighted.

CYRIL: (*to* JOYCE *who is signing to him to desist*) Oh, what's the use of our keeping it dark any longer?

JOYCE: We promised mother –

CYRIL: Ages ago. But you heard what father said to uncle Stephen – it's all over the town. Young Pither says there's something about it in the paper.

HELEN: The paper?

CYRIL: The *Courier* – that fellow Hammond's paper. Hammond was beastly sarcastic about it last week, Pither says. (*going to the door*) I don't read the *Courier* myself (*At the door he beckons to* JOYCE. *She joins him and his voice drops to a whisper.*) Besides – (*glancing significantly at* HELEN, *whose back is turned to*

them) it'll make it easier for *us*. (*nudging her*) Now's your chance; do it now.
(*aloud*) Give me five minutes, you two. I can't be seen at the flower-show in
these togs.

> (*He withdraws. Having assured herself that the door is closed,* JOYCE
> *advances to* HELEN.)

JOYCE: Helen –
HELEN: Hallo?
JOYCE: (*gravely*) Have you a minute to spare?
HELEN: (*coming to the round table*) Yes, dear.
JOYCE: Helen, it's quite true we've come into a great deal of money. Uncle
    Edward, who lived at Linchpool – oh, you knew him, didn't you? – he was a
    friend of yours –
HELEN: (*nodding*) He was a friend of mine.
JOYCE: Uncle Edward has left his fortune to the family – (*breaking off*) you've been
    told already! –
HELEN: Well – yes.
JOYCE: We haven't received our share yet; but we *shall*, as soon as it's all divided up.
    (*timidly*) Helen – (HELEN *seats herself upon the ottoman in an attitude of*
    attention.) I needn't tell you this will very much improve father and mother's
    position.
HELEN: Naturally.
JOYCE: And mine and Cyril's too. I'm to finish abroad, I believe.
HELEN: Lucky brat.
JOYCE: But it's Cyril I want to talk to you about – my brother Cyril –
HELEN: Cyril?
JOYCE: Cyril is to be entered for one of the principal public schools.
HELEN: Is he?
JOYCE: One of those schools which stamp a boy a gentleman for the rest of his life.
HELEN: He is a gentleman, as it is. I've a high opinion of Cyril.
JOYCE: Oh, I *am* glad to hear you say so, because – because –
HELEN: Because what? (JOYCE *turns away in silence to the settee by the piano.*)
    What are you driving at, Joicey?
JOYCE: (*lounging on the settee uneasily and inelegantly*) Of course, Cyril's only
    fourteen at present; there's no denying that.
HELEN: I suppose there isn't.
JOYCE: But in three years' time he'll be seventeen, and in another three he'll be
    twenty.
HELEN: (*puzzled*) Well?
JOYCE: And at twenty you're a young man, aren't you?
HELEN: A young man.
JOYCE: (*seating herself, her elbows on her knees, examining her fingers*) And even
    then he'd be content to wait.
HELEN: To wait? What for?
JOYCE: (*in a low voice*) Cyril wishes to marry you some day, Helen.
HELEN: (*after a pause gently*) Does he?
JOYCE: He consulted me about it soon after you came to us, and I advised him to be
    quite sure of himself before he spoke to you. And he *is*, quite sure of himself.

HELEN: And he's asked you to speak *for* him.?

JOYCE: He prefers my doing it. (*looking, under her lashes, at* HELEN) Are you furious?

HELEN: Not a scrap.

JOYCE: (*transferring herself from the settee to the floor at* HELEN'*s feet – embracing her*) Oh, that's lovely of you! I was afraid you might be.

HELEN: Furious?

JOYCE: (*gazing at her admiringly*) At our aiming so high. I was afraid you might consider that marrying Cyril would be marrying beneath you.

HELEN: (*tenderly*) The girl who marries Cyril will have to be a far grander person than I am, Joyce, to be marrying beneath her.

JOYCE: Oh, Cyril's all right in himself, and so is father. Father's very retiring, but he's as clever a musician as any in the midlands. And mother is all right in *herself*. (*backing away from* HELEN) It's not mother's fault; it's her misfortune –

HELEN: Her misfortune – ?

JOYCE: (*bitterly*) Oh, I'll be bound they mentioned it at 'Ivanhoe' or at the Crescent.

HELEN: Mentioned – ?

JOYCE: (*between her teeth*) The shop – grandfather's shop –

HELEN: Ah, yes.

JOYCE: (*clenching her hands*) Ah! (*squatting upon her heels, her shoulders hunched*) Grandfather was a grocer, Helen – a grocer. Oh, mother has suffered terribly through it – agonies.

HELEN: Poor mother!

JOYCE: We've all suffered. Sometimes it's been as much as Cyril and I could do to keep our heads up; (*proudly, with flashing eyes*) but we've done it. The Singlehampton people are beasts.

HELEN: Joyce!

JOYCE: If it's the last word I ever utter – beasts. (*swallowing a tear*) And only half of it was grocery – only half.

HELEN: Only half – ?

JOYCE: It was a double shop. There were two windows; the other half was bottles of wine. They forget that; they forget that!

HELEN: A shame.

JOYCE: (*embracing* HELEN *again*) What shall I say to him, then?

HELEN: Say to him?

JOYCE: Cyril – what answer shall I give him?

HELEN: Oh, tell Cyril that I am highly complimented by his offer –

JOYCE: (*eagerly*) Complimented – yes – ?

HELEN: And that, if he's of the same mind when he's a man, and I am still single, he may propose to me again.

JOYCE: (*in alarm*) If you're – still single – ?

HELEN: Yes – (*shaking her head*) and if he's of the same mind.

> (*There is a sharp, prolonged rapping on the door.* JOYCE *and* HELEN *rise.*)

JOYCE: (*going to the door*) It's that frightful tease.

(*She opens the door and* TRIST *enters, carrying his hat, gloves and walking-stick.*)

TRIST: Ladies, I have reason to believe that several choice specimens of the *Dianthus Caryophyllus* refuse to raise their heads until you grace the flower-show with your presence.

    (JOYCE *slaps his hand playfully and disappears.* HELEN *takes her hat from the round table and, standing before the mirror at the mantelpiece, pins it on her head.* TRIST *watches her.*)

HELEN (*after a silence, her back to* TRIST) The glass reflects more than one face, Mr Trist.

TRIST: (*moving*) I beg your pardon.

HELEN: You were thinking – ?

TRIST: Philosophising – observing your way of putting on your hat.

HELEN: I put it on carelessly?

TRIST: Quickly. A convincing sign of youth. After you are five-and-twenty the process will take at least ten minutes.

HELEN: And at thirty?

TRIST: Half-an hour. Add another half-hour for each succeeding decade –

HELEN: (*turning to him*) I'm afraid you're a knowing, worldly parson.

TRIST: (*laughing*) No, no; a tolerant, human parson.

HELEN: We shall see. (*picking up her gloves*) If ever you get a living in London, Mr Trist, I shall make a point of sitting under you.

TRIST: I bind you to that.

HELEN: (*pulling on a glove*) By-the-bye, I set out to seek *my* London living to-morrow.

TRIST: (*with a change of manner*) To-morrow?

HELEN: To-morrow.

TRIST: (*blankly*) I – I'm sorry.

HELEN: Very polite of you. I'm glad.

TRIST: Glad?

HELEN: It sounds rather unkind, doesn't it? Oh, I'm extremely fond of everybody in this house – Mr and Mrs Tad and the children, I mean. But I'm sure it isn't good, morally, for me to be here, even if there were no other reasons for my departure.

TRIST: Morally?

HELEN: Yes; if I remained here, all that's bad in my nature would come out on top. Do you know that I've the makings in me of a most accomplished liar and hypocrite?

TRIST: I shouldn't have suspected it.

HELEN: I have (*coming nearer to him*) What do you think takes place this afternoon?

TRIST: What?

HELEN: (*with gradually increasing excitement*) There's to be a meeting of the Mortimore family at James Mortimore's house at four o'clock. He and his brother Stephen have just informed me, with the delicacy which is characteristic

---

sitting under: i.e. attending his church.

of them, that they are going to arrange with the lawyers to administer my father's estate without any more delay. And I was double-faced enough to receive the news smilingly and agreeably, and all the time I could have struck them – I could have seen them drop dead in this room without a pang of regret –

TRIST: No, no –

HELEN: I could. (*walking away and pacing the room on the left*) Oh, it isn't father's money I covet. I said so to the family in Linchpool and I say it again. But I deceived myself.

TRIST: Deceived yourself?

HELEN: Deceived myself. I can't *bear* that father should have forgotten me. I can't bear it; I can't resign myself to it; I shall never resign myself to it. I thought I should be able to, but I was mistaken. I told Mr Thaddeus that I've been suffering no suspense this last month. It's a falsehood; I've been suffering intense suspense. I've been watching the posts, for letters from Elkin; I've been praying, daily, hourly, that something – anything – might be found to prove that father had remembered me. And I loathe these people, who step over me and stand between me and the being I loved best on earth; I loathe them. I detest the whole posse of them, except the Thaddeuses; and I wish this money may bring them, and those belonging to them, every ill that's conceivable. (*confronting* TRIST, *her bosom heaving*) Don't you lecture me!

TRIST: (*good-humouredly*) I haven't the faintest intention of doing so.

HELEN: Ha! (*at the piano, mimicking* JAMES) Here's Gordon Street –

TRIST: Eh?

HELEN: You come along here, to Albert Terrace – taking in Clark's piano factory –

TRIST: Who does?

HELEN: (*fiercely*) Here – here's the pub at the corner!

TRIST: (*bewildered*) I – I don't –

HELEN: (*speaking to him across the piano*) James Mortimore is buying land and building a new street in the town.

TRIST: Really?

HELEN: And Stephen is putting twelve thousand pounds into his old-fashioned paper, to freshen it up; and the Pontings are moving into a big house in London – near Burkeley Square, as James calls it; and they must needs discuss their affairs in my hearing, brutes that they are! (*coming to the chair on the left of the table at the end of the piano*) Oh, thank God, I'm leaving the town to-morrow! It was only a sort of curiosity that brought me here. (*sitting and producing her handkerchief*) Thank God, I'm leaving to-morrow!

> (*He walks to the window on the right, to allow her to recover herself, and then returns to her.*)

TRIST: My dear child, may I speak plainly to you?

HELEN: (*wiping her eyes*) If you don't lecture me.

TRIST: I won't lecture you. I merely venture to suggest that you are a trifle illogical.

HELEN: I dare say.

TRIST: After all, recollect, our friends James and Stephen are not to be blamed for the position they find themselves in.

HELEN: Their manners are insufferable.

TRIST: Hardly insufferable. Nothing is insufferable.

HELEN: There you go!

TRIST: Their faults of manner and breeding are precisely the faults a reasonable, dispassionate person would have no difficulty in excusing. And I shall be much astonished, when the bitterness of your mortification has worn off –

HELEN: You *are* lecturing!

TRIST: I'm not; I give you my word I'm not.

HELEN: It sounds uncommonly like it. What did I tell you the other day – that you were different from the clergymen I'd met hitherto, because you were – ?

TRIST: Jolly.

HELEN: (*with a shrug*) Jolly! (*wearily*) Oh, please go and hurry the children up, and let's be off to the flowers.

TRIST: (*not stirring*) My dear Miss Thornhill –

HELEN: (*impatiently*) I'll fetch them –

TRIST: Don't. (*deliberately*) My dear Miss Thornhill, to show you how little I regard myself as worthy of the privilege of lecturing you; (*smiling*) to show you how the seeds of selfishness may germinate and flourish even in the breast of a cleric – may I make a confession to you?

HELEN: Confession – ?

TRIST: I – I want to confess to you that the circumstance of your having been left as you are – cast adrift on the world, unprotected, without means apart from your own talent and exertions – is one that fills me with – hope.

HELEN: Hope?

TRIST: Fills me with hope, though it may scarcely justify my presumption. (*sitting opposite to her*) You were assuming a minute ago, in joke perhaps, the possibility of my obtaining a living some day.

HELEN: (*graciously, but with growing uneasiness*) Not altogether a joke.

TRIST: Anyhow, there *is* a decided possibility of a living coming my way – and practically in London, as it chances.

HELEN: I – I'm pleased.

TRIST: Yes, in the natural order of events a living will be vacant within the next few years which is in the gift of a father of an old college chum of mine. It's a suburban parish – close to Twickenham – and I'm promised it.

HELEN: That would be – nice for you.

TRIST: (*gazing at her fixedly*) Jolly.

HELEN: (*her eyes drooping*) Very – jolly.

TRIST: I should still be a poor man – that I shall always be; but poverty is relative. It would be riches compared with my curacy here. (*after a pause*) The vicarage has a garden with some grand old trees.

HELEN: Many of the old gardens – in the suburbs – are charming.

TRIST: I – I could let the vicarage during the summer, to increase my income.

HELEN: May a vicar – let – his vicarage?

TRIST: It's done. Some Bishops object to it; (*innocently*) but you can dodge the old boy.

HELEN: Dodge the – old boy!

TRIST: There are all sorts of legal fictions to help you. I know of a Bishop's son-in-law who let his vicarage for a term under the pretence of letting only the furniture.

HELEN: Wicked.

TRIST: (*leaning forward*) But I shouldn't dream of letting my vicarage if my income
– proved sufficient –
HELEN: It would be wealth – you say – in comparison –
TRIST: Yes, but I – I might – marry.
HELEN: (*hastily*) Oh – oh, of course.

> (*The door opens and* JOYCE *and* CYRIL *enter, dressed for going out.*
> CYRIL *is in his best suit, is gloved and swings a cane which is too long
> for him. At the same moment* THADDEUS *lets himself into the garden
> at the gate. He is accompanied by* DENYER, *an ordinary-looking
> person with whiskers and moustache.* HELEN *and* TRIST *rise, and
> she goes to the mirror in some confusion and gives a last touch to her
> hat.*)

JOYCE: Have we kept you waiting?
CYRIL: Sorry. Couldn't get my tie to go right.
THADDEUS: (*in the garden*) Come in, Denyer. (*at the window, to those in the
room*) What, haven't you folks gone yet?
TRIST: (*with the children, following* HELEN *into the garden*) Just off.
THADDEUS: (*to* HELEN, *as she passes him*) Hope you'll enjoy yourself.
TRIST: (*to* DENYER) Ah, Mr Denyer, how are you?
DENYER: How are you, Mr Trist?
JOYCE *and* CYRIL: (*to* THADDEUS) Good-bye, father.
THADDEUS: (*kissing them*) Good-bye, my dears.

> (TRIST *opens the gate and* HELEN *and the children pass out into the
> lane.* TRIST *follows them, closing the gate.* THADDEUS *and*
> DENYER *enter the room.* DENYER *is carrying a newspaper.*)

CYRIL: (*out of sight, shrilly*) Which way?
TRIST: Through Parker Street.
JOYCE: Who walks with who?
HELEN: I walk with Cyril.

> (*The sound of the chatter dies in the distance.*)

DENYER: (*to* THADDEUS) Then I can put up the bill at once, Mr Mortimore?
THADDEUS: (*laying his hat upon the table on the left*) Do, Denyer, To-morrow –
to-day –
DENYER: I'll send a man round in the morning (*producing a note-book and writing
in it*) Let's see – your lease is seven, fourteen, twenty-one?
THADDEUS: That's it.
DENYER: How much of the first seven is there to run – I ought to remember – ?
THADDEUS: Two-years-and-a-half from Michaelmas.
DENYER: Rent?
THADDEUS: Forty.

> (*The door opens a little way and* PHYLLIS *peeps in. Her features are
> drawn, her lips white and set.*)

DENYER: Fixtures at a valuation, I s'pose?
THADDEUS: Ha, ha! The costly fixtures at a valuation.

---

bill: 'To Let' bill.
twenty-one: i.e. years.

DENYER: You may as well sell 'em, if they only fetch tuppence. (*seeing* PHYLLIS, *who has entered softly*) Good afternoon, ma'am.

PHYLLIS: (*in a low voice*) Good afternoon.

THADDEUS: (*turning to her*) Phyl, dear! I met Mr Denyer in the lane. (*gleefully*) The bill goes up to-morrow – 'house to let' – to-morrow morning – (*to* DENYER) first thing –

> (PHYLLIS *moves to the bay-window without speaking.*)

DENYER: First thing. (*putting his pocket-book away*) Excuse me – you're on the look out for a new residence?

THADDEUS: Oh – er – one must live somewhere, Denyer.

DENYER: And a much superior house to *this*, Mr Mortimore, I lay a guinea.

THADDEUS: (*walking about with his hands in his pockets*) The children are springing up – getting to be tremendous people.

DENYER: (*genially*) Oh, come sir! *We* know.

THADDEUS: (*pausing in his walk*) Eh?

DENYER: Everybody in the town knows of your luck, and the family's. (*picking up his hat and newspaper which he has laid upon the ottoman*) Here's another allusion to it in this week's *Courier*.

THADDEUS: The *Courier*?

DENYER: (*handing him the paper*) Just out. You keep it; I've got another at 'ome. (THADDEUS *is searching the paper.*) Middle page – 'Town Topics'.

THADDEUS: Thanks.

DENYER: Mr Hammond – he will poke his fun. (*going to the window*) P'r'aps you'll give us a call, sir?

THADDEUS: (*following him absently, reading*) Yes, I'll call in.

DENYER: (*to* PHYLLIS, *who is sitting in the chair by the bay-window*) Good-day, ma'am. (*in the garden, to* THADDEUS, *persuasively*) Now, you won't forget Gibson and Denyer, Mr Mortimore?

THADDEUS: (*at the window*) I won't; I won't.

DENYER: The old firm. (*opening the gate*) What we haven't got on our books isn't worth considering, you take it from me.

> (*He disappears, closing the gate.* THADDEUS *comes back into the room.*)

THADDEUS: Upon my soul, this is too bad of Hammond. This'll annoy Jim and Stephen frightfully – drive 'em mad. (*flinging the paper on to the settee by the piano*) Oh, well – ! (*putting his necktie in order at the mirror*) By Jove, we've done it at last, old lady! 'House to let', hey? I believe I'm keener about it than you are, now it's come to it. What a sensation it'll cause at 'Ivanhoe', and at the Crescent! I tell you what, you and I must have a solemn talk to-night – a parliament – when the children have gone to bed; a regular, serious talk. (*turning*) You know, I'm still for Cheltenham. Cheltenham seems to me to offer so many advantages. (PHYLLIS *rises slowly.*) There's the town itself – bright and healthy; then the College, for Cyril. As for its musical tastes – (*breaking off and looking at the clock*) I say, do get your things on, Phyl. (*comparing his watch with the clock and then timing and winding it*) We shall catch it if we're not punctual.

PHYLLIS: I – I'm not going, Tad.

THADDEUS: Not going, dear?
PHYLLIS: No – I – (*He advances to the right of the piano solicitously.*) I can't go.
THADDEUS: Aren't you up to it?
        (*She moves to the open window and looks into the garden.*)
PHYLLIS: They won't – be back – for a long while?
. THADDEUS: The children, and Trist and Helen? Not for an hour or two.
PHYLLIS: (*turning*) Tad – that girl – that girl –
THADDEUS: Helen?
PHYLLIS: (*coming forward a little*) We're robbing her; we're robbing her. (*shaking*) We're all robbing her.
THADDEUS: (*at her side*) You've got another bad attack of nerves this afternoon – an extra bad one –
PHYLLIS: (*suddenly, grasping his coat*) Tad – I – I've broken down –
THADDEUS: Broken down?
PHYLLIS: I've broken down under it. I – I can't endure it.
THADDEUS: (*soothingly*) What – what – ?
PHYLLIS: Your brother – Edward – your brother – Edward –
THADDEUS: Yes?
PHYLLIS: Everything – everything – belongs to her – Helen –
THADDEUS: My dear, the family were prepared to offer Helen –
PHYLLIS: No, no! He left every penny to her – *left* it to her. (*staring into his face*) There was a will.
THADDEUS: A will?
PHYLLIS: I saw it.
THADDEUS: You saw it?
PHYLLIS: I read it – I had it in my hand –
THADDEUS: (*incredulously*) *You* did!
PHYLLIS: Yes, I – I did away with it –
THADDEUS: Did away with it?
PHYLLIS: Destroyed it.
THADDEUS: A will – Ned's will – !
        (*She turns from him and sinks helplessly on to the settee by the fireplace. He stands looking down upon her in a half-frightened, half-puzzled way; then his face clears and he looks at the clock again.*)
THADDEUS: (*calmly*) Phyl, I wish you'd let me have Chapman in.
PHYLLIS: (*in a faint voice*) No – no –
THADDEUS: My dear, we can afford a doctor now, if we require one. That bromide stuff he prescribed for you once – that did you no end of good. (*going towards the door*) I'll send Kate.
PHYLLIS: (*raising herself*) Tad –
THADDEUS: (*reassuringly*) I'll stay with you till he comes.
PHYLLIS: Tad – (*getting to her feet*) you – you think I'm not right in my head. Tad, I – I know what I'm saying. I'm telling the truth. I'm telling you the truth.
THADDEUS: A will – ?
PHYLLIS: (*at the round table*) Yes – yes –
THADDEUS: No, no, you're talking nonsense. (*He goes to the door and there pauses, his hand on the door-knob.*) When – when – ?

PHYLLIS: When – ?

THADDEUS: When did you see it?

PHYLLIS: On the – on the Wednesday night.

THADDEUS: The Wednesday night?

PHYLLIS: You remember – the night there was no night-nurse – ?

THADDEUS: I remember of course.

PHYLLIS: Ann and Louisa had gone to the hotel to lie down, and – and I was alone with him.

THADDEUS: I remember it all perfectly.

PHYLLIS: (*moving towards the ottoman, supporting herself by the table*) I was with him from eight o'clock till nearly eleven.

THADDEUS: Till the others came back. That was the night he – the night he sank.

PHYLLIS: Yes; it was just before than that he – that he –

THADDEUS: (*leaving the door*) Just before then – ?

PHYLLIS: It was just before the change set in that he – that he sent me downstairs.

THADDEUS: Downstairs?

PHYLLIS: To the library.

THADDEUS: The library?

PHYLLIS: With the keys.

THADDEUS: Keys?

PHYLLIS: His bunch of keys.

THADDEUS: Sent you downstairs – to the library – with his keys?

PHYLLIS: Yes.

THADDEUS: What for?

PHYLLIS: To fetch something.

THADDEUS: Fetch something?

PHYLLIS: From the safe.

THADDEUS: The safe?

PHYLLIS: The safe in the library – (*sitting on the ottoman*) the safe in the bookcase in the library.

THADDEUS: (*coming to her*) What – what did he send you to fetch, dear?

PHYLLIS: Some – some jewellery.

THADDEUS: Jewellery?

PHYLLIS: Some pieces of jewellery. He had some pieces of jewellery in his safe in the library, that he'd picked up, he said, at odd times, and he wanted to make me a present of one of them –

THADDEUS: Make you a present – ?

PHYLLIS: As a keepsake. (*her elbows on her knees, digging her fingers into her hair*) It was about half-past nine. I was sitting beside his bed, thinking he was asleep, and I found him looking at me. He recollected seeing me when I was a child, he said, skating on the ponds at Claybrook; and he said he was sure I – I was a good wife to you – and a good mother to my children. And then he spoke of the jewellery – and opened the drawer of the table by the bed – and took out his keys – and explained to me how to open the safe.

THADDEUS: (*his manner gradually changing as he listens to her recital*) You – you went down – ?

PHYLLIS: Yes.

THADDEUS: And – and – ?

PHYLLIS: And unlocked the safe. And in the lower drawer I – I came across it.

THADDEUS: Came across – ?

PHYLLIS: He told me I should find four small boxes – and I could find only three – and that made me look into the drawer – and – and under a lot of other papers – I – I saw it.

THADDEUS: *It?*

PHYLLIS: A big envelope with 'My Will' written upon it.

> (*There is a short silence; then he seats himself upon the settee by the piano.*)

THADDEUS: (*in a whisper*) Well?

PHYLLIS: (*raising her head*) I put it back into the drawer, and locked the safe, and went upstairs with the jewellery. Outside the bedroom door I found Heath. I'd given him permission to run out for an hour, to get some air, with Pearce and Sadler, the housemaids. He asked me if they could do anything for me before they started. I told him no, and that Mr Mortimore seemed brighter and stronger. I heard him going down the servant's staircase; and then I went into the room – up to the bed – and – and he was altered.

THADDEUS: (*moistening his lips with his tongue*) Ned – ?

PHYLLIS: His cheeks were more shrunken, and his jaw had dropped slightly, and his lips were quite blue; and his breathing was short and quick. I measured the medicine which he was to have if there was any sign of collapse, and lifted him up and gave it to him. Then I rang the bell, and by-and-by the woman from the kitchen answered it. He was easier then – dozing, but I told her to put on her hat and jacket and go for Dr Oswald. And then I stood watching him, and – and the idea – came to me.

THADDEUS: The – the idea?

PHYLLIS: My head suddenly became very clear. Every word of the argument in the train came back to me –

THADDEUS: Argument?

PHYLLIS: Between James and the others – in the train, going to Linchpool, on the Tuesday –

THADDEUS: Oh – oh, yes.

PHYLLIS: If Edward died, how much would he die worth? Who would come in for all his money? Would he remember the family, to the extent of a mourning ring or so, in his will? If he should die leaving *no* will! Of course Ned would leave a will, but – where did a man's money go to when he *didn't* leave a will?

THADDEUS: (*under his breath*) To his – next-of-kin – !

PHYLLIS: (*rising painfully*) After a time, I – I went downstairs again. At first I persuaded myself that I only wanted to replace the jewellery – that I didn't want to have to explain about the jewellery to Ann and Lou; (*moving about the room on the left*) but when I got downstairs I *knew* what I was going to do. And I did it as if it was the most ordinary thing in the world. I put back the little boxes – and took out the big envelope – and locked up the safe again, and read the will. (*pausing at the piano*) Everything – everything – to some person – some woman living in Paris. (*leaning upon the piano, a clenched hand against her brow*) 'Everything I die possessed of to Helen Thornhill, now or late of' – such-and-

such an address, 'spinster, absolutely'; and she was to be his executrix – 'sole
executrix'. That was all, except that he begged her to reward his old servants –
his old servants at his house and at the brewery. Just a few lines – on one sheet of
paper –

THADDEUS: Written – in his own – hand?

PHYLLIS: I think so.

THADDEUS: You – you've seen his writing – since –

PHYLLIS: (*leaving the piano*) Yes – I'm sure – in his own hand.

THADDEUS: (*heavily*) That clears it up, then.

PHYLLIS: Yes.

THADDEUS: He'd made his will – himself – himself –

PHYLLIS: (*her strength failing a little*) Three years ago. I – noticed the date –
   (*dropping into the chair on the extreme left*) it was three years ago –
      (*Again there is a silence; then he rises and walks about aimlessly.*)

THADDEUS: (*trying to collect his thoughts*) Yes – yes; this clears it up. This clears it
   all up. There *was* a will. There *was* a will. He *didn't* forget his child; he didn't
   forget her. What fools – what fools we were to suppose he *could* have forgotten
   his own daughter!

PHYLLIS: (*writhing in her chair*) Oh, I didn't know – I didn't guess – ! His daughter!
   (*moaning*) Oh! oh!

THADDEUS: Don't; don't, old lady. (*She continues her moaning.*) Oh, don't, don't!
   Let's think; let's think, now; let's think. (*He seats himself opposite to her.*) Now,
   let's think. Helen – this'll put Helen in a different position entirely; a different
   position entirely – won't it? I – I wonder – I wonder what's the proper course for
   the family to take. (*stretching out a trembling hand to her*) You'll have to write
   down – to write down carefully – very carefully – (*breaking off, with a change of
   tone*) Phyl –

PHYLLIS: Oh! oh!

THADDEUS: Don't, dear, don't! Phyllis, perhaps you – didn't – destroy the will; not
   – actually – destroy it? (*imploringly*) You didn't destroy it, dear!

PHYLLIS: I did – I did –

THADDEUS: (*leaning back in his chair, dazed*) I – I'm afraid – it – it's rather – a
   serious matter – to – to destroy –

PHYLLIS: (*starting up*) I did destroy it; I did destroy it. (*pacing the room on the right*)
   I kept it – I'd have burnt it then and there if there'd been a fire – but I kept it – I
   grew terrified at what I'd done – oh, I kept it till you left me at Roper's on the
   Thursday morning; and then I – I went to the Ford Street bridge – and tore it into
   pieces – and threw them into the water. (*wringing her hands*) Oh! oh!

THADDEUS: (*his chin on his breast*) Well – well – we've got to go through with it.
   We've got – to go – through – (*rising and walking about unsteadily on the left*)
   Yes, yes, yes; what a difference it'll make to everybody – not only to Helen!
   What a difference it'll make at 'Ivanhoe', and at the Crescent – and to Rose – !

PHYLLIS: They'll curse me! They'll curse me more than ever!

THADDEUS: And to – to us!

PHYLLIS: To us – the children – !

THADDEUS: (*shaking a finger at her across the piano, cunningly*) Ah – ah – ah, but
   when the affair's really settled, we'll still carry out our intention. We – we'll still –

PHYLLIS: (*facing him*) Our intention? Our – ?

THADDEUS: Our intention – of leaving the town –

PHYLLIS: (*wildly*) Leaving the town! Oh, my God, we shall *have* to leave the town!

THADDEUS: (*recoiling*) Oh – !

PHYLLIS: Leave it as beggars and outcasts!

THADDEUS: (*quietly*) Oh, yes, we shall – *have* – to leave the town – now –
> (*The door opens and a little maidservant enters.* THADDEUS *looks at her with dull eyes.*)

THE SERVANT: Please, sir –

THADDEUS: Eh?

THE SERVANT: Maud's just come down from 'Ivanhoe'. They're waiting for you.

THADDEUS: W – waiting?

THE SERVANT: That's the message, sir. Mr James and the family's waiting for Mr Thaddeus.

THADDEUS: Oh, I – (*taking out his watch and fingering it*) Yes, of course – (*to the servant*) I – I'm coming up.
> (*The servant withdraws.* THADDEUS *picks up his hat from the table on the left and turns to* PHYLLIS.)

THADDEUS: (*to* PHYLLIS) Good-bye, dear. (*taking her in his arms and kissing her, simply*) I – I'll go up.
> (*He puts his hat on, finds his way to the door with uncertain steps, and disappears.*)
> END OF THE SECOND ACT

THE THIRD ACT

The scene is the dining-room in JAMES MORTIMORE's *house. In the wall facing the spectator there is an arched recess with a fireplace at the back of it, and on either side of the fireplace, within the recess, there is a chimney-seat. On the right of the recess a door opens into the room from a hall or passage.*

Standing out in the middle of the room is a large, oblong dining-table, uncovered. On the table are a couple of inkstands, some pens, paper, and blotting-paper. Ten chairs are placed at regular intervals at the table – three at each side and two at the ends. Against the wall on the right, near the door, stands a heavy sideboard. On it are several pieces of ugly-looking, showy plate, a carafe of water and a tumbler, and, upon a tray, a decanter of red wine and some wine-glasses. Against the same wall, but nearer to the spectator, there is a cabinet. In front of the cabinet there is a round table, covered with a white cloth, on which tea-cups and saucers are laid for ten persons. Also on the table are tea caddy and tea-pot, a plated kettle-stand, a plum-cake, and other accompaniments of afternoon tea. On each side of the tea-table there is an arm-chair belonging to the same set of chairs that surround the dining-table.

Against the left-hand wall is another heavy piece of furniture. Except for this, and the sideboard and the cabinet, the walls, below the dado rail, are bare.

---

dado: 'any lining, papering, or painting of the lower part of an interior wall, if a different material or colour from that of the upper part' (*OED*).

The architecture, decorations and furniture are pseudo-artistic and vulgar. The whole suggests the home of a common person of moderate means who has built himself a 'fine house'.

JAMES *and* STEPHEN *are seated at the further side of the dining-table with a newspaper spread out before them. Standing by them, reading the paper over their husbands' shoulders, are* ANN *and* LOUISA. ROSE *is sitting, looking bored, at the right-hand end of the table, and* PONTING, *smoking a cigar, is pacing the room on the left.* LOUISA *and* ROSE, *the latter dressed in rich half-mourning, are wearing their hats.*

JAMES: (*scowling at the paper*) It's infamous.

LOUISA: Abominable!

ANN: It oughtn't to be allowed, James.

STEPHEN: Ah, now James is stabbed at as well as myself.

JAMES: The man's a blackguard; that's what he is.

LOUISA: His wife's a most unpleasant woman.

STEPHEN: (*leaning back and wiping his spectacles*) Hitherto *I* have been the chief object of Mr Hammond's malice.

LOUISA: You'll soon have your revenge now, Stephen. (*to the others*) Stephen will soon have his revenge now.

JAMES: By George, I've half a mind to ask Vallance to give me his opinion on this!

STEPHEN: We might consult Vallance, certainly.

LOUISA: And tell him what Mrs Hammond *was*.

ANN: When she was plain Nelly Robson.

STEPHEN: Sssh, sssh! Do, pray, keep the wife out of it.

PONTING: (*looking at his watch as he walks across to the right*) I say, my friends, it's four o'clock, you know. (*The* MORTIMORES *stiffen themselves and regard him coldly.*) Where are these lawyer chaps?

JAMES: (*folding the newspaper*) They're not in my pocket, Colonel.

STEPHEN: No, we're not in the habit of carrying them about with us.

LOUISA: (*laughing sillily*) Oh, Stephen!

ROSE: We mustn't lose the – what's the train back, Toby?

PONTING: (*behind her chair, annoyed*) Five fifty-seven.

ROSE: I shall be dead with fatigue; I've two parties to-night.

JAMES: Parties?

ROSE: (*to* PONTING) Destinn is singing at the Trench's, Toby.

STEPHEN: (*rising*) H'm! Indeed?

ANN: (*in an undertone, withdrawing with* LOUISA *to the fireplace*) Singing!

JAMES: (*rising*) So you're going to parties, are you, Rose? Pretty sharp work, with Ned only a month in his grave.

PONTING: We're not conventional people.

ROSE: (*rising and walking away to the left*) No, we don't mourn openly.

PONTING: We don't carry our hearts on our what-d ye-call-it – sleeve.

ROSE: And Edward wasn't in the least known in London society.

JAMES: (*walking about on the right*) *You* knew him.

PONTING: (*seating himself on the nearer side of the dining-table in the middle chair*)

Destinn: Emmy Destinn (1878–1930), celebrated Czech soprano, who first appeared at Covent Garden in 1904.

In London, my friends, reg'lar mournin' is confined to the suburbs nowadays.
May I have an ash-tray?

ROSE: (*walking about on the left*) And we go to Harrogate on the twenty-ninth.

PONTING: Good lord, yes; I'm kept devilish quiet *there*.

> (ANN *takes a metal ash-tray from the mantelpiece and gives it to*
> STEPHEN *who almost flings it on to the table. The door opens and a*
> *maidservant enters followed by* ELKIN *and* VALLANCE. *The lawyers*
> *carry small leather bags. The servant retires.*)

JAMES: (*shaking hands heartily with* ELKIN *and* VALLANCE) Here you are!

ELKIN: A minute or two behind time – my fault.

STEPHEN: How d'ye do, Mr Elkin? (*shaking hands with* VALLANCE) Good
afternoon.

ELKIN: (*to* PONTING) How d'ye do?

PONTING (*shortly, not rising*) H'ah you?

VALLANCE: (*shaking hands with* ANN *and* LOUISA *and bowing to* ROSE) How
do you do?

ELKIN: (*to* ROSE) Hope you're very well, Mrs Ponting.

ROSE: Thanks.

VALLANCE: (*to* PONTING, *who nods in return*) Good afternoon.

PONTING: (*bringing the palm of his hand down upon the table*) Now, then!

JAMES: (*to* ELKIN *and* VALLANCE, *inviting them by a gesture to be seated*)
Excuse the dining-room, gentlemen; looks more like business than the drawing-
room.

STEPHEN: (*on the left*) Where's Tad?

ANN: (*seating herself at the further side of the dining-table in the middle chair*) Yes,
where's Tad?

LOUISA: (*sitting beside her*) Where are Tad and Phyllis?

JAMES: (*looking at his watch*) Five past, by my watch.

ROSE: (*sitting at the left hand end of the table*) Oh, never mind *them*.

JAMES: (*to* STEPHEN) P'r'aps you told 'em four-thirty?

STEPHEN: (*nettled*) Perhaps *I* told them!

JAMES: All right, all right; don't flare up! P'r'aps *I* did; there *was* a talk of making it
half-past.

STEPHEN: (*raising his arms*) On the day I go to press –

JAMES: Ring the bell. (*opening the door and calling*) Maud! Maud – !

> (STEPHEN *rings the bell.* ELKIN *and* VALLANCE *are now seated.*
> ELKIN *in the further chair at the right-hand end of the dining-table,*
> VALLANCE *in the chair between* ELKIN *and* ANN. *They open their*
> *bags and sort and arrange their papers.*)

PONTING: We shall be here till midnight.

JAMES: Maud – !

ROSE: (*pushing her chair away from the table*) How vexing!

PONTING: (*with a sneer*) I suppose one can buy a soot of pyjamas in the town, eh,
Mrs James?

Harrogate: a spa in Yorkshire.

ELKIN: *I* sha'n't detain you long.
    (*The servant appears at the door.*)
JAMES: Maud, run down to Nelson Villas – just as you are –
ROSE: (*satirically*) Don't hurry them, Jim. Phyllis is smartening herself up.
STEPHEN: (*seating himself in the further chair at the left-hand end of the dining-table, loudly*) Say we are waiting for Mr Thaddeus.
JAMES: (*to the girl*) Mr James and the family are waiting for Mr Thaddeus. (*as he closes the door*) Go along Collier Street; you may meet him.
PONTING: (*fussily*) We can deal with preliminaries, at any rate. Kindly push that ash-tray a little nearer. (*to* VALLANCE) Mr Vallance –
JAMES: (*leaving the door, resenting* PONTING'*s assumption of authority*) I beg your pardon, Colonel; we'll give my brother another five minutes' grace, with your permission.
PONTING: (*shrugging his shoulders*) By all means – ten – twenty –
JAMES: (*finding that he has the newspaper in his hand*) Oh – here – ! (*opening the paper*) While we're waiting for Tad –
STEPHEN: Ah, yes. Read it aloud, Jim.
PONTING: (*rising and moving away impatiently*) Tsch!
JAMES: Mr Vallance – Mr Elkin – oblige us by listening to this. It's from the *Courier*.
STEPHEN: This week's *Courier* – published to-day –
VALLANCE: (*to* ELKIN) One of our local papers.
JAMES: Owned by a feller o' the name of Hammond. (*reading*) 'Town Topics'.
ANN: He married a Miss Robson.
LOUISA: A dreadful woman.
STEPHEN: Sssh, sssh! Mr Hammond's offensive remarks are usually directed against *myself*, but in this instance –
JAMES: (*walking about as he reads*) 'A curious complication arises in connection with the estate of the late Mr Edward Mortimore of Linchpool.'
STEPHEN: He doesn't cloak his attack, you see.
JAMES: 'As many of our readers are aware – (*running his hands over his pockets*) as many of our readers are aware –'
STEPHEN: He has *made* them aware of it.
JAMES: (*to* ANN) Where did I put them, mother?
ANN: (*producing her spectacles*) Try mine, James.
    (ANN *gives her spectacles to* STEPHEN, STEPHEN *gives them to* ROSE, *and* ROSE *presents them to* JAMES.)
JAMES: I'm getting as blear-eyed as Stephen. (*resuming*) 'As many of our readers are aware, the whole of that gentleman's wealth passes, in consequence of his having died intestate, to a well-known Singlehampton family, –'
LOUISA: That points to us.
STEPHEN: (*irritably*) Of course it does; of course it does.
LOUISA: There's no better-known family in Singlehampton than ours.
STEPHEN: Sssh, sssh!
JAMES: ' – two members of which –'
ANN: The Mockfords were an older family – but where *are* the Mockfords?
JAMES: (*to* ANN) Give me a chance, Ann. (*continuing*) ' – two members of which

have been for many years prominently associated with the temperance movement in this town.'

STEPHEN: (*rising*) My brother James and myself.

JAMES: (*standing at the table, facing* ELKIN *and* VALLANCE, *in his oratorical manner*) Twelve years ago, gentlemen, I was instrumental in founding the Singlehampton and Claybrook Temperance League –

LOUISA: Stephen was another of the founders.

STEPHEN: (*joining* JAMES) I was another.

JAMES: And day in and day out I have devoted my best energies to furthering the objects of the League in Singlehampton *and* in Claybrook.

STEPHEN: Very materially aided by the *Times and Mirror*, a temperance organ.

JAMES: And I submit that it's holding us up to ridicule and contempt – holding us up to public obloquy and derision –

VALLANCE: (*to* JAMES) What is your objection to the paragraph, Mr Mortimore?

JAMES: Objection!

ELKIN: There's more to come, I expect.

JAMES: (*grimly*) Aye, a bit more. (*sitting at the table*) What d'ye think of this? (*reading*) 'When it is remembered that the late Mr Mortimore's fortune was derived from the brewing and the sale of *beer* –'

STEPHEN: (*sitting beside* JAMES) The word 'beer' is in italics.

VALLANCE: Oh, I see.

JAMES: '– it will be understood that our two distinguished fellow-townsmen are placed in an extremely difficult position.'

STEPHEN: This is the most spiteful part of it.

JAMES: 'We have no doubt, however, that, as conscientious men, they will prove fully equal to the occasion by either renouncing their share of their late brother's property or by dedicating it entirely to the advancement of the cause they have at heart.' (*throwing the newspaper to* ELKIN *and* VALLANCE) There it is, gentlemen.

> (*In wandering round the room,* PONTING *has come upon the decanter of wine and the wine-glasses standing on the sideboard. He is now filling a glass.*)

PONTING: Every man has a right to his convictions. (*taking the glass in his hand*) A little alcohol hurts nobody –

JAMES: You won't find any in *my* house.

PONTING: What's this, then?

JAMES: Currant.

PONTING: (*replacing the glass, with a wry face*) My dear Mortimore – !

> (*He sits at the right-hand end of the table beside* ELKIN, *and pries at the document which* ELKIN *has taken from his bag.* VALLANCE *and* ELKIN *are reading the paragraph together,* VALLANCE *drawing his chair closer to* ELKIN's *for that purpose.*)

JAMES: (*to* VALLANCE) Well, what's your opinion, Mr Vallance? Is that libellous, or isn't it?

Currant: home-made wines were apparently admissible in teetotal homes.

STEPHEN: Does it, or does it not, go beyond the bounds of fair comment – eh, Mr Elkin?

VALLANCE: (*pacifically*) Oh, but aren't you attaching a great deal too much importance to this?

JAMES: Too much – !

ELKIN: Why not ignore it?

STEPHEN: Ignore it!

VALLANCE: Treat it as a piece of pure chaff – badinage –

ELKIN: In more or less bad taste.

VALLANCE: Take no notice of it whatever.

JAMES: (*rising and walking away to the fireplace*) Take no notice of it! The townspeople will take notice of it pretty quickly.

STEPHEN: (*rising*) In *my* opinion, that paragraph renders our position in the League absolutely untenable.

JAMES: (*standing over* VALLANCE) Unless that paragraph is apologised for, withdrawn –

STEPHEN: (*standing over* ELKIN) Explained away –

JAMES: Aye, explained away –

VALLANCE: I don't see how it can be explained away.

ELKIN: (*dryly*) The proposition is a perfectly accurate one, whatever you may think of the corollary.

VALLANCE: You *are* ardent advocates of temperance.

ELKIN: Your late brother's property *was* amassed mainly by beer.

VALLANCE: It can hardly be explained away.

STEPHEN: (*walking to the left*) Good heavens above, I've explained things away often enough in *my* paper!

JAMES: (*coming forward on the right*) This does us at the League, then – *does* us, knocks our influence into a cocked hat.

ELKIN: (*to* JAMES *and* STEPHEN, *while* VALLANCE *holds the paper*) After all, gentlemen, when you come to reflect upon it, the laugh is with *you*.

JAMES: *Is* it?

ELKIN: (*genially*) The *Courier* has its little joke, but *you've* got the money, remember.

JAMES: Oh, that's true.

STEPHEN: (*walking about on the left*) That's true; that's true.

JAMES: (*walking about on the right, rattling his loose cash*) Aye, *we've* got the mopuses

ROSE: (*tilting her chair on its hind legs*) I say, Jim – Stephen – why don't you two boys, between you, present the League with a handsome hall – ?

JAMES: (*pausing in his walk*) Hall?

ROSE: Build the temperance folk a meeting-place of their own – a head-quarters –

PONTING: (*mischievously*) He, he, he! That 'ud smooth 'em down. Capital idea, Rosie!

JAMES *and* STEPHEN: We!

---

mopus: slang: 'a halfpenny or farthing, in plural, money in general' (*OED*).

JAMES: I'd see 'em damned first. (*to the ladies*) I beg pardon –

ANN: (*with unusual animation*) No, no; you're quite right, James.

STEPHEN: (*at the fireplace*) That would be playing into Mr Hammond's hands with a vengeance.

JAMES: (*walking across to the left, derisively*) Ha! Wouldn't Hammond crow, hey! Ha, ha, ha!

STEPHEN: No, if the situation becomes too acute – painful as it would be to me – I shall resign.

JAMES: (*determinedly*) Resign.

STEPHEN: Sever my connection with the League.

JAMES: Leave 'em to swill themselves with their lemonade and boiled tea – !

STEPHEN: (*coming forward on the right*) And to find out how they get on without us.

JAMES: Serve 'em up in their own juice!

STEPHEN: (*meeting* JAMES *in the middle of the room on the nearer side of the dining-table*) You know, Jim, we've never gone *quite* so far – you and I – with our principles of temperance as some.

JAMES: (*eyeing him curiously*) Never gone so far?

STEPHEN: As old Bob Amphlett, for example – never.

JAMES: Oh, yes, we have, and a deuced sight further.

STEPHEN: Excuse me – I've *always* been for moderation rather than for total abstinence.

JAMES: Have yer? (*walking away to the left*) First I've heard of it.

STEPHEN: Anyhow, a man may broaden his views with years and experience. (*argumentatively*) Take the hygienic aspect of the case. Only the other day, Sir Vincent West, probably the ablest physician in England –

LOUISA: (*abruptly*) Stephen – !

STEPHEN: (*angrily*) Don't interrupt me.

LOUISA: (*with energy, rising*) I've maintained it throughout my life – it's nothing new from my lips –

STEPHEN: What – ?

LOUISA: There are two sides to every question.

STEPHEN: (*hurrying round the table to join* LOUISA) Exactly – exactly – as Lou says –

LOUISA: It's been almost a second religion with me. I've preached it in season and out of season –

STEPHEN: (*with conviction*) There *are* two sides –

LOUISA: Two sides to every question.

JAMES: (*to* ANN, *pointing to the door*) Mother –

> (*The door has been opened by another maid-servant, who carries a tray on which are a plated kettle, a dish of toast, and a plentiful supply of bread-and-butter. The girl remains in the doorway.* ANN *rises and goes to her and takes the kettle from the tray.*)

JAMES: (*coming forward and seating himself on the nearer side of the dining-table in the middle chair*) Look here; I don't wait another minute for the Tads – not a second.

PONTING: Ah!

(LOUISA *follows* ANN *and takes the toast and the bread-and-butter from the servant, who then disappears, closing the door.*)

STEPHEN: (*again sitting in the further chair at the left-hand end of the dining-table*) Inexcusable of them – inexcusable.

(ANN *and* LOUISA *come to the tea-table and drawing the two arm-chairs up to it, seat themselves and prepare the tea. The kettle is set upon the stand, the spirit-lamp is lighted.* ANN *measures the tea from the caddy into the pot, and* LOUISA *cuts the plum-cake.*)

JAMES: Mr Elkin – Mr Vallance –

PONTING: Now, Mr Vallance; now, Mr Elkin!

ELKIN: (*to* VALLANCE) Will you – ?

VALLANCE: No, no – you –

ELKIN: Well, gentlemen – (*to* ROSE) – Mrs Ponting – Mr Vallance and I have to report to you that we've received no communication of any kind in answer to our circulars and advertisements –

JAMES: (*to* ANN, *who is making a clatter with the kettle*) Steady, mother!

PONTING: (*to the ladies at the tea-table*) Sssh, sssh, sssh!

ELKIN: No communication from any solicitor who has prepared a will for your late brother, nor from anybody who has knowingly witnessed a will executed by him.

STEPHEN: Mr Vallance has apprised us of this already.

JAMES: (*raising a hand*) Order! There's a formal way of doing things and a lax way.

STEPHEN: I merely mentioned –

(PONTING *raps the table sharply with his knuckles.*)

ELKIN: I may say that, in addition to the issuing of the circulars and advertisements, I have made search in every place I could think of, and have enquired of every person likely to be of help in the matter. In fact, I've taken every possible step to find, or trace, a will.

VALLANCE: Without success.

ELKIN: Without success.

JAMES: (*magnanimously*) And *I* say that the family bears no grudge to Mr Elkin for doing his duty.

STEPHEN: (*in the same spirit*) Hear, hear!

PONTING: (*testily*) Of course not; of course not.

ROSE: It's all the more satisfactory, it seems to me, that he *has* worried round.

JAMES: The family *thanks* Mr Elkin.

STEPHEN: We thank Mr Elkin.

ELKIN: (*after a stiff inclination of the head*) The only other observation I wish to make is that several gentlemen employed in the office of the brewery in Linchpool have at different times witnessed the late Mr Mortimore's signature to documents which have apparently required the attestation of two witnesses.

PONTING: (*curtly*) That amounts to nothing.

JAMES: There are a good many documents, aren't there, where two witnesses are required to a signature?

ELKIN: Deeds under seal, certainly.

STEPHEN: I remember having to sign, some years ago –

(PONTING *again raps the table.*)

VALLANCE: But none of these gentlemen at the brewery can recall that any particular document appeared to him to be a will, which is not a document under seal.

JAMES: Besides, a man signing a will always tells the witnesses that it *is* his will they're witnessing, doesn't he, Mr Vallance?

VALLANCE: A solicitor would, in the ordinary course of practice, inform the witnesses to a will of the nature of the document they were attesting, undoubtedly.

ELKIN: Granted; but a testator, supposing he were executing his will in his own house or office, and not in the presence of a solicitor, is under no legal necessity to do so, and may omit to do so.

JAMES: (*rolling about in his chair*) Oh, well, we needn't –

PONTING: (*looking at his watch*) In heaven's name – !

STEPHEN: We needn't go into all this.

ELKIN: No, no; I simply draw attention to the point. (*unfolding a document*) Well, gentlemen – Mrs Ponting – this is a statement – (*handing another document to* VALLANCE) here is a copy of it, Mr Vallance – this is a statement of particulars of stocks, shares and other items of estate, with their values at the death of the late Mr Mortimore, and a schedule of the debts so far as they are known to me.

> (*There is a general movement.* JAMES *rises and goes to* VALLANCE. STEPHEN *also rises stretching out an eager hand towards* VALLANCE. ROSE *draws nearer to the table,* PONTING *still closer to* ELKIN. ANN *and* LOUISA, *too, show a disposition to desert the tea-table.*)

JAMES: (*to* ANN, *as he passes her*) You get on with the tea, mother. (*to* VALLANCE) Allow me, Mr Vallance –

> (VALLANCE *gives him the duplicate of the statement.*)

PONTING: What's it come out at; what's it come out at?

STEPHEN: What's it come out at?

ROSE: Yes, what does it come out at? Jim –

STEPHEN: Jim –

> (JAMES *joins* STEPHEN *and they examine the duplicate together.* ROSE *rises and endeavours to read it with them.*)

ELKIN: I estimate the gross value of the estate, which, as you will see, consists entirely of personal property, at one hundred and ninety-two thousand pounds,

PONTING: The *gross* value.

STEPHEN: Yes, but what do *we* get?

PONTING *and* ROSE: What do *we* get?

JAMES: After all deductions.

ELKIN: Roughly speaking, after payment of debts, death duties and expenses, there will be about a hundred and seventy thousand pounds to divide. (*Those who are standing sit again.* JAMES *seats himself next to* STEPHEN *and, with pen and ink, they make calculations on paper.* PONTING *does the same.* ROSE, *closing her eyes, fans herself happily, and the two ladies at the tea-table resume their preparations with beaming countenances.* ELKIN *leans back in his chair.*) Mr Vallance –

VALLANCE: (*to* ROSE, JAMES *and* STEPHEN) Mrs Ponting and gentlemen –

(PONTING *raps the table and* JAMES *and* STEPHEN *look up*.) I advise you that, as next-of-kin of the late Mr Mortimore, if you are satisfied – and in my opinion you may reasonably be satisfied – that he died intestate – I advise you that any one or more of you, not exceeding three, (*The door opens quietly and* THADDEUS *appears. He is very pale, but is outwardly calm. After a look in the direction of the table, he closes the door*) may apply for Letters of Administration of your late brother's estate. It isn't necessary or usual, however, I may tell you, to have more than one administrator, and I suggest –
> (*Hearing the click of the lock as* THADDEUS *shuts the door, everybody turns and glances at him.*)

ROSE: (*opening her eyes*) Here's Tad.
STEPHEN: (*grumpily*) Oh –
ROSE: (*tossing* THADDEUS *a greeting*) Hallo!
JAMES: (*to* THADDEUS, *with a growl*) Oh, you've arrived.
STEPHEN: (*to* THADDEUS) Did I say four or half-past – ?
LOUISA: Where's Phyllis?
ANN: Where's Phyllis?
THADDEUS: (*in a low voice, advancing*) She – she didn't feel well enough –
> (PONTING *raps the inkstand with his pen-holder.*)

JAMES: (*pointing to the chair beside him, imperatively*) Sit down; sit down.
> (THADDEUS *sits, his elbows on the table, his eyes cast down.*) Mr Vallance –

VALLANCE: (*to* THADDEUS) Good afternoon, Mr Mortimore.
ELKIN: (*nodding to* THADDEUS) How d'ye do?
THADDEUS (*almost inaudibly*) Good afternoon.
VALLANCE: (*to the others*) I suppose we needn't go back – ?
A MURMUR: No, no; no, no.
JAMES: (*pushing the duplicate of the statement under* THADDEUS's *eyes*) A hundred and seventy thousand pound to divide.
STEPHEN: A hundred and seventy thousand.
PONTING: (*finishing his sum*) Forty-two thousand five hundred apiece.
VALLANCE: (*resuming*) I was saying that it isn't usual to have more than one administrator, and I was about to suggest that the best course will be for you, Mr James, to act in that capacity, and for you, Mr Stephen, and you, Mr Thaddeus, or one of you, and Colonel Ponting, to be the sureties to the bond for the due administration of the estate.
JAMES: (*cheerfully*) I'm in your hands, Mr Vallance.
STEPHEN: I'm agreeable.
PONTING: And I.
VALLANCE: The procedure is this – perhaps I'd better explain it (*producing a form of 'Oath for Administrators' which is among his papers*) The intended administrator will make an affidavit stating when and where the deceased died, that he died intestate (THADDEUS *looks up*) a bachelor without a parent, and that the deponent is a natural and lawful brother and one of the next-of-kin of the deceased –
THADDEUS (*touching* VALLANCE's *arm*) Mr Vallance –
VALLANCE: Eh?
THADDEUS: We – we mustn't go on with this.

VALLANCE: I beg pardon?

THADDEUS: The family mustn't go on with this.

VALLANCE: Mustn't go on – ?

JAMES: (*to* THADDEUS) What a'yer talking about?

THADDEUS: (*after a hurried look round*) There – there was a will.

VALLANCE: A will?

THADDEUS: He – he made a will.

JAMES: *Who* did?

THADDEUS: Edward. He – he left a will.

JAMES: (*roughly*) What the – !

ELKIN: (*to* JAMES, *interrupting him*) One moment. Your brother has something to say to us, Mr Mortimore.

STEPHEN: What – what's he mean by – ?

ELKIN: (*to* STEPHEN) Please – (*to* THADDEUS) Yes, sir? (THADDEUS *is silent.*) What about a will? (THADDEUS *is still silent.*) Eh?

THADDEUS: I – I saw it.

ELKIN: Saw a will?

THADDEUS: I – I opened it – I read it –

ELKIN: Read it?

THADDEUS: I – tore it up – got rid of it.

> (*Again there is silence, the* MORTIMORES *and the* PONTINGS *sitting open-mouthed and motionless.*)

ELKIN: (*after a while*) Mr Vallance, I think we ought to tell Mr Mortimore that he appears to be making a confession of the gravest kind –

VALLANCE: Yes.

ELKIN: One that puts him in a very serious position.

VALLANCE: (*to* THADDEUS, *after a further pause*) Mr Mortimore – ?

> (THADDEUS *makes no response.*)

ELKIN: If, understanding that, he chooses to continue there is nothing to prevent our hearing him.

THADDEUS: (*looking straight before him, his arms still upon the table, locking and unlocking his hands as he speaks*) It – it happened on the Wednesday night – in Cannon Row – in Ned's house – the night before he died – the night we were left without a nurse. (*Another pause.* VALLANCE *takes a sheet of paper and selects a pen.* ELKIN *pushes the inkstand nearer to him.*) Mrs James – and – and Mrs Stephen – my – my sisters-in-law –

> (ANN *and* LOUISA *get to their feet and advance a step or two.*)

ELKIN: (*hearing the rustle of their skirts and turning to them*) Keep your seats, ladies, please.

> (*They sit again, drawing their chairs close together.*)

THADDEUS: My sisters-in-law had gone home – that is, to their hotel – to get a few hours' sleep in case of their having to sit up through the night. Jim and Stephen and I were out and about, trying to find a night-nurse who'd take Nurse Ralston's place temporarily. At about nine o'clock, I looked in at Cannon Row, to see how things were getting on.

VALLANCE: (*who is writing*) The Wednesday? Mr Edward Mortimore dying on Thursday, the twentieth of June –

ELKIN: On the morning of Thursday, the twentieth.

VALLANCE: That makes the Wednesday we are speaking of, Wednesday, June the nineteenth.

ELKIN: (*to* THADDEUS) You looked in at Cannon Row – ?

VALLANCE: At about nine o'clock on the night of Wednesday, June the nineteenth.

THADDEUS: I – I went upstairs and sat by Ned's bed, and by-and-by he began talking to me about – about Phyllis. He – he'd taken rather a fancy to her, he said, and he wanted to give her a memento – a keepsake.

ELKIN: Phyllis – ?

VALLANCE: (*to* ELKIN) His wife. (*to* THADDEUS) Your wife?
        (THADDEUS *nods.*)

ELKIN: (*recollecting*) Of course.

THADDEUS: (*moistening his lips with his tongue*) He – he had some little bits of jewellery in his safe, and he – he asked me to go downstairs and – and to bring them up to him.

ELKIN: (*keenly*) In his safe?

VALLANCE: The safe in the library?
        (THADDEUS *nods again.*)

ELKIN: Quite so.

VALLANCE: And – er – ?

THADDEUS: He – he gave me his keys, and I – I went down – I –
        (*He stops suddenly and* VALLANCE *glances at him. Noticing his extreme pallor,* VALLANCE *looks round the room. Seeing the water-bottle upon the sideboard,* VALLANCE *rises and fills the tumbler. Returning to the table, he places the glass before* THADDEUS *and resumes his seat.*)

THADDEUS: (*after a gulp of water*) It was – it was in the drawer of the safe – the drawer –

ELKIN: What was?

THADDEUS: (*wiping his mouth with his handkerchief*) A large envelope – a large envelope – the envelope containing the will.

VALLANCE: How did you know – ?

THADDEUS: 'My Will' was written on it.

VALLANCE: (*writing*) 'My Will' –

ELKIN: On the envelope? (THADDEUS *nods.*) You say you opened it?
        (THADDEUS *nods.*)

VALLANCE: Opened the envelope –

ELKIN: And inside – you found – ?

VALLANCE: What did you find?

THADDEUS: Ned's will.

VALLANCE: (*writing*) What appeared to be your brother Edward's will.

ELKIN: You read it? (THADDEUS *nods.*) You recollect who was interested under it? (THADDEUS *nods.*) Will you tell us – ?
        (*The* MORTIMORES *and the* PONTINGS *crane their necks forward, listening breathlessly.*)

THADDEUS: He left everything – (*taking another gulp of water*) everything – to Miss Thornhill.

(*There is a slight, undecided movement on the part of the* MORTIMORES *and the* PONTINGS.)

ELKIN: (*calmly but firmly*) Keep your seats; keep your seats, *please*. (*to* THADDEUS) Can you recall the general form of the will?

.THADDEUS: (*straining his memory*) Everything he had – died possessed of – to Helen Thornhill – spinster – of some address in Paris – absolutely. And – and he appointed her his sole executrix.

ELKIN: Do you recollect the date?

THADDEUS: Date – ?

ELKIN: Did you observe the date of the will?

THADDEUS: (*quickly*) Oh, yes; it was made three years ago.

ELKIN: (*to* VALLANCE) When she came of age.

THADDEUS: Oh, and he asked her to remember his servants – old servants at the brewery and in Cannon Row. (*leaning back, exhausted*) There was nothing else. It was very short – written by Ned –

ELKIN: The whole of it? (THADDEUS *nods, with half-closed eyes.*) The whole of it was in his handwriting? (THADDEUS *nods again.*) Ah! (*to* VALLANCE, *with a note of triumph in his voice*) A holograph will, Mr Vallance, prepared by the man himself.

VALLANCE: (*now taking up the questioning of* THADDEUS) Tell me, Mr Mortimore – have you any exact recollection as to whether this document, which you describe as a will, was duly signed and witnessed?

THADDEUS: (*rousing himself*) It was – it was – signed by Ned.

VALLANCE: Was it signed, not only by your brother, but by two witnesses under an attestation clause stating that the testator signed in the joint presence of those witnesses and that each of them signed in his presence?

THADDEUS: I – I don't recollect that.

VALLANCE: (*writing*) You've no recollection of that.

(JAMES, STEPHEN *and* PONTING *stir themselves.*)

JAMES: (*hoarsely*) He doesn't recollect that, Mr Vallance.

STEPHEN: (*in quavering tones*) No, he – he doesn't recollect that.

PONTING: (*pulling at his moustache with trembling fingers*) That's most important, Mr Vallance, isn't it – isn't it?

VALLANCE: (*to* THADDEUS, *not heeding the interruption*) You say you destroyed this document –

ELKIN: Tore it up.

VALLANCE: When – and where? In the room – in the library?

THADDEUS: (*thinking*) N–no – out of doors.

VALLANCE: Out of doors. When?

THADDEUS: (*at a loss*) When – ?

VALLANCE: (*looking at him in surprise*) You can't remember – ?

THADDEUS: (*recollecting*) Oh, yes, yes, yes, yes. Some time between ten and eleven on the Thursday morning, after I left Phyllis – after I left my wife at Roper's to be measured for her black.

VALLANCE: (*writing*) What did you do then?

THADDEUS: (*readily*) I went to Ford Street bridge, and tore up the paper, and dropped the pieces into the Linch.

VALLANCE: (*writing*) Into the river –

ELKIN: One more question, Mr Mortimore – to make your motive perfectly clear to us. May we assume that, on the night of June the nineteenth, you were sufficiently acquainted with the law of intestacy to know that, if this dying man left no will, you would be likely to benefit considerably?

THADDEUS: Well, I – I had – the idea –

ELKIN: The idea?

THADDEUS: I – I – (*recollecting*) Oh, yes; there'd been a discussion in the train, you see, on the Tuesday, going to Linchpool –

ELKIN: Discussion?

THADDEUS: Among us all, as to how a man's money is disposed of, if he dies intestate.

ELKIN: (*nodding*) Precisely. (*to* JAMES *and* STEPHEN) You remember that conversation taking place, gentlemen?

JAMES: Oh, I – I dessay.

ELKIN: (*to* THADDEUS) So that, when you came upon the envelope with the endorsement upon it – 'My Will' – ?

THADDEUS: (*leaning his head upon his hands*) Yes – yes –

VALLANCE: (*running his eyes over his notes, to* THADDEUS) Have you anything to add, Mr Mortimore?

THADDEUS: (*in a muffled voice*) No. (*quickly*) Oh, there is one thing I should like to add. (*brokenly*) With regard to Miss Thornhill – I – I hope you'll bear in mind that I – that none of us – heard from Mr Elkin of the existence of a child – a daughter – till the Thursday – middle-day –

ELKIN: That is so.

THADDEUS: It doesn't make it much better; only – a girl – alone in the world – one wouldn't – (*breaking off*) no, I've nothing more to say.

ELKIN: (*to* THADDEUS) And we may take it that your present act, Mr Mortimore, is an act of conscience, purely?

> (THADDEUS *inclines his head. There is silence again, the* MORTIMORES *and the* PONTINGS *presenting a picture of utter wretchedness. The ladies' tears begin to flow.*)

JAMES: (*after a time, speaking with some difficulty*) Well –

STEPHEN: (*piteously*) Mr Vallance – ?

JAMES: What – what's to be done, Mr Vallance?

PONTING: (*to the ladies*) For God's sake, be quiet!

JAMES: (*a clenched fist on the table*) What we want to know is – what we want to know is – who does my brother Edward's money belong to now – *her* or us?

STEPHEN: (*in agony*) Her!

PONTING: Don't be a dam' fool, Mortimore.

VALLANCE: Well, gentlemen, I confess I am hardly prepared to express an opinion off-hand on the legal aspect of the case –

PONTING: The will's torn up – it's destroyed – !

STEPHEN: It's destroyed – gone – gone!

PONTING: Gone.

VALLANCE: But I need not remind you, there is another aspect –

PONTING: I don't care a rap for any other aspect –

STEPHEN: We want the *law* explained to us – the law –

PONTING: The law – !

JAMES: (*to* ELKIN) Mr Elkin – ?

ELKIN: You appeal to me, gentlemen?

STEPHEN *and* PONTING: Yes – yes –

ELKIN: Then I feel bound to tell you that *I* shall advise Miss Thornhill, as the executrix named in the will, to apply to the Court for probate of its substance and effect –

VALLANCE: (*to* ELKIN) Ask the Court to presume the will to have been made in due form – ?

ELKIN: Decidedly.

> (STEPHEN *and* PONTING *fall back in their seats in a stupor, and once more there is silence, broken only by the sound of the women snivelling.* ELKIN *and* VALLANCE *slowly proceed to collect their papers.*)

JAMES: (*turning upon* THADDEUS, *brutally*) Have you – have you told Phyllis – have you told your wife what you've been up to?

> (*At the mention of* PHYLLIS, *there is a movement of indignation on the part of the ladies.*)

ROSE: Ha!

JAMES: (*to* THADDEUS) Have yer?

THADDEUS: Y–yes – just before I came out. (*weakly*) That – that's what made me so late.

JAMES: (*between his teeth*) What does *she* think of yer?

THADDEUS: Oh, she – she's dreadfully – cut up – of course.

ROSE: (*hysterically*) The jewellery! Ha, ha, ha! (*rising*) She managed to get hold of some of the jewellery, at any rate.

ANN: (*with a sob*) Yes, she – she managed *that*.

LOUISA: (*mopping her face*) She's kept that from us artfully enough.

ROSE: (*going over to* ANN *and* LOUISA, *who rise to receive her*) Ha, ha! Edward's 'little bits' of jewellery!

ANN: Little bits!

ROSE: They're little bits that are *left*.

LOUISA: How many did she have of them, I wonder!

ROSE: She shall be made to restore them –

LOUISA: Every one of them.

THADDEUS: No, no, no – (*stretching out a hand towards the ladies*) Rosie – Ann – Lou – Phyllis hadn't any of the jewellery – not a scrap. I put it all back into the safe. I – I swear she hadn't any of it.

ELKIN: Why did you do that?

THADDEUS: (*agitatedly*) Why, you see, Mr Elkin, when I carried it upstairs, I found my brother Edward in a state of collapse – a sort of faint –

ELKIN: (*with a nod*) Ah –

THADDEUS: And Phyllis – my wife – she sent me off at once for the doctor. It was on the Wednesday evening, you know –

VALLANCE: (*pricking up his ears*) Your wife, Mr Mortimore – ?

THADDEUS: It was on the Wednesday evening that the change set in.

VALLANCE: (*to* THADDEUS) Your wife sent you off at once – ?

THADDEUS: (*to* VALLANCE) To fetch the doctor.

VALLANCE: (*raising his eyebrows*) Oh, Mrs Mortimore was in the house while all this was going on?

THADDEUS: Y–yes; she was left in charge of him – in charge of Ned –

ELKIN: (*to* VALLANCE, *in explanation*) To allow these other ladies to rest preparatory to their taking charge later.

THADDEUS: Yes.

VALLANCE: I hadn't gathered –

JAMES: (*who has been sitting glaring into space, thoughtfully*) Hold hard. (*to* THADDEUS) *You* didn't go for the doctor.

THADDEUS: Yes, I – I went –

STEPHEN: (*awakening from his trance*) Phyllis sent the cook for the doctor.

THADDEUS: Yes, yes; you're quite right. The cook was the first to go –

ELKIN: (*to* THADDEUS) You followed?

THADDEUS: I followed.

JAMES: (*knitting his brows*) It must have been a good time afterwards.

THADDEUS: Y–yes, perhaps it was.

JAMES: I was at Dr Oswald's when the woman arrived. The doctor was out, and –

VALLANCE: (*to* THADDEUS) You said your wife sent you at once.

THADDEUS: Told me to go at once. There – there was the jewellery to put back into the safe –

VALLANCE: (*eyeing* THADDEUS) What time was it when you *got* to the doctor's?

THADDEUS: Oh – ten, I should say – or a quarter-past.

JAMES: (*shaking his head*) No. I sat there, waiting for Dr Oswald to come in –

STEPHEN: (*to* THADDEUS) Besides, that couldn't have been; you were with me then.

JAMES: (*to* STEPHEN) Was he?

STEPHEN: Why, yes; he and I were at the Nurses' Home in Wharton Street from half-past nine till ten.

JAMES: Half-past nine – ?

STEPHEN: (*becoming more confident as he proceeds*) And we never left each other till we went back to Cannon Row.

VALLANCE: Let us understand this –

PONTING: (*who has gradually revived, eagerly*) Yes – yes – (*to the ladies*) Sssh!

STEPHEN: And, what's more, we allowed ourselves a quarter-of-an-hour to walk to Wharton Street.

JAMES: (*quietly, looking round*) Hallo – !

THADDEUS: It – it's evident that I – that I'm mistaken in thinking that I – that I went to Dr Oswald's –

VALLANCE: Mistaken?

THADDEUS: I – I suppose that, as the woman had already gone, I – I considered it – wasn't necessary – (*to* ELKIN *and* VALLANCE, *passing his hand before his eyes*) You must excuse my stupidity, gentlemen.

VALLANCE: (*to* THADDEUS, *distrustfully*) Then, according to your brother Stephen, Mr Mortimore, you were in Cannon Row, on the occasion of this particular visit, no longer than from nine o'clock till a quarter-past?

STEPHEN: Not so long, because we met, by arrangement, at a quarter-past-nine, in the hall of the Grand Hotel –

JAMES: The hotel's six or seven minutes' walk from Cannon Row –

PONTING: Quite, quite.

THADDEUS: (*a little wildly*) I said I called in at Cannon Row at *about* nine o'clock. It may have been half-past eight; it may have been eight –

JAMES: Ann and Lou didn't leave Cannon Row till past eight –

LOUISA: (*standing, with* ANN *and* ROSE, *by the tea-table*) It had gone eight –

JAMES: I walked 'em round to the Grand –

STEPHEN: The *three* of us walked with them to the Grand – !

LOUISA: All three –

JAMES: So we did.

STEPHEN: (*to* JAMES *excitedly*) And then Thaddeus went off to the Clarence Hospital with a note from Dr Oswald –

JAMES: By George, yes!

STEPHEN: I left him opposite the Exchange – it must have been nearly half-past eight *then* – !

(JAMES *rises. The ladies draw nearer to the dining-table.*)

THADDEUS: Ah, but I didn't go to the hospital – I didn't go to the hospital –

STEPHEN: (*rising*) Yes, you did. You brought a note *back* from the hospital, for us to take to Wharton Street –

VALLANCE: (*to* ELKIN:) How far is the Clarence Hospital from the Exchange?

ELKIN: A ten minutes' drive. It's on the other side of the water.

THADDEUS: I – I – I'd forgotten the hospital –

JAMES: (*scowling at* THADDEUS) Forgotten – ?

THADDEUS: I – I – I mean I – I thought the hospital came later – after I'd been to Wharton Street –

JAMES: (*going to* VALLANCE: *and tapping him to the shoulder*) Mr Vallance –

THADDEUS: I – I must have gone to Cannon Row *between* my return from the hospital and my meeting Stephen at the Grand –

JAMES: (*to* ELKIN *and* VALLANCE) Why, he couldn't have *done* it, gentlemen –

PONTING: Impossible!

STEPHEN: It's obvious; he *couldn't* have done it.

THADDEUS: I – I was only a few minutes at the hospital –

ELKIN: (*scribbling on the back of a document*) Oh, yes, he could have done it – barely –

VALLANCE: (*making a mental calculation*) Assuming that he left his brother at the Exchange at eight-twenty –

ELKIN: Ten minutes *to* the hospital.

VALLANCE: If he drove there –

THADDEUS: I did drive – I did drive –

PONTING: (*who is also figuring it out on paper*) Ten minutes back –

ELKIN: Ten minutes *at* the hospital –

PONTING: Eight-fifty –

THADDEUS: Eight-fifty in Cannon Row! That was it – that was it, Mr Elkin –

JAMES: Give him twenty minutes in Cannon Row – *give* it him! He couldn't have done all he says he did in the time, gentlemen –

STEPHEN: He couldn't have *done* it –

PONTING: Impossible!

ELKIN: (*to* PONTING) No, no, please – not impossible.

VALLANCE: (*to* STEPHEN) When you met Mr Thaddeus Mortimore – you – when you met him in the hall of the Grand Hotel, before starting for Wharton Street, did he say anything to you as to his having just called at the house – ?

STEPHEN: No.

VALLANCE: Nothing as to an alarming change in your brother's condition?

STEPHEN: Not a syllable.

JAMES: (*to* ELKIN *and* VALLANCE) Oh, there's a screw loose here, gentlemen, surely?

STEPHEN: (*joining* JAMES) This is *most* extraordinary, Mr Vallance – isn't it? Not a syllable!

> (ANN *and* LOUISA *join their husbands and the four gather round* ELKIN *and* VALLANCE. ROSE *stands behind* PONTING's *chair.*)

THADDEUS: You see – Edward – Edward had rallied before I left Cannon Row. He – he'd fallen into a nice, quiet sleep –

JAMES: All in twenty minutes, gentlemen – twenty minutes at the outside!

VALLANCE: (*to* THADDEUS) Mr Mortimore –

ANN: I remember –

PONTING: (*to* ANN) Hold your tongue!

VALLANCE: Mr Mortimore, *who let you into the house* in Cannon Row on the night of June the nineteenth – ?

PONTING: Ah, yes –

VALLANCE: At *any* time between the hours of eight o'clock –

STEPHEN: And eleven.

ELKIN: (*to* THADDEUS) Who gave you admittance – which of the servants?

THADDEUS: I – I can't – I don't – (*blankly, addressing* VALLANCE) was it the – the butler? –

VALLANCE: No, no; I ask *you*. (*to* ELKIN, *who nods in reply*) Have you the servants' addresses?

THADDEUS: But you wouldn't – you wouldn't trust to the servants' memories as to – as to which of them opened the front-door to me a month ago! (*with an attempt at a laugh*) It's ridiculous!

ELKIN: (*reprovingly*) Ah, now, now, Mr Mortimore!

THADDEUS: (*starting up from the table*) Oh, it isn't fair – it isn't fair of you to badger me like this; it isn't fair!

VALLANCE: Nobody desires to 'badger' you –

THADDEUS: Trip me up, then – confuse me. (*at the left-hand end of the table, clutching the back of a chair*) The will – the will's the main point – Ned's will. What does it matter – what can it matter, to a quarter-of-an-hour or so – when I was in Cannon Row, or how long I was there? One would think, by the way I'm being treated, gentlemen, that I'd something to gain by this, instead of everything to lose – everything to lose!

JAMES: (*coming forward, on the further side of the table*) Don't you whine about what *you've* got to lose – !

STEPHEN: (*joining him*) What about *us*?

THE LADIES: Us!

PONTING: (*hitting the table*) Yes, confound you!

VALLANCE: Colonel Ponting – !

ELKIN: (*to* JAMES *and* STEPHEN) It seems to me – if my friend Mr Vallance will allow me to say so – that you are really bearing a little hardly on your brother Thaddeus.

THADDEUS: (*gratefully*) Thank you, Mr Elkin.

ELKIN: What reason – what possible reason can there be for doubting his good faith?

THADDEUS: Thank you.

ELKIN: Here is a man who forfeits a considerable sum of money, and deliberately places himself in peril, in order to right a wrong which nobody on earth would have suspected him of committing. Mr Mortimore is *accusing* himself of a serious offence, not defending himself from it.

VALLANCE: (*obstinately*) What we beg of Mr Mortimore to do, for the sake of all parties, is to clear up certain inconsistencies in his story with his brothers' account of his movements and conduct on this Wednesday evening. We are entitled to ask that.

JAMES: Aye – entitled.

STEPHEN *and* PONTING: Entitled.

ELKIN: (*to* JAMES *and* STEPHEN) Yes, and Mr Mortimore is equally entitled to refuse it.

JAMES, STEPHEN *and* PONTING: (*indignantly*) Oh – !

THADDEUS: But I – I haven't refused. I – I've done my best –

ELKIN: On the other hand, if he has no objection to her doing so, the person to assist you, I suggest – distressing as it may be to her – is the wife.

VALLANCE: (*assentingly*) The wife –

(THADDEUS *pushes aside the chair which he is holding and comes to the table.*)

ELKIN: *She* ought to be able to satisfy you as to what time he was with her –

VALLANCE: (*to everybody*) By-the-bye, has she ever mentioned this visit of her husband's to Cannon Row – ?

ANN *and* LOUISA: Never – never –

ELKIN: Attaching no importance to it. But now –

THADDEUS: (*stretching out a quivering hand to them all*) No. No, no. Don't you – don't you drag my wife into this. I – I won't have my wife dragged into this –

JAMES: (*in a blaze*) Why not?

STEPHEN: Why not?

THE LADIES: (*indignantly*) Ah – !

THADDEUS: You – you leave my wife out of it –

JAMES: (*to* THADDEUS, *furiously*) Who the hell's your wife – !

ELKIN: *and* VALLANCE: Gentlemen – gentlemen –

LOUISA: Who's Phyllis – !

ANN: Who's *she* – !

ROSE: Ha!

JAMES *and* STEPHEN: (*derisively*) Ha, ha, ha!

THADDEUS: Anyhow, I do object – I do object to your dragging her into it – (*his show of courage flickering away*) I – I do object – (*coming to the nearer side of the table, rather unsteadily*) Mr Elkin – Mr Vallance – I – I don't think I can be of any further assistance to you to-day –

> (VALLANCE *shrugs his shoulders at* ELKIN.)

ELKIN: (*to* THADDEUS, *kindly*) One minute – one minute more. Mr Vallance has taken down your statement roughly. (*to* VALLANCE) If you'll read us your notes, Mr Vallance, Mr Mortimore will tell us whether they are substantially correct – (*to* THADDEUS) perhaps he will even be willing to attach his name to them –

> (*With a nod of patient acquiescence,* THADDEUS *sinks into the middle chair.* VALLANCE *prepares to read the notes, first making some additions to them.*)

JAMES: (*to* THADDEUS, *from the other side of the table*) Look here – !

THADDEUS: (*feebly*) No – no more questions. I – I'm advised I – I may refuse –

JAMES: Mr Vallance asked you just now about your conscience –

THADDEUS: I – I'm not going to answer any more questions –

STEPHEN: (*to* JAMES) It was Mr Elkin –

JAMES: I don't care a curse which it was –

THADDEUS: No more questions –

JAMES: (*leaning across the table towards* THADDEUS, *fiercely*) Why the devil did your conscience begin to prick you over this? Hey?

STEPHEN: (*to* THADDEUS) Yes, you've been in excellent spirits apparently this last month – excellent spirits.

JAMES: (*hammering on the table*) Hey?

STEPHEN: (*to* ELKIN *and* VALLANCE) There was no sign of anything amiss when we were with him this afternoon, gentlemen – none whatever, I give you my word.

JAMES: Less than two hours ago – not a symptom!

STEPHEN: (*to* JAMES) He was gay enough at the club dinner on Tuesday night. It was remarked – commented on.

LOUISA: (*at* STEPHEN's *elbow, unconsciously*) It's Phyllis who's been ill all the month, not Thaddeus.

JAMES: (*in the same way, with a hoarse laugh*) Ha! If it had been his precious wife who'd come to us and told us this tale –

STEPHEN: Yes, if it had been the lady –

JAMES: If it had been –

> (*Struck by the idea which occurs to him,* JAMES *breaks off.*
> THADDEUS *doesn't stir.*)

JAMES: (*after a pause, thoughtfully*) If it had been –

STEPHEN: (*holding his breath, to* JAMES) Eh?

JAMES: (*slowly stroking his beard*) One might have understood it –

ELKIN: (*who has been listening attentively, in a tone of polite interest*) How long has Mrs Mortimore been indisposed?

JAMES: (*disturbed*) Oh – er – a few weeks –

VALLANCE: (*quietly*) Ever since – ?

JAMES: (*with a nod*) Aye.

> (ELKIN *and* VALLANCE *look at each other enquiringly.*)

STEPHEN: (*staring into space*) Ever since – Edward – as a matter of fact –

ROSE: (*going to* ANN *and* LOUISA) What's wrong with her? What's wrong with his wife?

ANN: (*obtusely*) She's not sleeping.

LOUISA: (*looking from one to the other*) No – she isn't –
(*There is a further pause, and then* THADDEUS, *slowly turning from the table, rises.*)

THADDEUS: (*in a strange voice, his hands fumbling at the buttons of his jacket*) Well, gentlemen – whatever my sins are – I – decline to sit still and hear my wife insulted in this style. If it's all the same to you, I'll call round on Mr Vallance in the morning and – and sign the paper –
(*While* THADDEUS *is speaking,* JAMES *and* STEPHEN *come forward on the left,* ELKIN *and* VALLANCE *on the right. The three women get together at the back and look on with wide-open eyes. The movement is made gradually and noiselessly, so that when* THADDEUS *turns to go he is startled at finding his way obstructed. After a time* PONTING *also leaves the table, watching the proceedings, with a falling jaw, from a little distance on the right.*)

ELKIN: (*rubbing his chin meditatively, to* THADDEUS) Mr Mortimore, your wife travelled with you and the other members of the family to Linchpool on the Tuesday – ?

JAMES: Aye, she was with us –

ELKIN: (*to* THADDEUS) She was in the railway-carriage when the – when the discussion arose – ?

STEPHEN: Yes, yes –

ELKIN: The discussion as to where a man's money goes to, in the absence of a will?

ANN: (*from the other side of the table*) Yes –

LOUISA: (*close to* ANN) Of course she was.

ELKIN: (*nodding*) H'm. (*to* THADDEUS) I – I am most anxious not to pain you unnecessarily. Er – the conversation you had with your brother Edward at the bedside, in reference to Mrs Thaddeus Mortimore – when he said that he – that he –

JAMES: (*breathing heavily*) He'd taken a fancy to her –

ELKIN: That he wished to make her a present of jewellery – she was within hearing during that talk?

THADDEUS: (*avoiding everybody's gaze, his hands twitching involuntarily at his side*) She – she may have been.

ELKIN: (*piercingly*) He was left in her charge, you know.

THADDEUS: She – she was moving about the room –

ELKIN: She would scarcely have been far away from him.

THADDEUS: (*moistening his lips with his tongue*) N–no.

ELKIN: And when he handed you his keys and asked you to go downstairs and open the safe – did she hear and witness that also?

THADDEUS: She – she – very likely.

ELKIN: (*raising his voice*) There was nothing at all confidential in this transaction between you and your brother?

THADDEUS: Why – why should there have been?

ELKIN: Why *should* there have been? (*coming a step nearer to him*) So that, feeling towards her as he did, there was no reason why, if you hadn't chanced to be on the spot – there was no reason why he shouldn't have held that conversation with *her*, and intrusted *her* with the keys?

THADDEUS: She – she was almost a stranger to him. He – he hadn't seen her since she was a child –

ELKIN: (*interrupting him*) Tell us – this illness of Mrs Mortimore's – ?

THADDEUS: My – my wife's a nervous, delicate woman – always has been –

ELKIN: (*nodding*) Quite so.

THADDEUS: She – she was upset at being alone with Edward when he – when he swooned –

JAMES: That was the tale –

ELKIN: (*to* THADDEUS) Although you happened to be in the library, a floor or two below, at the time?

THADDEUS: He – he might have died suddenly, in her arms. She's a nervous, sensitive woman –

ELKIN: (*nodding*) And she's been unwell ever since. (*with an abrupt change of manner*) Mr Mortimore, how is the lock of the safe opened?

THADDEUS: Opened – ?

ELKIN: (*sharply*) The safe in the library in Cannon Row – how do you open it? (THADDEUS *is silent.*) Is it a simple lock, or is there anything unusual about it?

THADDEUS: He – he gave me directions how to open it.

ELKIN: Tell us –

THADDEUS: I – I forget –

ELKIN: Forget?

THADDEUS: It – it's gone from me –

JAMES: (*in a low voice*) Gentlemen, you couldn't forget *that* –

STEPHEN: (*in the same way*) You *couldn't* forget it.

ELKIN: (*to* THADDEUS, *solemnly*) Mr Mortimore, are you sure that the conversation at the bedside didn't take place between your brother and your wife solely, and that it wasn't *she* who was sent downstairs to fetch the jewellery?

THADDEUS: (*drawing himself up, with a last effort*) Sure – ?

ELKIN: Are you positive that *she* didn't open the safe?

THADDEUS: It – it's ridiculous –

ELKIN: (*quickly*) When you took her to Roper's, the draper's, on the Thursday – you left her there?

THADDEUS: Yes, I – I left her –

ELKIN: Are you sure that *she* didn't then go on to the bridge, and tear up the will, and throw the pieces into the river?

THADDEUS: I – I decline to answer any more questions –

ELKIN: (*raising his voice again*) Were you in Cannon Row, sir, on the night of June the nineteenth, for a *single moment* between eight o'clock and eleven – ?

THADDEUS: (*losing his head completely*) Ah! Ah! I know – I know! You mean to drag my wife into this – !

ELKIN: (*to* THADDEUS) You were late in coming here this afternoon, Mr Mortimore –

THADDEUS: (*to* ELKIN, *threateningly*) Don't you – don't you dare to do it – !

ELKIN: Owing, you say, to your having made a communication to Mrs Mortimore about this affair –

THADDEUS: (*clinging to the chair which is behind him*) You – you leave my wife out of it – !

ELKIN: Are you sure that you were not delayed through having to *receive* a communication from her – ?

THADDEUS: (*dropping into the chair*) Don't you – drag her – into it – !

ELKIN: Are you sure that the story you have told us, substituting yourself for the principal person of that story, is not exactly the story which she has just told *you*? (*There is a pause.* PONTING *goes to* ROSE.) Mr Vallance –

VALLANCE: Yes?

ELKIN: I propose to see Mrs Mortimore in this matter, without delay.

VALLANCE: Very good.

ELKIN: Will you – ?

VALLANCE: Certainly.

>   (*Quietly,* VALLANCE *returns to the table and, seating himself, again collects his papers.* ELKIN *is following him.*)

JAMES: Mr Elkin –

ELKIN: (*stopping*) Eh?

JAMES: Stealing a will – destroying a will – what is it?

ELKIN: What *is* it?

JAMES: The law – what's the law – ?

ELKIN: (*to* JAMES) I – I'm sorry to have to say, sir – it's a felony.

THADDEUS: (*with a look of horror*) Oh – !

>   (ANN *and* LOUISA *come to* JAMES *and* STEPHEN *hurriedly.*
>   ELKIN *sits beside* VALLANCE, *and, picking up their bags from the floor, they put away their papers.*)

JAMES: (*standing over* THADDEUS) Well! Are yer proud of her now?

STEPHEN: *This* is what his marriage has ended in!

LOUISA: I'm not in the least surprised.

ANN: Old Burdock's daughter!

ROSE: (*from the other side of the table*) Thank heaven, my name isn't Mortimore!

THADDEUS: (*leaping to his feet in a frenzy*) Don't you touch her! Don't any of you touch her! Don't you harm a hair of her head! (*to the group on the left*) You've helped to bring this on her! You've helped to make her life unendurable! You've helped to bring her to this! She's been a good wife to me. Oh, my God, let me get her away! (*turning towards the door*) Mr Elkin – Mr Vallance – do let me get her away! Don't you harm a hair of her head! Don't you touch her! (*at the door*) She's been a good wife to me! (*opening the door and disappearing*) She's been a good wife to me – !

JAMES: (*moving over to the right, shouting after* THADDEUS) Been a good wife to you, has she!

STEPHEN: (*also moving to the right*) A disgrace – a disgrace to the family!

LOUISA: (*following* STEPHEN) I always said so – I said so till I was tired –

JAMES: *We've* helped to bring her to this!

ANN: (*sitting in a chair on the nearer side of the dining-table*) A vile creature!

PONTING: (*coming forward on the left with* ROSE) Damn the woman! Damn the woman! My position is a cruel one –

STEPHEN: (*raising his arms as he paces the room on the right*) Here's a triumph for Hammond!

JAMES: (*to* PONTING, *contemptuously*) *Your* position – !

LOUISA: Nelly Robson's got the better of me now!

PONTING: (*to* JAMES) I'm landed with an enormous house in Carlos Place – my builders are in it –

ROSE: (*pacing the room on the left*) Oh, we're in a shocking scrape! We're up to our necks – !

JAMES: (*approaching* PONTING) D'ye think you're the only sufferer – !

STEPHEN: (*wildly*) A triumph for Hammond! A triumph for Hammond!

JAMES: (*to* PONTING) I've bought all that dirt at the bottom of Gordon Street – acres of it – !

PONTING: (*passing him and walking away to the right*) That's *your* business.

STEPHEN: (*now, with* LOUISA, *at the further side of the dining-table*) Hammond and his filthy rag!

JAMES: (*going after* PONTING, *in a fury*) Aye, it *is* my business –

PONTING: (*turning upon him viciously*) I wish to God, sir, I'd never seen or heard of you, *or* your family.

ROSE: (*coming forward*) Oh, Toby, don't – !

JAMES: (*to* PONTING) You wish that, do yer – !

ANN: (*rising and putting herself between* JAMES *and* PONTING) James – !

STEPHEN: (*shaking his fists in the air*) Blast Hammond and his filthy rag.

JAMES: (*to* PONTING) You patronising little pauper – !

ROSE: (*to* JAMES) Don't you speak to my husband like that – !

PONTING: You're a pack of low, common people – !

ROSE: (*going to* PONTING) He's the only gentleman among you.

JAMES: The only gentleman among us – !

STEPHEN: (*coming forward, with* LOUISA, *on the left*) The only gentleman – !

JAMES: We could have done without such a gentleman in our family – (*to* ANN, *who is forcing him, coaxingly, towards the left*) hey, mother?

STEPHEN: (*advancing to* PONTING, *still followed by* LOUISA) Exceedingly well – exceedingly well –

LOUISA: (*taking* STEPHEN's *arm*) Don't lower yourself – !

JAMES: (*over* ANN's *shoulder*) The Colonel never came near us till the other day he saw a chance o' picking up the pieces – !

STEPHEN: Nor Rose either – neither of them did!

JAMES: It's six o' one and half a dozen o' the other!

ROSE: (*to* JAMES *and* STEPHEN) Oh, you cads, you boys – !

JAMES: (*mockingly*) Didn't they bustle down to Linchpool in a hurry *then*! Ha, ha, ha!

STEPHEN: (*waving his hand in* PONTING's *face*) This serves you right, Colonel; this serves you right.

ROSE: (*leading* PONTING *towards the door*) Don't notice them – don't notice them –

JAMES: (*walking about on the left, to* ANN) I'm in a mess, mother; I'm in a dreadful mess!

STEPHEN: (*sinking into a chair by the tea-table*) On I go at the broken-down rat-hole in King Street; on I go with my worn-out old plant – !

    (*On getting to the door,* PONTING *discovers that* ELKIN *and* VALLANCE *have taken their departure. He returns, with* ROSE, *to the further side of the dining-table.*)

ANN: (*to* JAMES) You must get rid of the contract, James.

JAMES: Who'll take it – who'll take it – !

STEPHEN: I've always been behind the times –

LOUISA: Nelly will laugh her teeth out of her head –

PONTING: (*to* JAMES *and* STEPHEN, *trying to attract their attention*) Mortimore – Mortimore –

ANN: (*to* JAMES) It's splendid land, isn't it?

JAMES: Nobody's been ass enough to touch it but me!

STEPHEN: (*rocking himself to and fro*) Always behind the times – no need to tell me that –

PONTING: (*to* JAMES) Mortimore –

JAMES: (*to* PONTING) What?

PONTING: (*pointing to the empty chairs*) They've gone –

JAMES: (*sobering down*) Hooked it –

STEPHEN: (*looking round*) Gone – ?

JAMES: Elkin –

STEPHEN: (*weakly*) And Vallance –

JAMES: They might have had the common civility –

PONTING: (*coming forward slowly and dejectedly*) They've gone to that woman –

ROSE: (*at the further side of the table*) I hope they send her to jail – the trull – the baggage – !

    (ANN *and* LOUISA *join* ROSE.)

PONTING: The whole business will be settled between 'em in ten minutes – the whole business –

JAMES: (*coming to* PONTING) Aye, the whole concern.

STEPHEN: (*who has risen, holding his head*) Oh, it's awful!

PONTING: (*laying a hand on* JAMES *and* STEPHEN, *who are on either side of him*) My friends, don't let us disagree – we're all in the same boat –

JAMES: (*grimly, looking into space*) Aye, they'll be talking it over nicely –

PONTING: Let us stick to each other. Aren't we throwing up the sponge prematurely – ?

JAMES: (*not heeding him*) Tad and his wife and the lawyers – ha, ha! –

STEPHEN: And that girl –

JAMES: (*nodding*) The young lady.

PONTING: What girl?

STEPHEN: Miss Thornhill.

PONTING: Thornhill – ?

JAMES: She's staying with 'em.

PONTING: *She* is?

Hooked it: disappeared (slang).

ROSE: (*coming forward on the left*) Staying with the Tads – ?

PONTING: In their house? Elkin and Vallance will find her there!

JAMES: (*nodding*) Aye.

PONTING: (*violently*) It's a conspiracy – !

JAMES: Conspiracy – ?

PONTING: I see it! The Thornhill girl's in it! She's at the bottom of it! (*going to ROSE as* ANN *and* LOUISA *come forward on the left*) They're cheating us – they're cheating us. I tell you we ought to be present. They're robbing us behind our backs –

STEPHEN: (*looking at* JAMES) Jim – ?

JAMES: (*shaking his head*) No, it's no conspiracy –

PONTING: It is! They're robbing us – !

STEPHEN: (*to* JAMES) Still, I – I really think –

PONTING: Behind our backs!

THE LADIES: Yes – yes – yes –

JAMES: (*after a pause, quietly stroking his beard*) By George, we'll go down – !
(*Instantly they all make for the door.*)

STEPHEN: We'll be there as soon as Elkin –

PONTING: A foul conspiracy – !

ANN: (*in the rear*) Wait till I put on my hat –

ROSE: Jim, you follow with Ann.

PONTING: (*to* STEPHEN) We'll go on ahead.

STEPHEN: Yes, we'll go first.

LOUISA: I'm ready.

JAMES: No, no; we'll all go together.

PONTING: Robbing us behind our backs – !

JAMES: Look sharp, mother!

THE OTHERS: Be quick – be quick – be quick – !
(*Seizing* ANN *and pushing her before them, they struggle through the doorway.*)
END OF THE THIRD ACT

THE FOURTH ACT

The scene is the same, in every respect, as that of the Second Act.
VALLANCE *is seated at the writing-table by the bay-window, reading aloud from a written paper.* PHYLLIS, *in deep abasement, is upon the settee by the piano, and* THADDEUS *is standing by her, holding her left hand in both of his. On the left of the table at the end of the piano sits* HELEN, *pale, calm and erect, and opposite to her, in the chair on the other side of the table, is* ELKIN. PONTING *is sitting in the bay-window,* STEPHEN *is standing upon the hearth-rug, and the rest of the 'family' are seated about the room – all looking very humble and downcast.* ANN *and* LOUISA *are upon the settee on the right,* ROSE *is in the arm-chair on the nearer side of the fireplace,* JAMES *on the ottoman.* ROSE, ANN *and* LOUISA *are in their out-door things.*

VALLANCE: (*reading*) 'It was broad daylight before my husband and I got back to our lodgings. The document was then in a pocket I was wearing under my dress. Before going to bed I hid the pocket in a drawer. At about eleven o'clock on the same morning my husband took me to Roper's, the draper's, in Ford Street, and left me there. After my measurements were taken I went up Ford Street and on to the bridge. I then tore up both the paper and the envelope and dropped the pieces into the water.'

ELKIN: (*half-turning to* PHYLLIS) You declare that that is correct in every particular, Mrs Mortimore?

(PHYLLIS *bursts into a paroxysm of tears.*)

THADDEUS: (*to* PHYLLIS, *as if comforting a child*) All right, dear; all right. I'm with you – I'm with you. (*She sobs helplessly.*) Tell Mr Elkin – tell him – is that correct?

PHYLLIS: (*through her sobs*) Yes.

ELKIN: (*to* PHYLLIS) You've nothing further to say?

(*Her sobbing continues.*)

THADDEUS: (*to* PHYLLIS) Have you anything more to say, dear? (*encouragingly, as she tries to speak*) I'm here, dear – I'm with you. Is there anything – anything more –

PHYLLIS: Only – only that I beg Miss Thornhill's pardon. I beg her pardon. Oh, I beg her pardon.

(ELKIN *looks at* HELEN, *who, however, makes no response.*)

THADDEUS: (*to* PHYLLIS, *glancing at the others*) And – and –

PHYLLIS: And – and Ann and Jim – and Stephen – and Lou – and Rose and Colonel Ponting – I beg their pardon – I beg their pardon.

(*She sinks back upon the settee, and her fit of weeping gradually exhausts itself.*)

THADDEUS: And I – and I, Mr Elkin – I wish to offer *my* apologies – my humble apologies – to you and Mr Vallance – and to everybody – for what took place this afternoon in my brother's dining-room.

ELKIN: (*kindly*) Perhaps it isn't necessary –

THADDEUS: Perhaps not – but it's on my mind. (*to* ELKIN *and* VALLANCE) I assure you and Mr Vallance – (*to the others*) and I assure every member of my family – that when I went away from here I had no intention of inventing the story I attempted to tell you at 'Ivanhoe'. It came into my head suddenly – quite suddenly – on my way to Claybrook Road – almost at the gate of the house. I must have been mad to think I could succeed in imposing on you all. I believe I *was* mad, gentlemen; and that's my excuse, and I – I hope you'll accept it.

ELKIN: Speaking for myself, I accept it freely.

VALLANCE: And I.

THADDEUS: Thank you – thank you.

(*He looks at the others wistfully, but they are all staring at the carpet, and they, too, make no response. Then he seats himself beside* PHYLLIS *and again takes her hand.*)

ELKIN: (*after a pause*) Well, Mr Vallance – (VALLANCE *rises, the written paper in his hand, and comes forward on the left.*) I think – (*glancing over his shoulder at* PHYLLIS) I think that this lady makes it perfectly clear to any reasonable person that the document which she abstracted from the safe in Cannon Row, and subsequently destroyed, was the late Mr Edward Mortimore's will, and that Miss Thornhill was the universal legatee under it, and was named as the sole executrix. (VALLANCE *seats himself in the chair on the extreme left.*) As I said in Mr James Mortimore's house, the advice I shall give to Miss Thornhill is that she applies to the Court for probate of the substance and effect of this will.

VALLANCE: Upon an affidavit by Mrs Thaddeus Mortimore – ?

ELKIN: An affidavit disclosing what she has done and verifying a statement of the contents of the will.

VALLANCE: And how, may I ask, are you going to get over your great difficulty?

ELKIN: My great difficulty – ?

VALLANCE: The fact that Mrs Thaddeus Mortimore is unable to swear that the will was duly witnessed.

PONTING: Ah (*rising and coming forward, but discreetly keeping behind* HELEN) That seems to me to be insuperable – insuperable. (*anxiously*) Eh, Mr Vallance?

STEPHEN: (*advancing a step or two*) An obstacle which cannot be got over.

PONTING: (*eyeing* HELEN *furtively*) It – ah – may appear rather ungracious to Miss Thornhill – a young lady we hold in the highest esteem – and to whom I express regret for any hasty word I may have used on arriving here – unreserved regret – (HELEN's *eyes flash, and her shoulders contract; otherwise she makes no acknowledgment.*) It may appear ungracious to Miss Thornhill to discuss this point in her presence; (*pulling at his moustache*) but she will be the first to recognise that there are many – ah – interests at stake.

STEPHEN: Many interests – many interests –

PONTING: And where so many interests are involved, one mustn't – ah – allow oneself to be swayed by anything like sentiment.

STEPHEN: (*at the round table*) In justice, one *oughtn't* to be sentimental.

PONTING: One *daren't* be sentimental.

LOUISA: (*meekly, raising her head*) I always maintain –

STEPHEN: (*to* LOUISA) Yes, yes. yes.

LOUISA: There are two sides –

STEPHEN: Yes, yes.

ELKIN: (*ignoring the interruption*) Mrs Thaddeus Mortimore is prepared to swear, Mr Vallance, that she believes there were other signatures besides the signature of the late Mr Mortimore.

VALLANCE: But she has no recollection of the names of witnesses –

PONTING: None whatever.

STEPHEN: Not the faintest.

VALLANCE: Nor as to whether there was an attestation clause at all.

PONTING: Her memory is an utter blank as to that.

STEPHEN: An utter blank.

> (*As* PONTING *and* STEPHEN *perk up, there is a rise in the spirits of the ladies at the fire-place.* ROSE *twists her chair round to face the men.* JAMES *doesn't stir.*)

ELKIN: Notwithstanding that, I can't help considering it reasonably probable that, in the circumstances, the Court would presume the will to have been made in due form.

PONTING: (*walking about agitatedly*) I differ.

STEPHEN: (*walking about*) So do I.

PONTING: I don't pretend to a profound knowledge of the law –

STEPHEN: As a mere layman, *I* consider it extremely *im*probable – extremely *im*probable.

VALLANCE: (*to* STEPHEN *and* PONTING) Well, gentlemen, there I am inclined to agree with you –

PONTING: (*pulling himself up*) Ah!

STEPHEN: (*returning to the round table*) Ah!

VALLANCE: I think it doubtful whether, on the evidence of Mrs Thaddeus Mortimore, the will could be upheld.

PONTING: Exactly (*to everybody*) You've only to look at the thing in the light of common sense –

STEPHEN: (*argumentatively, rapping the table*) A will exists or it does not exist –

PONTING: If it ever existed, and has been destroyed –

STEPHEN: It must be shown that it was a complete will –

PONTING: Shown beyond dispute.

STEPHEN: Complete down to the smallest detail.

VALLANCE: (*continuing*) At the same time, in my opinion, the facts do not warrant the making of an affidavit that the late Mr Mortimore died intestate.

PONTING: (*stiffly*) Indeed?

STEPHEN: (*depressed*) Really?

VALLANCE: And the question of whether or not he left a duly executed will is clearly one for the Court to decide

ELKIN: Quite so – quite so.

VALLANCE: I advise, therefore, that, to get the question determined, the next-of-kin should consent to the course of procedure suggested by Mr Elkin.

ELKIN: I am assuming their consent.

PONTING: (*blustering*) And supposing the next-of-kin do *not* consent, Mr Vallance – ?

STEPHEN: Supposing we do *not* consent – ?

PONTING: Supposing we are convinced – convinced – that the late Mr Mortimore died without leaving a properly executed will?

ELKIN: Then the application, instead of being by motion to the judge in Court, must take the form of an action by writ. (*to* VALLANCE) In any case, perhaps it should do so.

> (*There is a pause.* STEPHEN *wanders disconsolately to the window on the right and stands gazing into the garden.* PONTING *leans his elbows on the piano and stares at vacancy.*)

ELKIN: (*to* HELEN, *looking at his watch*) Well, my dear Miss Thornhill – ?

> (VALLANCE *rises.*)

HELEN: Wait – wait a moment –

> (*The sound of* HELEN's *voice turns everybody, except* JAMES, THADDEUS *and* PHYLLIS, *in her direction.*)

ELKIN: (*to* VALLANCE) Eh?

HELEN: Wait a moment please. There is something I want to be told – there's something I want to be told plainly.

ELKIN: What?

HELEN: Mrs Thaddeus Mortimore –

ELKIN: Yes?

HELEN: (*slowly*) I want to know whether it is necessary, whatever proceedings are taken on my behalf – whether it is necessary that she should be publicly disgraced. I want to know that.

ELKIN: Whichever course is adopted – motion to the judge or action by writ – Mrs Thaddeus Mortimore's act must be disclosed in open Court.

HELEN: There are no means of avoiding it?

ELKIN: None.

HELEN: And the offence she has commited is – felony, you say?

> (ELKIN *inclines his head. Again there is silence, during which* HELEN *sits with knitted brows, and then* JAMES *rouses himself and looks up.*)

JAMES: (*to* ELKIN) What's the – what's the penalty?

ELKIN: (*turning to him*) The – the penalty?

JAMES: The legal punishment.

ELKIN: I think – another occasion –

> (*Suddenly* THADDEUS *and* PHYLLIS *rise together, he with an arm round her, supporting her, and they stand side by side like criminals in the dock.*)

THADDEUS: (*quickly*) No, no – now –

PHYLLIS: (*faintly*) Yes – now –

THADDEUS: (*to* ELKIN *and* VALLANCE) We – we should like to know the worst, gentlemen. I – I had the idea from the first that it was a serious offence – but hardly so serious –

ELKIN: (*with a wave of the hand*) By-and-by –

THADDEUS: Oh, you needn't hesitate, Mr Elkin. (*drawing* PHYLLIS *closer to him*) We – we shall go through with it. We shall go through with it to the end. (*A pause*) Imprisonment, sir?

ELKIN: (*gravely*) A person convicted of stealing or destroying a will for a fraudulent purpose is liable under the statute to varying terms of penal servitude, or to imprisonment with or without hard labour. In this instance, we should be justified, I am sure, in hoping for a considerable amount of leniency.

> (THADDEUS *and* PHYLLIS *slowly look at one another with expressionless faces.* JAMES *rises and moves away to the fireplace, where he stands looking down upon the flowers in the grate.*
> VALLANCE *goes to the writing-table and puts the written paper into his bag.* ELKIN *rises, takes up his bag from the table at the end of the piano, and is following* VALLANCE. *As he passes* HELEN, *she lays her hand upon his arm.*)

HELEN: Mr Elkin –

ELKIN: (*stopping*) Yes?

HELEN: Oh, but this is impossible.

ELKIN: Impossible.

HELEN: Quite impossible. I couldn't be a party – please understand me – I refuse to be a party – to any steps which would bring ruin on Mrs Mortimore.

ELKIN: (*politely*) You refuse – ?

HELEN: Absolutely. At any cost – at any cost to me – we must all unite in sparing her and her husband and children.

ELKIN: My dear young lady, I join you heartily in your desire not to bring suffering upon innocent people. But if you decline to take proceedings –

HELEN: There is no 'if' in the matter –

ELKIN:If you decline to take proceedings, there is a dead-lock.

HELEN: A dead-lock?

ELKIN: As Mr Vallance tells us, it's out of the question that the next-of-kin should now apply for Letters of Administration in the usual way.

HELEN: Why? I don't see why – I can't see why.

ELKIN: (*pointing to* JAMES *and* STEPHEN) You don't see why neither of these gentlemen can make an affidavit that Mr Edward Mortimore died intestate!

HELEN: (*with a movement of the head towards* PHYLLIS) She has no remembrance of a – what is it called –

PONTING: (*eagerly*) Attestation clause.

STEPHEN: (*coming to the head of the piano*) Attestation clause.

HELEN: (*haughtily, without turning*) Thank you. (*to* ELKIN) Only the vaguest notion that there *were* witnesses.

PONTING: The vaguest notion.

STEPHEN: The haziest.

ELKIN: Her memory is uncertain there. (*to* HELEN) But you know – *you know*, Miss Thornhill – as we all know – that it was your father's will that was found in the safe at Cannon Row and destroyed.

HELEN: (*looking up at him, gripping the arms of her chair*) Yes, of course I know it. Thank God I know it! I'm happy in knowing it. I know he didn't forget me; I know I was all to him that I imagined myself to be. And it's because I've come to know this at last – through *her* – that I can afford to be a little generous to her. Oh, please don't think that I want to introduce sentimentality into this affair – (*with a contemptuous glance at* PONTING *and* STEPHEN) any more than Colonel Ponting does – or Mr Stephen Mortimore. Mrs Thaddeus did a cruel thing when she destroyed that will. It's no excuse for her to say that she wasn't aware of my existence. She was defrauding *some* woman, not only of money, but of what is more valuable than money – of peace of mind, contentment, belief in one who could never speak, never explain, never defend himself. However, she has made the best reparation it is in her power to make – and she has gone through a bad time – and I forgive her. (PHYLLIS *releases herself from* THADDEUS *and drops down upon the settee. He sits upon the ottoman burying his face in his hands.* HELEN *rises, struggling to keep back her tears, and turns to the door.*) I – I'll go upstairs – if you'll allow me –

ELKIN: (*between her and the door*) Miss Thornhill, you put us in a position of great difficulty –

HELEN: (*impatiently*) I say again, I don't see why. Where is the difficulty? (*to* VALLANCE *and* ELKIN) If there's a difficulty, it's you gentlemen who are raising it. Let the affair go on as it was going on. (*turning to* JAMES) Mr Mortimore! (*to* ELKIN) I say, let Mr James Mortimore and the others administer the estate as they intended to do. (*to* JAMES, *who has left the fireplace and slowly advanced to her*) Mr Mortimore –

ELKIN: (*to* HELEN) Then you would have Mr James Mortimore deliberately swear that he believes his late brother died without leaving a will?

HELEN: Certainly, if necessary. Who would be hurt by it?

ELKIN: (*pursing his lips*) Miss Thornhill –

HELEN: (*hotly*) Why, which do you think would be the more acceptable to the Almighty – that I should send this poor lady to prison, or that Mr James should make a false oath?

ELKIN: H'm! I won't attempt to follow you quite so far. But even then a most important point would remain to be settled.

HELEN: Even then – ?

ELKIN: Assuming that Mr James Mortimore did make this affidavit – that he were permitted to make such an affidavit –

HELEN: Yes?

ELKIN: What about the disposition of the estate?

HELEN: (*nodding, slowly and thoughtfully*) The – the disposition of the estate –
        (STEPHEN *steals over to* PONTING, *and* ROSE, ANN *and* LOUISA *quietly rise and gather together. They all listen with painful interest.*)

ELKIN: (*to* HELEN) Morally, at all events, the whole of the late Mr Mortimore's estate belongs to you.

HELEN: (*simply*) It was his intention that it should do so. (*looking at* JAMES, *as if inviting him to speak*) Well – ?

JAMES: (*stroking his beard*) Look here. Miss Thornhill. (*pointing to the chair on the extreme left*) Sit down a minute. (*She sits.* JAMES *also seats himself, facing her, at the right of the table at the end of the piano.* VALLANCE *joins* ELKIN *and they stand near* HELEN, *occasionally exchanging remarks with each other.*) Look here. (*in a deep, gruff voice*) There *is* no doubt that my brother Ned's money rightfully belongs to you.

PONTING: (*nervously*) Mortimore –

JAMES: (*turning upon him*) You leave us alone. Don't you interfere. (*to* HELEN) I've no more doubt about it, Miss Thornhill, than that I'm sitting here. Very good. Say I make the affidavit, and that we – the family – obtain Letters of Administration. What then? The money comes to *us*. Still – it's *yours*. We get hold of it, but it's *yours*. Now! What if we offer to throw the whole lot, so to speak, into your lap?

STEPHEN: (*biting his nails*) Jim –

JAMES: (*to* STEPHEN) Don't you interfere. (*to* HELEN) I repeat, what if we offer to throw the whole lot into your lap? (*leaning forward, very earnestly*) Miss Thornhill –

PONTING: May I – ?

JAMES: (*to* PONTING) If you can't be silent – ! (*to* HELEN) Miss Thornhill, we're poor, we Mortimores. I won't say anything about Rose – (*with a sneer*) it wouldn't be polite to the Colonel; nor Tad – you see what he's come to. But Stephen and me – take our case. (*to* ELKIN *and* VALLANCE) Mr Vallance – Mr Elkin – this is sacred. (*to* HELEN) My dear, we're prominent men in the town, both of us; we're looked up to as being fairly warm and comfortable; but in reality we're not much better off than the others. My trade's being cut into on all sides; Stephen's business has run to seed; we've no capital; we've never had any capital. What we might have saved has been spent on educating our children, and keeping up appearances; and when the times comes for us to be

knocked out, there'll be precious little – bar a stroke of luck – precious little for
us to end our days on. So this is a terrible disappointment to us – an awful
disappointment. Aye, the money's yours – it's yours – but – (*opening his hands*)
what are you going to do for the family?

>   (*There is a pause. The* PONTINGS, STEPHEN, ANN *and* LOUISA
>   *draw a little nearer.*)

HELEN: (*to* JAMES) Well – since you put it in this way – I'll tell you what I'll do.
(*another pause*) I'll share with you all.

JAMES: (*to the others*) You leave us alone; you leave us alone. (*to* HELEN) Share
and share alike?

HELEN: (*thinking*) Share and share alike – after discharging my obligations.

JAMES: Obligations?

PONTING *and* STEPHEN: Obligations?

HELEN: After carrying out my father's instructions with regard to his old servants.

JAMES: (*nodding*) Oh, aye.

PONTING: (*walking about excitedly*) That's a small matter.

STEPHEN: (*also walking about*) A trifle – a trifle –

PONTING: Then what it amounts to is this – the estate will be divided into five parts
instead of four.

STEPHEN: Five instead of four – obviously.

HELEN: (*still thinking*) No – into six.

JAMES: Six?

PONTING *and* STEPHEN: Six!

ROSE *and* LOUISA: (*who, with* ANN, *are moving round the head of the piano, to join*
PONTING *and* STEPHEN) Six!

HELEN: (*firmly*) Six. A share must be given, as a memorial of my father, to one of the
hospitals in Linchpool.

PONTING *and* STEPHEN: (*protestingly*) Oh – !

ROSE, ANN *and* LOUISA: Oh – !

PONTING: Entirely unnecessary.

STEPHEN: Uncalled for.

HELEN: I insist.

PONTING: (*coming to* HELEN) My dear Miss Thornhill, believe me – believe me –
these cadging hospitals are a great deal too well off as it is.

HELEN: I insist that a share be given to a Linchpool hospital.

PONTING: I could furnish you with details of maladministration on the part of
hospital-boards –

ROSE: Shocking mismanagement –

STEPHEN: There's our own hospital –

LOUISA: A scandal.

STEPHEN: Our Jubilee hospital –

ANN: It's scarcely fit to send your servants to.

HELEN: (*to* JAMES, *rising*) Mr Mortimore –

JAMES: (*rising, to* PONTING *and the rest*) Miss Thornhill says that one share of the
estate's to go to a Linchpool hospital. D'ye hear? (*moving towards them*
authoritatively) That's enough.

>   (PONTING *and* STEPHEN *bustle to the writing-table, where they each*

seize a sheet of paper and proceed to reckon. ROSE, ANN *and* LOUISA *surround them.* JAMES *stands by, his hands in his pockets, looking on.*)

PONTING: (*sitting at the writing–table – in an undertone*) A hundred and seventy thousand pounds –

STEPHEN: (*bending over the table – in an undertone*) Six into seventeen – two and carry five –

PONTING: Six into fifty – eight and carry two –

STEPHEN: Six into twenty –

PONTING: Three –

(HELEN *seats herself in the chair on the right of the table at the end of the piano.* ELKIN *and* VALLANCE *are now in earnest conversation on the extreme left. While the calculation is going on,* THADDEUS *and* PHYLLIS *raise their heads and look at each other.*)

STEPHEN: Carry two –

PONTING: Six into twenty again – three and carry two –

STEPHEN: Again, six into twenty – three and carry two –

PONTING: Six into forty – six and carry four –

STEPHEN: Six into forty-eight –

PONTING: Eight –

STEPHEN: Twenty-eight thousand, three hundred and thirty-three pounds, six shillings and eight pence.

PONTING: (*rising, his paper in his hand*) Twenty-eight thousand apiece.

THADDEUS: (*rising*) No –

PHYLLIS: (*rising*) No –

THADDEUS: (*as everybody turns to him*) No, no –

JAMES: Eh?

PONTING: (*to* THADDEUS) What do you mean, sir?

STEPHEN: (*to* THADDEUS:) What do you mean?

THADDEUS: (*agitatedly*) I don't take my share – my wife and I don't take our share – we don't touch it –

PHYLLIS: (*clinging to* THADDEUS) We won't touch it – oh, no, no, no, no – !

JAMES: (*to* THADDEUS) Don't be a fool – don't be a fool!

THADDEUS: Fool or no fool – not a penny –

PHYLLIS: Not a penny of it –

THADDEUS: Not a penny.

HELEN: Very well, then. (*in a clear voice*) Very well; Mr Thaddeus Mortimore will not accept his share.

PONTING: (*with alacrity*) He declines it

HELEN: He declines it.

PONTING: That alters the figures – alters the figures –

STEPHEN: Very materially.

ROSE: (*to* ANN *and* LOUISA) Only five to share instead of six.

ANN: (*bewildered*) I don't understand –

LOUISA: (*shaking her arm*) Five instead of six!

(*Laying his paper on the top of the piano,* PONTING *produces his*

> *pocket-pencil and makes a fresh calculation.* STEPHEN *stands at his elbow.* ROSE, ANN *and* LOUISA *gather round them.*)

STEPHEN: (*in an undertone*) A hundred and seventy thousand –

PONTING: (*in an undertone*) *Five* into seventeen –

STEPHEN: Three –

PONTING: Five into twenty –

STEPHEN: Thirty-four thousand exactly.

PONTING: Thirty-four thousand apiece.

ROSE, ANN *and* LOUISA: (*to each other*) Thirty-four thousand!

HELEN: Wait – wait. Wait, please. (*after a short pause*) Mr Thaddeus Mortimore refuses to accept his share. I am sorry – but he appears determined.

THADDEUS: Determined – determined –

PHYLLIS: Determined –

HELEN: That being so, I ask that his share shall be settled upon his boy and girl. (*to* ELKIN) Mr Elkin – (ELKIN *advances to her.*) I suppose an arrangement of that kind can easily be made?

ELKIN: (*with a shrug*) Mr Thaddeus Mortimore can assent to his share being handed over to the trustees of a Deed of Settlement for the benefit of his children, giving a release to the administrator from all claims in respect of his share.

HELEN: (*turning to* THADDEUS) You've no objection to this? (THADDEUS *and* PHYLLIS *stare at* HELEN *dumbly, with parted lips.*) They are great friends of mine – Cyril and Joyce – and I hope they'll remain so. (*A pause*) Well? You've no right to stand in their light. (*a pause*) You won't, surely, stand in their light? (*a pause*) Don't.

> (*Again there is a silence, and then* PHYLLIS, *leaving* THADDEUS, *totters forward, and drops on her knees before* HELEN, *bowing her head in* HELEN's *lap.*)

PHYLLIS: (*weeping*) Oh–oh–oh – !

> (*Calmly,* HELEN *disengages herself from* PHYLLIS, *rises, and walks away to the fire-place.* THADDEUS *lifts* PHYLLIS *from the ground and leads her to the open window. They stand there, facing the garden, she crying upon his shoulder.*)

ELKIN: (*advancing to the middle of the room, with the air of a man who is about to perform an unpleasant task*) Miss Thornhill – (HELEN *turns to him.*) Mr Vallance and I – (*to* VALLANCE) Mr Vallance – (VALLANCE *advances.*) Mr Vallance and I have come to the conclusion that as all persons interested in this business are *sui juris* and agreeable to the compromise which has been proposed, nobody would be injured by the next of kin applying for Letters of Administration.

VALLANCE: (*to* ELKIN) Except the Revenue.

ELKIN: (*indifferently, with a nod*) The Revenue.

VALLANCE: The legacy duty being at three-per-cent. instead of ten.

ELKIN: (*nodding*) H'm h'm! (*to* HELEN) But, my dear young lady, we have also to say that, with the information we possess, we do not see our way clear to act in the matter any further.

---

sui juris: legal term, literally 'of his own law' *i.e.* of full age and capacity.

VALLANCE: (*to* JAMES, *who has come forward on the left*) We certainly could not be parties to the making of an affidavit that the deceased died intestate.

ELKIN: We couldn't reconcile ourselves to *that*.

VALLANCE: We leave it, therefore, to the next-of-kin to take their own course for obtaining Letters of Administration.

ELKIN: In fact, we beg to be allowed to withdraw from the affair altogether. I speak for myself, at any rate.

VALLANCE: (*emphatically*) Altogether.

JAMES: (*after a pause*) Oh – all right, Mr Elkin; all right, Mr Vallance.

HELEN: (*to* ELKIN) Then – do I lose you – ?

ELKIN: I am afraid – for the present –

HELEN: (*with dignity*) As you please. I am very grateful to you for what you *have* done for me.

ELKIN: (*looking round*) If I may offer a last word of advice, it is that you should avoid putting the terms of this compromise into writing.

VALLANCE: (*assentingly*) Each party must rely upon the other to fulfil the terms honourably.

ELKIN: (*to* HELEN) You have no *legal* right to enforce those terms; but pray remember that, in the event of any breach of faith, there would be nothing to prevent you from propounding the will even after Letters of Administration have been granted.

JAMES: Breach of faith, sir – !

PONTING *and* STEPHEN: (*indignantly*) Oh – !

JAMES: There's no need, Mr Elkin –

ELKIN: (*to* JAMES) No, no, no – not the slightest, I'm convinced. (*to* HELEN, *taking her hand*) The little hotel in London – Norfolk Street – ?

HELEN: Till I'm suited with lodgings.

ELKIN: Mrs Elkin will write.

HELEN: My love to her.

> (*He smiles at her and leaves her, as* VALLANCE *comes to her and shakes her hand.*)

VALLANCE: (*to* HELEN) Good-bye.

HELEN: (*to* VALLANCE) Good-bye.

ELKIN: (*to those on the left*) Good afternoon.

A MURMUR: Good afternoon.

VALLANCE: (*to those on the left*) Good afternoon.

A MURMUR: Good afternoon.

> (JAMES *has opened the door.* ELKIN *and* VALLANCE, *carrying their bags, go out.* JAMES *follows them, closing the door.*)

PONTING: (*coming forward*) Ha! We can replace *those* gentlemen without much difficulty.

STEPHEN: (*coming forward*) Old Crake has gone to pieces and this fellow Vallance is playing ducks and drakes with the practice – ducks and drakes.

PONTING: (*offering his hand to* HELEN *who takes it perfunctorily*) Greatly indebted to you – greatly indebted to you for meeting us half-way and saving unpleasantness.

STEPHEN: Pratt is the best lawyer in the town – the best by far.

PONTING: (*to* HELEN) Nothing like a compromise, provided it can be arrived at – ah –

STEPHEN: Without loss of self-respect on both sides.

(JAMES *returns*.)

PONTING: (*to* JAMES) Mortimore, we'll go back to your house. There are two or three things to talk over –

(ROSE *comes to* HELEN *as* PONTING *goes to* STEPHEN *and* JAMES.)

ROSE: (*shaking hands with* HELEN) We sha'n't be settled in Carlos Place till the autumn, but directly we *are* settled –

HELEN: (*distantly*) Thank you.

ROSE: Everybody flocks to my Tuesdays. Let me have your address and I'll send you a card.

(ROSE *leaves* HELEN, *making way for* LOUISA *and* STEPHEN.)

LOUISA: (*to* HELEN) Don't forget the Crescent. Whenever you want to visit your dear father's birth-place –

STEPHEN: (*benevolently*) And if there should be any little ceremony over laying the foundation-stone of the new *Times and Mirror* building –

LOUISA: There's the spare bedroom.

(*They shake hands with her and, making way for* ANN *and* JAMES, *follow the* PONTINGS, *who have gone out*.)

ANN: (*shaking hands with* HELEN, *gloomily*) The next time you stay at 'Ivanhoe', I hope you'll unpack more than one small trunk. But, there – (*kissing her*) I bear no malice.

(*She follows the others, leaving* JAMES *with* HELEN.)

JAMES: (*to* HELEN, *gruffly, wringing her hand*) Much obliged to you, my dear; much obliged to you.

HELEN: (*after glancing over her shoulder, in a whisper*) Mr Mortimore –

JAMES: Eh?

HELEN: (*with a motion of her head in the direction of* THADDEUS *and* PHYLLIS) These two – these two –

JAMES: (*lowering his voice*) What about 'em?

HELEN: She's done a wrong thing, but recollect – you all profit by it. You don't disdain, any of you, to profit by it. (*He looks at her queerly, but straight in the eyes*.) Try to make their lives a little easier for them.

JAMES: Easier – ?

HELEN: Happier. You can influence the others, if you will. (*a pause*) Will you?

(*He reflects, shakes her hand again, and goes to the door*.)

JAMES: (*at the door, sharply*) Tad – ! (THADDEUS *turns*.) See you in the morning. Phyllis – ! (*She also turns to him, half-scared at his tone*.) See you both in the morning. (*nodding to her*) good-bye, old girl.

(*He disappears.* HELEN *is now standing upon the hearthrug, her hands behind her, looking down into the grate.* THADDEUS *and* PHYLLIS

Tuesdays: i.e. 'At Homes' each Tuesday.

glance at her; then, guiltily, they too move to the door, passing round the head of the piano.)

PHYLLIS: (*at the door, in a low, hard voice*) Helen – (HELEN *partly turns.*) You're leaving to-morrow. I'll keep out of your way – I'll keep upstairs in my room – till you've gone.

(*She goes out.* THADDEUS *is following her when* HELEN *calls to him.*)

HELEN: Mr Thaddeus – (*He closes the door and advances to her humbly. She comes forward.*) There's no reason why I should put your wife to that trouble. It's equally convenient to me to return to London this evening. (*He bows.*) Will you kindly ask Kate to pack me?

THADDEUS: Certainly.

HELEN: Er – (*thinking*) Mr Trist had some calls to make after we left the flower-show. If I've gone before he comes back, tell him I'll write –

THADDEUS: (*bowing again*) You'll write.

HELEN: And explain.

THADDEUS: (*under his breath, looking up quickly*) Explain – !

HELEN: Explain, among other things, that I've yielded to the desire of the family –

THADDEUS: Desire – ?

HELEN: That I should accept a share of my father's property.

THADDEUS: (*falteringly*) Thank you – thank you –

HELEN: (*after a while*) That's all, I think.

THADDEUS: (*offering his hand to her*) I – I wish you every happiness, Miss Thornhill. (*She places her hand in his.*) I – I wish you every happiness.

(*She inclines her head in acknowledgement and again he goes to the door; and again, turning away to the round table where she trifles with a book, she calls him.*)

HELEN: Oh, Mr Tad – (*He halts.*) Mr Tad, I propose that we allow six months to pass in complete silence – six months from to-day –

THADDEUS: (*dully, not understanding*) Six months – silence – ?

HELEN: I mean, without my hearing from your wife. Then, perhaps, she – she will send me another invitation –

THADDEUS: (*leaving the door, staring at her*) Invitation – ?

HELEN: By that time, we shall, all of us, have forgotten a great deal – sha'n't we? (*facing him*) You'll say that to her for me?

(*He hesitates, then he takes her hands and, bending over them, kisses them repeatedly.*)

THADDEUS: God bless you. God bless you. God bless you.

HELEN: (*withdrawing her hands*) Find – Kate –

(*Once more he makes for the door.*)

THADDEUS: (*stopping half-way and pulling himself together*) Miss Thornhill – my wife – my wife – you've seen her at a disadvantage – a terrible disadvantage. Few – few pass through life without being seen – once – or oftener – at a disadvantage. She – she's a splendid woman – a splendid woman – a splendid wife and mother. (*moving to the door*) They haven't appreciated her – the family haven't appreciated her. They've treated her abominably; for sixteen years she's been treated abominably. (*At the door*) But I've never regretted my marriage – (*defiantly*) I've never regretted it – never, for a single moment – never regretted it – never – never regretted it –

> (*He disappears. She goes to the table at the end of the piano and takes up her drawing-block and box of crayons. As she does so,* TRIST *lets himself into the garden. She pauses, listening, and presently he enters the room at the open window.*)

TRIST: (*throwing his hat on the round table*) Ah –

HELEN: (*animatedly*) Mr Trist –

TRIST: Yes?

HELEN: Run out to the post-office for me – send a telegram in my name –

TRIST: With pleasure.

HELEN: Gregory's Hotel, Norfolk Street, Strand, London – the manager. Miss Thornhill will arrive to-night – prepare her room –

TRIST: (*his face falling*) To-night!

HELEN: I've altered my plans. Gregory's Hotel – Gregory's –

TRIST: (*picking up his hat*) Norfolk Street, Strand –

HELEN: (*at the door*) Mr Trist – I want you to know – I – I've come into a small fortune.

TRIST: A fortune – ?

HELEN: Nearly thirty thousand pounds.

TRIST: Thirty thousand – !

HELEN: They've persuaded me – persuaded me to take a share of my poor father's money.

TRIST: I – I'm glad.

HELEN: You – you think I'm doing rightly?

TRIST: (*depressed*) Why – of course.

> (*She opens the door and he goes to the window.*)

HELEN: Mr Trist – ! (*she comes back into the room*) Mr Trist – ! (*he approaches her*) Mr Trist – don't – don't –

TRIST: What?

HELEN: (*her head drooping*) Don't let this make any difference between us – will you? –

> (*She raises her eyes to his and they stand looking at each other in silence. Then she turns away abruptly and leaves the room as he hurries through the garden.*)

THE END

APPENDIX C

THE THUNDERBOLT: table of events

(This typed Table of Events (originally headed 'Chronology') in the Pinero Archive at the Garrick Club shows the playwright's scrupulous planning of his work. The exact moment of Edward Mortimore's death has been delayed by a week, and the events surrounding it adjusted accordingly. Even the time of the first member of the family returning to Cannon Row, Edward's home, has been amended from 11 o'clock to 'a quarter to' (thus limiting the period available to Phyllis to purloin his will), and the postal service between the English Midlands and metropolitan and provincial France carefully considered.)

The play opens at half-past eleven o'clock on the morning of Friday, June [14th deleted] 21st.

Edward Mortimore dies at a quarter-past three o'clock on the previous morning (Thursday, June [13th deleted; 21st deleted] 20th). The funeral is fixed for Monday, the [17th deleted] 24th.

Mr and Mrs James, Mr and Mrs Stephen, and Mr and Mrs Thaddeus reach Linchpool in the course of Tuesday, the [11th deleted] 18th. On the Tuesday night the invalid is nursed by the night-nurse who has been attending him throughout his illness. On the following – that is, the Wednesday – afternoon this night-nurse suddenly sends word that she is ill and cannot attend to her duties. Difficulties arise in procuring another night-nurse. It is arranged that Phyllis – in the event of a qualified night-nurse not being found – shall nurse the sick man during the early hours of the Wednesday night, the other ladies taking their turn later. The day-nurse goes off duty at eight o'clock on the Wednesday evening, and at that hour Phyllis takes her place at the bedside. Whereupon Mrs James and Mrs Stephen go to their hotel, leaving James, Stephen, and Thaddeus to search for a night-nurse.

At [MS insertion: a quarter to] eleven o'clock Stephen returns to Cannon Row with Mrs Stephen; at half-past eleven James returns with Mrs James; at twelve Thaddeus returns alone. The search for a night-nurse has been only partially successful, one having been found who will come in on Thursday night.

The invalid showing signs of increasing weakness, all the members of the family remain in the house, spending the time between the bedside and the various rooms.

At two o'clock in the morning – Thursday morning – the doctor is summoned.

It must, therefore, have been between the hours of eight and eleven on the Wednesday night that the occurrence took place which led to the temptation of Phyllis.

Colonel Ponting and his wife, kept informed of the progress of events by telegram, arrive in Linchpool on the Thursday afternoon.

Elkin writes to the Mortimore family and to Miss Thornhill on Monday June [10th deleted] 17th, catching the post.

The Mortimores receive their letters by the first post on the morning of Tuesday, the [11th deleted] 18th.

Helen's letter reaches Paris on the Tuesday night. It is reposted and finds her at St Etienne on Wednesday morning, the [12th deleted] 19th. She at once leaves St Etienne and gets to Paris late on the Wednesday night. She leaves Paris for London early on the morning of Thursday, the [13th deleted] 20th, reaching Linchpool on the night of that day.

[MS addition]

The action of Acts II, III, and IV takes place on Friday July 19th.

CHRONOLOGY

Edward Mortimore dies at the age of 53. Helen is 24; he was, therefore, 29 when she was born. He cut himself adrift from Singlehampton 26 years before the opening of the story.

Next in order of birth comes James, who is 51; then Stephen who is 49; then Rose, who is 44; then Thaddeus, who is 42. Thaddeus was 26, Phyllis 19, at the time of their marriage. They have been married 16 years, which makes her 35. Joyce, their eldest child, is 15. Cyril, the boy, 14. Mrs James Mortimore (Ann) is 50, Mrs Stephen (Louisa) 46, Colonel Ponting is 55.

THE PLAYS OF A. W. PINERO

The date and place are of the first London performance, unless otherwise stated. The number of performances, where ascertainable, follows in parentheses.

£200 a Year. Globe, 6 October 1877. (36)
La Comète; or, Two Hearts. Theatre Royal, Croydon, 22 April 1878.
Two Can Play at that Game. Lyceum, 20 May 1878 (40)
Daisy's Escape. Lyceum, 20 September, 1879. (31)
Hester's Mystery. Folly, 5 June 1880. (308)
Bygones. Lyceum, 18 September 1880. (89)
The Money-Spinner. St James's, 8 January, 1881 (98)
Imprudence. Folly, 27 July 1881. (54)
The Squire. St James's, 29 December 1881. (170)
Girls and Boys: A Nursery Tale. Toole's, 1 November 1882. (53)
The Rector: The Story of Four Friends. Court, 24 March 1882. (16)
The Rocket. Gaiety, 10 December 1883. (51)
Lords and Commons. Haymarket, 24 November 1883. (70)
Low Water. Globe, 12 January 1884. (7)
The Iron-Master (from Georges Ohnet, *Le Maître de Forges*). St James's, 17 April
    1884. (200)
In Chancery. Gaiety, 24 December 1884. (36)
The Magistrate. Court, 21 March 1885. (363)
Mayfair (from Victorien Sardou, *La Maison Neuve*). St James's, 31 October 1885. (53)
The Schoolmistress. Court, 27 March 1886. (291)
The Hobby-Horse. St James's, 23 October 1886. (109)
Dandy Dick. Court, 27 January 1887. (262)
Sweet Lavender. Terry's, 21 March 1888. (684)
The Weaker Sex. Court, 16 March 1889. (61)
The Profligate. Garrick, 24 April 1889. (129)
The Cabinet Minister. Court, 23 April 1890. (199)
Lady Bountiful. Garrick, 7 March 1891. (65)
The Times. Terry's, 24 October 1891. (155)
The Amazons. Court, 7 March 1893. (114)
The Second Mrs Tanqueray. St James's, 27 May 1893. (225)
The Notorious Mrs Ebbsmith. Garrick, 13 March 1895. (86)
The Benefit of the Doubt. Comedy, 16 October 1895. (74)
The Princess and the Butterfly; or, The Fantastics. St James's, 29 March 1897. (97)
Trelawny of the 'Wells'. Court, 20 January 1898. (135)
The Beauty Stone. With J. Comyns Carr. Music by Sullivan. Savoy, 28 May 1898. (50)
The Gay Lord Quex. Globe, 8 April 1899. (300)

287

Iris. Garrick, 21 September 1901. (115)

Letty. Duke of York's, 8 October 1903. (123)

A Wife without a Smile. Wyndham's, 12 October 1904. (77)

His House in Order. St James's, 1 February 1906. (430)

The Thunderbolt: An Episode in the History of a Provincial Family. St James's, 9 May 1908. (58)

Mid-Channel. St James's, 2 September 1909. (58)

Preserving Mr Panmure. Comedy, 19 January 1911. (99)

The 'Mind-the-Paint' Girl. Duke of York's, 17 February 1912. (126)

The Widow of Wasdale Head. Duke of York's, 14 October 1912. (26)

Playgoers: A Domestic Episode. St James's, 31 March 1913. (70)

The Big Drum. St James's, 1 September 1915. (111)

Mr Livermore's Dream. Coliseum, 15 January 1917. (12)

The Freaks: An Idyll of Suburbia. New, 14 February 1918. (51)

Monica's Blue Boy: A Wordless Play. New, 8 April 1918. (38)

Quick Work. Stamford Theatre (Stamford, Conn.), 14 November 1919

A Seat in the Park. Winter Garden, 21 February 1922. (1)

The Enchanted Cottage: A Fable. Duke of York's, 1 March 1922. (64)

A Private Room. Little, 14 May 1928. (23)

Dr Harmer's Holidays. Shubert-Belasco (Washington, DC), 16 March 1931.

A Cold June. Duchess, 29 May 1932. (19)

SELECT BIBLIOGRAPHY

The uniform edition of Pinero's plays was published by Heinemann between 1891 and 1922. The following titles appeared:

The Amazons	1894
The Benefit of the Doubt	1895
The Big Drum	1915
The Cabinet Minister	1892
Dandy Dick	1893
The Enchanted Cottage	1922
The Freaks	1922
The Gay Lord Quex	1900
His House in Order	1906
The Hobby-Horse	1892
Iris	1902
Lady Bountiful	1891
Letty	1904
The Magistrate	1892
Mid-Channel	1911
The 'Mind-the-Paint' Girl	1913
The Notorious Mrs Ebbsmith	1895
Preserving Mr Panmure	1912
The Princess and the Butterfly	1898
The Profligate	1891
The Schoolmistress	1894
The Second Mrs Tanqueray	1895
Sweet Lavender	1893
Trelawney of the 'Wells'	1899
The Thunderbolt	1909
The Times	1891
The Weaker Sex	1894
A Wife without a Smile	1905

Pinero's other published plays are:

The Beauty Stone	Chappell, 1898
The Bulkeley Peerage	*Pearson's Magazine*, Christmas 1914
Hester's Mystery	French, 1893
In Chancery	French, 1905
The Money-Spinner	French, 1900
Playgoers	French, 1913
A Private Room	French, 1928

289

The Rocket	French, 1905
A Seat in the Park	French, 1922
The Squire	French, 1905
Two Plays (*Dr Harmer's Holidays* and	Heinemann, 1930
Child Man)	
The Widow of Wasdale Head	Barrett H. Clark (ed.), *Representative*
	One-Act Plays (Boston, Mass., 1921)
A Cold June	(privately printed, Chiswick Press, 1932)

The Social Plays of Arthur Wing Pinero (four volumes), edited by Clayton Hamilton, were published by Dutton, New York, between 1917 and 1922, and reprinted by AMS Press, New York, in 1967. They contain
Vol. 1: *The Second Mrs Tanqueray*
         The Notorious Mrs Ebbsmith
Vol. 2: *The Gay Lord Quex*
         Iris
Vol. 3: *Letty*
         His House in Order
Vol. 4: *The Thunderbolt*
         Mid-Channel
Arthur Wing Pinero, *Three Plays* (*The Magistrate*, *The Second Mrs Tanqueray*, *Trelawny of the 'Wells'*), introduced by Stephen Wyatt, published in the series Methuen Master Playwrights, London, 1985.
Unpublished and Unperformed Plays:
Bound to Marry (earlier, rejected titles: *The Breadwinner*; *The Captain*) (1881). TS in the Garrick Club Library
Late of Mockford's (1934). TS in British Library
The archives of Samuel French, London, contain TS of *Quick Work* (1919; unproduced in UK); and of *Up to Date* and *Sir Sandford*.

Amongst published accounts of Pinero are:
Archer, William, *The Old Drama and the New* (London, 1923)
    Play-Making (London, 1914)
    Real Conversations (London, 1901)
Booth, Michael R. Introduction to *English Plays of the Nineteenth Century*, vols. II
    (*Dramas: 1850–1900*) and IV (*Farces*) (Oxford, 1969, 1973)
Dawick, John. 'The First Night of *The Second Mrs. Tanqueray*', *Theatre Quarterly*,
    9:35 (1979)
Dunkel, Wilbur Dwight. *Sir Arthur Pinero: A Critical Biography with Letters*
    (Chicago, Ill., 1941)
Ervine, St. John. 'Sir Arthur Wing Pinero', in the *Dictionary of National Biography
    1931–1940* (London, 1949)
Fyfe, H. Hamilton. *Arthur Wing Pinero, Playwright* (London, 1902)
    Sir Arthur Pinero's Plays and Players (London, 1930)
Hamilton, Clayton. General Introduction (vol. I) and Introductions (vols. I–IV) to *The
    Social Plays of Arthur Wing Pinero* (see above)

Lazenby, Walter. *Arthur Wing Pinero* (New York, 1972)

Nicoll, Allardyce. *A History of English Drama 1660–1900*, Vol. v: Late Nineteenth Century Drama (Cambridge, 1959)

　English Drama 1900–1930: The Beginnings of the Modern Period (London, 1973)

Rowell, George. *Theatre in the Age of Irving* (Oxford, 1981)

　The Victorian Theatre 1791–1914 (London, 1978)

Wearing, J. P. (ed.). *The Collected Letters of Sir Arthur Pinero* (Minneapolis, Minn., 1974)

　'Pinero the Actor' and 'Pinero's Professional Dramatic Roles 1874–1884', *Theatre Notebook*, 26:4 (1972), 133–44

Weaver, J. W., and E. J. Wilson. 'A. W. Pinero: An Annotated Bibliography' *English Literature in Transition*, 23 (1981), 231–9

Weintraub, Stanley (ed.) *Modern British Dramatists 1900–1945* (Detroit, Ill., 1982), *sub* 'Arthur Wing Pinero' (by J. P. Wearing)

West, E. J. 'The Playwright as Producer: Sir Arthur Pinero, the Autocrat-Dictator', *University of Colorado Studies in Language and Literature*, 6 (1957), 79–102